Whereas, We have noticed with pleasure the action taken in different parts of our Confederacy in response to the call of the President for the Soldiers to reenlist for the war, and whereas we feel with pride the interests that bind us together in a common brotherhood struggling for the same common rights and liberties, and earnestly desiring to emulate the example of those who have resolved to serve their Country until the last armed foe shall be driven beyond the borders of our land,

Therefore be it:

Resolved that having already enlisted unconditionally for the war, we take this method of renewing our pledge to stand by our brethren in the field, until we have achieved an honourable independence among the nations of the world, and have avenged the death of our gallant commanders, who have sealed their devotion to our Country's cause, and enriched the soil of every State in the Confederacy by their blood.

Captain L.A. Whilden
Company E, 5th Regiment, South Carolina Cavalry
1864

SOUTH CAROLINA'S MILITARY
ORGANIZATIONS DURING THE WAR BETWEEN
THE STATES

VOLUME I: THE LOWCOUNTRY & PEE DEE
VOLUME II: THE MIDLANDS
VOLUME III: THE UPSTATE
VOLUME IV: STATEWIDE UNITS, MILITIA
AND RESERVES

SOUTH CAROLINA'S

MILITARY ORGANIZATIONS DURING THE

WAR BETWEEN THE STATES

THE LOWCOUNTRY & PEE DEE

ROBERT S. SEIGLER

Charleston · London

THE
History
PRESS

Cover image: Fort Johnson, James Island. Fort Sumter in distance. *Courtesy Library of Congress.*
Cover design by Marshall Hudson

First published 2008

Manufactured in the United States

ISBN 978.1.59629.158.4

Library of Congress Cataloging-in-Publication Data

Seigler, Robert S.
South Carolina's military organizations during the War between the States / Robert S. Seigler.
p. cm.
Includes bibliographical references and index.
ISBN 978-1-59629-158-4 (alk. paper)
1. South Carolina--History--Civil War, 1861-1865--Regimental histories. 2. United States--History--Civil War, 1861-1865--Regimental histories. 3. Confederate States of America--Armed Forces. I. Title.
E577.4.S45 2008
973.7'457--dc22
                          2007049670

In memory of:
Milledge Rivers Gunter
Company F
Palmetto Sharpshooters
Bratton's Brigade
Field's Division
Longstreet's Corps
A.N.V.

Joseph O'Hear Sanders
The Citadel Cadets, and
The Stono Scouts

Andrew Altman Seigler
Percival's Company
Colcock's Regiment
South Carolina State Troops

A.J. Bulkley
Company A, 17th Battalion, South Carolina Cavalry
Company D, 5th Regiment, South Carolina Cavalry

CONTENTS

CONTENTS

ACKNOWLEDGEMENTS

The following people offered invaluable assistance in the production of this work: John Mills Bigham, Curator of Education, South Carolina Confederate Relic Room and Museum, Columbia, South Carolina; Beth Bilderbeck, Visual Materials Archivist, South Caroliniana Library, University of South Carolina, Columbia, South Carolina; Suzanne Case, Supervisor, South Carolina Room, Greenville County Library System, Greenville, South Carolina; Doris Gandy, Director, Darlington County Historical Society, Darlington, South Carolina; Carl Hill, Director, The War Between The States Museum, Florence, South Carolina; Stephen L. Johnson, President, The State Printing Company, Columbia, South Carolina; Webster Jones, The 16th Regiment Museum, Greenville, South Carolina; Ola Jean Kelly, Director, Union County Museum, Union, South Carolina; Sidney R. Thompson, Executive Director, Greenville County Historical Society, Greenville, South Carolina; Jane Yates, Director, Archives and Museum, The Citadel, Charleston, South Carolina.

I deeply appreciate the expert editorial assistance of Ann Bowen of Greenwood, South Carolina, whose knowledge and guiding hand molded this work.

Finally and most importantly, I would like to thank my wife, Patti, and my children, Carrie and Robert, for their remarkable patience and encouragement throughout the fifteen or so years that I researched and wrote this book. I dedicate it to them.

INTRODUCTION

More than a century has passed since a comprehensive account of the organization of South Carolinians for military service in the War Between the States has appeared in print. In 1899 Professor William J. Rivers published *Rivers's Account of the Raising of Troops in South Carolina for State and Confederate Service 1861–1865*, and in the same year, Rivers's collaborator and then-state historian of Confederate records, John Peyre Thomas, issued an augmented version of Rivers's work as a report to the South Carolina legislature entitled *Annual Report of the State Historian of Confederate Records For The Year 1899*.[1] Since that time, a great many historical works dealing with South Carolina's Confederate history have been published. None, however, has attempted to update or expand upon Rivers's and Thomas's seminal works. This book attempts to do just that. It records the history of the infantry, cavalry, artillery, and reserve units organized in South Carolina immediately before and during the War Between the States.

OVERVIEW

On November 13, 1860, the South Carolina General Assembly authorized the creation of a convention of the people to be called the South Carolina Secession Convention. In late 1860 and early 1861, both the General Assembly and the Secession Convention approved several acts and resolutions creating a significant state military force. The South Carolina General Assembly passed its first act related to the raising of troops for possible armed conflict on December 17, 1860, just three days before the Ordinance of Secession passed the Convention. In a precautionary move designed to arm ten thousand men, the legislature authorized the governor to call up troops for the defense of the state by "engrafting a volunteer system on the existing militia" thus creating an "Armed Military Force."[1] The act directed "that whenever it shall appear that an armed force is about to be employed against the State, or in opposition to its authority, the Governor be, and he is hereby, authorized to repel the same; and for that purpose to call into the service of the State…such a portion of the militia as he may deem necessary and proper."[2] It also directed the governor to call at once for one volunteer company of infantry from each militia infantry battalion, two rifle companies from each militia infantry brigade, one or more cavalry companies from each militia cavalry regiment and one regiment of artillery from Charleston. In addition, he was allowed to call for three artillery companies, one each from Columbia, Georgetown and Beaufort.[3]

This act also authorized the governor to receive into service any volunteer organization that had a full complement of officers and men and to draft men from any militia battalion that did not furnish its quota within thirty days.[4] These volunteer units were to be organized into battalions or regiments, which, in turn, were to be organized into four brigades. Then the entire organization was to be incorporated into a single division under the command of a major general. The men in ranks were to elect officers up to and including the rank of colonel. The governor, with the advice and consent of the Senate, was to appoint the four brigadier generals and the sole major general. The governor could call any or all elements of this organization into service for no more than twelve months. Governor Pickens duly appointed Milledge L. Bonham of Edgefield as major general; Patrick H. Nelson of Sumter, T.G. Rhett and Samuel McGowan of Abbeville and Albert C. Garlington of Newberry would be the four brigadier generals.

On December 26, 1860, Major Robert Anderson of the United States Army withdrew his troops from Fort Moultrie to Fort Sumter. On December 29, Governor Pickens responded by issuing the call to begin raising troops as authorized by the act of December 17.[5] The first regiments to be raised were called "South Carolina Volunteers." Initially there were to be ten of these volunteer regiments. They were given numeric designations—2nd Regiment Infantry, South Carolina Volunteers, for example—and were usually abbreviated "SCV." In 1860 South Carolina was divided into thirty districts.[6] These thirty districts were further divided into ten "regions" for the purpose of raising the ten regiments created by the December 17 act.[7] It is possible the first ten regiments were numbered based on their geographical origin. It is also possible that they were based on the dates of elections for field officers. In fact, Johnson Hagood said his regiment was the first to volunteer and for that reason was designated the 1st Regiment, SCV.[8]

While these volunteer regiments were being organized, the South Carolina legislature and the Secession Convention realized that the state militia, as it existed, was unable to meet the immediate needs of the state to defend itself. On January 1, 1861, the Secession Convention passed two resolutions. One created a Board of Ordnance and a Corps of Military Engineers. The other authorized the immediate enlistment of volunteer companies to be formed into a single regiment to serve for six months[9] and allowed the governor to accept volunteer companies attached to the South Carolina Militia to serve until they could be replaced by the forces raised under the legislature's December 17 act.[10] Acting on this resolution, the governor, on January 8, accepted Maxcy Gregg's regiment, known as the 1st Regiment Infantry, SCV, for six months' service as infantry support for Sullivan's Island and Fort Moultrie in the event of a Federal land attack.[11] He also employed the 4th Brigade, South Carolina Militia, as the primary military force in and around Charleston during the first few months of 1861.

The preceding day the Secession Convention had passed a resolution authorizing the creation of one or two regiments that would soon become known as the Regular Army of South Carolina. The first regiment was to have eight companies whose 640 privates who would enlist for twelve months. Company officers and field officers were to be appointed by the governor and confirmed by the Senate. The governor could enlist a second regiment following the same guidelines "whenever the public interest, in his opinion, may require it."[12] Originally, these "regular troops" were created to relieve the volunteers who were then in possession of the forts in the state, primarily in and around Charleston Harbor. On January 19, 23 and 28 the Senate confirmed Governor Pickens's recommendations for many of the field-grade and company-grade officers.

On January 28 the South Carolina legislature passed an act entitled "An act for creating a military establishment for the State of South Carolina, and for other purposes." This act modified the Secession Convention's resolution of December 31, 1860.[13] It created a state military establishment to be known as the Regular Army of South Carolina, and it extended the men's term of service to three years unless they were discharged earlier. All officers were to be approved by the governor and confirmed by the Senate. The organization was modified to comprise one infantry regiment, one artillery battalion and one cavalry squadron. Between them, the resolution of December 31 and the act of January 28 created the following units: the 1st Regiment, South Carolina Infantry, Regulars; the 1st Battalion, South Carolina Artillery, Regulars; and DeSaussure's Squadron, South Carolina Cavalry, Regulars. Brigadier General R.G.M. Dunovant commanded the Regular Army of South Carolina. Colonel R.H. Anderson commanded the infantry regiment, Lieutenant Colonel Roswell Ripley commanded the artillery battalion, and Major W.D. DeSaussure commanded the cavalry squadron.[14]

In March 1861 the Secession Convention passed a resolution allowing the South Carolina Regular Army to be transferred to Confederate service for the remainder of its three-year term.[15] The intention was to have these troops form the nucleus of the Confederate Regular Army. Although these men enlisted in Confederate service as state volunteers, not regulars, they remained in and around Charleston Harbor until February 1865.[16] In December 1861, the legislature passed an amendment that augmented the artillery battalion to a regiment of eight companies and the cavalry to four squadrons.[17] Consequently, the 1st Battalion Artillery, South Carolina Regulars, was redesignated the 1st Regiment Artillery, South Carolina Regulars, on March 25, 1862. Although four cavalry squadrons were allowed, DeSaussure's Squadron was the only cavalry organization accepted into the South Carolina Regular Army, and it was converted to artillery within a few months of its organization. In fact, all three branches of the South Carolina Regular Army—infantry, artillery and cavalry—served as artillery units from shortly after their creation in 1861 until February 1865.

Meanwhile, South Carolinians were volunteering for twelve months' service under the act of December 17, 1860. By March 6, 1861, nearly nine thousand volunteers had enlisted in 104 companies. These companies of twelve-month volunteers were organized into the mandated ten regiments, four brigades and one division, with the ten regiments numbered one through ten.[18] The organization of the South Carolina volunteer infantry regiments numbered two through eight and ten was fairly straightforward. But it is easy to confuse some of the other regiments, especially the 1st, 9th and 11th. Johnson Hagood, for example, commanded one of the original regiments called the 1st Regiment, SCV. But Hagood's regiment should not be confused with either Colonel Maxcy Gregg's 1st Regiment (six-month), SCV; Colonel Butler's 1st Regiment, South Carolina Regulars; or Colonel Orr's 1st Regiment of Rifles, SCV. Colonel Nathaniel Heyward commanded the 9th Regiment, SCV, which was later redesignated the 11th Regiment, SCV, and it is usually referred to as such. Colonel J.D. Blanding's 9th Regiment, SCV, was not one of the original ten volunteer regiments, even though most of the companies of Blanding's regiment were among the initial 104 companies. The nucleus of Blanding's 9th Regiment was created by the consolidation of some of the original companies of the 2nd Regiment that refused to volunteer for service in Virginia in the spring of 1861 and some additional companies. In addition to these regiments, the 2nd Battalion, South Carolina Artillery, enlisted under the South Carolina General Assembly's act of December 17, 1860.[19]

On February 28, 1861, the Confederate Congress passed an act creating the Confederate States Provisional Army, usually abbreviated P.A.C.S. or C.S.P.A. After the bombardment of Fort Sumter in April 1861, President Davis called for eight thousand volunteers from South Carolina to enlist in the P.A.C.S., and Governor Pickens urged existing state troops to volunteer for Confederate service.[20] Though the response was generally positive, Davis's and Pickens's actions caused a great deal of disruption and confusion among South Carolina organizations. John Peyre Thomas wrote:

> *The Act of the Confederate States to raise provisional forces conferred upon the President the appointment of officers above the rank of Colonel. In transferring the enlisted troops of the state to the Confederate Government, the Governor was instructed by the Convention to endeavor to preserve the rank of State officers and obtain for them commissions of the same grade for at least the period of their enlistment. But many officers, natives of Southern states, were now resigning from the United States Army and seeking commissions in the Army of the Confederacy; and it was the policy of the government to hold in its own hands the appointment of all superior*

officers. Indeed, it was their desire to accept volunteers only by companies, and such alone as volunteered for the whole war; although, through the necessity of bringing large forces rapidly forward, it was accorded to the volunteer troops to retain their regimental organizations.[21]

Every one of the original eleven regiments ultimately enlisted in part or in whole in Confederate service. Many of the men and companies who had enlisted for twelve months of state service, however, refused to enter Confederate service with their original regiments in the spring of 1861. Many South Carolina regiments were affected by this switch from state to Confederate service. Severely affected were Maxcy Gregg's reorganized 1st Regiment, Johnson Hagood's 1st Regiment, J.B. Kershaw's 2nd Regiment and J.D. Blanding's 9th Regiment. Moderately affected were the 3rd, 4th, 5th, 6th, 10th and 11th Regiments. Least affected were the 7th and 8th Regiments. On April 25, 1861, Governor Pickens, who believed the troops should be transferred under certain conditions, wrote: "Hardly any full regiment with all its companies was prepared to go suddenly [to Virginia]."[22] William W. East, a corporal in the 5th Regiment who wrote to the *Yorkville Enquirer* under the sobriquet "Our Corporal," explained the feelings of the men in May 1861: "Some think there is no danger and therefore, no need of us here [in South Carolina]; others wish to go to Virginia; others shrink from encountering the yellow fever or other disease during the idle garrison life…; and others still, feeling that the state is secure, are desirous of returning to their work-shops, their farms, or their merchandise."[23] At that time, many of the twelve-month volunteer companies, which had been in existence for only a few months, refused to enter Confederate service and were disbanded altogether, but the regiments quickly enlisted new companies to replace them. The 2nd Regiment, SCV, was split into two regiments–the 2nd Regiment, SCV, and Blanding's 9th Regiment, SCV. Another regiment, Johnson Hagood's 1st, SCV, was temporarily disbanded until the men and the governor could settle their differences. John Peyre Thomas wrote that in the summer of 1861, "the Governor exhorted the lately formed regiments from the upcountry to re-volunteer for Virginia. It was understood that such volunteering for Confederate service among the twelve months State troops would not bind them to the new service beyond the term of their first enlistment."[24] In June and July 1861, the 3rd, 4th, 5th, 6th, 7th and 8th Regiments, SCV, mustered in Confederate service and were sent to Virginia, where Maxcy Gregg's reorganized 1st Regiment and J.B. Kershaw's 2nd Regiment had been since April. The men of Johnson Hagood's 1st Regiment were still uncommitted and remained in South Carolina. Blanding's 9th Regiment, Manigault's 10th Regiment and Heyward's 11th Regiment also remained in the state. When the dust settled in the late spring and summer of 1861, the original ten regiments were intact. They had recruited back to full strength and had spawned one new regiment, Blanding's 9th. All eleven regiments had mustered in Confederate service. The eleven South Carolina Volunteer regiments, however, contained many new companies, which had replaced those that had refused to enter Confederate service.

Another organization, the Hampton Legion, mustered in Confederate service in 1861. In April, President Davis authorized its creation as a combined force of infantry, cavalry and artillery, which had originally enlisted for twelve months' service in the Provisional Army of the Confederate States.

On June 30, 1861, President Davis called for the creation of a thirty-thousand-man reserve army corps. This new call-up included an additional three thousand South Carolinians, who would enlist "for the duration of the war."[25] Under the plan, the three thousand men were to be organized into companies at two camps of instruction, and President Davis was to appoint the field officers for the new regiments. As the sites for the camps of instruction, Governor Pickens chose Lightwood Knot Springs, located about seven miles north of Columbia, and Camp Butler, near Polecat (now Montmorenci) in Barnwell District. A later modification of the terms of the call-up said a combination of ten companies could form a regiment, men could elect their field officers, and the regiment could enter service with this organizational structure.[26] In early September, there were forty-two infantry companies, three cavalry companies and two artillery companies at Lightwood Knot Springs. Except for one cavalry company, this contingent completed South Carolina's quota.[27] President Davis's call for three thousand new troops resulted in the creation of the 12th, 13th, 14th and 15th Regiments, SCV.

On July 1, 1861, President Davis called for two additional regiments to enlist for the duration of the war. This call resulted in the organization of two infantry regiments and one infantry battalion. The two regiments were Maxcy Gregg's 1st Regiment, SCV, which had reorganized for the duration after its initial six-month term of enlistment expired in early July 1861, and James L. Orr's 1st Regiment, South Carolina Rifles, the first South Carolina regiment to enlist for the duration of the war. Sixteen companies offered their services to Colonel Orr. He accepted ten; the remaining six were organized into the 5th Battalion Rifles, SCV, which was later augmented to become the 2nd Regiment Rifles, SCV.

By November 1, 1861, nineteen volunteer infantry regiments and one volunteer infantry battalion had been raised. One—Maxcy Gregg's 1st (six-month) Regiment—disbanded at the end of its term of enlistment in

July 1861, and it reorganized shortly thereafter. Gregg's regiment, along with five others and the 2nd Battalion, had enlisted for the duration of the war. Eleven regiments and the Hampton Legion signed on for twelve months. In addition, the South Carolina Regular Army, consisting of one infantry regiment, one artillery battalion and one cavalry squadron, had enlisted for three years. Several artillery batteries and about twenty-one independent companies of cavalry and mounted infantry were also organized during this period. Some of the cavalry companies were raised under a special resolution of the Secession Convention, with their terms of service limited to ten days after the adjournment of the regular session of the legislature.[28] It is difficult to determine exactly which company was which, but most likely they were the undersized companies of Martin's 1st Regiment Cavalry, South Carolina Militia. These troops were stationed along the South Carolina coast.

In November 1861, the South Carolina legislature met in special session to appoint electors for president and vice-president under the permanent Confederate Constitution. In response to the fall of Port Royal in early November and the subsequent threat to Charleston, the legislators passed a resolution authorizing the governor to call for volunteers to defend the state either against an actual invasion or against one he believed to be imminent.[29] Acting under a Confederate act entitled "an act to provide for local defense and special service" passed on August 21, 1861, the governor, on November 11, called for volunteers to enter Confederate service in special defense of the state. The response was slow.[30] As a result, the General Assembly amended the South Carolina Militia Law of 1841 on December 7, 1861, by passing an "Act to amend and suspend certain portions of the Militia and Patrol laws of the State."[31] This act stated that unless exempt, all free white males between the ages of sixteen and sixty years were liable to perform ordinary military duty during the war. In addition, it made eighteen- to forty-five-year-old men liable to be called for twelve months' service either in South Carolina or in any other Confederate state instead of the previously allowed three months' service inside and two months' service outside the state. The governor was authorized to call out these troops at any time.[32] If the South Carolina Militia did not furnish the allotted number of men, a draft would follow.[33] The law also tried to revitalize the South Carolina militia system by calling for new elections of officers and more frequent drilling. On December 9, 1861, Governor Pickens called for twelve thousand volunteers to enlist for twelve months' service, unless they were discharged before that time.[34] As a result, the 16th and 17th Infantry Regiments, SCV, and the 3rd Infantry Battalion, SCV, were organized. The 18th, 19th, 20th, 21st, 22nd, 23rd and 24th Infantry Regiments, SCV, were also organized under this call.

By the end of 1861, more than 7,000 men had enlisted "for and during the war" and 20,251 for shorter terms, usually either twelve or thirty-six months. A total of 27,362 men were in uniform, and an additional sixty-four companies were either in camp or under marching orders.[35] In 1861, a number of organizations enlisted for the duration of the war. These were the infantry regiments of Gregg's 1st SCV, the 12th SCV, 13th SCV, 14th SCV, 15th SCV and Orr's regiment of rifles; the 5th Battalion Rifles Infantry, Edward Manigault's Battalion, four companies of Hatch's Battalion of Coast Rangers and the 1st Battalion Cavalry; the artillery organizations of the 2nd Battalion, the 3rd Battalion (Palmetto Battalion) Light Artillery and the Chesterfield Light Artillery. Captain Boyce's Company, Captain Mangum's Company, Captain Boykin's Cavalry Company and Captain Shannon's Cavalry Company also signed on for the duration in 1861.

Many units enlisted in 1861 for shorter terms of service, usually for twelve months. Infantry regiments included Hagood's 1st SCV, the 2nd through the 11th SCV, the 16th SCV, the 17th SCV, the Hampton Legion and the Holcombe Legion. Infantry battalions were the 3rd (James's) Battalion and six companies of Hatch's Battalion of Coast Rangers. Artillery organizations were Bachman's Battery, the Beaufort Volunteer Artillery, Bonneau's Artillery, the Calhoun Light Artillery, the Santee Light Artillery, the Macbeth Artillery, the Marion Artillery and the Washington (Hart's) Artillery. Cavalry units were Boykin's Cavalry Troop, J.G. Harlan's Company, Lipscomb's Cavalry Troop, St. James Mounted Riflemen, Tucker's Squadron and Trenholm's Squadron. In addition, the 18th, 19th, 20th, 21st, 22nd, 23rd and 24th Regiments, SCV, along with some companies of Hatch's Battalion of Coast Rangers, were raised late in 1861 and early in 1862 for twelve months' service.

The South Carolina Regular Army, consisting of the 1st Regiment, South Carolina Infantry (Regulars), the 1st Battalion, South Carolina Artillery (Regulars) and the 15th Battalion, South Carolina Artillery (Regulars), also enlisted for three years in 1861. Other organizations enlisting for three years were the Pee Dee Legion Militia, Martin's Cavalry Regiment Militia, the 4th Brigade Militia, the Battalion of South Carolina Cadets and several independent cavalry companies.[36]

After the close of 1861, the record of the raising of troops for service in South Carolina is less clear. The accounts of both Professor Rivers and J.P. Thomas become ever more vague about which organizations were created under which act, resolution, law or authority in 1862.

On December 11, 1861, the Confederate Congress passed the first Confederate Conscription Act, also called the Bounty and Furlough Act. On February 19, 1862, the *Mercury* reprinted that act, along with subsequent orders from the War Department dated January 1, 1862.[37] The Conscription Act dictated a reorganization of existing Confederate military forces and provided for the following: (1) a bounty of fifty dollars would be paid to all privates, musicians and non-commissioned officers who would enlist in the Confederate States Provisional Army for three years, or for those men already enlisted for twelve months who would re-enlist for two additional years; (2) a furlough, not to exceed sixty days, would be granted "to all twelve months men now in service, who shall, prior to the expiration of their present term of service, volunteer or enlist for the next two ensuing years subsequent to the expiration of their present term of service, or for three years, or the war." The secretary of war would issue the furloughs at such times and in such number as he deemed most compatible with the public interest; (3) the act applied to any man who had already enlisted for twelve months or more in the service of any Confederate state; (4) all men who re-enlisted would be allowed, at the expiration of their original terms of service, to reorganize themselves into new companies and to elect new company officers. The new companies would be allowed to organize into new battalions or regiments, and the men would elect new field officers. Subsequent vacancies among the officer corps would be filled by promotion within the ranks of the existing officers of the unit. If the lowest ranking officer in a company had to be replaced, an election would be held to fill that vacancy. When a vacancy arose within the units of any state's Regular Army, new officers would be appointed and not elected; (5) further provisions were made for the reorganization of new companies into battalions and regiments.[38]

On February 2, 1862, the secretary of war called on Governor Pickens for South Carolina to fill its quota of troops to be furnished "for and during the war."[39] This quota—6 percent of the white male population of the state— translated to about 18,000 men.[40] An estimated 6,000 South Carolinians had already enlisted for the duration of the war. To meet the requisition of an additional 12,590 men, the secretary of war projected the need to enlist at least five new regiments and to re-enlist enough of the twelve months' troops whose terms were about to expire to make up the difference.[41] On February 20, 1862, the South Carolina adjutant and inspector general provided more accurate figures. His report showed that, of 30,670 South Carolinians currently in uniform, 9,349 had enlisted for the duration of the war and 21,321 had signed on for twelve months. At about the same time, by contrast, the secretary of war counted 6,260 South Carolinians enlisted for the duration and 23,975 enlisted for twelve months.[42] James Chesnut Jr., a member of the South Carolina Executive Council, urged the twelve months' troops to re-enlist for the duration to meet the quota of 18,000 men.

As a part of this call for additional troops, the *Mercury* reported on February 21, 1862, that President Davis had issued a call for 5,000 more men—approximately five regiments—from South Carolina. Another call for 5,000 men went out on March 5, 1862, with a notice that said until five regiments were raised, no man could enter any organization then in service for less than the duration of the war.[43] On March 6, 1862, the *Mercury* reprinted a proclamation from Governor Pickens stating that President Davis called for an additional 12,590 men from the state, a number that included the two previous calls for 5,000 men each.[44] To meet the state's quota, including the five new regiments called for, the governor and Executive Council, on March 5, 1862, adopted a system of conscription.[45] They also directed South Carolina Adjutant and Inspector General States Rights Gist to issue a statement in early March. Gist's proclamation, issued on March 7, declared a reorganization of the South Carolina Military System to bring it into compliance with the Executive Council's decision.[46] The statement contained several major points, among them: the system of volunteering by individuals or by companies would be in place until March 20, 1862, when all volunteering would be discarded and a system of conscription, as provided for by law, would be instituted; all male citizens between the ages of eighteen and forty-five would be required to enroll for active duty and would not be allowed to serve in the reserves; all eligible men must report for duty within ten days of being called or be liable for the draft; volunteer companies already in service would be required to re-enlist ten days before their term of service expired; any individuals who refused to re-enlist would be eligible for the draft; and the governor would appoint all field officers in new regiments and company-grade officers in new companies.[47] In addition, boards of exemption were to be created throughout the state, a system of conscription was to be established and a method for substitution was to be set in place.[48] Troops were to be received at Lightwood Knot Springs, north of Columbia.[49]

Even before the cutoff date of March 20, 1862, more than 22,000 South Carolinians had volunteered for the duration of the war, and an additional 17,210 men had enrolled for twelve months.[50] On March 21, the governor and Executive Council responded to this positive news by extending the deadline to April 15 and allowing the men to elect their officers, subject to approval by the Executive Council.[51] Under this proclamation, the 24th Regiment, SCV, was accepted for the duration of the war, and Lamar's 2nd Artillery Battalion was increased to regiment strength.

The Confederate Congress passed a new conscription law, entitled "An Act to further provide for the public defense," on April 16, 1862.[52] It contained even more details concerning re-enlistment of soldiers and distribution of conscripted men than had the law passed the previous December. And it authorized the president to call into service all white male residents of the Confederate States between the ages of eighteen and thirty-five years who were not legally exempted from duty. The term of service would be "three years, unless the war shall have been sooner ended."[53] In addition, all the twelve-month volunteers were to serve two additional years from the expiration of their original terms. Any men younger than eighteen and older than thirty-five were required to remain in service for ninety days unless their places were filled by recruits. Bounties were granted to the twelve-month men, and furloughs would be granted at the discretion of the secretary of war. Transfers from one organization to another and the creation of new organizations were cancelled unless they could be completed within thirty days. All the twelve-month men who re-enlisted were allowed to hold elections for their officers within forty days of April 16.[54] This act had little effect on the creation of new units in South Carolina because most eligible men were already in the service. About five thousand South Carolinians enlisted or re-enlisted in existing units in response.

According to estimates of the state's adjutant and inspector general, 39,274 South Carolinians were in the field by April 28, 1862. Of this number, 22,064—some 4,000 more than required—had enlisted for the duration and 17,210 had enlisted for twelve months.[55] By August 30, the number of men enlisted for service in all South Carolina military organizations had grown to 42,973. At that time, the infantry comprised twenty-eight regiments, two legions, eight battalions and two unattached companies. The artillery comprised two regiments, one battalion and eighteen unattached companies; the cavalry units numbered two regiments, five battalions and seven unattached companies.[56]

The conscription laws, especially the Conscription Act of April 16, set the stage for significant reorganization of the entire Confederate army in the spring of 1862; the laws greatly affected the organization of South Carolina troops as well. D.A. Dickert, captain of Company H of the 3rd Regiment, wrote of the Conscript Laws:

> *The Conscript Act was condemned in unmeasured terms in many places at the South, but its necessity and expediency was never doubted. To have allowed so great a number to absent themselves from the army at this time, in the face of an overwhelming enemy, and that enemy advancing upon our Capitol, was more than the morale of the army would admit. Not altogether would the absence of the soldiers themselves effect the army, but in the breaking up of organizations, for in some companies all had re-enlisted,*

while in others one-half, and in many cases none. New regiments would have to be formed out of the re-enlisted companies, and new companies out of the large number of recruits, now in camps of instruction. So by keeping up the old organizations, and filling up the ranks by the conscripts at home, the army would be greatly benefited.[57]

The term of enlistment for most of the men who originally signed up for twelve months was set to expire in the spring of 1862. Twelve-month men not otherwise exempt were required to re-enlist "for three years or the duration of the war," meaning three years from their initial date of enlistment. Most men of eligible age who were exempt from re-enlistment in the spring of 1862 were those who had originally signed on for a term greater than twelve months; all new recruits were required to enlist "for three years or the duration of the war." This phrase caused some confusion. Some men interpreted it to mean three years, or for the duration of the war, whichever was shorter. Others interpreted it to mean the opposite—three years, or for the duration of the war, whichever was longer. In his discussion of the re-enlistment for "three years or the war," Douglas Southall Freeman wrote in *Lee's Lieutenants* that the soldiers took the phrase to mean a maximum of three years. This position is supported by the original wording, "three years, unless the war shall have been sooner ended."[58] D.A. Dickert, captain of Company H of the 3rd Regiment, held a similar view: "It was during our stay in winter quarters, March 1864, that the term of our second enlistment expired." Dickert explained that the troops who had originally enlisted for twelve months in the spring of 1861 and who had then re-enlisted for "three years" in the spring of 1862 were due to re-enlist a third time in the spring of 1864. He held that the men had re-enlisted in the spring of 1862 for three years, or for the duration of the war, whichever was the shorter of the two terms. Dickert wrote further that the re-enlistment in March 1864 was "only a form, no change in officers or organization."[59]

All but a few men voluntarily re-enlisted in March 1864, but because of the conscription laws, no one was allowed to leave the army or change his branch of service. An interesting example of the effect on the ranks lies in the 1st Regiment, SC Infantry (Regulars). The men in that regiment clearly believed that their original term of service expired in early 1864, and they were right. On February 8, 1864, P.G.T. Beauregard published the following statement: "Soldiers of the Department of South Carolina, Georgia and Florida. The term of service of some of you is about to expire. You must have observed from the newspapers of your city that your brothers in arms of the veteran armies of Northern Virginia and of Tennessee have re-enlisted as was to be expected of such men, by entire companies, battalions, regiments and brigades, proudly retaining the organizations intact under which they have won renown. Will the men who have defended Forts Sumter and Moultrie, and Battery Wagner fail to follow these examples of soldierly patriotism?"[60] Beauregard's goal, of course, was to preserve the integrity of the 1st Regiment, and his method was to appeal to honor and patriotism. Left unsaid was the stark fact that, under the law, if the men did not re-enlist in the 1st Regiment, they would not be allowed to leave the service.[61]

Lieutenant J.F.J. Caldwell, historian of McGowan's Brigade, also discussed the issue of "three years or the duration of the war" and arrived at a different conclusion:

> *In February* [1864], *there was a general call for re-enlistment in the Confederate armies. It will be remembered that almost all the regiments organized in the summer of 1861 enlisted for "three years or the war." I always held the expression to mean a consent to serve three years, whether the war lasted so long or not; and to serve for the war, should it last for even longer than three years. But as there was doubt about it; as there were many originally twelve-month regiments, who reenlisted, it is said, for two years from the expiration of their first year, so making their term expire in the spring of 1864; and as, above all things, the weary citizens at home needed encouragement; a renewal of enlistment and of allegiance to the Confederacy was invited. The army adopted the suggestion most cordially, and declared afresh their determination never to lay down their arms until the independence of the South should be achieved.*[62]

To avoid a catastrophe of disorganization in early 1864 when the three-year terms would expire, and perhaps also to clarify the issue, the Confederate Congress, in early 1864, passed "A Bill to Organize Forces to Serve During the War."[63] This bill required all white males between seventeen and fifty years of age to serve during the war. All men between eighteen and forty-five currently in service were to remain in their units. Men between seventeen and eighteen and between forty-five and fifty would form companies and regiments of reserves, which would serve within the borders of their states. Consequently, in the first few months of 1864, most South Carolinians then in service either re-enlisted if their three-year term had expired or reaffirmed their commitment to the Confederacy if it had not; there were no major changes in organizational structure.

As a part of the reorganization in the spring of 1862, a Confederate soldier between eighteen and thirty-five years of age whose twelve-month term of enlistment had expired was required to re-enlist in the service. In the process, however, he could change to a different company or regiment, enlist in a new unit entirely, change to a unit from another state, or even select a different branch of service. Men were also allowed to form new companies and regiments and re-elect both company-grade (lieutenants and captains) and field-grade (colonels, lieutenant colonels and majors) officers.[64] J.P. Thomas wrote: "The State Adjutant General reported that 'entire companies and even regiments were lost, and new companies and regiments formed; in most instances retaining their names, but the regiments in all instances were composed to a great extent of new company organizations. The original 9th [Blanding's] Regiment was, in this way, wholly lost; and the old 4th [Regiment] was reduced to a mere battalion.'"[65]

When the men were allowed to choose their own officers, many were not re-elected because they were judged either too old or too incompetent to perform their duties. It should be noted, however, that many efficient officers were not re-elected simply because they were unpopular. Thomas wrote that the reorganization act of February 1862 should have been named the disorganization act since it caused the loss of many of the Confederacy's best officers, the disciplinarian being turned out by the politician.[66]

Many new organizations were created in South Carolina during the first half of 1862. Infantry regiments created in early 1862 and not already mentioned were the 2nd (Moore's) Regiment of Rifles and the Palmetto Sharpshooters. Several infantry battalions were raised in the first half of 1862 as well, including the 1st (Charleston), the 1st Battalion Sharpshooters, the 13th (4th), the 6th (Byrd's), the 7th, the 9th (Pee Dee), the 11th (Eutaw) and Dunlop's Battalion of Sharpshooters. The only cavalry regiment created in the first half of 1862 was the 1st Regiment. Cavalry battalions created were the 1st (14th), the 2nd (10th), the 3rd (4th), the 6th (17th), the 8th (2nd Battalion Reserves) and the 12th (4th Squadron). Independent cavalry units created during this time were the German Hussars, the Rebel Troop, the Charleston Light Dragoons, Harlan's Company, the Yeadon Rangers, Whitner's Troop, Hough's Company, the Ripley Rangers, A.C. Earle's Company, M.J. Kirk's Squadron, Keitt's Mounted Riflemen and E.M. Boykin's Squadron. Two artillery regiments were created in early 1862, the 1st Regulars, an augmentation of the 1st Battalion, and the 2nd (Lamar's) Regiment. The 18th Artillery Battalion and several other batteries were also created, including the Brooks Guard Artillery, the Inglis Artillery, the Palmetto Light Battery, the German Artillery, the Gist Guards Battery and the McQueen Light Artillery. Still other batteries were the Lafayette Artillery, the Pee Dee Artillery, the Washington (Walter's) Artillery, the Waccamaw Light Artillery, Ferguson's Light Artillery, the Edisto Artillery, B.E. Dickson's Battery, the Carolina Artillery, the Silverton Artillery, Willis's Battery and S.D. Lee's

Battery. Thomas wrote, "In addition to these organizations, under the call for all arms-bearing men between eighteen and thirty-five years of age for Confederate service, many separate companies of infantry, artillery and cavalry were raised, most of which became merged into regiments or other organizations."[67]

Organizations created in the second half of 1862 or later were the 25th, 26th and 27th Regiments, SCV; Brooks's Partisan Rifles, later designated Company H of the 7th Battalion; and the 2nd Battalion Sharpshooters. Six of the seven South Carolina cavalry regiments, the 2nd–7th, as well as the 19th Cavalry Battalion, were created in July 1862 or were created later in the war.

The South Carolina militia played an important role in the organization of troops for military service. As an effective fighting force, the militia's role was limited to the first few months of 1861 when the 4th Brigade, South Carolina Militia, supplied most of the manpower around Charleston Harbor. Several militia regiments remained in active service until early 1862, but by that time the militia no longer existed as a fighting force. Its major contribution between late 1862 and late 1864 lay in providing an organizational structure upon which the governor could call for reserve troops as needed. The South Carolina Militia Law of 1841 had created forty-six regiments organized into ten brigades and five divisions, with the governor as commander-in-chief. Men between sixteen and sixty years of age were eligible for service, while those between eighteen and forty-five were liable to serve for three months in South Carolina and two months outside the state. Men elected their company and field officers, brigade officers elected brigadier generals and division officers elected major generals.[68]

The first Conscription Act of April 16, 1862, which claimed for active duty all white males between eighteen and thirty-five years of age, significantly depleted the ranks of the South Carolina militia.[69] The second Conscription Act passed on September 27, 1862, further depleted the militia. The new law allowed the president to call up men between the ages of thirty-five and forty-five for three years unless the war ended sooner, an option that he implemented in stages.[70] These acts took "all the material of armies between the ages mentioned, from the control of the state."[71] The South Carolina Executive Council wrote: "To meet this new condition of things, it becomes necessary that the State shall adopt further measures to organize its forces and provide for its defence."[72] Soon after the passage of the conscription laws, the Executive Council decided to separate the remainder of the men between thirty-five and fifty from the militia and organize them into companies and regiments to be held in reserve for defense of the state or other service at the discretion of the governor.[73]

Consequently, on April 23, 1862, the Executive Council of South Carolina passed resolutions creating two corps of state reserves.[74] The 1st Corps was composed of thirty-five-year old to fifty-year-old men conscripted from within the existing South Carolina militia regiments and battalions to be held for active service anywhere the state required, as the occasion dictated.[75] They were also subject to patrol and police duty until called to active service.[76] Men of the 1st Corps were allowed to elect their company officers—the lieutenants and captains. The governor and the Executive Council were to appoint field officers—the colonels, lieutenant colonels and majors.[77] When not on active duty, men of the 1st Corps of reserves were to perform patrol duty under the command of the officers of the 2nd Corps.[78]

On May 13, 1862, the governor and the Executive Council called for the organization of five regiments, each to consist of men between thirty-five and fifty years of age in one set of companies and men between sixteen and eighteen years of age in a second set. Each company would elect its own officers, and the Executive Council would appoint the field officers of any battalions or regiments formed from the companies.[79] These regiments were to be held in reserve until ordered into active service. At all times, one company was to remain in each regiment's camp of instruction without pay, with this duty rotating among companies every two weeks.[80] Unfortunately, whether these five regiments were ever actually organized is unclear. By August 30, 1862, the 1st Corps comprised ten regiments called regiments of reserves; these regiments consisted of about eight thousand men with elected company-grade officers. Each of the ten regiments was assigned a numeric designation of two through eleven.[81] To avoid confusion with the 1st Regiment, Charleston Reserves, which was organized in October 1861, none of these new regiments were designated the "1st Regiment." Originally, the Executive Council's resolution creating the reserve corps did not apply to the 1st Regiment of Charleston Reserves. By August 22, 1862, however, the Charleston unit was officially designated the 1st Regiment of the 1st Corps of Reserves, a modification that gave the 1st Corps of Reserves eleven regiments.[82]

Between October 4, 1862, and October 31, 1862, Governor Pickens reviewed nine of the eleven reserve regiments.[83] On October 25, Secretary of War G.W. Randolph wrote James Chesnut that the Confederate States Government would accept four regiments—the 2nd, 3rd, 8th and 11th—for local service and that the remaining seven would be disbanded. Randolph also wrote that he would accept men over forty years of age for service in the reserve regiments, and that the men between thirty-five and forty, along with conscripts from the seven disbanded regiments, would be placed in existing South Carolina regiments. These four regiments, consisting of about three thousand men, were expected to be in camp in about twenty days.[84] On November 11, President Davis modified the plan to accept eight of the reserve regiments into service, with the result that, on November 18, eight of the ten new regiments of the 1st Corps Reserves entered Confederate service for state defense for ninety days.[85] These were the 2nd, 3rd, 5th, 6th, 7th, 8th, 9th and 11th. At least four of these regiments were ordered to report to Lightwood Knot Springs north of Columbia and then on to Charleston.[86] The 4th and the 10th Regiments were disbanded on November 7 because of disaffection among the men.[87]

The Secession Convention expired by its own ordinance on December 12, 1862. The very next day, the South Carolina General Assembly declared many of the Executive Council's decisions invalid.[88] In one action it revoked the Council's order to disband the 4th and 10th Regiments. On December 18, it passed an act forbidding the reserve regiments to serve more than ninety days. It also called for the replacement of council-appointed field officers through elections to be held on January 1, 1863.[89] P.G.T. Beauregard criticized this provision, and Governor M.L. Bonham requested and received an appeal. As a result, new elections were never held.[90] On February 10, 1863, after ninety days' service, the reserve regiments of the 1st Corps were disbanded.[91] The thirty-five- to forty-year-old men of the 1st Corps who had not been called to active service because of their age, however, were now required by the second Conscription Act of September 27, 1862, to enter active service. On February 18, 1863, Governor Bonham ordered the 1st, 4th and 10th Regiments back into the field. He held the remainder in reserve in anticipation of an immediate Federal assault.[92] On March 9, 1863, the governor suspended his order, and the reserves stayed at home.[93]

The 2nd Corps of Reserves was composed of men between sixteen and eighteen years of age, fifty and sixty-five years of age, alien residents and all others exempt from ordinary military duty. After organization into companies and regiments, the 2nd Corps was placed under the command of South Carolina militia officers, who were already commissioned but who could not, for some reason, serve in the 1st Corps. The 2nd Corps was used for patrol and police duty and for internal defense as required by the state. Since the 2nd Corps did not enter Confederate service, virtually no information about it appears in the *Compiled Service Records* (CSR). Additionally, little extant information about its organizational structure exists. On July 21, 1862, the Executive Council amended resolutions that said if the 1st and 2nd Corps of Reserves were brought into active service at the same time, the 1st Corps was to act as regulars and the 2nd Corps as militia.[94] When not under orders, both the 1st and 2nd Corps would perform patrol duty.[95]

To further shore up the South Carolina militia, the Executive Council passed a resolution on November 7, 1862, that contained the following directive: "the public safety imperiously demands that all white male residents of the State of South Carolina capable of bearing arms should be immediately placed into military organizations and armed." The Executive Council ordered the formation of companies to include practically all males between sixteen and sixty-five. Drill under pain of court martial was required every two weeks. The order included members of the legislature, doctors, ministers, millers and others; it exempted only a few groups like the Executive Council, judges and state treasurers. The force as a whole was designed as a district police with access to arms deposited at each courthouse.[96] To have troops available to serve as "alarm men" for military service in the South Carolina militia,[97] the commanding officer of each beat was ordered to keep a separate roll of men between forty and fifty years of age. Subject to the call of the commander in chief, these men would constitute a reserve force for the defense of the state.[98]

In the summer of 1863, Federal assaults were anticipated along the South Carolina coast. On June 6, and again on July 31, President Davis called on the governor of South Carolina to provide 5,384 volunteers for local defense and special service.[99] On June 16, Governor Bonham ordered South Carolina militia regiments to respond to President Davis's 5,000-man quota.[100] The president's authority was based on two acts passed by the Confederate Congress: the first, passed on August 21, 1861, was entitled "An act to provide for local defense and special service"; the other, passed on October 13, 1862, was called "An act to authorize the formation of volunteer companies for local defense."[101] The 1861 act authorized the president to accept volunteers to serve in a capacity and for a duration prescribed by him for the defense of exposed places or for special service.[102] Under this act, the volunteers would be mustered in Confederate service, and the president would appoint the field officers. Men were to be between forty and forty-five years of age and, beginning August 1, 1863, would serve in South Carolina for six months.[103] The governor was instructed to ask for volunteers from this age group. If the quota of 5,384 men went unmet, then the governor was authorized to draft men between forty and fifty years of age. Sixteen- and seventeen-year-old-men in the South Carolina militia were not subject to the draft. South Carolina militia regiments were ordered to assemble at their muster grounds on July 7 and to organize new companies either by volunteering or, if necessary, by means of a draft.[104] Each company was to carry between 64 and 125 privates on its roster, and each regiment was to contain ten companies.[105] The men elected their company-grade officers in early July.[106] Since all the men were volunteers, President Davis agreed on July 23 to allow them to elect their field officers as well. He set a date of July 31 for elections in all five regiments,[107] and he required the regiments to be ready for immediate service after elections were held.

As a result of the presidential call-up, about five thousand South Carolinians volunteered for service in five new regiments, known as the "South Carolina State Troops (Six Months)." It was understood that the regiments were raised only for local defense and special service—most importantly, the defense of Charleston.[108] The five regiments, numbered one through five, were ready for service on August 1. Beauregard, however, did not call them to active duty until September 5.[109] At that time, one regiment was sent to Pocotaligo, the other four to Charleston and their six months' service began.[110] In December 1863, Governor Bonham argued successfully that the six-month service should date from August 1; consequently, the five regiments of South Carolina state troops were mustered out on February 3, 1864.[111] Men between forty and forty-five years of age who were mustered out, however, were almost immediately conscripted into service again[112]

The Conscription Act passed on February 17, 1864, was entitled "An act to organize forces to serve during the war."[113] On March 1, 1864, Adjutant General Samuel Cooper implemented the new law.[114] Under it, all white male citizens of the Confederate States between seventeen and fifty years of age were liable for service within their respective states for the duration of the war.[115] Men between eighteen and forty-five were to remain with their respective organizations. Seventeen-year-old men and forty-five- to fifty-year-olds were required to form a reserve corps and were allowed to elect their own company and field officers. They were ordered to organize themselves first into companies and then into either battalions or regiments.[116] Within thirty days from March 15, the men were required either to enroll in an existing local defense company or to organize a new company. "Those between seventeen and eighteen and between forty-five and fifty were organized and commanded by General (James) Chesnut under an appointment by President Davis; some were called into active service at Charleston, of course, at Confederate expense."[117] Camps of instruction were established and provisions were made for exemptions.[118]

Eight new battalions, designated the "1st to 8th Battalions, South Carolina Reserves," were created under this law. These battalions were later referred to as the Battalions of Senior Reserves to distinguish them from the regiments of Junior Reserves. The *Yorkville Enquirer* reported in late March that the new battalions were not to be called into active service "unless a greater emergency occurs."[119] In early April 1864, the *Daily South Carolinian* reported that all eligible men were to enroll before April 16 and that the new battalions were to serve as a "reserve for state defense" within the boundaries of the state.[120] The *Yorkville Enquirer* reported on June 15 that eight new battalions had been organized.[121] On June 24, General Chesnut ordered each battalion to elect a major to command it.[122] On July 13, he issued another order calling the reserve battalions to active duty "at once" because infantry support of the artillery on John's Island and James Island was needed.[123] By July 20, several of the reserve battalions were in the field.[124] Throughout the summer of 1864, the reserve battalions continued to muster in state service, and in December, they became part of the Confederate forces. Though some of the reserve battalions were disbanded shortly before the end of the war, others were merged into nonreserve South Carolina regiments on April 9, 1865.

In August and early September 1864 South Carolina required all white males between sixteen and sixty years of age to be liable for service in the South Carolina Militia.[125] Each regiment of militia provided one new company toward the creation of four new regiments designated the "1st, 2nd, 3rd and 4th Regiments, Junior Reserves, South Carolina State Troops." They were also called "Regiments of South Carolina Militia" and "Regiments of State Troops" and might also have been known to as Battalions of State Troops.[126] These new regiments should not be confused with the 1st, 2nd, 3rd and 4th Regiments, South Carolina Militia, all of which had existed before and continued during the war. The Junior Reserves consisted of sixteen-year-old men. Before this call-up, the militia was a strictly local force, on duty as home guards and in other capacities.[127] All regiments of South Carolina Militia were ordered to rendezvous on September 12, 1864, so each could raise one company of Junior Reserves.[128] The men then went home and reassembled at Hamburg in late November. On March 29, 1865, Governor Magrath ordered militiamen who were between sixteen and seventeen years of age to assemble by April 1 in Spartanburg for the defense of the state. The Citadel and Arsenal cadets were to be placed in command of the camp of instruction.[129] By early April, all four of the regiments of Junior Reserves had been disbanded.[130] Older men were allowed to go home, but the "boys," called "State Troops, First Class Militia," were required to remain in service.[131] In early April, about seven hundred sixteen-year-olds were being held for state service and drilling at Spartanburg.[132] On April 3, they were ordered to reorganize immediately and report to Captain J.P. Thomas at Greenville. This move never took place, and on April 8, the State Troops, First Class Militia, was disbanded.

John Peyre Thomas offered an in-depth enumeration of South Carolinians who served in the War Between the States.[133] He estimated that 64,903 men were enrolled in Confederate service; of those, some 56,661 were considered effective. Thomas also estimated that 6,180 men were enrolled in state service, and that all but 3 of these were effective. Thus, of the 71,083 South Carolinians enrolled, a full 62,838 were effective. This service population of 71,083 men was drawn from an 1860 voting population of only 60,000 men.[134] In 1899 Thomas estimated that 20,101 South Carolinians were killed or died in service during the war. He noted that because many rolls were missing or incomplete, this number could run as high as 21,146. In a further breakdown, he estimated infantry deaths at 17,918, cavalry at 1,467 and artillery at 716. In his book *Broken Fortunes*, B.F. Kirkland records the deaths of South Carolinians as 18,666, but he suggests that the actual number could have been as high as 21,166 because the records of 2,500 men were missing.[135]

Thomas records a total of thirty-four infantry regiments and four infantry battalions; seven cavalry regiments, one cavalry squadron and one cavalry company; and three artillery regiments, two artillery battalions and nineteen unattached artillery batteries.[136] The accounting is actually somewhat more complicated because of duplications and other ramifications. Many independent companies, for example, were subsequently attached to battalions or regiments, and many battalions eventually merged into regiments. Additionally, a number of companies, battalions and regiments ceased to exist before the end of the war. If all duplications are avoided, the following summarizes South Carolina units in Confederate service during the war: thirty-six infantry regiments, seven infantry battalions, two artillery regiments, three artillery battalions, twenty-seven independent artillery batteries, seven cavalry regiments and one cavalry battalion. This listing includes neither the militia nor the reserves.

The basic building block of all military units during the War Between the States was the company. Men mustered in service as part of a company, and it was at the company level that all official records of individuals were kept. In the infantry, companies were referred to as such; in the cavalry, they were usually called a troop; and in the artillery, the words company and battery were used interchangeably. At the start of the war, a company was composed of 80 to 104 officers and men. Under the first Conscription Act passed in the spring of 1862, an infantry company consisted of 125 men, rank and file; each cavalry company consisted of 80 men; and a field artillery battery was made up of 150 men.[137] A captain commanded each company, with lieutenants as his immediate subordinates. Numerous independent companies were raised for local defense purposes early on, but most were consolidated into battalions or regiments before the end of the war.

Usually ten companies formed a regiment, and each regiment was commanded by a colonel, whose immediate subordinates were the lieutenant colonel and major. Four to eight companies normally formed a battalion, which was commanded by a lieutenant colonel or a major. Some battalions maintained their integrity throughout the war, but often two battalions or one battalion and several independent companies were merged to create a new regiment. Such mergers or consolidations typically occurred in South Carolina's cavalry regiments, and sometimes with the infantry and artillery as well—the creation, for example, of the 23rd, 24th, 25th, 26th and 27th Regiments, SCV, and the 2nd Regiment, South Carolina Artillery. In one instance the 4th Regiment, SCV, was raised as a regiment, but was downsized to the 13th Battalion at the reorganization as a result of losses from combat and disease. Subsequently, the 13th Battalion was disbanded and the remaining companies consolidated into just two that merged into the Hampton Legion. The cavalry branch of the service had a subdivision called the squadron, which was usually made up of two companies or troops. As the war progressed, most South Carolina cavalry squadrons were incorporated into cavalry regiments. Three to five regiments or battalions usually formed a brigade, which was commanded by a brigadier general. Three to five brigades usually formed a division, which was commanded by a major general. Three to five divisions usually formed a corps, which was under the command of a lieutenant general. Two or three corps usually formed an army.

This work concentrates on the company, battalion and regimental levels of South Carolina military organizations during the War Between the States. Companies were usually designated alphabetically, though several exceptions to this rule arose early in the war, when some regiments designated their companies numerically. The letter J was eliminated from military nomenclature because of the difficulty in distinguishing between the letters J and I when written by hand. An exception was that of the 4th Regiment, SCV, which had a Company J—the Confederate Guards. This company was composed of men from Anderson whose backgrounds were not military. Because other letter designations were already in use when they enlisted, these men innocently chose the letter J and opted to retain it even after they discovered their error.[138]

Early in the war before many companies were attached to regiments, companies were designated by the name of their first captain; Captain Bill Smith's Company, SCV, for example. When companies became attached to a regiment or battalion, they were given an alphabetic designation, such as Company B, 3rd Regiment, SCV. A common practice in most companies was to allow the men to choose a company nickname, often some brief and colorful term, in addition to its alphabetic designation or its captain's name. Many of these nicknames reflected upon the men's hometown or district, their desire to defend their rights or some person whom they wished to honor. Nicknames included the Enoree Mosquitoes, the Meeting Street Saludas, the Horry Rough and Readys, the Lancaster Invincibles and the Bozeman Guards. Some companies had more than one popular name. This practice of nicknames was common among infantry companies and almost universal among cavalry companies and independent artillery batteries, but it was virtually nonexistent among companies of the South Carolina Regular Army. A good deal of evidence suggests that most of South Carolina's volunteer companies had a popular name or nickname. Many such names have been recorded in various newspapers, books and other records. Unfortunately, others probably existed but were not preserved and thus are lost forever. Multiple sources exist for the 14th Regiment, SCV, for example, and most of its companies' popular names are well documented. None of the known regimental records for Company G of the 14th Regiment, SCV, however, contain the company nickname—the McGowan Greys; the only known source that documents this popular name is an obituary in the *Due West Times*.[139]

Keeping track of companies and individuals throughout their service is usually straightforward but can sometimes be quite confusing. Some men whose original enlistments were for the duration never re-enlisted because the companies they first joined managed to maintain their integrity throughout the war. Many companies, however, had at least one opportunity, and some even a second, to re-enlist. The first such opportunity for many South Carolina companies came in the spring and summer of 1861 when they voluntarily left state service and joined the Confederate forces. This change of service offered at least three possibilities: men and officers could transfer individually to a different company; a company could remain intact, but it could transfer to a different regiment; and some companies could disband altogether. The second opportunity for many companies to re-enlist came when the army reorganized in the spring of 1862 at the expiration of the initial twelve-month term of enlistment. This reorganization offered much the same possibilities for individuals and companies as had the changes of the preceding year. An extreme example of change can be found in the records of the Wee Nee Volunteers, which served with four different regiments and one battalion between 1861 and 1865.

At the reorganization of the Confederate army in the spring of 1862, many companies and regiments remained intact; some companies remained relatively intact but transferred to a different regiment; others disbanded completely and the men re-enlisted elsewhere. In some cases most of the men from one company re-enlisted together in a new company. The 9th Regiment, SCV, was completely disbanded, and the 4th Regiment, SCV, converted to a battalion. Further confusion arose from the practice of allowing individuals to transfer to a different company, though this did not happen on a large scale after the 1862 reorganization. Occasionally, companies were granted special permission to transfer to a different battalion or regiment, and sometimes regiments were transferred to a different brigade.

Every South Carolina company, squadron, battalion and regiment was provided with an official designation. While companies in Confederate service received alphabetic designations, regiments, battalions and cavalry squadrons were usually given numeric designations—the 1st Regiment, SCV, for example. In addition, most regiments were referred to unofficially by the name of their colonel—Gregg's regiment, for instance. Some, like the Eutaw Regiment (25th SCV) or the Pee Dee Regiment (8th SCV), had unofficial names. Three South Carolina regiments and one battalion in Confederate service received no numeric designation: the Hampton Legion, the Holcombe Legion, the Palmetto Sharpshooters and Manigault's Battalion.

Regiments and battalions in each service—infantry, cavalry and artillery—were given sequential numerical designations in 1861. All three services duplicated the use of numbers for regiments throughout the war. Numbering of battalions, on the other hand, was different. There was some duplication in the use of numbers among the three services during the first year of the war, and gaps in available information suggest that other numbers were probably skipped over and not used at all. In 1861, for example, infantry battalions were numbered the 1st, 3rd and 5th; cavalry battalions were designated the 1st, 2nd, 3rd and 4th; and artillery battalions used the designations 1st, 2nd and 3rd. At or shortly after the reorganization of the armies in 1862, all battalions in the state, regardless of service branch, seem to have been incorporated into a system of numerical designation that both avoided duplication of numbering among the various branches and started the numbering sequence all over again. There is, however, no documentation for this theory; it is simply an observation. At the reorganization, some battalions became full regiments, others remained unchanged and a few ceased to exist altogether. After that, the infantry battalions, some old and others new, were the 1st, 2nd, 3rd, 5th, 6th, 7th, 9th, 11th and 13th. The cavalry used the 4th, 8th, 10th, 12th, 14th, 16th, 17th and 19th. Artillery had the 15th and 18th Battalions. The artillery also carried the 3rd Battalion, which appears to duplicate the 3rd Infantry Battalion, but the artillery battalion, which failed in an effort to become a regiment, probably retained its designation for that reason.

An officer could lose his commission in several ways. Many, some excellent and some downright incompetent, were simply not re-elected at the reorganization of the Confederate armies in the spring of 1862 and were consequently dropped from the rolls of their respective organizations.

Such officers were then required to serve elsewhere unless they were overage or otherwise exempt. An officer could resign his commission by tendering a letter of resignation to the secretary of war through his commanding officer, who would either recommend approval or, rarely, denial and forward the letter up the chain of command. Most officers who resigned did so because chronic or severe illness, advanced age or the effect of wounds left them unable to perform their duties. A few resigned because they realized they lacked the intellect or leadership ability needed for their position. Confederate law gave an officer the option of resigning his commission if he held certain offices in the civil government, and some individuals resigned on those grounds. A few officers were cashiered or discharged by court martial, usually for drunkenness on duty or some other crime. The Invalid Corps was created by the Confederate Congress on February 17, 1864, to retain competent officers who wished to remain in the service but who had been disabled for further duty in the field. Many officers were retired to the Invalid Corps after approval from a medical examiners' board upon documentation by means of a surgeon's certificate. These men were usually assigned to light duty as officers in camps of instruction, at military posts or as enrolling officers.

This work will emphasize the company, battalion and regimental organization of South Carolina troops during the War Between the States. To obtain proper perspective, however, it is also necessary to present a basic outline of the relationship of battalions and regiments to higher levels of organization—brigades, divisions, corps and armies, as well as departments and their sub-units of military districts and subdivisions. This work gives a cursory overview of this relationship so readers can relate regiments and battalions to each other in their respective higher levels of organization. An excellent, and quite exhaustive, review of these higher levels of organization can be found in *Compendium of the Confederate Armies, South Carolina and Georgia* by Stewart Sifakis.

This work presents a history of South Carolina's military organizations in the War Between the States in four volumes. Within each volume, the order of presentation is: first, infantry, followed by cavalry and artillery. Volume I discusses those organizations whose men came from the Lowcountry and the Pee Dee; Volume II discusses those whose men came from the Midlands; Volume III discusses those whose men came from the Upstate; and Volume IV discusses those units that drew from all over the state, militia, reserves and miscellaneous organizations. Within each volume, each organization is set forth and described in numeric order—the 1st Infantry Regiment, for example. This order generally follows that of the *Compiled Service Records*, but, for the sake of clarity, there are exceptions. In numeric order, regiments are listed first, followed by battalions, squadrons and, finally, independent companies. The presentation of each regiment and battalion follows the same pattern. First, it gives a history of the organization of each unit followed by a brief wartime biography of each field officer (colonels, lieutenant colonels and majors). Next, it presents a synopsis of the origins and commanders (captains) of each company. Finally, it summarizes the brigade affiliations and the major movements and engagements of each regiment or battalion.

Unit Designation	When Organized	Under What Authority	Initial Enlistment
1st Regiment, SCV (Gregg's 6-month Regiment)	01/08/61	2	6 months
1st Regiment, South Carolina Infantry, Regulars	01/28/61	3 and 4	3 years
1st Battalion, South Carolina Artillery, Regulars	01/28/61	3 and 4	3 years
DeSaussure's Cavalry Squadron, Regulars	01/28/61	3 and 4	3 years
1st SCV Infantry(Hagood's)	04/12/61	1	12 months
2nd SCV Infantry	04/09/61	1	12 months
3rd SCV Infantry	04/14/61	1	12 months
4th SCV Infantry	04/14/61	1	12 months
5th SCV Infantry	04/13/61	1	12 months
6th SCV Infantry	04/11/61	1	12 months
7th SCV Infantry	04/15/61	1	12 months
8th SCV Infantry	04/14/61	1	12 months
9th SCV Infantry	07/12/61 to date from 04/08/61	1	12 months
10th SCV Infantry	~05/31/61	1	12 months
11th SCV Infantry	05/20/61	1	12 months
12th SCV Infantry	08/30/61	7	war
13th SCV Infantry	09/04/61	7	war
14th SCV Infantry	09/10/61	7	war
15th SCV Infantry	09/10/61	7	war
Gregg's (reorganized) 1st SCV Infantry	08–09/61	8	war
Orr's Regiment Rifles	07/20/61	8	war
5th Battalion Infantry	12/10/61	8	war
1st Battalion Cavalry	10/31/61	25	war

Unit Designation	When Organized	Under What Authority	Initial Enlistment
2nd Battalion Artillery	10/61	1	war
3rd Battalion Artillery	07–12/61	7	war
Manigault's Battalion	12/61	17	war
Chesterfield Light Artillery	08/25/61	—	war
16th SCV Infantry	12/12/61	10	12 months
17th SCV Infantry	12/18/61	6	12 months
Holcombe Legion	11/21/61	22	12 months
Hatch's Battalion Coast Rangers	09/61	—	mixed
3rd Battalion Infantry	12/04/61	10	12 months
Pee Dee Legion, South Carolina Militia	12/60–01/61	—	12 months
1st (Martin's) Cavalry Regiment, South Carolina Militia	11/61	2	90 days
4th Brigade, South Carolina Militia	1861	2	—
Stono Scouts	11/10/61	—	—
W.F. Percival's Company	11/61	—	—
South Carolina College Cadets	01/19/61	—	—
German Light Artillery	08/22/61	—	5 years
Beaufort Volunteer Artillery	05/61	1	12 months
Bonneau's Artillery	10/01/61	—	—
Calhoun Light Artillery	~04/26/61	—	~90 days
Santee Light Artillery	10/30/61	prob. 17	war
Macbeth Artillery	09/16/61	—	war
Marion Artillery	09/61	—	—
Washington (Hart's) Artillery	05/18/61	6	12 months
1st Regiment Charleston Guards	—	—	—
1st Regiment Reserves, South Carolina Militia	11/11/61	—	—
A.H.Boykin's Cavalry Troop	06/26/61	—	war
J.G.Harlan's Company	12/30/61	—	—
Lipscomb's Cavalry Troop	12/61	—	—
St. James Mounted Riflemen, Company A	04/15/61	9	war
Marion Men of Winyah	05/05/61	—	—
Trenholm's Squadron	09/09/61	—	12 months
Battalion South Carolina Cadets	01/28/61	24	—
6th Battalion Infantry	05/29/62	prob. 18	war

Unit Designation	When Organized	Under What Authority	Initial Enlistment
18th SCV Infantry	01/02/62	10	12 months
19th SCV Infantry	01/03/62	10	12 months
20th SCV Infantry	01/11/62	10	12 months
21st SCV Infantry	11/12/61	10	12 months
22nd SCV Infantry	12/61	10	12 months
23rd SCV Infantry	11/15/61	10, 39	mixed
24th SCV Infantry	12/61–04/62	10, 11	war
25th SCV Infantry	07/22/62	11 and 38	war
26th SCV Infantry	09/09/62	20	mixed
27th SCV Infantry	09/30/63	21	war
2nd Regiment Rifles	04/27/62	35	war
2nd Battalion Sharpshooters	09/01/62	prob. 10	—
4th (13th) Battalion Infantry	04/21/62	36	3 years or war
15th Battalion Artillery Regulars	summer 1861	37	3 years
18th Battalion Artillery	05/01/62	—	war
Palmetto Sharpshooters	04/16/62	23	2 years or war
1st Regiment Artillery Regulars	03/25/62	5	war
2nd Regiment Artillery	04/12/62	34	war
1st Regiment Cavalry	06/25/62	26	war
2nd Regiment Cavalry	08/22/62	27	war
3rd Regiment Cavalry	08/62	29	war
4th Regiment Cavalry	12/16/62	30	war
5th Regiment Cavalry	01/18/63	31	war
6th Regiment Cavalry	11/01/62	32	war
7th Regiment Cavalry	03/18/64	33	war
7th Battalion Infantry	02/22/62	19	war
1st (Charleston) Battalion Infantry	02/17/62	15	12 months
1st Battalion Sharpshooters	06/62	16	—
11th Battalion Infantry	~02/22/62	10	12 months
9th Battalion Infantry	01–03/62	prob. 10	12 months
1st (14th) Battalion Cavalry	01/62	—	12 months
3rd (4th) Battalion Cavalry	01–02/62	prob. 10	12 months
2nd (10th) Battalion Cavalry	01/19/62	—	12 months
6th (17th) Battalion Cavalry	03/62	—	mixed
Brooks Guard Artillery	01/28/62	17	2 years and 3 months
Inglis Light Artillery	03/20/62	17	war

Unit Designation	When Organized	Under What Authority	Initial Enlistment
Palmetto Light Battery	~04/08/62	—	—
German Artillery	02/12/62	prob. 10	—
Gist Guards Artillery	02/62	prob. 10	3 years
McQueen Light Artillery	04/14/62	—	—
Lafayette Artillery	03/13/62	prob. 10	12 months
12th Battalion (4th Squadron Cavalry)	01/01/62	—	mixed
16th (6th) Battalion Cavalry	07/21/62	prob. 10 and 11	war
19th Battalion Cavalry	12/20/64	—	war
Pee Dee Artillery	03/62	—	war
Washington (Walter's) Artillery	02/20/62	prob. 10 or 11	3 years or war
Waccamaw Light Artillery	01/20/62	prob. 10	war
Ferguson's Light Battery	04/62	—	—
Edisto Artillery	03/19/62	—	war
B.E.Dickson's Battery	03/19/62	—	war
Carolina Artillery	04/12/62	—	war
Silverton Artillery	04/09/62	—	2 years or war
Willis's Battery	spring 1862	—	—
S.D. Lee's Battery	~05/12/61	—	—
South Carolina Reserve Regiments	11/62	12, 40	90 days
South Carolina State Troops	08/04/63	14	6 months
South Carolina Reserve Battalions	09/64	13	war
South Carolina Junior Reserves	summer 1864	41	—
Brooks Foreign Battalion	10/10/64	—	—
Dunlop's Battalion Sharpshooters	05/03/62	—	—
8th Battalion (2nd Battalion Reserves) Cavalry	05/30/62	28	war
St. Peters Guards	1861	9	—
German Hussars	1861	prob. 9	—
Rebel Troop	01/17/62	prob. 10	—
Charleston Light Dragoons	04/61	prob. 10	—
Yeadon Rangers	07/27/62	—	war
Whitner's Troop	—	—	—
Hough's Company	01/01/62	—	war

Unit Designation	When Organized	Under What Authority	Initial Enlistment
Ripley Rangers	04/03/62	—	war
A.C. Earle's Company	04/15/62	—	war
M.J. Kirk's Squadron	07/11/62	—	war
Keitt's Mounted Riflemen	06/10/63	—	—
E.M. Boykin's Squadron	11/05/62	—	—
Brooks Infantry Partisan Rangers	07/14/62	17	war

1. South Carolina legislature act of December 17, 1860.
2. South Carolina Convention resolution of January 1, 1861.
3. South Carolina Convention resolution of December 31, 1860.
4. South Carolina legislature act of January 28, 1861.
5. South Carolina legislature act of December 1861.
6. President Davis authorized the Hampton Legion on April 27, 1861.
7. President Davis called for three thousand men to enlist for the duration of the war on June 30, 1861.
8. President Davis called for two regiments to enlist for the duration of the war on July 1, 1861.
9. Special resolution of the South Carolina Convention in 1861 calling for twenty-one cavalry companies to serve until the end of the legislative session.
10. South Carolina legislature resolutions of November 1861 and December 7, 1861, and Governor Pickens's calls on November 11, 1861, and December 9, 1861, for special local defense troops.
11. Confederate Congress act of February 28, 1862.
12. South Carolina Executive Council created two corps of reserves in the summer of 1862.
13. Confederate Conscription Act of February 17, 1864.
14. Confederate Congress act of August 21 1861, and Confederate Congress act of October 13, 1862 and President Davis's call for troops.
15. Arose from a failed scheme of John Pemberton to raise a battalion of sharpshooters in late 1861 and early 1862.
16. Primarily compulsory draft and a few volunteers.
17. Special permission from the Confederate War Department.
18. A series of calls in 1862 (February 2, 21 and 28, 1862, and March 5, 1862) for eighteen thousand South Carolinians to enlist for the duration of the war.
19. Confederate Congress called for twenty-five hundred men for the duration of the war.

20. Consolidation of the 6th and 9th Infantry Battalions.
21. Consolidation of the 1st (Charleston) Battalion and the 1st Battalion Sharpshooters.
22. Governor Pickens authorized the Holcombe Legion in the fall of 1861.
23. Act of Congress and permission of the secretary of war.
24. South Carolina legislature created the South Carolina Military Academy (The Citadel and The Arsenal) as well as the Battalion State Cadets.
25. Governor Pickens called up the 1st Battalion in the fall of 1861.
26. Augmentation of the 1st Battalion Cavalry.
27. Alignment of the Hampton Legion Cavalry Battalion with the 4th (3rd) Cavalry Battalion, Lipscomb's Company and A.H. Boykin's Company.
28. Consolidation of eight independent companies.
29. Consolidation of the 8th cavalry Battalion (2nd Battalion Reserves) with three independent companies.
30. Augmentation of the 10th and 12th Cavalry Battalions with B.H. Rutledge's Company and Thomas Pinckney's Company.
31. Augmentation of the 14th and 17th Cavalry Battalions with Harlan's Company and Whilden's Company.
32. Augmentation of the 16th (6th) Cavalry Battalion with three companies.
33. Augmentation of the Holcombe Legion Cavalry Battalion with Tucker's Squadron, Trenholm's Squadron and E. Boykin's Squadron.
34. Augmentation of the 2nd (Lamar's) Artillery Battalion with six companies when the secretary of war called for additional troops on February 2, 1862.
35. Augmentation of the 5th Battalion Infantry.
36. Abatement of the 4th Regiment Infantry.
37. Formed from DeSaussure's Cavalry Squadron Regulars.
38. Augmentation of the 11th Battalion Infantry.
39. Augmentation of Hatch's Battalion Coast Rangers.
40. Confederate Conscription Act of September 17, 1862, and South Carolina Executive Council resolutions of April 23, 1862 and November 7, 1862.
41. South Carolina Militia Laws, not Confederate States troops.

1.

THE 1ˢᵀ (CHARLESTON) BATTALION, INFANTRY

T he 1ˢᵗ (Charleston) Battalion, Infantry, was also known as Gaillard's Battalion, the Charleston Battalion and the 1ˢᵗ Infantry Battalion. It was raised in Charleston in early 1862, and its muster in state service dated from February 17. Four of its companies—the Charleston Riflemen, the Sumter Guard, the Calhoun Guard and the Charleston Light Infantry—went into camp on March 10.[1] Following the addition of two new companies, the original six, designated with the letters A to F, mustered in Confederate service between March 17 and March 28 for twelve months service, primarily for local defense.[2] A seventh company, G, was added to the battalion in August 1863. All officers and many of the enlisted men were Charlestonians who had previously served in one or another of Charleston's militia units. In February 1862, the *Mercury* reported that a new battalion had been organized by assimilating several of the companies in Charleston's 1ˢᵗ and 17ᵗʰ South Carolina Militia Regiments.[3] These militia companies included the Union Light Infantry, the Irish Volunteers, the Emerald Light Infantry, the Sarsfield Light Infantry, the Jasper Greens and the Montgomery Guards. The battalion was reorganized on May 3, 1862, for three years, or for the duration of the war. The 1ˢᵗ (Charleston) Battalion was consolidated with a smaller battalion, the First Battalion of Sharpshooters, to form the 27ᵗʰ Regiment, SCV, on September 30, 1863.

FIELD OFFICERS

Peter Charles Gaillard, a Charleston lawyer and the only commander of the battalion, graduated from the United States Military Academy at West Point in 1835 and served in the United States Army until 1838. He saw state service as well—as colonel of the 17ᵗʰ Regiment, South

Carolina Militia—before Adjutant and Inspector General States Rights Gist appointed him lieutenant colonel of the battalion in March 1862.[4] His subsequent election to the post came on April 14, 1862, but the *Mercury* charged that the procedure was illegal.[5] In accordance with the Conscription Act regarding the reorganization of Confederate armies, a new election was held, and Gaillard was re-elected lieutenant colonel on May 3, 1862.[6] He was slightly wounded in the knee at Secessionville on June 16, 1862, and, while stationed at Battery Wagner on August 23, 1863, he was wounded in the leg and left hand. His left hand and wrist were so badly mangled by a shell that amputation above the wrist was necessary.[7] Gaillard was promoted to colonel of the newly-created 27th Regiment, SCV, on October 17, 1863, with rank from October 2. Krick records Gaillard's middle name as Cheves, but the marker honoring him at the French Protestant Church in Charleston shows the name Charles.[8] Gaillard was regarded as "efficient and brave" as well as "gallant and distinguished."[9]

J.M. Harleston was chosen major at the disputed election of April 14, 1862. He served less than a month and was not re-elected on May 3, 1862.[10] The CSR, in fact, does not list Harleston as major at all, but J.P. Thomas shows him as senior major of the battalion.[11]

David Ramsay, a Charleston lawyer and captain of Company F, was elected major on May 3, 1862.[12] On July 18, 1863, while leading a detachment of the Charleston Battalion in an effort to retake a sea face battery occupied by Federal troops at Battery Wagner, Ramsay sustained a mortal wound in the back, probably from friendly fire.[13] He died at his home in Charleston at nine thirty on the evening of August 4.[14] The CSR states the date of his death, incorrectly, as both August 5 and August 6. The White Point Battery in Charleston was renamed Battery Ramsay in his honor.

Julius Augustus Blake of Charleston was promoted from captain of Company A to major as a replacement for Ramsay in mid-August 1863.[15] The CSR does not give the date of his promotion, but Blake signed as "major-commanding" the battalion in October 1863. He was promoted to lieutenant colonel of the 27th Regiment on October 17, 1863, with rank from October 2.

COMPANIES

Company A, the Charleston Riflemen, was organized in 1806 and was part of the 17th Regiment, South Carolina Militia, before the war.[16] It was also designated Company A from February to the reorganization in May 1862. Some of its men had also served in the Sarsfield Light Infantry and Emerald Light Infantry of the 1st Regiment Rifles, South Carolina Militia, before February 1862. Julius A. Blake was elected captain on August 7, 1861, while the company was still a militia unit.[17] When it entered state service as part of the 1st Battalion on February 17, 1862, Blake was re-elected captain; his commission bore the same date.[18] The company mustered in Confederate service in Charleston on March 17 for twelve months' service as local defense troops.[19] Blake retained the captain's post with rank from March 18. He was slightly wounded at Secessionville on June 16, 1862, and was promoted to major in August 1863.[20] William Dove Walter was promoted from first lieutenant to captain as Blake's replacement in mid-August.[21] When the battalion merged into the 27th Regiment, Company A became Company I but retained the name of Charleston Riflemen. J.P. Thomas wrote, incorrectly, that the Charleston Riflemen became Company A of the 27th Regiment.[22]

Thomas Y. Simons, who was elected captain in state service on February 17, 1862, commanded Company B, the Charleston Light Infantry. It was also designated Company B from February to the reorganization in May 1862. Simons, who had served previously as captain of the Jamison Rifles, 1st Regiment Rifles, South Carolina Militia, mustered in Confederate service as captain of Company B on March 24. The *Mercury* reported in February that the men of the Montgomery Guard and the Jasper Greens of the 17th Regiment, South Carolina Militia, united with the Sarsfield Light Infantry and the Emerald Light Infantry of the 1st Regiment, South Carolina Militia, to create a new company called the Charleston Light Infantry, which then joined the 1st Battalion on February 22.[23] The Charleston Light Infantry mustered in Confederate service for twelve months on March 24.[24] Most of its men were from Charleston, Spartanburg and Ireland, although several other South Carolina towns were represented as well. Simons was bruised and stunned by a shell at Battery Wagner on July 18, 1863.[25] At about 200 members, Company B was too large. It was subdivided on August 14, 1863: about 125 men remained as Company B, and the rest went into the newly-created Company G, also called the Charleston Light Infantry.[26] At that time, the men of Company B re-elected Simons captain.[27] Company B of the Charleston Battalion became Company B of the 27th Regiment in September 1863, and Company G became Company K of the 27th.

Company C, the Irish Volunteers, evolved from a prewar Charleston militia company of the same name created about 1783.[28] This original company of Irishmen was part of the 17th Regiment, South Carolina Militia. The prewar Irish Volunteers raised two companies from their ranks for Confederate service, Company K of Gregg's 1st Regiment, SCV, and Company C of the Charleston Battalion; both were called Irish Volunteers. Company C mustered in Confederate service in Charleston on April 7,

1862, for one year. Edward Magrath was captain of both the militia unit and Company C. His election to captain in state service came on February 17, 1862, and he mustered in Confederate service on March 17. Poor health forced Magrath to resign in April 1862.[29] He later commanded the 1st Regiment of Charleston Guards. First Lieutenant William Hasett Ryan replaced Magrath as captain in April 1862. During a night assault on July 18, 1863, Ryan was killed instantly as he led his men in a counterattack on Federal troops who had entered Battery Wagner.[30] A battery on the east side of James Island was named in Ryan's memory.[31] First Lieutenant James M. Mulvaney was promoted to captain with rank from July 18.[32] Charleston's Irish Volunteers of Company C became Company H of the 27th Regiment in September 1863. J.P. Thomas records, probably incorrectly, that the Irish Volunteers became Company F of the 27th Regiment.[33]

Company D, the Sumter Guards, was also known as the Sumter Guard Volunteers and the Gamecocks, both names referring to Revolutionary War General Thomas Sumter.[34] Before the war, the company was part of Charleston's 17th Regiment, South Carolina Militia. It was also designated Company C from February to the reorganization in May 1862. Henry Campbell King, a Charleston lawyer and the original first lieutenant, was promoted to captain on May 20, 1861, when the first captain resigned.[35] King was re-elected on February 17, 1862, when the company entered state service.[36] Company D mustered in Confederate service for twelve months on March 24.[37] Mortally wounded in the breast at the battle of Secessionville on June 16, 1862, King died in Charleston in the afternoon of the following day.[38] J. Ward Hopkins, who had been wounded in the shoulder at Legare's place on June 3, 1862, was promoted to captain as King's replacement on June 17 and retained command when the company became Company D in the 27th Regiment in September 1863.[39] J.P. Thomas concurred that the Sumter Guards became Company D of the 27th Regiment.[40]

Company E, the Calhoun Guards, or Guard, was also part of Charleston's 17th Regiment, South Carolina Militia. The company mustered in Confederate service for twelve months on March 24, 1862.[41] It was also designated Company D from February to the reorganization in May 1862. Francis Turquand Miles, MD, was elected captain on February 17, although his commission was actually dated March 24.[42] Miles was severely wounded in the thigh at Secessionville on June 16, 1862.[43] While serving as heavy artillery in the summer of 1863, a detachment from Company E was sent to Battery Wagner.[44] Miles and his entire gun crew were either wounded or stunned when a shell burst among them on August 17.[45] Miles retained command of the company when it became Company A of the 27th

Regiment in September 1863. J.P. Thomas records, probably incorrectly, that the Calhoun Guards became Company C of the 27th Regiment.[46]

Company F, the Union Light Infantry Volunteers, was also called the "Union Light Infantry Volunteers and German Fusiliers," the result of a consolidation of two companies—the Union Light Infantry Volunteers and the German Fusiliers—from the 17th Regiment, South Carolina Militia.[47] Organized from Charleston's Scottish population about 1812, the Union Light Infantry Volunteers was part of Charleston's prewar 17th Regiment, South Carolina Militia; the German Fusiliers had been organized in May 1775, making it the oldest volunteer corps in the state at the outbreak of the war. In February 1862, the conscription laws severely depleted the ranks of the militia companies—most of the German Fusiliers became too old for Confederate service and the members who were still eligible were too few to create a complete company. As a result, the men were consolidated with the Union Light Infantry to form Company F, which mustered in Confederate service in Charleston on March 15 for twelve months' service.[48] Most of the men were from Charleston, but many were from York and Spartanburg.[49] David Ramsay, who had been captain of the militia company, was re-elected on February 17. Ramsay was elected major of the Charleston Battalion on May 3, and First Lieutenant Samuel Lord Jr. was promoted to captain on April 16 with rank from May 3, 1862.[50] Lord was bruised in the side by a shell at Battery Wagner on August 17, 1863.[51] Company F became Company C of the 27th Regiment in September 1863. J.P. Thomas records, probably incorrectly, that Company F became Company E of the 27th Regiment.[52]

Company G, the Charleston Light Infantry, was created on August 14, 1863, by a special order dividing Company B into two companies.[53] Its men were from Charleston, Spartanburg, Ireland and various other parts of the state. William Clarkson, previously first lieutenant in Company B, was elected captain on August 14.[54] He had been wounded at Battery Wagner on July 18, 1863, and retained command when Company G became Company K of the 27th Regiment in September. Unfortunately, Company K of the 27th Regiment was disbanded in 1864; the secretary of war gave the order on April 1, but the company was probably not disbanded until July 11, at which time Captain Clarkson returned to his original company, now designated Company B of the 27th Regiment, with the rank of first lieutenant.

BRIGADE AFFILIATIONS

The Charleston Battalion was assigned to the 1st South Carolina Military District of the Department of South Carolina, Georgia and Florida. It was attached to Johnson Hagood's Brigade on September 20, 1863, ten days before the creation of the 27th Regiment.[55]

MAJOR MOVEMENTS AND ENGAGEMENTS

Prior to merging with the 1st Battalion of Sharpshooters to form the 27th Regiment, SCV, on September 30, 1863, the Charleston Battalion spent its entire nineteen-month existence in the vicinity of Charleston and the surrounding islands. On March 9, 1862, Company A, and probably some, if not all the other companies, entered Camp Gist at Magnolia for a period of instruction. On April 14 and 15, the battalion left the city with its six companies, A to F, for the James Island fortifications.[56] It was sent to Secessionville on April 22. During May and the first half of June, the Charleston Battalion performed picket duty on Legare's and Grimball's plantations near Secessionville. A brief skirmish with enemy forces erupted on June 3 while a group of men worked to recover three artillery pieces from Chichester's Battery, which had been lost in the marsh the day before at Legare's plantation on Sol Legare Island.[57] The battalion was engaged inside the Tower Battery during the battle of Secessionville on June 16. It was ordered to camp at the St. Stephens railroad station on July 8.[58] It returned to Charleston for provost guard duty on July 20 and, with few exceptions, was based in Charleston until early July 1863.[59] In what was a common practice for many of the battalions and regiments stationed around Charleston at that time, companies were temporarily detached and sent elsewhere. Company A, for example, was stationed at Camp Limehouse in Charleston in September 1862. A detachment of twenty-five men from Company B went to Fort Sumter where they were engaged as sharpshooters during the Federal ironclad attack on April 7, 1863.[60] Company E served as heavy artillery at White Point Gardens on the tip of the Charleston peninsula from January to July 1863.[61]

On July 11, 1863, the battalion was transferred to Secessionville and then to Fort Johnson on James Island.[62] On July 15 five companies were transferred to the hotly contested Battery Wagner to serve the first of three tours of duty as part of the garrison there.[63] The battalion endured four days of heavy shelling, which culminated on July 18, when Federal forces threw nine thousand shells at the battery, where the Charleston Battalion was posted in an exposed position on the parapet. Eight men from the battalion were killed and twenty were wounded that day. Companies A and B fought outside Battery Wagner, and Companies C, D and F fought inside during the night assault on July 18.[64] The battalion returned to Charleston on July

20 and remained until the thirty-first.[65] It was sent back to Battery Wagner on August 1 and remained there until the evening of the sixth, when it returned to Charleston.[66] Company E, serving as heavy artillery, was sent to Battery Wagner on July 31 and again on August 16.[67] Various companies of the Charleston Battalion were engaged at Battery Wagner from August 19 to 27; a particularly heavy engagement occurred on August 23.[68] The battalion was relieved at Battery Wagner on either August 24 or 25, but some elements remained there through the twenty-seventh.[69] From late August to early September the battalion was in Charleston, but at ten o'clock on the night of September 4 it was sent to relieve the 1st Regiment, South Carolina Artillery, at Fort Sumter because heavy artillery was no longer needed there.[70] The Charleston Battalion was the first infantry unit to garrison the fort after it was abandoned as an artillery post, and the battalion performed garrison duty there for the next three weeks.[71] At about one in the morning on September 9, the men of the battalion repelled a combined Federal army and navy boat assault on the fort by hurling bricks at the enemy when they ran low on ammunition. For this, the unit earned the sobriquet "Brickbat Battalion."[72] On September 20 the Charleston Battalion was sent back to Charleston and assigned to provost guard duty.[73] It merged with the 1st Battalion of Sharpshooters on September 30, 1863, to become the 27th Regiment, SCV. The 27th Regiment was the last, and highest numbered, infantry regiment to be created in South Carolina.

2.

THE 1ST REGIMENT, CHARLESTON (SOUTH CAROLINA) GUARDS

Although the record is unclear as to whether or not the 1st Regiment, Charleston (South Carolina) Guards, was originally part of the South Carolina Militia, we know it was in the service of the Confederate States in the summer of 1863, well before the regiments of state troops were called up on September 5.

Colonel Edward McGrath, who had been captain of the Charleston Battalion's Company C, the Irish Volunteers, commanded the regiment until April 1862. The regimental major was W.A. Wardlaw, who had also served as the major of the 1st Regiment Reserves, South Carolina Militia. The CSR does not show a lieutenant colonel for the regiment.

J.H. Taylor commanded Company A, and A. Mercer commanded Company D until July 19, 1863, when he resigned because he was appointed assistant surgeon of the regiment. First Lieutenant A. Moroso replaced him. E. Prendergast commanded Company F; T.W. Holwell was captain of Company G; S.Y. Tupper led Company H. Tupper, who was captain of the Vigilant Rifles before the war, tendered the services of the company to the governor of South Carolina on November 19, 1860. Tupper and the Vigilant Rifles served in the 4th Brigade, South Carolina Militia, early in 1861, and later that year he served in the 1st Regiment, South Carolina Artillery Militia. On July 10, 1863, Tupper enlisted as captain of Company H of the 1st Regiment Charleston Guards. An order dated May 29, 1864, authorized him to raise a company of citizens and volunteers, who were then exempt from immediate military duty, for service in the batteries in and around the city of Charleston. This force served under Tupper's command as an auxiliary to the army in the defense of Charleston.[1] Another order, dated September 23, 1864, detached Tupper for duty as an agent of state commissioners charged with removing noncombatants from Charleston. Tupper also signed official documents as the commanding officer of Company F of the

Bureau Battalion on December 10, 1864. During this assignment, he was stationed at Battery Waring at Chisholm's Mill. His name appears again on January 31, 1865, as captain of Tupper's section of artillery in the South Carolina militia.[2] M.W. Blythewood commanded Company I. Companies B, C and E are not mentioned in the CSR.

The regiment was part of the 5th Subdivision under DeSaussure in the 1st South Carolina Military District commanded by Ripley in the summer of 1863. The exact dates of its organization are unknown, but it served from July 10 to September 26, 1863, at the Military Hall in Charleston.[3]

3.

MANIGAULT'S BATTALION, SOUTH CAROLINA VOLUNTEERS

Manigault's Battalion, SCV, did not have a numeric designation. It is included here for convenience since three of its final complement of seven companies became the 6th, or Byrd's, Battalion in May 1862. In September 1861, some South Carolinians, finding themselves disillusioned with the militia units assigned to protect the area between Charleston and the Santee River, sought permission for Edward Manigault to raise a battalion as a replacement.[1] The War Department gave its consent in December, authorizing a battalion for special service; that is, local defense. Officially organized at McClellanville on December 22, 1861, Manigault's Battalion was similar to the "legion" concept in that it consisted of all three military branches: artillery, infantry and cavalry. The battalion's whole purpose was to provide local defense between the North Santee River and Charleston. Although J.P. Thomas wrote that all the companies enlisted for the duration of the war, only four of the original seven did so; the rest mustered in for twelve months' service.[2] Manigault's Battalion disbanded at the reorganization in May 1862. At that time, two of the twelve-month companies re-enlisted, and the other was disbanded. Those that originally enlisted for the duration were unaffected by the reorganization.

FIELD OFFICER

Edward Manigault, brother of Brigadier General Arthur Manigault and veteran of the Mexican War, was major and the only field officer of Manigault's Battalion. In mid-1861, he had served as the chief of ordnance for South Carolina with the rank of colonel but resigned that position on October 1.[3] Manigault was commissioned major of the new battalion upon its organization and assumed command on December 22,

1861. Ripley states that Manigault became major on October 31.[4] He was not re-elected at the reorganization.[5] The *Mercury* reported that Manigault was one of the three most capable South Carolina officers displaced by the elections at the reorganization in the spring of 1862.[6] Manigault's record over the next year is unclear. We know only that he served as a volunteer aide to Brigadier General Roswell Ripley and that he was present at Fort Sumter during the "Ironclad Attack" on April 7, 1863. The record picks him up again on June 8, 1863, when he was appointed major in command of the 18th Battalion South Carolina Artillery, also called the South Carolina Siege Train, with rank from May 23, 1863.

COMPANIES

Company A, the St. James Santee Mounted Riflemen, was also called the Mounted Rifles Company and Captain Thomas Pinckney's Company. Following a resolution of the South Carolina Convention, it was organized on April 15, 1861, as Thomas Pinckney's Independent Mounted Riflemen. The company tendered its services to President Davis some time in 1861 and performed local service on the South Carolina coast between Charleston and the North Santee River. At McClellanville on October 31, the company mustered in Confederate service for the duration of the war. The St. James Santee Mounted Riflemen joined Manigault's Battalion upon its organization in December. Its men were from Charleston, Georgetown, Clarendon and Beaufort Districts, with a few from Orangeburg and Horry Districts.[7] The company derived its name from the St. James Santee area around McClellanville. Thomas Pinckney was commissioned captain on April 15, 1861. On February 10, 1862, General Roswell Ripley ordered the company increased to squadron size, about 160 men, and then subdivided into two companies of roughly equal size. About May 1, 1862, the company became two, both of which served in Manigault's Battalion for a couple of weeks before the battalion was disbanded about the eighteenth. Pinckney retained command of one company, and Louis A. Whilden, who was promoted from first lieutenant to captain on May 1, led the other. His middle name is shown as both Augustus and Angstree.[8] Later in May, Pinckney's Company, officially Company A, St. James Mounted Riflemen, was attached to Byrd's 6th Battalion, South Carolina Infantry, and in December it became Company D of the 4th Regiment, South Carolina Cavalry. Whilden's Company, called Company B, St. James Mounted Riflemen, mustered in Confederate service for the duration of the war on May 1, 1862, at Camp Palmer on the South Santee River. After Manigault's Battalion was disbanded, Whilden's Company was attached to Byrd's 6th

Battalion without a letter designation. In January 1863, it became Company E of the 5th Regiment, South Carolina Cavalry.

Company B, the Santee Light Artillery, was the artillery component of Manigault's Battalion. Its captain was Christopher "Kit" Gaillard. Many of its men had been in the first Company G of the 10th Regiment, SCV, and when that company disbanded in September 1861, they had enlisted in the Santee Light Artillery. They mustered in Confederate service on October 31, 1861, at St. James Santee for the duration of the war.[9] Shortly after that, their battery was attached to Manigault's Battalion. After the reorganization in May 1862, the Santee Light Artillery was attached to Byrd's 6th Battalion as an unlettered company. It then became an independent artillery battery called the Santee Light Artillery or Gaillard's Company of Light Artillery, SCV, for the remainder of the war. Gaillard's Company was a six-gun battery for about two years before it converted to a four-gun battery.[10] Most of its men were from Williamsburg and Charleston Districts, but a few came from Richland, Barnwell, Clarendon and Marion Districts.

John A. Leland, who was elected captain on November 18, 1861, commanded Company C, the Trenholm Rifles.[11] This company was also called the Infantry Company–Trenholm Rifles and Company A.[12] On November 18, 1861, at Mount Pleasant, the company mustered in Confederate service for twelve months.[13] Originally called the Palmer Rifles, the company changed its name to the Trenholm Rifles in December to honor George A. Trenholm.[14] It arrived at McClellanville on December 7 and was stationed there as part of Manigault's Battalion for its entire existence. The Trenholm Rifles refused to reorganize in the spring of 1862 and was disbanded on May 31.

Henry S. Dickinson commanded Company D, the Infantry Company–Chesnut Guards. Most Company D men were from Sumter and Clarendon Districts, with a few from Williamsburg, Charleston and Darlington Districts. The company mustered in Confederate service for twelve months on December 4, 1861, at Mount Pleasant; Dickinson was elected captain the same day. In May 1862, this company became Company B, Byrd's 6th Battalion; Dickinson probably retained command for only a few days. He was not re-elected at the reorganization on May 24, 1862. The company later became Company H of the 26th Regiment, SCV.

Cornelius D. Rowell commanded a second Company D. This one, from Marion Court House, mustered in Confederate service on March 22, 1862, for the duration of the war. Rowell was elected captain on March 22, a date that has also been shown as the twenty-fourth. The original complement was sixty-seven men, but only forty were present when the company arrived in Charleston on April 2. Rowell's Company left Charleston on April 10 and arrived at McClellanville the next day. From April 11 to late May, both companies designated D appear to have served in Manigault's Battalion. Rowell's Company became Company A of Byrd's 6th Battalion at the reorganization in May 1862, with Rowell still in command. The company became Company C of the 26th Regiment, SCV, on October 31, 1862.

Stephen Decatur Miller Byrd, MD, commanded Company E, the Kickapoo Riflemen. Most of its men were from Williamsburg and Clarendon Districts, with a few from Sumter District. Elected captain on January 13, 1862, Byrd and his company mustered in service for twelve months at Mount Pleasant. On May 29 the men reorganized and re-enlisted for the duration of the war as Company C, Byrd's 6th Battalion. Byrd had been elected major of the 6th Battalion four days earlier. Company E later became Company I, 26th Regiment, SCV.

BRIGADE AFFILIATIONS

Manigault's Battalion was stationed in the Department of South Carolina, Georgia and Florida.

MAJOR MOVEMENTS AND ENGAGEMENTS

Company A was ordered into service by detachments, and its men served as vedettes on Bull Island from September 10 to November 13, 1861. By December 31, Company A was stationed at the South Santee River. It was based at Camp Palmer near McClellanville from January to April 1862. Company B was also stationed at Camp Palmer from October 31, 1861, to the following April. Company C left Mount Pleasant on December 6, 1861, and arrived at McClellanville on the seventh. It remained there until April 1862. Dickinson's Company D was based at Mount Pleasant from December 4, 1861, to January 3, 1862, when it was sent to McClellanville. Company E left Charleston on January 18, 1862, and arrived at McClellanville the next day. The battalion remained near McClellanville until it was disbanded about May 18, 1862, by the operations of the Conscription Act. During its brief existence, Manigault's Battalion participated in no engagements. Its only action of any significance was a march to Anderson's place in Christ Church Parish on April 17, 1862, in anticipation of an attack by the Federal blockading force off Bulls Bay—an attack that failed to materialize. Three of its four infantry companies joined Byrd's 6th Battalion in May, and one disbanded. The cavalry company split into two companies, and they eventually joined South Carolina cavalry regiments. The artillery battery became an independent organization.

4.

THE 6ᵀᴴ BATTALION, SOUTH CAROLINA INFANTRY

The 6ᵗʰ Battalion South Carolina Infantry, also called Byrd's Battalion, was organized at the reorganization in May 1862; it was to provide local defense. The exact date of organization is not recorded in the CSR, but it was probably the twenty-fifth, the day S.D.M. Byrd was commissioned its commanding major. The battalion comprised three infantry companies that had been part of Manigault's Battalion. Several additional companies were attached to the battalion temporarily but never assigned alphabetic designations. The three companies of Byrd's Battalion were consolidated with the 9ᵗʰ Battalion, SCV, to form the 26ᵗʰ Regiment, SCV, on September 9, 1862.[1]

FIELD OFFICERS

Stephen Decatur Miller Byrd of Williamsburg District had been captain of Company E of Manigault's Battalion. Elected major of the 6ᵗʰ Battalion on May 24, 1862, his commission dated from the twenty-fifth. One card in the CSR refers to Byrd as lieutenant colonel of the 6ᵗʰ Battalion, but this is probably an error. For if Byrd, who was the only field officer in the battalion, had been promoted to lieutenant colonel, someone else would have been serving as major. Byrd assumed command of the battalion on May 30. He was appointed major of the 26ᵗʰ Regiment, SCV, on October 7, 1862, with rank from the date of its organization, September 9.

COMPANIES

Cornelius D. Rowell commanded Company A from Marion District. The company originally mustered in service on March 22, 1862, for the duration of the war. One of two companies designated D, it was attached to Edward Manigault's Battalion from April 11, 1862, until the battalion disbanded in late May. When the 6th Battalion merged into the 26th Regiment that September, Rowell's Company became Company C.

Company B, the Chesnut Guards, was made up of men primarily from Sumter and Clarendon Districts, although a few were from Williamsburg, Charleston and Darlington Districts. The Chesnut Guards had originally mustered in for twelve months' service on December 4, 1861, as Captain Henry S. Dickinson's Company, one of the two companies designated D in Manigault's Battalion. After the battalion disbanded in late May 1862, the Chesnut Guards became Company B in Byrd's 6th Battalion; Dickinson probably retained command for a few days. He was not re-elected at the reorganization on the twenty-fourth. The Chesnut Guards was reorganized, and its men re-enlisted for the duration of the war five days later. Robert E. Wheeler was elected captain at the reorganization. When the 6th Battalion merged into the 26th Regiment that September, Company B became Company H.

Company C, the Kickapoo Riflemen, was previously Company E of Manigault's Battalion until the battalion disbanded in May 1862. Its men were mostly from Williamsburg and Clarendon Districts, with a few from Sumter District. Having originally mustered in for twelve months' service on January 13, 1862, the company was reorganized, and the men re-enlisted on May 29, at which time they elected Ceth Smith Land captain. The Kickapoo Riflemen became Company I when the 6th Battalion merged into the 26th Regiment in September 1862.

Several other companies that had been in Manigault's Battalion before May 1862 and were temporarily attached to Byrd's Battalion between May and September were not given alphabetic designations. According to the CSR one of those companies, Company B, Christopher Gaillard's Santee Light Artillery, was mustered in Byrd's Battalion but was not recognized officially as part of that organization. The Santee Light Artillery became an independent artillery company sometime between May and September 1862, and it remained independent for the remainder of the war. The other two companies were Thomas Pinckney's Company A, St. James Santee Mounted Riflemen, and L.A. Whilden's Company B, St. James Mounted Riflemen. The CSR shows Pinckney's Company as Company A of Byrd's Battalion. This designation, however, is probably in CSR in error because C.D. Rowell's Company was designated Company A. Most likely the confusion arose over the fact that Pinckney's Company was called Company A, St. James Mounted Riflemen. Pinckney's Company was probably independent from September to December 16, 1862, when it became Company D of the 4th Regiment, South Carolina Cavalry. Whilden's Company, on the other hand, was independent from September 1862 to January 18, 1863, when it became Company E of the 5th Regiment, South Carolina Cavalry. Company A of the German Artillery, SCV, commanded by Captain Didrich Werner, was also attached temporarily to Byrd's Battalion.

BRIGADE AFFILIATIONS

The 6th Battalion was assigned to the Department of South Carolina, Georgia and Florida.

MAJOR MOVEMENTS AND ENGAGEMENTS

Byrd's Battalion spent its brief three-month existence near McClellanville. Company C was stationed at Pinckney's Bluff on the Santee River in June 1862, and the rest of the battalion was at McClellanville. Company C was based at Camp Warren on the Santee River from June 22 to sometime in August 1862. A Federal steamer entered the South Santee River on June 24 and continued upriver the next day. Ordered to respond, Company A and a section of Gaillard's Santee Light Artillery followed the steamer; the artillery battery shelled the steamer on the twenty-sixth.[2] The next day Federal troops landed at the Alvarado house on the South Santee River, where Company B, one section of Company A and the Santee Light Artillery, all under the command of Major Byrd, skirmished with them.[3] A sketch in *Recollections and Reminiscences* states that the skirmish took place at the Blake plantation.[4] Byrd's Battalion merged into the 26th Regiment, SCV, on September 9, 1862.

5.

THE 8ᵀᴴ REGIMENT, SOUTH CAROLINA VOLUNTEERS

The 8th Regiment, SCV, was also called the 8th South Carolina Infantry and the Pee Dee regiment.[1] It was authorized by a South Carolina legislative act of December 17, 1860, calling for ten regiments of twelve-month volunteers. Governor Pickens received the regiment on March 6, 1861, and it was officially organized on April 14, 1861, either at Marion or Charleston. The regiment originally comprised ten companies, A to I and K. It mustered in Confederate service on June 1, 1861, for twelve months' service from April 13.[2] Unlike other South Carolina volunteer regiments converting from state to Confederate service in the spring of 1861, virtually no disruption of the regimental structure occurred within the 8th Regiment, but at the reorganization in the spring of 1862, the 8th did not re-elect its colonel, major and six of its ten captains. The reorganization left the ten original companies unchanged except that two more were recruited from within the ranks, leaving the regiment with twelve companies, A to I and K to M, for the remainder of the war. The men re-enlisted on May 13, 1862, for two additional years and again in March 1864 for the duration of the war. On April 9, 1865, the 8th was consolidated with the 3rd Regiment, SCV, and the 3rd Battalion, South Carolina Infantry, to form the (New) or Consolidated 3rd Regiment, SCV.[3] At that time, the 8th Regiment ceased to exist.

FIELD OFFICERS

Ellerbe Boggan Crawford Cash of Chesterfield District, a major general in the South Carolina militia at the start of the war, was forty-seven years old when, on March 20, 1861, he was elected colonel of the 8th Regiment; he mustered in Confederate service with the regiment on June 1.[4] Cash was not re-elected at the reorganization and was dropped from the rolls on May 14, 1862. Dickert wrote that he did not run for re-election.[5] Cash was colonel of the 2nd Regiment of South Carolina Reserves for ninety days in late 1862 and early 1863. Many years after the war ended, on July 5, 1880, Cash killed William McCreight Shannon in a duel in present-day Lee County. Shannon was formerly captain of Company E of the Holcombe Legion Cavalry Battalion. Dickert wrote: "Colonel Cash was a man of strong character, fearless, brave, generous and true, a good friend and patriot. He made no religious profession. He was charitable to the extreme, and was the soul of honor, and while he had many enemies, being a fearless man and a good hater, he had such qualities as inspired the respect and admiration of his fellowmen."[6]

John Williford Henagan of Marlboro District was commissioned lieutenant colonel of the regiment on April 13, 1861.[7] The CSR states that he was appointed to the post on March 20, but this was probably the date of the election.[8] Henagan mustered in Confederate service with the regiment on June 1. He was elected colonel at the reorganization on May 14, 1862. On September 13, 1862, while carrying the regimental flag after Captain Harlee was wounded, Henagan was severely wounded at Maryland Heights near Harpers Ferry.[9] With J.B. Kershaw's endorsement he applied for promotion to brigadier general in February 1864. Henagan was wounded again and captured on September 13, 1864, on the Winchester and Berryville Pike near Opequon, Virginia, when all but two companies of the regiment were captured while on picket duty.[10] He was taken to Johnson's Island, Ohio, on September 24, 1864.[11] On October 11, while still a prisoner of war, Henagan was elected to the South Carolina House of Representatives.[12] Described as a brave officer, he died of pneumonia on April 26, 1865, at Johnson's Island and was buried there.[13] Dickert wrote: "There was little or no fear in him to move into battle, and he was always sure, during the thickest of the fight, cheering on his men to victory."[14]

Thomas Ephraim Lucas, MD, of Chesterfield was commissioned major of the regiment on April 13, 1861.[15] The CSR gives a date of March 20, but this was probably the date of his election.[16] Lucas was also not re-elected at the reorganization and was dropped from the rolls on May 14, 1862. He was appointed a lieutenant in Company A of the 15th Battalion South Carolina Artillery, an organization of South Carolina Regulars, on December 5, 1863, but he resigned that commission on November 3, 1864, on the grounds that he was a member of the South Carolina legislature.

Axalla John Hoole of Darlington District was elected lieutenant colonel on May 14, 1862. Previously captain of Company A, Hoole was killed at Chickamauga on September 20, 1863.[17] The CSR gives the date of his death as September 18, obviously incorrect since the regiment was not engaged that day. Dickert wrote: "No officer in the brigade had a more soldierly bearing, high attainments, and knightly qualities than Colonel Hoole, and not only the regiment, but the whole brigade felt his loss."[18] Kershaw wrote that Hoole was "an officer of much merit."[19]

Donald McDearmid McLeod of Marlboro District was elected major on May 14, 1862. The records have trouble with McLeod's name: the CSR shows the first name as both Donald and Daniel and the middle name as both McDonald and McDearmid. Dickert spells the name Donald McDiarmid McLeod, and Krick uses McDairmed.[20] McLeod was severely wounded in the right hip at Gettysburg on July 2, 1864, while leading the regiment's charge through the Peach Orchard. He was taken along when the Army of Northern Virginia withdrew, and he died of the wound on July 5 at Cashtown, Pennsylvania.[21] Although most cards in the CSR state that he died on July 5, a few give the date of death as the fourth, as do two articles in the *Charleston Daily Courier*.[22] Dickert wrote: "On the field of battle his gallantry was conspicuous, and he exhibited undaunted courage, and was faithful to every trust."[23] Kershaw wrote that McLeod was "a gallant and estimable officer."[24]

Eli Thomas Stackhouse of Marion District, a "brave and efficient officer," was promoted from captain of Company L to major on September 17, 1863, effective July 5, a date also shown in the record as July 4.[25] Stackhouse was promoted to lieutenant colonel on February 11, 1864, with rank from September 20, 1863, when Lieutenant Colonel Hoole was killed. The CSR dates the rank of lieutenant colonel from September 18. After Henagan's capture in September 1864, Stackhouse commanded the regiment for the rest of the war. He was wounded first at Sharpsburg and again at Gettysburg, where he suffered a chest wound from a shell. About July 1, 1864, at Deep Bottom, a shell again wounded him, this time in the abdomen and chest. Stackhouse commanded the Consolidated 3rd Regiment from April 9, 1865, until the end of the war. He was paroled with the rank of colonel at Greensboro on May 2, 1865. Dickert wrote that Stackhouse was a "sterling farmer, soldier, and statesman," adding, "in battle he was cool, collected, and brave; in camp or on the march he was sociable, moral—a Christian gentleman. As a tactician and disciplinarian, Colonel Stackhouse could not be called an exemplar soldier, as viewed in the light of the Regular Army, but as an officer of volunteers he had those elements in him to cause men to take on that same unflinching courage, indomitable spirit, and bold daring that actuated him in danger and in battle. He had not that sternness of command nor niceties nor notion of superiority that made machines of men, but he had that peculiar faculty of endowing his soldiers with confidence and a willingness to follow where he led."[26]

COMPANIES

Company A, the Darlington Riflemen, was composed of men from Darlington District.[27] The company had existed as early as 1854, and all but one man volunteered when the call came in the spring of 1861.[28] The company was in Charleston in early April and returned to Florence to become Company A of the 8th Regiment in mid-month. Axalla John Hoole commanded the company on at least two occasions in the mid-1850s. Its captain since January 14, 1861, he was re-elected on April 13. He was elected lieutenant colonel at the reorganization on May 14, 1862. Hoole was killed at Chickamauga in September 1863. John H. Muldrow, a private in Company A, was elected captain on May 13, 1862. He was killed at Malvern Hill on July 1, 1862.[29] First Lieutenant William Odom, "an ordinary officer," was promoted to captain as his replacement on July 1 or 2.[30] Odom was captured on the Winchester and Berryville Pike near Opequon, Virginia, on September 13, 1864, and taken to Harpers Ferry. He was moved to Johnson's Island on the twenty-fourth and released on June 16, 1865.[31]

Company B, the Chesterfield Rifles, was composed of men from Chesterfield District.[32] Its first captain, Minor Jackson Hough, was probably elected on March 9, 1861, although his commission dated from April 13. Hough was re-elected on May 13, 1862, but on May 21 he resigned because of poor health— he had been unfit for duty for over a year. Miles P. Thurman, previously a corporal in Company B, was elected captain as Hough's replacement probably shortly after the reorganization, although the exact date is unclear. Thurman tendered his resignation on July 20, 1862; it was accepted on August 1. Richard T. Powell was promoted from first lieutenant to captain the same day. At Gettysburg on July 2, 1863, Powell was severely wounded in the left thigh. He was captured on the Winchester and Berryville Pike near Opequon Creek, Virginia, on September 13, 1864,[33] and was taken to Harpers Ferry. He was moved to Johnson's Island, Ohio, on the twenty-fourth, and he was released there on June 16, 1865.[34]

Company C, the Chesterfield Guards, was the first company raised in Chesterfield District.[35] William Henry Coit had been its captain since January 1, 1861. He mustered in state service on April 13 and in Confederate service on June 1, 1861, both times as captain. Coit was not re-elected at the reorganization and was dropped from the rolls on May 13, 1862. He transferred to the Palmetto Light Artillery, commanded by Captain Hugh R. Garden, at the rank of senior first lieutenant. Thomas E. Powe Jr., a lawyer from Cheraw and previously first lieutenant in Company C, was elected captain of the company on May 13, 1862.[36] At Gettysburg on July 2, 1863, Powe sustained wounds to the forehead and both legs. As a result, his left leg was amputated at the thigh. He was captured and died of tetanus in a hospital near Gettysburg.[37] Most of the cards in the CSR indicate he died on July 10; some, however, give July 22 as the date he was either wounded or died, but those cards have been corrected to show July 2 as the date he was wounded. The *Memory Roll* gives the date of Powe's death as July 20, and the *Mercury*, the *Charleston Daily Courier* and the *Roll of the Dead* all show July 22.[38] The date Powe's successor was promoted fails to clarify the issue of which day Powe died because the CSR gives the same conflicting days. Powe was "loved, respected, and honored by his comrades."[39] Theodore F. Malloy of Cheraw was promoted from first lieutenant to captain on October 5, with rank from either July 10, 20 or 22.[40] Most cards in the CSR, however, show the date as the tenth. Malloy, "an efficient officer," was wounded at Fredericksburg and paroled at Greensboro on May 2, 1865.[41]

Company D, the Jackson Guards, was also composed of men from Chesterfield District.[42] Its men mustered in Confederate service on June 1, 1861, effective from April 13. John S. Miller, elected captain on April 13, 1861, resigned on November 12.[43] Miller's letter of resignation was not preserved, but he probably cited poor health since the record shows he was in the hospital at Danville, Virginia, with fever on December 19, 1861. Robert Peele Miller was promoted from first lieutenant to captain on November 12 as John Miller's replacement. Re-elected on April 16, 1862, he resigned on January 7, 1863, citing ill health as the reason. Robert Miller was an inefficient officer; J.B. Kershaw recommended accepting his resignation for the good of the service and the command.[44] First Lieutenant Phineas F. Spofford was promoted to captain on January 7, 1863, but this date is also shown as both the eighth and the thirteenth. He was severely wounded in the foot at Gettysburg.[45] Spofford, considered an efficient officer, was paroled at Greensboro on May 2, 1865. The *Mercury* spelled the name both Spofferd and Shafford.[46]

Company E, the Timmonsville Minute Men, was composed of men from Timmonsville in Darlington District.[47] It was raised from the Lower Battalion of the 29th Regiment, South Carolina Militia, on January 10, 1861.[48] James W. Owens, the first captain, resigned on June 1, when the company mustered in Confederate service.[49] Owens immediately raised a company that served in Harlee's Legion from early August until the legion was disbanded in January 1862. Silas Mercer Keith was promoted from first lieutenant to captain, replacing Owens on June 1. Keith, who had typhoid pneumonia, suffered from fragile health and tendered his resignation on

January 1, 1862. He was granted a leave of absence on January 4, and his resignation was forwarded on the thirty-first. Keith was killed in a railroad accident in Wilmington, North Carolina, on February 4, two days before his resignation was accepted.[50] The CSR, probably confusing him with his successor, states that Keith was dropped from the rolls of the 8th Regiment on May 13, 1862. First Lieutenant John Dove Young commanded the company after Keith's death. One CSR card reads that Young was promoted to captain, but no date is given. Young was not re-elected at the reorganization and was dropped from the rolls at the rank of first lieutenant on May 13, 1862. William R. Joy, previously third sergeant of Company E, was elected captain the same day. Joy was an inefficient officer.[51] He was the last captain of the company; no information on his parole is shown in the CSR.

Company F, the Darlington Grays, was organized in early 1861.[52] Its men were from Society Hill, Dovesville, Lydia and Stokes Bridge in Darlington District. The company was raised from the Upper Battalion of the 29th Regiment, South Carolina Militia, on January 10, 1861.[53] William H. Evans, colonel of the 29th Regiment, South Carolina Militia, at the outbreak of the war, raised the company and served as its first captain. Although he mustered in service on April 13, Evans resigned on November 29, 1861. James L. Orr gave the reason nearly a year later when he wrote, in October 1862, that Evans was "compelled to resign by a serious affliction in his family, greatly to his own regret and equally to his command."[54] Although Orr recommended him for a position as field officer in the Confederate States Provisional Army, Evans did not receive the commission. In late 1862, Governor Pickens appointed him lieutenant colonel of the 2nd Regiment, South Carolina Reserves.

Thomas Epaphroditus Howle was promoted from first lieutenant to captain on November 29, 1861. At the reorganization in the spring of 1862, Howle recruited half the men from his own company and added some new recruits to create a new company designated Company M of the 8th Regiment. The men promptly elected Howle captain on May 13, and he was dropped as captain of Company F. John Kolb McIver, second lieutenant in Company F before the reorganization, was elected captain of Company F on May 13. Kirkland spells McIver's middle name as Kalb.[55] At Gettysburg on July 2, 1863, McIver was severely wounded in the forehead and both his eyes were shot out.[56] He was borne with the retreating Confederate army to Williamsport, where he was reported alert albeit "in a dying condition and suffering untold agony."[57] He was left in a private house there and was captured when Federal troops occupied the town. McIver recovered sufficiently for transfer to a Federal hospital in Chester, Pennsylvania, on September 17. His frontal bone was resected because of compression of the brain. On October 4 he was moved to Hammond General Hospital at Point Lookout, Maryland, where he died. John L. Black, colonel of the 1st Regiment, South Carolina Cavalry, wrote that McIver died from exposure during the trip to Point Lookout.[58] Most CSR cards show the date of his death as October 15, although a few show the eighth. The *Roll of the Dead* gives the date of October 13, and the *Mercury*, gives the fifteenth.[59] The company's last captain, James Edward Bass, was promoted from first lieutenant on October 8, 1863. Bass was wounded at Sharpsburg, when he was third lieutenant, and at Berryville on September 3, 1864. He was considered a "very efficient officer."[60] One source gives his middle name as Edwin.[61]

Company G, the Marlboro Guards, was also called the Marlborough Guards and Harrington's Company.[62] Its men were from Marlboro District. John W. Harrington was elected captain on January 18, 1861. He was slightly wounded in the face by a musket ball at First Manassas but did not leave the field. Harrington was not re-elected at the reorganization and was dropped from the rolls on May 13, 1862. First Lieutenant Charles Pinckney Townsend was elected captain the same day. Slightly wounded at Malvern Hill on July 1, 1862, Townsend was not considered an efficient officer.[63] He was a member of the South Carolina legislature. Townsend was cashiered on October 25, 1864, but the action was revoked on December 1.

Company H, the Jeffries Creek Company, was also called the Jeffries Volunteers.[64] Its men were from that part of Marion District now in the eastern section of Florence County. The company was organized at Hopewell Church.[65] Robert L. Singletary was elected captain on January 26, 1861, and mustered in state service on April 13. He was not re-elected at the reorganization and was dropped from the rolls on May 13, 1862. Singletary served as president of the Charleston and Savannah Railroad for the remainder of the war.[66] Duncan McIntyre, first lieutenant of Company H before the reorganization, was elected its captain on May 13, 1862. He was slightly wounded in the chest at Fredericksburg on December 13, 1862. The CSR states, erroneously, that McIntyre was killed on July 2, 1863, at Gettysburg and that R.D. Cooper replaced him. One card in the CSR shows, also erroneously, that Cooper was promoted to captain on July 2, 1863; he was actually promoted to first lieutenant on that date. Cooper was retired to the Invalid Corps on February 3, 1865, at the rank of first lieutenant. Records show McIntyre present in October 1863. He was shot through the right thigh at Deep Bottom on July 27, 1864. He was paroled at Greensboro.

Company I, the Marion Guards, was the color company of the 8th Regiment.[67] Its men were from Marion District. Eli Thomas Stackhouse, elected captain on January 26, mustered in state service on April 13, 1861. At the reorganization, Stackhouse transferred to the newly created Company L as its captain and was dropped from the rolls of Company I on May 13, 1862. Andrew Turpin Harlee, nephew of William Wallace Harlee and second lieutenant in Company I before the reorganization, was elected its captain the same day. Harlee was wounded at either Savage's Station or Malvern Hill in 1862. At Maryland Heights on September 13, 1862, he was shot through both thighs by a Minié ball while carrying the flag and rallying the company.[68] He sustained a slight wound to the thigh at Gettysburg and was also wounded at Bean's Station.[69] Harlee was an "efficient officer and loved pleasure."[70] Dickert calls him "a daring and intrepid officer."[71] Some Company I men served in Company L after the reorganization.

Company K, the McQueen Guards, was composed of men from Marlboro District. Donald McDearmid McLeod was elected its captain on April 13, 1861. He was elected major of the regiment on May 14, 1862. Franklin Manning, previously a second lieutenant in Company K, was elected its captain on May 13. Manning was wounded at Maryland Heights on September 13, 1862, and was left behind in Maryland, where he was captured three days later. He was sent to Fortress Monroe on December 8 and exchanged at City Point, Virginia, along with sixty-four other prisoners of war. On the tenth Manning was furloughed home for a few weeks, but in January 1863, he was assigned to serve as the enrolling officer for Chesterfield District. Disabled by his wounds, he retired to the Invalid Corps on January 24, 1865, and was assigned to the superintendent of the bureau of conscription three days later. Manning never returned to the company after he was wounded. First Lieutenant Benjamin A. Rogers assumed command after September 1862. Rogers himself was wounded at Sharpsburg. He was captured there and paroled soon afterward. He was wounded in the left arm at Gettysburg on July 2, 1863, and was wounded again at Deep Bottom on July 28, 1864. The CSR states that Rogers was promoted to captain on January 24, 1864, which probably should read January 24, 1865, the day Manning retired to the Invalid Corps. An "efficient officer," Rogers was appointed captain of Company G of the 3rd Consolidated Regiment in April 1865, and he was paroled with the rank of captain on May 2 at Greensboro.[72] J.M. Henagan, assistant quartermaster of the 8th Regiment, probably commanded Company K in the absence of both Captain Manning and Lieutenant Rogers.[73]

Company L, the Spartan Band, was created about May 13, 1862, when the regiment was reorganized.[74] Most of its men were from Marion District and had previously served in Company I. Some were from Darlington District and others from North Carolina. Eli Thomas Stackhouse and

William D. Carmichael raised the company. Stackhouse, captain of Company I before the reorganization, was elected captain of Company L on May 13. He was promoted to major on July 5, 1863, and was replaced by First Lieutenant William D. Carmichael the same day. Before he became captain, Carmichael had been wounded at Malvern Hill and again in the left thigh at Gettysburg just before his promotion. At Deep Bottom on July 28, 1864, Carmichael was struck in the mouth by a Minié ball. He retired to the Invalid Corps on January 16, 1865, and on the twentieth was assigned to the Quartermaster Department at the military station at Florence. Dickert wrote that Carmichael was "one of the most gallant and most trusted officers of that gallant regiment."[75]

Company M was created about May 13, 1862, when the regiment was reorganized. William C. Coker and Thomas Epaphroditus Howle filled the new company with men from Darlington District by drawing about half of them from Company F and the other half from recruits. Howle, captain of Company F before the reorganization, was elected captain on May 13, 1862. He was wounded, either on June 29 at Savage's Station or on July 1 at Malvern Hill.[76] Howle was mortally wounded in the back on September 17, 1862, at Sharpsburg and died on the field at Lavinia Grove's farm.[77] William C. Coker was promoted to captain as his replacement on September 17.[78] Coker had been slightly wounded at Malvern Hill, and on July 2, 1863, at Gettysburg, he was severely wounded in the left foot. Captured at Williamsport on July 14, 1863, Coker was taken to the Seminary Hospital in Hagerstown, Maryland, in August.[79] He was moved to Point Lookout, Maryland, on February 14, 1864, and to Fort Delaware on June 23.[80] In November 1863, the *Charleston Daily Courier* reported that Coker was in prison at Johnson's Island.[81] He was paroled at Fort Delaware in February 1865, and he was exchanged at City Point, Virginia, on March 7. Coker was the brother of James L. Coker, major of the 6th Regiment.

BRIGADE AFFILIATIONS

The 8th Regiment, SCV, and the 7th Regiment, SCV, constituted A.C. Garlington's 3rd Brigade from April to early June 1861.[82] After the 8th Regiment went to Virginia, it was part of M.L. Bonham's Brigade from July 1, 1861, to February 1862, along with the 2nd, 3rd and 7th Regiments, SCV, and Kemper's Virginia Artillery.[83] From February 1862 to December 1863, J.B. Kershaw commanded the brigade. On November 15, 1862, it added the 15th Regiment, SCV, and the 3rd Battalion, South Carolina Infantry. On May 28, 1864, the brigade also added the 20th Regiment, SCV. James

Conner commanded the brigade from August to October 1864, and John D. Kennedy commanded it from October 1864 until the end of the war. On April 9, 1865, the regiments of Kennedy's Brigade were consolidated; afterward the brigade consisted of the (New) or Consolidated 2nd, 3rd and 7th Regiments, SCV. The 8th Regiment was consolidated with the 3rd Regiment and the 3rd Battalion to form the (New) or Consolidated 3rd Regiment. The 3rd Battalion and the 8th, 15th and 20th Regiments ceased to exist at that time.[84]

MAJOR MOVEMENTS AND ENGAGEMENTS

The 8th Regiment was present but was held in reserve in Charleston during the bombardment of Fort Sumter on April 12 and 13, 1861. According to a sketch in *Recollections and Reminiscences*, the regiment was called to Charleston after the surrender of Fort Sumter.[85] Companies A, E and F left Darlington for Charleston by train on April 15.[86] It is probable that some companies were in the city during the bombardment and some arrived after the battle. The regiment was stationed on Sullivan's Island by April 18, and by the twenty-third it was encamped at Charleston's racecourse, where it remained until it was ordered to transfer to another encampment at Florence on May 2.[87] The regiment moved to Florence on the fourth and was still there when the men volunteered for Confederate service in late May or early June. The *Mercury* gives the date as May 23, but the CSR makes it June 1.[88] The 8th Regiment left Florence by rail for Virginia on June 2.[89] Before June 15, the 8th, along with the 7th Regiment, was in camp at Howard's Grove about two miles from Richmond.[90] The regiment was transferred to the vicinity of Bull Run about June 15.[91] It then marched to the vicinity of Fairfax Court House, and on July 16 and 17 it marched back to Bull Run. On July 18 the brigade, consisting of the 2nd, 3rd, 7th and 8th Regiments, SCV, was shelled at Mitchell's Ford during the battle of Bull Run, or Blackburn's Ford.[92]

The men of the 8th Regiment built earthworks at Mitchell's Ford from July 18 to 20. The 2nd and 8th Regiments were engaged in a charge at the Henry House Hill during the battle of First Manassas on July 21. That day the 3rd and 7th Regiments were on the field and endured heavy shellfire but were not actively engaged; the 3rd and 7th Regiments pursued Federal troops later in the day;[93] the 3rd Regiment sustained no casualties. On August 14, the brigade moved toward Washington and established a new camp at Flint Hill. The 2nd Regiment skirmished alone near Lewinsville and Georgetown on September 27.[94] The brigade was stationed at Flint Hill until mid-October, when it moved to Centreville.[95] The men left Centreville on January 10,

1862, and moved into winter quarters near Blackburn's Bridge at Bull Run.[96] The brigade left camp on March 9 and marched toward the Rappahannock River, moving from there to Orange Court House on the nineteenth. Between March 28 and April 6 the brigade marched and countermarched before departing Orange Court House by rail for Richmond.[97] The men took the York River Railroad to West Point the next day and embarked on a schooner for Yorktown, arriving there late that night.[98] They spent the next few weeks marching, performing picket duty and constructing fieldworks. The brigade skirmished near Yorktown while covering Johnston's retreat on May 2. It withdrew on the third and marched through Williamsburg on the fourth, then turned and marched back through the town. The 2nd and 8th Regiments were engaged there on the fourth, and the 3rd and 7th were shelled on the field but not actively engaged.[99] The brigade then withdrew to a position eight miles from Richmond. The brigade was held in reserve at Seven Pines on May 31 and June 1.[100] The 2nd and 3rd Regiments, but not the 7th and 8th, were engaged on the Nine Mile Road below Richmond on June 18. Since it was south of the Chickahominy River, the brigade was not engaged at Mechanicsville on the twenty-sixth, at Gaines's Mill on the twenty-seventh or at Garnett's Farm on the twenty-eighth. The 3rd, 7th and 8th Regiments skirmished south of the Chickahominy on the twenty-seventh.[101] The brigade was heavily engaged at Savage's Station on June 29 and at Malvern Hill on July 1, but not at Frayser's Farm on June 30.[102] The brigade remained below Richmond for about seven weeks before moving north toward Manassas. Since Kershaw's Brigade did not arrive at the battlefield until September 2, it did not participate in the battle of Second Manassas.[103] The brigade arrived at Leesburg on September 3 and crossed the Potomac River into Maryland on the sixth. It marched to Frederick City, Maryland, on September 7 and remained there until the tenth, when it moved toward Maryland Heights. The brigade was lightly engaged at the north end of Maryland Heights near Harpers Ferry on September 12 and heavily engaged there the next day.[104]

The brigade came down from Maryland Heights very early on September 15 and formed into a line of battle near Crampton's Gap, but Harpers Ferry surrendered that morning and Kershaw's Brigade was not engaged. Crossing the Potomac River into Virginia on the evening of the fifteenth, the brigade camped the next night about ten miles from Sharpsburg. The men recrossed the Potomac into Maryland at Boteler's Ford, near Shepherdstown, on the morning of September 17. The brigade was heavily engaged on the Confederate left near the Dunker Church at the battle of Sharpsburg on the seventeenth.[105] Recrossing the Potomac again late in the evening of September 18 and early in the morning of the nineteenth, the men marched to Martinsburg for a few days and then to Winchester, where they remained until October 28. They moved on to Culpeper, arriving on November 9, and left for Fredericksburg on the eighteenth, arriving two days later. The 3rd Battalion and the 15th Regiment, SCV, were reassigned to Kershaw's Brigade as it marched from Culpeper to Fredericksburg. Initially held in reserve, the brigade was fully engaged at Fredericksburg on December 13. The 2nd and 8th Regiments were engaged in the Sunken Road at Marye's Heights, and the 3rd and 7th Regiments were positioned on the plateau to the left of Marye's Mansion. The 3rd Regiment suffered particularly heavy casualties that day.[106] Company I, the Palmetto Guard of the 2nd Regiment, was detached and engaged to the right of Marye's Heights.[107] The 15th Regiment moved into the Sunken Road at Marye's Heights about four thirty in the afternoon and was engaged there.[108] The 3rd Battalion took up a position in the railroad cut running from Fredericksburg to Marye's Heights, but since the men were somewhat protected by the bluff and railroad cut, they did not suffer as greatly as the rest of the brigade. Company A of the 3rd Battalion was engaged that day, but Company B was held in reserve and received shellfire only. Companies C, D and E endured shelling while in line of battle but were not engaged because their line was not attacked. Company F was placed at the gristmill on the west side of town to guard the railroad cut and suffered heavy shelling. The brigade remained in line of battle until December 16, when the 2nd, 7th and 15th Regiments moved into Fredericksburg, which the Federal troops had vacated.[109] The brigade set up winter camp nearby and performed picket duty in January and February 1863. The men left camp on April 29 and marched toward Chancellorsville. The brigade was engaged on May 1 near Chancellorsville and skirmished while in line of battle the next day. At that time the 8th Regiment was temporarily assigned to Brigadier General Fitzhugh Lee's cavalry brigade to guard its wagon train. The men of the 8th were engaged as skirmishers and flankers without loss on May 1 and 2, and they rejoined the brigade the next day. The brigade saw action near the Chancellor house on May 3 before withdrawing toward Fredericksburg and engaging the enemy at Salem Church later the same day. On the fourth the brigade skirmished between Salem Church and Fredericksburg.

The men left camp near Fredericksburg on June 3 and crossed the Potomac River into Maryland at Williamsport on the twenty-fifth. On July 1, the first day of the battle of Gettysburg, the brigade was two miles away from the battlefield. Late in the afternoon of the second, however, the brigade was involved in Longstreet's attack, during which the 2nd Regiment suffered casualties of 52 percent.[110] Although present on the battlefield on July 3, the brigade was not actively engaged. It remained on the field the next day but only the 8th Regiment saw light skirmishing. Withdrawing about midnight, the brigade marched toward Hagerstown on the fifth and sixth.[111] The men entrenched between Williamsport and Falling Waters on July 6 and 7, and elements of the 3rd, 8th and 15th Regiments and 3rd Battalion skirmished at Antietam Creek near Hagerstown on the tenth and twelfth. The brigade remained in line of battle near Williamsport from July 11 to July 13 and finally crossed the Potomac into Virginia on July 14.[112] Only forty men of the 8th Regiment reported for duty after the Gettysburg campaign, and they skirmished near Front Royal on July 23.[113] The brigade arrived at Culpeper Court House on July 24 and on August 3 moved to the south side of the Rapidan River.

The brigade left its camp at Wallace's Tavern on September 8 and marched to Hanover Junction, where, on the tenth, the men boarded a train for Richmond. Transferred with Longstreet's corps to Tennessee, the brigade passed through Atlanta on the sixteenth, Dalton on the seventeenth and arrived at Catoosa Station, near Ringgold, Georgia, at about two in the afternoon on the eighteenth.[114] The men camped at Tunnel Hill that night and marched to Ringgold the next morning. They deployed about three that afternoon to guard a gap in the mountains nearby, but they were not engaged that day.[115] The brigade crossed the Chickamauga River after dark on the nineteenth and arrived on the battlefield at about one on the morning of the twentieth. Later that day, the brigade was heavily engaged during the battle of Chickamauga.[116] The brigade followed the retreating Federal army to Chattanooga on the twenty-second, but only the 8th Regiment saw action that day.[117] The brigade did not participate in the battle at Wauhatchie on the night of October 28, and it left Chattanooga for Knoxville on November 4. The men arrived at Sweetwater on November 8 and crossed the Tennessee River on November 13. They pursued the enemy and skirmished on the fifteenth, and they did the same again at Campbell's Station on the sixteenth.[118] The 3rd Regiment and 3rd Battalion skirmished without the rest of the brigade along Kingston Road near Knoxville on November 17. The brigade marched in line of battle for five miles and drove Federal troops from Armstrong's Hill into Knoxville on the eighteenth.[119] The brigade invested Knoxville the next day and spent the next sixteen days in the rifle pits around the town. The brigade was present but not heavily engaged during the attack on Fort Loudon, also called Fort Sanders, near Knoxville on November 29. Longstreet abandoned the siege and withdrew from Knoxville on December 4, arriving at Rogersville on the ninth. The brigade's last engagement in Tennessee was at Bean's Station on December 14.[120] The 3rd Regiment was on the field that day but was not actively engaged.[121] The brigade left Bean's Station on December 20, and two days later, it went into winter quarters on the east bank of the Tennessee River at Russellville, near Morristown. The 7th Regiment marched to Dandridge on December 28 but had returned to Russellville by the thirtieth. From January 4 to March 29, 1864, Companies H and M of the 7th Regiment were stationed at Broylesville, Tennessee, to guard the division shoe shop against bushwhackers. The brigade made a few brief excursions from Russellville that winter: to Dandridge from January 28 to February 1, to New Market on February 10 and to Greenville on February 21.

Leaving its winter quarters on February 22, the brigade ultimately arrived at Charlottesville, Virginia, on April 15 and at Gordonsville on the nineteenth. It left Gordonsville on May 4. Although the brigade missed the first day of the battle of the Wilderness on May 5, it was heavily engaged there on the sixth. After burying their dead on the seventh, the men marched slowly to their right until evening, when they were force-marched to Spotsylvania Court House, arriving after midnight.[122] Racing the Federal vanguard to a crucial crossroads near Spotsylvania Court House, the brigade successfully delayed the Federal troops near there on the Brock Road on May 8. The brigade saw skirmishing only during the heaviest fighting at Spotsylvania Court House on May 9, 10 and 12. It left Spotsylvania Court House on the twentieth. On May 23, the 8th and 15th Regiments were held in reserve when the rest of the brigade was heavily engaged near the Chesterfield Bridge on the North Anna River.[123] The 20th Regiment joined Kershaw's Brigade on the South Anna River on May 28. As the Overland campaign progressed, the brigade was engaged at Beulah Church near Cold Harbor on June 1 and skirmished near Gaines farm on the second and third.[124] The 20th Regiment suffered a few casualties on the fifth and twelfth.[125] The brigade left Cold Harbor on June 12 and marched to Malvern Hill by way of the old battlefield at Frayser's Farm. Leaving Malvern Hill on June 15, the men marched to Deep Bottom on the sixteenth and to Chaffin's Farm on the seventeenth. They crossed to the south side of the James River on the eighteenth and fought at Petersburg later that day.[126] The 2nd and 3rd Regiments were engaged there again on June 21, and the 20th Regiment suffered casualties from June 18 to 24.[127] The brigade remained in the trenches until June 25, when it was transferred into the city of Petersburg and, on July 13, to the north side of the James River at Chaffin's Bluff. The men skirmished near Deep Bottom on the north side of the James River on July 25 and 26 and were engaged there on the twenty-seventh and twenty-eighth.[128] Transferred to the Shenandoah Valley on August 6, the brigade skirmished at Halltown on August 21 and 26, near Berryville on September 3 and near Winchester on the thirteenth. When the 8th Regiment was performing picket duty that day on the Berryville and Winchester Pike near Winchester, all but two companies of the regiment were captured.[129] The remnants of the 8th were then temporarily consolidated with the 15th Regiment. The brigade left the Shenandoah Valley on September 14, missing the battles at Winchester on September 19 and at Fisher's Hill on the twenty-second. The brigade arrived at Gordonsville on September 23 but returned to the Valley on the twenty-fifth or twenty-sixth. The brigade was engaged at Strasburg on October 13, and it also participated in the debacle at Cedar Creek on the nineteenth, where most of the 3rd Battalion was captured.[130] It was transferred back to Richmond about November 15, arriving there on the twentieth. The men went into winter quarters about seven miles below Richmond north of the James River and occupied the extreme left of the Confederate defenses.

Ordered to the Carolinas to help slow Sherman's advance, the brigade left Richmond by rail on January 4, 1865, arriving in Charleston on the seventh. After camping west of the Ashley River for about a week, the men moved to the railroad bridge over the Salkehatchie River. The 8th Regiment, and probably other units of the brigade, performed picket duty at the Salkehatchie River in late January and skirmished there on the thirty-first.[131] The men also guarded railroad bridges over the Edisto River. The brigade served as the rear guard during the evacuation of Charleston on February 18, and it guarded the bridge over the Santee River from February 20 to February 23. The brigade was at Cheraw on February 25 and at Florence the next day.[132] The brigade skirmished lightly at Thompson's Creek about five miles west of Cheraw on the twenty-eighth. Continuing its northward withdrawal on March 3, the brigade arrived at Fayetteville on the tenth. It was engaged at Averasboro on March 16 and at Bentonville on the nineteenth and twentieth. All the regiments in the brigade, with the exception of the 8th, suffered casualties on the nineteenth.[133]

The 8th Regiment was consolidated with the 3rd Regiment and the 3rd Battalion on April 9, 1865, and ceased to exist as a separate entity. The consolidated regiment surrendered with the Army of Tennessee near Greensboro on April 26; the men were paroled on May 2 and 3.

6.

THE 9TH BATTALION, SOUTH CAROLINA INFANTRY

The 9th Battalion, South Carolina Infantry was also called the Pee Dee Legion, the Pee Dee Rifles, the Pee Dee Battalion, Smith's Battalion and the Horry Battalion. Its predecessor was Nesbit's Battalion of South Carolina State Troops, and sometimes the 9th was called by that name as well. The 9th Battalion was organized about March 24, 1862, around a nucleus of the battalion commanded by Lieutenant Colonel Ralph Nesbit, a seven-company unit attached to Harlee's Pee Dee Legion in 1861. Harlee's Legion was a militia unit that assembled initially at the Centenary Campground in Marion and was stationed at Camp Lookout on the Waccamaw Neck for the rest of its brief existence. When the Pee Dee Legion was dissolved in early January 1862, most of Nesbit's men enlisted in the 9th Battalion, South Carolina Infantry. Nesbit resigned as lieutenant colonel of state forces in May and never held a position as field officer in the 9th Battalion.[1] The seven companies–A to G–of Nesbit's Battalion remained together and made up the 9th Battalion, which mustered in Confederate service for twelve months in early 1862 at Camp Lookout. A.D. Smith was elected lieutenant colonel on March 24; the battalion was called Smith's Battalion until the reorganization later that spring. The companies mustered in state service at various times in 1862: one on January 1, four on the twenty-seventh and two on March 19. Company officers were re-elected on April 16, and the 9th Battalion was reorganized on May 5 when its men re-enlisted for the duration of the war. The 9th Battalion merged with the three companies of Byrd's 6th Battalion to create the 26th Regiment, SCV, on September 9, 1862, at Church Flats, below Charleston.[2]

FIELD OFFICERS

Alexander D. Smith of Bennettsville in Marlboro District, previously captain of Company C, was elected lieutenant colonel of the 9th Battalion on March 24, 1862, and re-elected at the reorganization in May. Following the merger of the 9th and 6th Battalions into the 26th Regiment in September, Smith was appointed colonel of the regiment on October 7, effective September 9, 1862.[3]

Richard D.F. Rollins of Darlington, who held the rank of major in Nesbit's Battalion, was elected major of the 9th Battalion on March 24 but was not re-elected at the reorganization. He was later major in the 7th Battalion, South Carolina Reserves.[4]

Joshua Hilary Hudson of Bennettsville in Marlboro District enlisted as a private in Company F of the 21st Regiment, SCV, in January 1862. He was soon promoted to adjutant of the 9th Battalion and elected major on May 19, 1862, when the battalion was reorganized. Hudson was promoted to lieutenant colonel of the 26th Regiment on April 29, 1863, with rank from September 9, 1862.

COMPANIES

Company A, the Bull Creek Guerillas, was composed of men from Horry District.[5] It had existed as a company as early as January 1, 1862, and was probably attached to the 33rd Regiment, South Carolina Militia, and to Harlee's Legion as the Bull Creek Rangers in late 1861.[6] The men mustered in service for twelve months on January 27, 1862, while stationed on the Waccamaw Neck. Samuel Smart, who enlisted on January 1, was elected as the company's only captain the same day. Smart was re-elected on April 16. Company A was also designated Company B before the reorganization. The company became Company A of the 26th Regiment at the merger in September 1862, and Smart remained its captain.

Company B was composed of men from Chesterfield District.[7] It was designated Company F before the reorganization and was also referred to as Company C.[8] While stationed on the Waccamaw Neck, the men mustered in service on March 19, 1862, for twelve months, the service to date from the seventeenth. John A. Evans was elected captain on January 19, 1862, and re-elected on April 16. This company became Company B of the 26th Regiment at the merger in September 1862. Evans retained command.

Company C, the Irby Rifles, was composed mostly of men from Marlboro District.[9] The *Mercury* called it the Erby Rifles.[10] Some Company

C men came from Robson and Brunswick Counties in North Carolina; Maryland, Ireland and Germany were also represented. The company was part of Harlee's Legion until it was dissolved at the end of its one-year term in January 1862. The company was designated Company G before the reorganization and was also referred to as Company E.[11] Alexander D. Smith, who had enlisted as a private in a company of cadets in Roanoke, Virginia, subsequently raised the Irby Rifles and was elected its captain on February 4, 1862. While stationed on the Waccamaw Neck, the men mustered in service on March 19, 1862, for twelve months. On March 24, 1862, Smith was elected lieutenant colonel of the 9th Battalion. That same day, Lieutenant Washington W. Davis replaced him as captain. Davis was re-elected on April 16. Company C became Company D of the 26th Regiment at the merger in September 1862, and Davis retained command.

Company D, the Watchesaw Rifles, was composed primarily of men from the All Saints Waccamaw area of Horry District, although a few came from Beaufort, Darlington, Charleston and Anderson Districts.[12] The company was probably attached to the 33rd Regiment, South Carolina Militia, and to Harlee's Legion as the Wachitaw Rifles under Captain Nesbit in late 1861.[13] The company was designated Company A in Smith's Battalion before the reorganization and was also referred to as Company G.[14] Joseph Blyth Allston was its first captain.[15] Allston, who had been elected on November 13, 1861, commanded the company when it was Allston's Company in Nesbit's Battalion of Harlee's Legion. Allston and his men mustered in Confederate service at Georgetown on January 1, 1862, for twelve months. He put together an incorrect payroll in the spring of 1862 and possibly because of that mistake was not re-elected at the reorganization on May 19. Sergeant John J. Best was elected captain instead. Company D became Company E of the 26th Regiment at the merger in September 1862, with Best retained as captain. Meanwhile, Allston was appointed captain of Company B of the 1st Battalion, South Carolina Sharpshooters on June 23. The CSR states, incorrectly, that Company D of the 9th Battalion became Company A of the 1st Battalion, South Carolina Sharpshooters. This mistake probably stems from Allston's appointment and the fact that some of the men probably followed him into that company.

Company E was probably called the Chesterfield Eagles. Its men were from Chesterfield District.[16] The company was designated Company D before the reorganization and was also referred to as Company F.[17] While stationed on the Waccamaw Neck, the men mustered in service on January 27, 1862, for twelve months. Neill F. Graham, who enlisted on December

21, 1861, was elected captain the same day. The CSR shows his name as both Neill and Neil. Graham was not re-elected at the reorganization the following May and subsequently served in a cavalry command. The CSR indicates that he was authorized to raise a company called the Chesterfield Eagles for special state service but does not specify whether Graham raised the company before or after the reorganization. Lieutenant D. Smilie, or Smily, Wadsworth replaced Graham as captain on May 19, 1862. Company E became Company F of the 26th Regiment at the merger in September; Wadsworth retained command.

Company F was composed of men from Darlington District.[18] Designated Company E before the reorganization, it was also referred to as Company D.[19] While stationed on the Waccamaw Neck, the men mustered in service on January 27, 1862, for twelve months. Richard D.F. Rollins, who enlisted on December 30, 1861, was the first captain of Company F. He was elected major of the battalion on March 24, 1862. Thomas D. Keith was promoted from first lieutenant to captain the same day. Not re-elected at the reorganization in May 19, Keith was elected lieutenant on November 11 and served at that rank until a court-martial cashiered him on March 28, 1864. Daniel W. Carter was elected captain on May 19, 1862.[20] Company F became Company G of the 26th Regiment at the merger in September. Carter retained command.

Company G, the Eutaw Rifles, was composed of men from Horry and Georgetown Districts.[21] It was probably attached to the 33rd Regiment, South Carolina Militia, and to Harlee's Legion as the Floyd Guerillas under Captain Grainger in late 1861.[22] Designated Company C before the reorganization, it was also referred to as Company B.[23] While stationed on the Waccamaw Neck, the men mustered in service on January 27, 1862, for twelve months. Levi Grainger, who was elected captain on January 1, was not re-elected at the reorganization and was dropped from the rolls on May 24. Lieutenant L. Dow Graham was elected captain on May 19. He resigned on August 7, a date also shown in the record as August 11, 1862, giving as his reason: "I find the charge greater than I was aware of and feel myself incompetent to fulfill the charge."[24] Company G became Company K of the 26th Regiment at the merger in September 1862.

Brigade Affiliations

The 9th Battalion was probably attached to the Department of South Carolina, Georgia and Florida.

MAJOR MOVEMENTS AND ENGAGEMENTS

The 9th Battalion was stationed on the South Carolina coast for its entire six-month existence. It was posted to Camp Lookout on the Waccamaw Neck near Georgetown until April 20, 1862, when it was sent to Charleston.[25] The battalion arrived at Camp Magnolia (Magnolia Cemetery), about two miles from Charleston, on the twenty-fifth and remained in and around Charleston in May. During that month and the first half of June 1862, the 9th Battalion performed picket duty on Legare's and Grimball's plantations near Secessionville on James Island. During the engagement at Secessionville on June 16, the 9th Battalion was engaged as part of the garrison of the Tower Battery, later known as Fort Lamar. It remained at Secessionville after the battle, and it was sent to Rantowles Station on the Charleston and Savannah Railroad on September 4 and to Church Flats, about three miles away, the next day. On September 9, 1862, while stationed at Church Flats, the 9th Battalion merged into the 26th Regiment.

7.

THE 10ᵀᴴ REGIMENT, SOUTH CAROLINA VOLUNTEERS

The 10ᵗʰ Regiment, SCV, was among those authorized by the General Assembly act of December 17, 1860, calling for ten regiments of twelve-month volunteers. Governor Pickens received it on March 6, 1861. Organization was considered complete and field officers were elected on May 31.[1] At the time, however, the company under Captain George was not accepted into the regiment because it was so disorganized when it reported that Colonel Manigault refused to accept it. The 10ᵗʰ was composed of companies from Horry, Marion, Georgetown, Williamsburg and Charleston Districts. Still in state service, it assembled at Camp Marion near White's Bridge in Georgetown District on July 19, 1861.[2] The regiment mustered in Confederate service on August 14 for twelve months to date from July 19, 1861. Three companies refused to enter Confederate service and were lost to the regiment at that time.[3] The 10ᵗʰ Regiment added three new companies in August and two more in October, giving it a complement of twelve companies by late 1861. On March 14, 1862, the regiment re-enlisted for three years or for the duration of the war, having already served eight months of its three-year term. Unlike many of the first ten volunteer regiments, the 10ᵗʰ lost no companies and few of its men at the reorganization in the spring of 1862. Its twelve companies were consolidated into six—Companies 1 to 6, in February 1863; the 19ᵗʰ Regiment's companies were consolidated into four—Companies 7 to 10.[4] The two regiments were then consolidated into one from February 1863 to April 1864. The field officers of the 10ᵗʰ initially commanded the Consolidated 10ᵗʰ/19ᵗʰ Regiment.[5] About February 13, 1864, the regiment unanimously and enthusiastically re-enlisted for the duration of the war.[6] Although the two regiments were relieved from consolidation in April 1864, they were combined again on April 9, 1865, to form Walker's South Carolina Battalion Infantry, also known as the 10ᵗʰ Battalion, South Carolina Infantry. Walker's Battalion consisted of Companies A, B, C, D, E and F. The men of the 10th Regiment, who made up Companies A and B of Walker's Battalion, were paroled at Greensboro on May 1, 1865.

FIELD OFFICERS

Arthur Middleton Manigault of Georgetown and Charleston was elected captain of a volunteer cavalry unit called the North Santee Mounted Rifles in December 1860. In the winter and spring of 1861, he supervised the construction of defenses around Winyah Bay and the North Santee River. On April 10, 1861, Manigault was appointed captain and named volunteer aide-de-camp to General P.G.T. Beauregard and was assigned to Morris Island during the bombardment of Fort Sumter in April. He was promoted to lieutenant colonel on May 2 as special acting assistant adjutant and inspector general for the provisional forces of General Beauregard's command. On May 31, 1861, Manigault was elected colonel of the 10th Regiment without opposition.[7] His Confederate commission was dated July 19. That fall Manigault commanded the 1st South Carolina Military District, an area extending from the Little River Inlet south to the South Santee River. He was re-elected colonel at the reorganization in the spring of 1862.[8] He was colonel in command of the Consolidated 10th/19th Regiment in February 1863.[9] Manigault was functioning as acting brigadier general as early as May 1862 and was officially promoted to that rank effective April 26, 1863. He was wounded in the hand by a rifle ball at Resaca, Georgia, on May 14, 1864.[10] During the battle of Franklin, Tennessee, on November 30, 1864, he was struck in the head by a Minié ball and was incapacitated for the rest of the war. Lingering effects of the wound contributed to his death on August 17, 1886.[11] Lieutenant Colonel C. Irvine Walker wrote in 1913: "He had high ideals of duty and to them was ever faithful. He was firm in his decisions, always formed after mature consideration and with the best of judgment. He was very even-tempered, never swayed by passion. He was pure in thought and had no vulgar impulses to clothe in blasphemous words. He was not only morally good, but a communicant of the church and a deeply religious man without fanaticism. His lofty character was an inspiration to his men. He was a guide in all noble things."[12]

James Fowler Pressley, a physician from Society Hill and graduate of The Citadel, was the first captain of Company E of the 10th Regiment.[13] He was elected lieutenant colonel on May 31, 1861, and mustered in Confederate service with the regiment at that rank on August 14.[14] His commission was dated July 19, 1861. Pressley was re-elected lieutenant colonel at the reorganization. General A.M. Manigault cited Pressley for his courage and coolness at the battle of Murfreesboro.[15] He was lieutenant colonel in command of the Consolidated 10th/19th Regiment from February to July 30, 1863.[16] Filling the vacancy when Manigault was promoted to brigadier general, Pressley was made colonel on July 30, with rank from April 26, 1863. He commanded the consolidated regiment as colonel until April 1864.[17] At the battle of Atlanta on July 22, 1864, Pressley was severely wounded in the left shoulder by a rifle ball "while wresting muskets from the hands of the enemy and mounting their breastworks."[18] Shell splinters also perforated his mouth and head. Manigault wrote that Pressley was shot while "fighting hand to hand with several Federal soldiers."[19] Incapacitated by the shoulder wound, Pressley never rejoined the regiment. In October 1864, he was elected to the South Carolina House of Representatives from Williamsburg District.[20] Pressley commanded Confederate troops at the battle of Dingle's Mill, near Sumter, on April 9, 1865.[21]

Richard Green White, a Georgetown physician, graduate of The Citadel and first major of the regiment, was elected sometime before June 1861, probably on May 31.[22] According to the *Mercury*, R.G. White was captain of Company A from 1859 until his resignation in early June 1861.[23] The Georgetown Confederate monument, erected in honor of Company A, however, does not include Captain White's name. This could be explained by the fact that he was captain of the company before it was attached to the 10th Regiment. A Georgetown County history mentions a Major R.G. White who resigned when his company went west. White resigned when the 10th Regiment mustered in Confederate service on August 14, 1861, nine months before his company went west with the regiment in April 1862.[24] One of his brothers was William Capers White, major of the 7th Regiment, SCV, who was killed at Sharpsburg. Another was James Benjamin White, superintendent of The Citadel Academy during the war and commanding officer of the Battalion of State Cadets.

Archibald James Shaw, a lawyer, was promoted from first lieutenant of Company A to major in August 1861.[25] The CSR states the date was August 4, but this might be a clerical error since the 10th Regiment mustered in Confederate service on August 14. Major White resigned when the regiment entered Confederate service in August 1861, and Shaw replaced him. All officers with ranks superior to Shaw's waived their right to promotion in his favor.[26] Not re-elected at the reorganization in the spring of 1862, he was dropped from the rolls on May 8. Lieutenant Colonel C.I. Walker later wrote of Shaw: "Brave, earnest, conscientious, a splendid officer, and a brave man, he discharged the duties of the Majoricy [*sic*] as honestly and as fearlessly as he, in after years, learnedly dispensed justice from the Bench. He was sacrificed, as many good men have been, and not re-elected at the reorganization."[27] Shaw served as a volunteer aide-de-camp to Brigadier General James H. Trapier and was a member of the South Carolina House of Representatives from 1863 to 1865.

Julius Theodore Porcher was promoted to major from captain of Company K on July 28, 1862, probably with rank from May.[28] S.E. McMillan, captain of Company L, had been elected major of the regiment at the reorganization, but he had declined the promotion. Although Porcher was not the senior captain at the time, captains senior to him recognized his ability and waived their claim to promotion in his favor.[29] Manigault cited Porcher's courage and coolness at the battle of Murfreesboro.[30] He served as major of the Consolidated 10th/19th Regiment from February 1863 until he was killed.[31] His promotion to lieutenant colonel was approved posthumously on February 16, 1864, effective April 26, 1863.[32] Wounded and captured at Missionary Ridge on November 25, 1863, Porcher died the same day.[33] Manigault wrote: "Several valuable officers were killed in this engagement but no one was more universally lamented and whose loss was a more serious one to the service than that of Lieutenant Colonel Julius Porcher...He was a brave, sagacious, and industrious officer. Fully alive to the responsibilities of his position, he never spared himself, and labored to perfect himself in all that pertained to the duty of a soldier, and made for himself an enviable reputation."[34] Walker saw Porcher as "brave, eminently pious, generous, cultivated, with the most winning manners, he was beloved by all and missed as a friend and officer."[35] The rank of major of the 10th Regiment was never filled after Porcher's death.

Cornelius Irvine Walker of Charleston was promoted from assistant adjutant general of Manigault's Brigade to lieutenant colonel on June 13, 1864, with rank from June 11.[36] All commissioned officers of the 10th Regiment waived their rights to promotion in deference to Walker. First honor graduate of The Citadel Academy's class of 1861, he was appointed adjutant of the 10th Regiment with the rank of captain on May 31 and appointed assistant adjutant general of Manigault's Brigade on August 5, 1863, with rank from May 2.[37] Wounded in the neck at Ezra Church near Atlanta on July 28, 1864, Walker was also struck in the upper right arm at Kinston, North Carolina, about March 15, 1865.[38] He commanded the brigade often and also led Walker's Battalion, which was formed on April 10, 1865, by the merger of the 10th and 19th Regiments. Walker was paroled with his battalion at Greensboro on May 1, 1865.[39]

COMPANIES

Three companies, D, G and I, which were part of the regiment while it was in state service, did not muster in Confederate service in August 1861. The company under Captain George sought to join the regiment for state service but was rejected by A.M. Manigault and never received a letter designation. In addition, all the original companies lost several men when the regiment mustered in Confederate service. Companies D, G and I were replaced by three new companies with the same letter designations. Companies A, B, C, E, F, H and K were the same before and after entering Confederate service. Companies L and M were added in the fall of 1861. The original Companies D, G and I, as well as George's Company, are listed below, and they are followed by a listing of the twelve companies that made up the 10th Regiment in Confederate service.

The original Company D was the Wee Nee Volunteers, a Williamsburg District company originally commanded by John Gotea Pressley.[40] Also known as the Williamsburg Company, the Wee Nee Volunteers was raised in Kingstree in Williamsburg District and given the American Indian name of the Black River running through Kingstree.[41] This company served as Company F in Maxcy Gregg's six-month regiment from January 4, 1861, until it refused to go to Virginia and was disbanded on April 26.[42] The Wee Nee Volunteers reorganized in May under command of Captain R.M. Gourdin and mustered in the 10th Regiment.[43] When the 10th entered in Confederate service on August 14, the company refused to do so, ending its association with the regiment.[44] The men of the Wee Nee Volunteers proceeded to reorganize themselves into two companies, one of which mustered in state service and the other in Confederate service. The company's original first lieutenant, Samuel W. Maurice, recruited one company, and its former captain, John G. Pressley, recruited the other. Pressley's Company mustered in Confederate service as Company E of Johnson Hagood's 1st Regiment, SCV, on September 11, 1861.[45] Maurice's Company mustered in state service in Harlee's Legion, South Carolina Militia, also called the Pee Dee Legion.

The original Company G was called the Coast Guards. Benjamin Jenkins Johnson, the loser to F.W. Pickens in a close gubernatorial election in November 1860, raised the Coast Guards from the 2nd Battalion of the 19th Regiment, South Carolina Militia.[46] The men, who were from Christ Church and St. Thomas Parishes in Charleston District, enlisted for service on April 11, 1861. The company, stationed at Sullivan's Island that month, participated in the engagement with Fort Sumter on April 12 and 13, 1861.[47] About April 27, Johnson was elected captain of a corps of volunteers from the Washington Light Infantry raised for the purpose of joining the Hampton Legion and serving in Virginia.[48] The *Horry Dispatch* lists Johnson as captain of the Coast Guards on May 23.[49] First Lieutenant Alfred H. DuPre replaced Johnson as captain sometime in May.[50] The company was stationed at Bull Island in July.[51] The *Charleston Daily Courier* places the Coast Guards in the 10th Regiment on July 24, but the company did not enter Confederate service with the regiment on August 14.[52] The Coast Guards remained in service until September 6, when it was disbanded.[53] On October 30 most of the men mustered for the duration of the war in a new local defense company in Confederate service.[54] This company, the Santee Light Artillery, subsequently served as Company B of Edward Manigault's Battalion, which, in December 1861, was raised for local defense. Some men of the Coast Guards served in other companies of Manigault's Battalion.

The original Company I was called the Carver's Bay Palmetto Rifle Guards or the Carver's Bay Sharpshooters.[55] Its men were from the Carver's Bay area in Georgetown District. A sketch in *Recollections and Reminiscences* lists William McAnge as captain.[56] An article in the *Horry Dispatch* on May 23, 1861, however, which purports to list all captains in the 10th Regiment, does not include McAnge; it does show that J.G. Henning of Georgetown commanded a company. Since Henning is not accounted for in any of the other companies, it appears, by process of elimination, that he must have commanded Company I.[57] The company did not muster in Confederate service with the regiment in August 1861. Its fate is unknown, but probably it was disbanded. McAnge enlisted in Company M as a private and rose to the rank of sergeant. He died at Holly Springs, Mississippi, in 1862 or 1863.

Captain George's Company was not included when the 10th Regiment mustered in state service. Captain J.J. George was in command of the company on May 23, 1861.[58] The company arrived at Camp Marion later that month in such a disorganized state that Colonel Manigault refused to accept it and sent the men back home. George's Company was never assigned a letter designation.

Following are the twelve companies of the 10th Regiment after it mustered in Confederate service in August 1861:

Company A, the Georgetown Rifle Guards, was composed of men from that town and district. Organized in 1859, the company was incorporated by the General Assembly on January 28, 1861.[59] Men from Williamsburg and Horry Districts joined the company that year.[60] In January 1861, the *Mercury* reported that the company had recruited fifty men and would soon make its appearance as a volunteer uniform company.[61] The Georgetown

Rifle Guards mustered in state service on January 2, went into garrison at South Island on February 4 and were relieved there on April 25, 1861.[62] The company mustered in as Company A of the 10th Regiment on May 31, and while it was stationed at Georgetown on August 14 mustered in Confederate service for twelve months to date from July 19.[63] Richard Green White, a graduate of The Citadel, was captain of the company from 1859 to May 1861.[64] He was elected major of the regiment about May 31 and replaced by Private Plowden Charles Jennet Weston.[65] Weston, a native of England, personally provided 155 English-manufactured Enfield rifles, accoutrements and knapsacks, as well as one summer uniform and one winter uniform for each man in the company. He also provided four of his slaves to act as pioneers for the company.[66] Weston also donated $5,000 to the state, a portion of which was used to purchase a rifled cannon from Cameron and McDurmid in Charleston. He mustered in Confederate service with the company on August 14, 1861; his commission as captain ranked from July 19. On March 28, 1862, the company re-enlisted for two additional years dating from July 19, 1862.[67] Weston declined promotion to major in the spring of 1862 but was re-elected captain of Company A.[68]

As Weston and ten or twelve of his sick or wounded men were on their way to the hospital in June 1862, they were captured by Federal pickets but were soon rescued by Confederate cavalry.[69] Worn down by the fatigues of the Kentucky campaign, Weston left the company on October 24, 1862, and went home, hoping that he could recover his health and return to duty with his company.[70] It was not to be. Weston, dubbed the "beloved captain," tendered his resignation on December 17 on the grounds that the General Assembly had elected him lieutenant governor of South Carolina.[71] Weston's resignation was accepted on January 27, 1863. He contracted tuberculosis during the Kentucky campaign and died from that disease in Conwayboro on January 25, 1864.[72] He was described as "a man of high, noble sentiments, [whose] age, pursuits, and responsibilities might fairly have excused him from service in the field and his wealth would easily have purchased immunity from hardship and danger."[73] First Lieutenant Charles Carroll White replaced Weston on January 27, 1863. White, who had been slightly wounded in the head near Corinth in May 1862, was promoted to captain for distinguished gallantry at Murfreesboro on December 29, 1862. On picket duty with Company A about a half mile in front of the Confederate battle line, White and eight of his men were cut off and captured by the 15th Regiment Pennsylvania Cavalry. White ordered the rest of the company to rally on the right group and "Commence firing! Don't mind us!" He and the men were able to escape in the ensuing fight. White was awarded the Medal of Honor on October 3, 1863, based on the extraordinary courage and valor he displayed at Murfreesboro. When the 10th and 19th Regiments were consolidated in February 1863, Company A was merged with Company G to form Company 1 in the consolidated regiment with White as captain.[74] He remained in command from September 1863 to April 1864.[75] White was shot through the body while on the picket line at Atlanta on August 4, 1864.[76] Initially left for dead, he began to shows signs of life as his body was prepared for burial. White eventually recovered, although the wound disabled him. General Manigault called White "one of my best officers, who lived through the war and distinguished himself on many occasions." [77] Emanuel wrote: "His record as an officer was without a superior."[78] White survived the war but received an almost identical wound during the affair at Cainhoy on October 17, 1876, and died from its effects.[79] The citizens of Georgetown erected a large monument to the memory of the men of Company A. Arthur Manigault called this company the best he ever saw in the service. The men of Company A formed part of Company A in Walker's Battalion in April 1865.

Company B, the Brooks Guards or Brooks Rifle Guards was composed of men from Conway in Horry District.[80] Organized in 1858 and incorporated in 1859, it was named in honor of Congressman Preston Brooks. Company B men were armed with the short Mississippi Rifle in early 1861.[81] Captain James H. Norman, MD, and the men mustered in state service with the 10th Regiment on May 31.[82] While stationed at Georgetown on August 14, the men mustered in Confederate service for twelve months to date from July 19, 1861. Norman mustered in Confederate service with the men; his commission dated from July 19. Norman, who had received some training at The Citadel Academy, was not re-elected at the reorganization and was dropped from the rolls on May 8, 1862. He returned to Conwayboro to resume the practice of medicine.[83] First Lieutenant William J. Tolar was elected captain on May 20. Tolar was one of nine brothers, all of whom served in the war.[84] When the 10th and 19th Regiments were consolidated in February 1863, Company B was consolidated with Company F to form Company 6 in the consolidated regiment with Tolar as captain.[85] He sustained severe wounds to the throat and face at Atlanta on July 22, 1864.[86] The bullet entered Tolar's face just below the left eye, fractured the facial bone and was extracted from the right side of the roof of his mouth. Initially thought to be mortally wounded, Tolar survived but remained disabled.[87] The men of Company B formed part of Company B in Walker's Battalion in April 1865. Walker wrote that he "felt satisfied when Captain Tolar commanded the skirmish line."[88]

Company C, the Lake Swamp Volunteers, was composed of men from Horry District. It mustered in state service with the 10th Regiment on May

31, 1861. While stationed at Georgetown on August 14, the men mustered in Confederate service for twelve months to date from July 19, 1861. Forty-year-old A.H. Johnson, captain of the company in May, mustered in Confederate service, along with his men, in August.[89] He was re-elected at the reorganization but resigned on November 25, 1862, citing poor health.[90] He had suffered for several months with dyspepsia and chronic diarrhea, and he also had lumbago and general debility. When the 10th and 19th Regiments were consolidated in February 1863, Company C merged with Company D to form Company 2 in the consolidated regiment.[91] Captain Harllee of Company D commanded the consolidated company. First Lieutenant Carmi Johnson, who commanded the consolidated company at times between September 1863 and April 1864, was promoted to captain of Company C in early 1864.[92] The CSR does not show a promotion date, but he first appears at that rank on the muster roll for March/April 1864. J.P. Thomas gives Johnson's name as Carnie, and other accounts show it as Cormi.[93] The men of Company C formed part of Company A in Walker's Battalion in April 1865.

Company D, the Marion Volunteers, was composed of men from that district.[94] In August 1861, this company was added to the regiment to replace the original Company D. While stationed at Georgetown on August 14, the men mustered in Confederate service for twelve months to date from July 19, 1861. Zack Godbold was commissioned captain on August 1. Not re-elected at the reorganization, he was dropped from the rolls on May 8, 1862, and was replaced by First Lieutenant Robert Z. Harllee.[95] When the 10th and 19th Regiments were consolidated in February 1863, Company D was consolidated with Company C to form Company 2 in the consolidated regiment with Harllee as captain.[96] Harllee was placed under arrest on May 7, 1863, for drunkenness. He was tried by general court-martial in June and relieved of command as of May 10. The officers of the regiment petitioned for Harllee's reinstatement, and both General Manigault and Colonel Pressley endorsed the petition. The sentence was either commuted or revoked, and Harllee resumed command of Company D on October 20. Company D was consolidated with Company C from February 1863 to April 1864.[97] Harllee was severely wounded in the hand and lost several fingers at Atlanta on July 28, 1864.[98] He was paroled at Greensboro on May 2, 1865. The men of Company D formed part of Company A in Walker's Battalion in April 1865. Harllee commanded Company A in Walker's Battalion.

Company E, the Black Mingo Rifle Guards or Black Mingo Riflemen, was composed of men from John G. Pressley's Company, the Wee Nee Volunteers, of the 31st Regiment, South Carolina Militia, before the war.[99]

As early as November 5, 1860, John G. Pressley was captain of a Kingstree company in the 31st Regiment.[100] Most of the men enlisted in state service as Company E, the Black Mingo Guards, 10th Regiment, on May 31, 1861. Company E men were mostly from Williamsburg and Georgetown Districts, although a few came from Marion and Clarendon Districts.[101] The men were originally armed with the Harpers Ferry Rifle. John G. Pressley raised a new company, also called the Wee Nee Volunteers, which enlisted on January 4, 1861, as Company F in Maxcy Gregg's 1st (six-month) Regiment and then became Company D in the 10th Regiment in April. James Fowler Pressley, the first captain of Company E, was elected lieutenant colonel of the 10th Regiment on May 31, 1861.[102] While stationed at Georgetown on August 14, the Black Mingo Rifle Guards mustered in Confederate service for twelve months to date from July 19, 1861. James F. Carraway replaced Pressley as captain, probably in May, and mustered in Confederate service at that rank on August 14. Not re-elected at the reorganization, he was dropped from the rolls on May 8, 1862, and was replaced by First Lieutenant Thomas McConnell Miller. Miller died of typhoid fever near Tupelo, Mississippi, on July 7, 1862.[103] First Sergeant George P. Anderson was promoted to captain the next day. When the 10th and 19th Regiments were consolidated in February 1863, Company E merged with Company L to form Company 5 with Anderson as captain.[104] Anderson sustained a severe chest wound on March 11, 1865, at Kinston, North Carolina. The men of Company E formed part of Company B in Walker's Battalion in April 1865 with Anderson as captain.

Company F, the Pee Dee Rangers, was composed of men from Marion District. It mustered in state service with the 10th Regiment on May 31, 1861, and on August 14 while stationed at Georgetown, mustered in Confederate service for twelve months to date from July 19, 1861. Edmund C. Miller was elected captain, probably before mid-May 1861, since the *Horry Dispatch* shows him in command on May 23.[105] Miller's commission was dated July 19, reflecting his entrance in Confederate service. Not re-elected at the reorganization, he was dropped from the rolls on May 8, 1862. Miller subsequently served as assistant surgeon at Chattanooga, Tennessee, until March 16, 1863, when he was sent to Ringgold, Georgia. On January 16, 1865, he was stationed at Tupelo, Mississippi. B.F. Davis enlisted on July 19, 1861, as first lieutenant in Miller's Company. The CSR shows Davis as captain in June 1862, but it does not give a promotion date. In fact, the CSR evidently has no records for Davis after June and his record remains unclear.[106] When the 10th and 19th Regiments were consolidated in February 1863, Company F was consolidated with Company B to form Company 6 with Captain Tolar of Company B in command.[107] Frank J.

Bostick was promoted from first lieutenant to captain on April 8, 1864, with rank from June 18, 1862. C. Irvine Walker records that Bostick was elected captain at the reorganization in the spring of 1862.[108] Bostick was wounded at Chickamauga and also at Missionary Ridge on November 25, 1863. Company F was consolidated with Company B from February 1863 to April 1864.[109] The men of Company F formed part of Company B in Walker's Battalion in April 1865.

Company G, the Horry Rough and Readys, was organized on August 23, 1861, and was added to the regiment in September after the original Company G, the Coast Guards, refused to enter Confederate service.[110] While stationed at Camp Marion near Georgetown on September 4, the Horry Rough and Readys mustered in Confederate service for twelve months. Company G men were from the Lake Swamp area of Horry District. Samuel Bell, previously first lieutenant in Company B, resigned that position on August 26, 1861, upon organizing the Rough and Readys. Bell was elected captain on August 23 and mustered in at that rank on September 4.[111] Not re-elected at the reorganization, Bell was dropped from the rolls on May 8, 1862, and was replaced by first Lieutenant Cornelius T. Ford, MD.[112] Slightly wounded at Murfreesboro, Ford resigned on May 14, 1863.[113] When the 10th and 19th Regiments were consolidated in February 1863, Company G was consolidated with Company A to form Company 1 in the consolidated regiment with C.C. White of Company A as captain.[114] Moses F. Sarvis was promoted from first lieutenant to captain at some point between December 1863 and February 1864. Company G was consolidated with Company A from September 1863 to April 1864.[115] The men of Company G formed part of Company A in Walker's Battalion in April 1865.

Company H, the Liberty Volunteers, was the original Company H of the 10th Regiment.[116] On August 14, 1861, while stationed at Georgetown, the Liberty Volunteers mustered in Confederate service for twelve months, to date from July 19, 1861. Most Liberty Volunteers were from Williamsburg District, but a few came from Marion and Darlington Districts. Captain John R. Nettles, who commanded the company as early as May 23, mustered in Confederate service as captain on August 14, 1861.[117] His commission dated from July 19. He was re-elected captain on May 31, 1862. Wounded three times, Nettles was captured at Murfreesboro on December 31, 1862, and died from his wounds while a prisoner of war. The *Roll of the Dead* states that he was killed on December 31, 1862, but the CSR gives the date of January 4, 1863. According to Captain Lee's letters, it was January 30, and Kirkland states that Nettles died on January 14, 1863, "in enemy hands."[118] General A.M. Manigault called him "an excellent and reliable officer" and cited Nettles for courage and coolness at the battle of Murfreesboro.[119] Nettles's name was engraved on one of the four cannon captured by the 10th and 19th Regiments at Murfreesboro.[120] The other three men were Colonel A.J. Lythgoe of the 19th Regiment; Captain Palmer, Company K of the 10th Regiment; and 2nd Lieutenant John T. Norris, Company A of the 19th Regiment. First Lieutenant William James McNeel Lee was promoted to captain with rank from January 14, 1863. When the 10th and 19th Regiments were consolidated in February 1863, Company H merged with Company I to form Company 3 in the consolidated regiment with Lee as captain.[121] He was a "fine officer, and he richly deserves the commission [to captain]."[122] The men of Company H formed part of Company A in Walker's Battalion in April 1865.

Company I, the Swamp Fox Guards, was composed of men from Marion and Williamsburg Districts. In August 1861, it was added to the 10th Regiment to replace the original Company I, the Carver's Bay Palmetto Rifle Guards.[123] On August 13, 1861, a date also shown in the record as August 31, while stationed at Camp Marion near Georgetown, the Swamp Fox Guards mustered in Confederate service for twelve months to date from July 19. The commission of the company's first captain, Henry Michael Lofton, bore the same date. Lofton resigned at some point between November 1 and December 26, 1861; he later served as captain of Company C, 26th Regiment, SCV. B.B. McWhite was promoted from first lieutenant to captain on December 26 and re-elected at the reorganization the following spring.[124] McWhite was severely wounded at Murfreesboro on December 31, 1862, and was hospitalized for a month; he was placed on recruiting and conscript duty until December 1863.[125] When the 10th and 19th Regiments were consolidated in February 1863, Company I merged with Company H to form Company 3 in the consolidated regiment with Lee of Company H as captain.[126] The men of Company I formed part of Company A in Walker's Battalion in April 1865.

Company K, the Eutaw Volunteers, was composed of men from St. John's Berkeley in Charleston District.[127] It probably mustered in state service with the 10th Regiment on May 31, 1861. The Eutaw Volunteers entered Confederate service for twelve months in Charleston on September 3.[128] The commission of the first captain, Julius Theodore Porcher, bore that date as well. Porcher had served as major of the Upper Battalion of the 19th Regiment, South Carolina Militia, in June.[129] He was promoted to major of the 10th Regiment on July 28, 1862, probably with rank from May. John Sanders Palmer was promoted from first lieutenant to captain effective May 24. When the 10th and 19th Regiments were consolidated in February 1863, Company K merged with Company M to form Company 4 in the consolidated regiment with Palmer as captain.[130] Palmer was slightly wounded at Murfreesboro on December 31, 1862. His is another of the names engraved on one of the four cannon captured at Murfreesboro.[131] Palmer was killed at Atlanta on July 28, 1864.[132] The men of Company K formed part of Company B in Walker's Battalion in April 1865.

Company L, the Liberty Guards, was composed of men from Marion District. While at Camp Marion near Georgetown on October 13, 1861, the Liberty Guards mustered in Confederate service for twelve months to date from September 30. Sidney E. McMillan was commissioned captain on the thirtieth as well. He was elected major at the reorganization, but he declined the office and was dropped from the rolls on May 8, 1862.[133] A sketch of McMillan's life states that he was promoted to captain in 1863, that he was later promoted to major, and that he served until the end of the war.[134] The CSR, however, shows no service record for McMillan after May 1862. First Lieutenant A.H. Ford was elected captain at the reorganization in May.[135] The CSR does not give a date for his commission to captain, but the first listing at that rank appears on the muster roll for November/December 1862. Ford was detached from the regiment on January 28, 1863, and was assigned to the recruiting service until at least September 1864. When the 10th and 19th Regiments were consolidated in February 1863, Company L was consolidated with Company E to form Company 5 in the consolidated regiment with Company E's Anderson as captain.[136] Ford was able-bodied on September 16, 1864, and it was recommended that he be sent back to the army. Company L was consolidated with Company E from September 1863 to April 1864.[137] The men of Company L formed part of Company B in Walker's Battalion in April 1865.

Company M, the Horry Dixie Boys, was also called the Horry Volunteers.[138] Another company called the Horry Volunteers was Company L of the 7th Regiment, SCV. Company M, composed of men from Horry and Marion Districts, was added to the 10th Regiment, probably on October 30, 1861, when it mustered in service for twelve months.[139] William J. Taylor, previously a private in Company B, organized Company M and was commissioned its captain on October 30. Not re-elected at the reorganization, Taylor was dropped from the rolls on May 8, 1862, and was replaced by First Sergeant J.P. Bessant.[140] The CSR spells the name both Bessant and Bessent, but his signature appears as Bessant. Bessant suffered from poor health, including chronic diarrhea and dropsy. When the 10th and 19th Regiments were consolidated in February 1863, Company M merged with Company K to form Company 4 in the consolidated regiment with Palmer of Company K as captain.[141] Bessant was not given command of a company at that time; he left on October 27, 1862, and resigned on January 9, 1863. His resignation was accepted on February 6. William C. Dubois was promoted from first lieutenant to captain on March 12, 1864, with rank from January 19, 1863. The men of Company M formed part of Company M in Walker's Battalion in April 1865.

A detachment of the North Santee Mounted Rifles under Captain A.W. Cordes was attached to the 10th Regiment in September and October 1861.

A Captain Forster and Lieutenant Joseph Jenkins Hucks commanded the Sampit Rangers from Georgetown District. It was also attached to the 10th Regiment for a short time in 1861 and 1862 and was disbanded in 1862.[142]

Captain Joshua Ward's Artillery Company, which subsequently became Captain Mayham Ward's Company, South Carolina Light Artillery, was temporarily attached to the 10th Regiment when it mustered in service. On August 31, 1862, it was mustered as a company of the 4th Squadron, later called the 12th Battalion, South Carolina Cavalry.

BRIGADE AFFILIATIONS

The 10th Regiment was part of Milledge L. Bonham's Brigade in South Carolina in 1861. The 10th Regiment was attached to the Department of South Carolina, Georgia and Florida until April 1862.[143] For a day or two that spring, the 10th Regiment was attached to David S. Donelson's Brigade, along with the 19th Regiment, SCV, and the 8th and 16th Tennessee Regiments. On April 28, 1862, the 10th and 19th Regiments, along with the 28th Alabama, the 44th Mississippi and Waters's Alabama Battery, were formed into James H. Trapier's 4th Brigade in the Army of the Mississippi. Trapier was soon sent back east, and Manigault took over command of the brigade. In June 1862, the 44th Mississippi was replaced with the 34th Alabama Regiment. On November 15, 1862, the 24th Alabama Regiment was added to the brigade. Thus, Manigault's Brigade consisted of the 10th and 19th South Carolina Regiments and the 24th, 28th and 34th Alabama Regiments.[144] Manigault's Brigade was transferred to the Army of Tennessee about November 1862.[145] In late March 1865, Manigault's Brigade consisted of the 10th and 19th South Carolina Regiments and the 24th and 34th Alabama Regiments.[146] On April 9, 1865, the 10th and 19th Regiments were consolidated into Walker's Battalion, and Manigault's Brigade was consolidated with Brigadier General Jacob H. Sharp's Brigade under command of Sharp.[147]

MAJOR MOVEMENTS AND ENGAGEMENTS

Some companies of the 10th Regiment were active before the regiment mustered in state service on May 31, 1861. The Georgetown Rifle Guards was stationed at the South Island Redoubt on February 4, and the Brooks Guards was at North Island from January to April.[148] Company G, stationed at Sullivan's Island in April, was engaged during the bombardment of Fort Sumter on the twelfth and thirteenth.[149] The Georgetown Rifle Guards was relieved of duty at South Island on April 25 and was ordered to Camp Marion near White's Bridge in Georgetown District.

The 10th Regiment elected field officers and mustered in state service on May 31, and some of its companies were stationed around Winyah Bay through the summer. Company E was posted to South Island and Company D to North Island.[150] The 10th Regiment, except for the two Charleston District companies—G (Coast Guards) and K (Eutaw Volunteers)—assembled at Camp Marion near White's Bridge about two miles west of Georgetown on July 19. Company G was stationed at Bull Island, and Company K was ordered to Bulls Bay in July.[151] The regiment mustered in Confederate service on August 14 for twelve months to date from July 19. In early September, eight companies of the regiment were at Camp Marion, with the other two expected shortly.[152] The regiment probably spent a brief period in Charleston in September, but it was back in the vicinity of Georgetown by October 1. The regiment served in the Georgetown area, particularly at Cat Island, throughout the remainder of 1861. From September 6 to November 10, Company K served as an artillery company at Fort Ripley and Fort Bonham on Bull Island, and by the fifteenth it had rejoined the regiment near Georgetown.[153] In the fall of 1861, Company H was sent to South Island, and Company F was sent to the fort on Cat Island, both near Georgetown. On December 15 and 16, Companies A, E, H and K were sent to South Island, Companies B and F to the Cat Island Fort, Company D to North Island and Companies C, G, I, L and M, to Cat Island near the South Island causeway.[154] The regiment remained in these positions for the rest of the winter.

On December 24, 1861, a picket detachment of seven men from Company D repelled a Federal boat party attempting to capture the grounded blockade-runner *Prince of Wales*.[155] On March 25, 1862, Major General Pemberton ordered Colonel Manigault to abandon and dismantle the Georgetown defenses and bring the 10th Regiment to Charleston.[156] Company A left Georgetown for Mount Pleasant on March 31.[157] The rest of the regiment arrived at Mount Pleasant on April 3.[158] At nine in the evening of April 11, one week after the battle of Shiloh, the regiment boarded the train in Charleston.[159] A few minutes before midnight, the train pulled out of Charleston.[160] A circuitous route by rail and steamer took the men through Augusta, Atlanta, Montgomery and Mobile; they arrived at Corinth, Mississippi, on April 25 and 26. The 10th Regiment suffered badly from disease at Corinth. From this time to the end of the war, the 10th Regiment served with the 19th Regiment. The major movements and engagements of both regiments are discussed below.

Both regiments were engaged in a skirmish at Farmington on May 17, 1862.[161] The two regiments evacuated Corinth on May 29 and arrived at Tupelo, Mississippi, on June 7. They left Tupelo about July 6 and marched fourteen miles north to Saltillo.[162] Leaving Saltillo by rail on July 30 or 31, the regiments arrived at Tyner's Station, near Chattanooga, in early August. On August 28, the regiments crossed the Tennessee River and on the thirtieth, they participated in the opening of Braxton Bragg's Kentucky campaign. The 10th and 19th Regiments were part of Bragg's march through Tennessee and Kentucky from August 30 to late October 1862. The men passed into Kentucky on September 10. On September 17, both regiments were engaged at Munfordville, where the 10th Regiment, being in advance of the brigade, drove in the Federal pickets. The regiments also participated in the attack on Lawrenceburg and took part in several smaller skirmishes in the Kentucky campaign, but they were not engaged at Perryville on October 8, 1862.

The regiments returned to Tennessee via Cumberland Gap on October 20 and marched to Knoxville on the twenty-fourth. Next, on November 1, they moved by rail to Bridgeport, Alabama, and then marched to Tullahoma, Tennessee, arriving there on November 24. The CSR's caption of events for the 19th Regiment shows it left Tullahoma on November 24 and arrived at Murfreesboro on the twenty-sixth. The 10th Regiment left Tullahoma and marched to Murfreesboro about the same time. Manigault's Brigade formed a line of battle there on December 28, 1862.[163] Company A of the 10th Regiment was engaged as brigade skirmishers near Murfreesboro on December 29.[164] Company I of the 19th Regiment skirmished at Murfreesboro on December 30. The two regiments were engaged in their first major action at Murfreesboro on December 30 and 31. The 10th and the 19th Regiments captured a Federal battery—Company C, 1st Illinois Light Artillery—that day, which General Bragg presented to General Beauregard, who was then commanding the Department of South Carolina, Georgia and Florida. The four captured guns—two Wiards and two Parrotts—were three-inch rifled, steel cannon, although another source records them as Napoleons.[165] The cannon were engraved with the names of four men who had shown outstanding bravery during the battle—two men from the 10th and two from the 19[166] Regiment. The men from the 10th Regiment were Captains John R. Nettles of Company H and John S. Palmer of Company K. The men from the 19th Regiment were Colonel A.J. Lythgoe and Second Lieutenant John T. Norris of Company A. In late February, the four cannon were shipped to Charleston for use there.[167] The Santee Light Artillery received two of the Murfreesboro cannon in March.

The men remained in line of battle on January 1, 2 and 3, 1863, and the regiments withdrew from Murfreesboro with the Army of Tennessee on January 4, marching twenty-five miles south in one day to Shelbyville. There they set up winter quarters.[168] In February 1863, the 10th and 19th Regiments were consolidated into one; the 10th Regiment furnished six companies, and the 19th supplied four.[169] Commissioned officers who no longer had a company to command were allowed to retain their commissions and were ordered to report to General Polk for duty.[170] The consolidated regiment remained in winter quarters near Shelbyville, performing picket and scout duty around that area and the Duck River until late June 1863.[171] The regiments arrived back at Tullahoma, Tennessee, on June 27, and on July 1 they retreated with Bragg's army from that place.[172] The army crossed the Tennessee River on July 4 and marched ninety miles to McFarland's Springs at the foot of Lookout Mountain near Chattanooga, arriving July 8.[173] The regiment left Chattanooga on August 30, arrived at Tyner's Station, near Chickamauga, the same day, then moved back to McFarland's Springs and left again on September 8.

From September 8 to September 12 the men marched and countermarched. During this time the consolidated regiment participated in unsuccessful maneuvers designed to entrap Thomas's Federal troops at McLemore's Cove on September 11 and at Lafayette, Georgia, on September 12.[174] The regiment left Lafayette on September 17 and went into line of battle the next day during a skirmish on the south side of the Chickamauga River near Lee's and Gordon's mills. The regiment also lay in line of battle near Chickamauga during most of September 19; at dusk it crossed the river and engaged in still another light skirmish. The lull ended on the twentieth, when the Consolidated 10th/19th Regiment found itself heavily engaged at the battle of Chickamauga. On September 21 the men pursued the enemy to Chattanooga and advanced the next day to the Chattanooga Valley. On September 23 the regiment was deployed as a heavy picket line at the foot of Missionary Ridge and participated in the siege of Chattanooga.[175] Engaged at the foot of Missionary Ridge on November 25, the regiment withdrew to its crest that afternoon. Later in the day it retreated from the Ridge, and it crossed Chickamauga Creek that night. The regiment moved through Ringgold, Georgia, on November 26 but was not engaged there.

Arriving at Dalton, Georgia, about November 27, the regiment went into winter quarters.

The men were placed in line of battle again on February 23 and 28, but no engagements ensued. The 10th/19th Consolidated Regiment was de-consolidated that spring. The 10th Regiment remained at Dalton until April 11, when the men left camp to repair the public road running between Dalton and Resaca. On April 23 the 19th Regiment left Dalton to build fortifications near the front at Ault's mill.

The 10th Regiment left Dalton on May 7, opening the Atlanta campaign. The regiments skirmished every day and were frequently engaged between May 7 and June 25.[176] The 19th and 10th were in line of battle at Rocky Face near Mill Creek Gap, but they were not engaged there on May 8. They suffered heavy shelling while in line of battle on the fourteenth at Resaca and were engaged during the second battle of Resaca, or Oostanaula, on May 15.[177] The regiments crossed the Oostanaula River that night and withdrew with the army in the direction of Atlanta. They marched to Adairsville on May 17, skirmished there the same day and marched to Cassville the next. The men skirmished near Cassville on May 19 and were engaged there on the twentieth as well. The two regiments withdrew from the lines near Cassville after dark on May 20 and crossed the Etowah River. They arrived at New Hope Church on May 25, were engaged that day and skirmished on May 26 and 27. Both regiments remained in line of battle, skirmishing daily near New Hope Church, until June 4, when they withdrew to Lost Mountain. By June 19 the men of the 10th and 19th Regiments were within two miles of Marietta. They were engaged again at Zion Church near Marietta on June 22 and remained in position until July 2.

Manigault's Brigade was not actively engaged during the battle of Kennesaw Mountain on June 27. On the night of July 2 the army evacuated Marietta. It withdrew on July 3 to Smyrna Church, and on the fifth to the Chattahoochee River. There it was engaged. The army crossed the river on July 9 and marched to within three miles of Atlanta, where, from July 10 to July 17, it experienced a week of relative calm. The 10th and 19th Regiments were not engaged at the battle of Peachtree Creek on July 20, but they skirmished on July 21 and fell back to the works surrounding Atlanta that night. On July 22 at the battle of Atlanta, the 10th and 19th Regiments were heavily engaged in attacking, capturing and then abandoning the same works they had evacuated the preceding night. The men rested in their trenches for the next five days. On July 27 the regiments moved through Atlanta to a point about two miles southwest of the city, where, on July 28, they were engaged at the battle of Ezra Church, also called the battle of the Poor House and the battle of Lick Skillet Road. Every captain of the 19th

Regiment was either killed or wounded in this battle, and Adjutant James O. Ferrell was forced to take command.[178] Company A of the 10ᵗʰ Regiment had only eight men present for duty on the morning of July 29. The regiments skirmished almost continuously for the next thirty days from their heavily fortified position about three to four miles southwest of Atlanta between the Lick Skillett Road and the Sandtown Road.[179] They evacuated their trenches on August 30, marched south of Atlanta toward Jonesboro and were engaged there on the thirty-first. The 10ᵗʰ and 19ᵗʰ Regiments marched northward toward Atlanta in the early morning hours of September 1, but they turned south and marched to Lovejoy's Station on the Macon and Atlanta Railroad as Hood's army evacuated Atlanta on September 2. The Federal army occupied Atlanta on the night of September 7, thus ending the Atlanta campaign. A.M. Manigault wrote that, except for twelve days, he had been under fire for the entire four-month period.[180]

Following a ten-day truce, the regiments marched northwest toward Palmetto Station on the Atlanta and West Point Railroad on September 18. The troops left by train from Palmetto Station on the twenty-ninth, crossed the Chattahoochee River and moved north. The army then moved through Dalton, Georgia, to Gadsden and Florence, Alabama. On November 20, Hood's army started for Tennessee, arriving at Spring Hill on the twenty-ninth. The consolidated 10ᵗʰ and 19ᵗʰ Regiments were engaged during the debacle at Franklin on November 30. Prior to that battle, the companies of the 10ᵗʰ Regiment had not been uniformly armed. Company A carried the English-made Enfield rifle, Company B carried the Mississippi rifle and Company E carried the Harpers Ferry rifle. The other nine companies were armed with smooth bore muskets, and it wasn't until after the battle of Murfreesboro that those were replaced with the Austrian rifle. After the battle of Franklin, the entire regiment was armed with Enfield rifles. After Franklin, the men moved to Nashville and were engaged there on December 15 and December 16. Manigault's Brigade managed to withdraw in an orderly manner during the chaotic retreat of Hood's army from Nashville on December 16. The regiments crossed over the Tennessee River on December 27 and arrived at Tupelo, Mississippi, on January 7, 1865. Hood's winter campaign took a severe toll on the men. The battered regiments left Tupelo by rail for South Carolina on January 19, passed through Augusta, Georgia, and Branchville, South Carolina, and arrived at the defensive lines along the Edisto River, where they were placed in position near Holman's Bridge. They soon moved to Jones's Bridge and then to a defensive line on Mill Creek, near Columbia. They crossed the Congaree River into the capital on February 16. The next day the regiments moved to Granby to support the artillery at the ferry there. On the evening of February 17, the 10ᵗʰ and 19ᵗʰ Regiments moved to the

Broad River Bridge, where their pickets were driven in the next morning. The regiments withdrew toward Winnsboro.

On February 18, 1865, about 150 men of the 10th Regiment took an unprecedented and unauthorized five-day leave of absence, leaving only about 83 men in the regiment. Many men from the 19th also took similar voluntary leave. Those from the 10th Regiment were unable to return because they were cut off by Sherman's troops, but some men did gather under Pressley's command at Marion Court House, thus avoiding the penalty for desertion.[181] Most of the men who left the 19th Regiment were able to return during its march through Winnsboro to Charlotte, North Carolina. In early March, the regiments moved to Smithfield, North Carolina; they were engaged at Kinston on March 8 and 9, and at Bentonville on the fifteenth. On April 10 the regiments retraced their steps to Smithfield.

On April 9, the 10th and 19th Regiments were consolidated into Cornelius I. Walker's Battalion, and the two regiments ceased to exist. There were only enough men left in the 10th Regiment to make up two companies in Walker's Battalion, but enough remained in the 19th to make up four companies. The men of the 10th Regiment made up Companies A and B of Walker's Consolidated Battalion and those from the 19th made up Companies C, D, E and F. Walker's Battalion surrendered near High Point, North Carolina, on April 26; the troops were paroled on May 1 at Greensboro.[182]

8.

THE 11ᵀᴴ REGIMENT, SOUTH CAROLINA VOLUNTEERS

The 11th Regiment, SCV, was originally called the 9th Regiment, SCV, and the 9th Regiment, South Carolina Infantry. It was also known as Heyward's and Gantt's regiment. Companies were raised in the first half of 1861 under authority of the South Carolina legislature's act of December 17, 1860, calling for ten thousand men to volunteer for twelve months. The men were organized into ten units designated 1st through 10th Regiments, SCV. In May 1861, Heyward's regiment was organized as the 9th Regiment, SCV; elections for field officers were held on the twentieth.[1] J.B. Kershaw's 2nd Regiment was divided in the spring of 1861 when many of its men volunteered for service in Virginia, and many others refused. Those who refused remained in South Carolina under command of Lieutenant Colonel J.D. Blanding; some formed the nucleus of a new regiment, which unfortunately was also designated the 9th. Heyward's regiment, in state service at the time, went into camp in July 1861.[2] Confusion arose immediately over the fact that Blanding's regiment, also in camp, carried the same designation as Heyward's.[3] The problem was unresolved until late July and early August. Blanding's regiment was the first of the two to enter Confederate service; it mustered in on July 12 for twelve months, and its official designation, the 9th Regiment, SCV, came no later than early August.[4] Heyward's regiment, originally designated the 9th, mustered in Confederate service on August 25 and became the 11th Regiment, SCV.[5] Captain Harrison of Company D continued to refer to the 11th Regiment as the 9th as late as November.[6]

The original organization of Heyward's regiment was atypical: although intended as an infantry regiment, its Company A was actually a light artillery battery; most of its companies mustered in Confederate service at different times in the summer of 1861; some companies refused to enter Confederate service at all and were disbanded as a result; others served on as state troops under Heyward's command until late 1861 or early 1862. When other infantry regiments converted from state to Confederate service in 1861, those companies declining to enter Confederate service were simply disbanded. Heyward's regiment, on the other hand, retained at least two—Sheridan's and Bellinger's—until late 1861 even though both had refused to muster in Confederate service. The regiment was reorganized early in 1862. While stationed at Hardeeville, the companies re-enlisted on March 14 for three years from the date of their original enlistment, or for the duration of the war, whichever came first. Elections for officers were held on May 3.[7] At the overall reorganization in the spring of 1862, the 11th Regiment lost its colonel, lieutenant colonel, major and seven of its nine captains, as well as all of Company A—a general bouleversement that caused serious and permanent damage.[8]

When Hagood's Brigade was created on September 20, 1863, the 11th Regiment, the only one in the brigade not equipped with Enfield rifles, was armed with smoothbore muskets. After the battle of Drewry's Bluff on May 16, 1864, the men abandoned their muskets on the battleground and picked up Enfield rifles left by Federal troops. In March 1865, the 11th Regiment was consolidated with the 7th Battalion, South Carolina Infantry, and the 21st, 25th and 27th Regiments, SCV, to form a new unit called Rion's Regiment.

FIELD OFFICERS

William Cruger Heyward, a West Point graduate from Combahee in Colleton District, was elected colonel on May 20, 1861.[9] He was not re-elected on May 3, 1862, and was dropped from the rolls on May 4, a date also shown in the record as the fifth. Heyward was among several good officers lost in this way.[10] Heyward enlisted in the 1st Regiment, Charleston Reserves.[11] The fifty-three-year-old Heyward died on September 1, 1863, from the effects of exposure.[12] He was called a "sterling and valuable citizen."[13]

William Murchey Shuler, MD, from George's Station in Colleton District, was elected lieutenant colonel on May 20, 1861.[14] Claiming his exemption as a physician, he resigned less than four months later, on September 9. He later commanded a company of Junior Reserves, probably Company A of the 2nd Regiment.

Robert Campbell of Walterboro in Colleton District was elected major on May 20, 1861.[15] He was promoted to lieutenant colonel as Shuler's replacement on September 10. Not re-elected on May 3, 1862, Campbell was dropped from the rolls on May 5. He enlisted as a private in the 3rd

Regiment, South Carolina Cavalry. By January 1863, Campbell was a lieutenant in Company I of the 11th Regiment. He retired to the Invalid Corps on December 15, 1864.[16]

Benjamin Burgh Smith Jr., also of Colleton District, was promoted from captain of Company B to major on September 19, 1861, to replace Campbell. Smith was not re-elected on May 3, 1862, and was dropped from the rolls on the fifth. He became major of the 2nd Battalion of South Carolina Sharpshooters on June 22, 1862.

Daniel Hix Ellis of Beaufort District was elected colonel on May 3, 1862, a date also shown in the record as May 5.[17] In the fall of 1862, General W.T. Walker offered Ellis the option of resigning or being charged with incompetence and facing a court martial.[18] Ellis resigned on November 27. He cited physical decline, feeble health and the fact that he was a member of the South Carolina legislature. Walker wrote: "the organization of the 11th Regiment and of this [military] district will be greatly benefited by the acceptance of Colonel Ellis's resignation."[19] Ellis sat in the South Carolina legislature and worked as a tax collector for the rest of the war.[20]

Frederick Hay Gantt of Barnwell District, previously first lieutenant of Company K, was elected lieutenant colonel on May 3, 1862, and was promoted to colonel when Ellis resigned on November 27.[21] Johnson Hagood wrote that Gantt was "a good drill officer and had his regiment in fair discipline when it reported to the brigade [in 1863]."[22] Gantt was in South Carolina gathering up members of the regiment at the end of the war and was paroled at Augusta, Georgia, on May 18, 1865.

John J. Harrison of Beaufort District, previously captain of Company D, was elected major on May 3, 1862.[23] When Federal forces ambushed a Confederate troop train near Coosawhatchie on October 22, 1862, Harrison, who was accompanying several companies of the 11th Regiment bound for Pocotaligo, was shot and killed.[24] His death was a "grievous loss" to the regiment. A positive tribute appeared the following month in the *Charleston Daily Courier*.[25]

Allen Cadwallader Izard of Colleton District, a graduate of the United States Naval Academy, resigned from the United States Navy in 1857. He was promoted from captain of Company I to major on October 22 as Harrison's replacement. The CSR gives the date as both October 22 and November 19, 1862. Izard was promoted to lieutenant colonel on November 27, 1862, when Gantt became colonel. Izard suffered from hemorrhoids and a prolapsed rectum from May 14 to October 8, 1864, when he entered General Hospital #4 in Richmond and was pronounced permanently disabled and unfit for field duty. Relieved of duty, Izard submitted his resignation on December 10 writing that he was "desirous of returning to the navy, which is my old profession."[26] The resignation was accepted on February 4, 1865.[27]

John Jacob Gooding of Beaufort was promoted to major from captain of Company D on November 5, 1863, with rank from November 27, 1862, when Izard became lieutenant colonel. On September 28, 1863, Company A of the 25th Regiment, SCV, replaced Gooding's Company as the garrison at Fort Sumter because Gooding, who was second in command to Major Stephen Elliott, was "reported incompetent to command the Fort in case of an accident to Major Elliott."[28] Johnson Hagood wrote that Gooding was "an incubus upon the command, without soldierly spirit, and yet with ability enough to keep clear of such derelictions of duty as would bring him before a court. Finally, however in the waning days of the Confederacy, he overstayed a leave under circumstances almost amounting to desertion and was dropped from the rolls."[29] The CSR states that Gooding was dropped from the rolls on March 2, 1865. He was paroled on May 25, 1865, at Augusta.

COMPANIES

Company A, the Beaufort Volunteer Artillery was organized in 1802 with men from Beaufort. Stephen Elliott Jr., who raised and equipped the company, was its only captain while it was part of the 11th Regiment. The Beaufort Volunteer Artillery mustered in Confederate service for twelve months on June 12, 1861, while stationed at Bay Point on Port Royal Sound. The exact dates of its attachment to the regiment are not well documented, although its company designation appears to date from as early as May and almost certainly before the regiment entered Confederate service in August 1861. The *Memory Roll* indicates that Company A was attached to the 11th Regiment for a few months after the battle of Port Royal on November 7, 1861. It also records that Hal M. Stewart Jr., then a first lieutenant and later captain of the company, felt that the attachment was a mistake.[30] On March 14, 1862, while it was based at Camp Sturgeon near Hardeeville, the Beaufort Volunteer Artillery was reorganized when its members re-enlisted for two years and twenty-eight days. Beginning in April, the Beaufort Volunteer Artillery was detached from the 11th Regiment, leaving it with only nine companies. After May 1862, the regiment did not have a Company A. The Beaufort Volunteer Artillery became an independent light artillery battery after April 1862, and it was permanently detached from the 11th Regiment by the secretary of war on or about September 20, 1863.[31]

Company B, the Calhoun Artillery, which was attached to the 11th Regiment for a few months in the spring of 1861, was a volunteer organization composed of men from Edisto, Fenwicke's and Musselboro Islands.[32] William M. Murray was captain.[33] The Calhoun Artillery built forts on the North and South Edisto Rivers in the spring of 1861 and garrisoned the North Edisto River from April 26 to June 19.[34] Its men furnished their own arms, ammunition and food. The Calhoun Artillery was relieved from duty on the seaboard by mid-June and disbanded on or about the nineteenth.[35] The St. Paul's Rifles, composed of men from Colleton District and organized about May 14, 1861, replaced the Calhoun Artillery as Company B about June 18. While stationed on the North Edisto River on September 5, 1861, the company mustered in Confederate service for twelve months dating from June 18. Although his commission was also dated June 18, an article in the *Mercury* said Captain Benjamin Burgh Smith Jr. had commanded the company since May 14.[36] This discrepancy can probably be explained by the fact that, although he had been in command since May, Smith's actual commission dated from the time his company joined the regiment. Smith was promoted to major on September 19, 1861. The *Mercury* reported that the company was finally organizing on September 22 at Adams Run.[37] William C. Meggett was promoted from first lieutenant to captain on November 21. While stationed at Camp Lee near Hardeeville, the men re-enlisted on March 14, 1862, for two years, three months and four days. Not re-elected at the reorganization, Meggett was dropped from the rolls on May 5, a date also shown in the record as the third.[38] Second Lieutenant Richard J. LaRoche was elected captain on May 3.[39] LaRoche was discharged within a week for an undisclosed reason, and Julius J. Wescoat Jr. was elected in his place on May 12, a date also shown in the record as the fifteenth.[40] Wescoat was severely wounded in his left leg while leading fifty men from Companies B and K as they drove Federal skirmishers out of a swamp in front of Hagood's Brigade after the main assault at Cold Harbor on June 3, 1864.[41] He was wounded again at Fort Harrison. Wescoat was captured near Town Creek, North Carolina, on February 20, 1865, and sent to Fort Anderson, Point Lookout, Maryland, eight days later. He was moved to the Old Capitol Prison in Washington, D.C., on March 1 and to Fort Delaware on the twenty-fourth. He was released on June 16, 1865.

Company C, the Summerville Guards, was composed of men from Charleston and Colleton Districts.[42] While stationed at Hilton Head Island, the men mustered in service for twelve months on July 6, 1861. Josiah S. Bedon mustered in as captain the same day, but his commission dated from August 25. Stationed the following March at Camp Sturgeon near

Hardeeville, the men re-enlisted on the fourteenth for two years, three months and twenty-two days, or for the duration of the war. Bedon, also not re-elected at the reorganization, was dropped from the rolls on May 3, 1862, a date also shown in the record as the fifth. He enlisted as a private in Company C, 6th Regiment, SCV, on May 26, 1862, and was wounded at Seven Pines five days later. Appointed first lieutenant of Company A, 2nd Battalion Sharpshooters in July or August 1862, he lost that slot when the battalion was disbanded in late December. Finally, he enlisted as a private in the Charleston Light Dragoons in April 1863. Several sources, including the CSR, state he was killed in action at Haw's Shop on May 28, 1864. His obituary in the *Mercury* of October 15, 1864, stated that he was still unaccounted for and presumed dead.[43] Bedon's name is listed, along with the other war dead of the Charleston Light Dragoons, on its monument at Magnolia Cemetery in Charleston. In contrast, one card in the CSR records Bedon's capture at Haw's Shop, and Baxley writes that he survived the war.[44] Thomas Deas Leadbetter was elected captain on May 3. He was mortally wounded at Drewry's Bluff on May 14, 1864, and died the next day.[45] The *Daily South Carolinian* states, incorrectly, that he died on May 9 at Swift Creek.[46] The *Mercury* spells his middle name as Days, while the *Roll of the Dead* makes it Theo Deas Ledbetter.[47] His own signature on official documents reads T.D. Leadbetter. The company served as artillery in 1863.[48]

Company D, the Whippy Swamp Guard, was composed of men from Crocketville in the part of Beaufort District now Hampton County.[49] A few were from just over the border in Barnwell District, and a few came from Georgetown and Prince William Parish.[50] Stationed at Bay Point in the summer of 1861, the men mustered in service for twelve months on July 15. John J. Harrison mustered in as captain the same day. The following spring, while stationed near Hardeeville, the men re-enlisted on March 14 for two years and four months, or for the duration of the war. Harrison was elected major on May 5. First Lieutenant John J. Gooding was elected captain at the reorganization on May 3, 1862. Gooding was promoted to major on November 5, 1863, with rank from November 27, 1862. Henry K. Hucks was promoted from second lieutenant to captain on November 27. Hucks was captured at Fort Fisher, North Carolina, on January 15, 1865, and taken to Fort Columbus in New York Harbor on the twenty-sixth.[51] He was paroled there on February 25 and sent to City Point, Virginia, for exchange. Suffering from pneumonia, he was admitted to Jackson Hospital in Richmond on March 6.

Company E, the Hamilton Guards, or Guard, was composed of men from Barnwell and Beaufort Districts.[52] Stationed at Bay Point during the summer of 1861, the men mustered in service on June 24 for twelve months.

Middleton Stuart mustered in as captain the same day. On March 15, at Camp Heyward near Hardeeville the following spring, the men re-enlisted for two years, three months and twenty days, or for the duration of the war. Stuart was not re-elected at the reorganization and was dropped from the rolls on May 5. First Sergeant John Henry Mickler from Bluffton in Beaufort District was elected captain on May 3, 1862, a date also shown in the record as the fifth.[53] An intrepid, although sometimes unlucky, scout, Mickler's exploits were printed regularly in the *Mercury*. Mickler was wounded by friendly fire at Pinckney Island on August 21 and was shot in the thigh by a Confederate picket on November 24, 1862.[54] During 1862 and 1863, he conducted scouting missions at various barrier islands: at Calliwassee in May 1862, Pinckney in July and August and Daufuskie and Hilton Head the following March.[55] The CSR's last record of Mickler's service as captain of Company E is a muster roll dated September/October 1864.[56] Baxley writes that Mickler was wounded in the summer of 1864, was furloughed home and was paroled at Augusta, Georgia, in May 1865.[57]

Company F, the Republican Blues, was previously Company I of Johnson Hagood's 1st Regiment, SCV. Having unanimously refused to enter Confederate service in May of 1861, the company under James White, who mustered in on June 26, joined Heyward's regiment. A.S. Salley wrote that Captain Rice's Company, probably Company F, of Heyward's regiment was exchanged with Captain White's Company of Hagood's 1st Regiment in the summer of 1861.[58] The Republican Blues disbanded soon afterward, on or about November 26, probably because the men refused to enter Confederate service. A few men later served in Company I of the 11th Regiment. It is unclear whether or not the Republican Blues was an independent company or remained as part of the 11th Regiment in state service from August 25 to November 26. We do know, however, that by July 26, 1861, a company called the Yemassee Volunteers had replaced the Republican Blues as Company F of the 11th Regiment.[59] Composed of men from Beaufort, the Yemassee Volunteers mustered in service on August 5, 1861, for twelve months while stationed at Braddock's Point.[60] Its captain, W.W. Elliott, mustered in the same day. On March 14 of the following spring while stationed near Hardeeville, the men re-enlisted for two years, four months and twenty-one days, or for the duration of the war. Captain Elliott, who was not re-elected at the reorganization, was dropped from the rolls on May 3, a date also shown in the record as the fifth. Ben F. Wyman was elected captain on May 3, 1862, to replace Elliott.[61] Wyman was paroled at Greensboro on May 1, 1865.

Company G, the Butler Guards or Butler Rifles, was composed of men from Charleston, Colleton and Beaufort Districts.[62] Stationed at Otter Island in St. Helena Sound during the summer of 1861, the men mustered in service for twelve months on August 20, along with their captain, John J. Maguire, a native of Ireland. On March 14 of the following spring, they re-enlisted for two years, five months and six days, or for the duration of the war. Not re-elected at the reorganization, Maguire was dropped from the rolls on May 3, a date also shown in the record as the fifth. Maguire proceeded to raise the Yeadon Rangers, which that November became Company H of the 6th Regiment, South Carolina Cavalry. W.D. McMillan was elected captain on May 12, with rank from the fifth. McMillan retired to the Invalid Corps on December 21, 1864, because of poor health. The *Memory Roll* states erroneously that McMillan was killed at Swift Creek on May 9, 1864, while in command of Company K. One card in the CSR indicates he was a prisoner of war on April 18, 1864, although no other cards support this assertion. Still another card lists McMillan as absent and sick in the hospital from April 18, 1864.

Company H, the St. George Volunteers or St. George's Volunteers, was composed mostly of men from Colleton and Charleston Districts; a few came from Orangeburg District.[63] Stationed at Hilton Head Island in the summer of 1861, the men mustered in service for twelve months, along with their captain, Jacob Weathers, on July 26. Weathers resigned later that year and was replaced by First Lieutenant Daniel S. Canaday.[64] On March 14 of the following spring while stationed at Camp Sturgeon near Hardeeville, the men re-enlisted for two years, four months and twelve days, or for the duration of the war. Not re-elected at the reorganization, Canaday was dropped from the rolls on May 5, 1862. Second Lieutenant Thomas E. Raysor, who was elected on May 3, followed him. Raysor was captured in battle on June 24, 1864, near Petersburg and taken to Fortress Monroe three days later. He was moved to the Old Capitol Prison in Washington, D.C., on the thirtieth and sent to Fort Delaware on July 22.[65] Raysor was released on June 27, 1865.

Company I, the Colleton Rifles, mustered in state service for twelve months on June 17, 1861, while it was stationed at one of the forts on the South Edisto River.[66] John D. Edwards served as captain from June 17 to August 31, when he probably resigned. J.S. Anderson was promoted from first lieutenant to captain about August 12, although the date appears to conflict with his predecessor's tenure as captain. Anderson's Company was among those that refused to enter Confederate service and was disbanded on November 25, 1861.[67] A second Company I was formed on January 4, 1862, from the remnants of other 11th Regiment companies disbanded for the same reason. The second Company I became the tenth company in the 11th Regiment. Josiah B. Perry, previously first lieutenant in Bellinger's

Company, was nominated for captain, but he was defeated on January 5 by Allen Cadwallader Izard, who, until November 26, 1861, had served as second lieutenant in Bellinger's Company.[68] Thus it was Izard who raised the second Company I in January and February. Stationed at Hardeeville, Company I mustered in Confederate service on February 25 for two years, ten months and nine days, or for the duration of the war. Commissioned as captain on February 25, 1862, Izard was re-elected on May 3 and promoted to major on October 22, a date also shown in the record as November 19, 1862. The CSR also records that Joseph Fraser was captain of Company I until he was relieved from duty on May 4, 1862, but this information conflicts with Izard's tenure. William L. Campbell was promoted from first lieutenant to captain on October 22. Campbell was captured at Swift Creek, Virginia, on May 9, 1864.[69] Sent to Fortress Monroe on May 11, he arrived there on the thirteenth.[70] Campbell was moved to Fort Delaware on June 23 and to Hilton Head on August 20 . He was among those who came to be known as the "Immortal Six Hundred," a group of six hundred Confederate officers intentionally exposed to fire of Confederate cannons while being held prisoner on Morris Island.[71] The officers, including Campbell, were returned to Federal prison at Fort Pulaski, Georgia, on October 24.[72] Campbell was sent back to Fort Delaware on March 12 and was released on June 16, 1865. Company I served as light artillery in 1862 and 1863.[73]

Company K, the Eutaw Volunteers, was composed of men from Colleton District. It mustered in for twelve months of Confederate service on September 7, 1861, along with its captain, Richard G. Hay, while it was stationed at Sam's Point. On March 3, 1862, the men of Company K re-enlisted at Camp Heyward near Hardeeville for two years, six months and fifteen days, or for the duration of the war. Not re-elected at the reorganization, Hay was dropped from the rolls on May 5. He served at the rank of major as the commissary of Hagood's Brigade and later died of wounds in Richmond. John Boatwright was elected captain in Hay's place on May 3, 1862. Having been suspended from both rank and command on October 29, 1863, by General Beauregard himself, Boatwright was dropped from the rolls on January 26, 1865.

Bellinger's Company, called the Colleton Guard or Colleton Rifles, was an unlettered company in the 11th Regiment.[74] Its men were from the old Parish of St. Bartholomew in Colleton District.[75] Raised by E. St.P. Bellinger about June 1, 1861, the company mustered in service on August 28 and served with the 11th Regiment until either November 7 or December 31, 1861.[76] This company was among the state troops attached to Heyward's regiment. About half the company was stationed at Field's Point and the remainder at Fenwick's Island. It declined to enter Confederate service in November. The CSR states that the Colleton Guard was disbanded in November 1861, but the muster roll continues through December 31. Some of its men continued to serve in the second Company I of the 11ᵗʰ Regiment after the Colleton Guard disbanded.

Sheridan's Company, called the Round O Guards, was another unlettered company in the 11ᵗʰ Regiment. Composed of men from Colleton and Barnwell Districts, its name originated from the town of Round O in Colleton District. The company mustered in state service on October 15, 1861. Hugo G. Sheridan was its only captain. The men refused to enter Confederate service, and the company was disbanded by the end of the year. It probably reorganized and became Company I of the 1ˢᵗ Regiment, South Carolina Cavalry, in April 1862. It is unclear if Sheridan retained command between late 1861 and April 1862.

BRIGADE AFFILIATIONS

The 11ᵗʰ Regiment was assigned to the Department of South Carolina, Georgia and Florida from November 1861 until its attachment to Hagood's Brigade in September 1863.[77] It was part of Anderson's Brigade in April 1862 and of W.S. Walker's Brigade in August of that year. On September 20, 1863, General P.G.T. Beauregard issued a special order creating a new brigade from the 7ᵗʰ Battalion and the Charleston Battalion, as well as the 11ᵗʰ, 21ˢᵗ and 25ᵗʰ Regiments, SCV, with Johnson Hagood commanding.[78] The 27ᵗʰ Regiment, an expansion of the Charleston Battalion, was added to the brigade on September 30, 1863. In March and April 1864, the 11ᵗʰ Regiment saw detached duty in the District of Florida, and in early March 1865, the 7ᵗʰ Battalion was consolidated with remnants of the 11ᵗʰ, 21ˢᵗ, 25ᵗʰ and 27ᵗʰ Regiments to form a new twelve-company regiment under the command of Lieutenant Colonel James H. Rion. This consolidated regiment of about five hundred men was placed in a new brigade commanded by Johnson Hagood. Other major components of the new brigade were the 40ᵗʰ North Carolina Regiment under Hedrick, Taylor's Consolidated 36ᵗʰ North Carolina and the 1ˢᵗ North Carolina Battalion of Heavy Artillery. When the North Carolina troops were reassigned to other brigades on March 31, 1865, Rion took command of Hagood's Brigade, which reverted back its original composition.

MAJOR MOVEMENTS AND ENGAGEMENTS

The 11th Regiment was ordered into camp at Grahamville in late June 1861, and elements of the regiment, including Company C, passed through Charleston on July 6 on their way to Hilton Head Island.[79] The regiment was posted on the North and South Edisto River, at Bay Point, at Hilton Head Island and at Braddock's Point by early August.[80] It was at Beaufort on October 1 and was engaged at the battle of Port Royal on November 7. Four companies, including C, F and H, were stationed at Fort Walker on Hilton Head Island. Six, including the Beaufort Volunteer Artillery, were posted at Fort Beauregard at Bay Point during the battle.[81] All the regiment's records and most of its equipment were lost during that engagement.[82] For about eighteen months—from November 1861 to summer 1863—the 11th Regiment was scattered among various camps and batteries in Beaufort District, with main concentrations around Hardeeville, McPhersonville, Pocotaligo, the Savannah River Trestle and Fort Drayton—a two-gun battery on the west bank of the New River. After the fall of Hilton Head Island in November 1861, Company I fell back to the Ashepoo Ferry, and the rest of the regiment fell back to Bluffton. From there, it fell back to Camp Heyward near Hardeeville. On December 6, the Beaufort Volunteer Artillery participated in an expedition to Port Royal Ferry, and on the fourteenth, Company A moved from Camp Lee near Hardeeville to Fort Drayton.[83]

In January and February 1862, Company A was stationed at Purysburg; it moved to Camp Sturgeon near Hardeeville on March 14. Companies A and C were in camp at the New River Bridge in April, and Company I was in camp at Hardeeville. In May, Companies B and C were at Camp Jones, F was at Coosawhatchie, H and K were at Camp Heyward and Company I was at McPhersonville. Although Companies F and I were deployed as skirmishers at the battle of Pocotaligo on May 29, neither was heavily engaged.[84] The Beaufort Volunteer Artillery, no longer officially part of the 11th Regiment, was also engaged that day. The two companies pursued the enemy to Port Royal Ferry the next day. Companies B, C, D, E, G, H and K were at Camp Lee in June, while Company F was still at Coosawhatchie and Company I at McPhersonville. On June 6 Company I supported the Beaufort Volunteer Artillery as it destroyed Federal flats at Port Royal Ferry.[85] Fifteen Company I men supported the same battery again on July 4 at Port Royal Ferry.[86] Captain John Mickler commanded ten men from Companies E and G, along with two other men, in a reconnaissance to Pinckney Island, near Hilton Head, also on July 4.[87] Men from Companies A and E, as well as a few from B, C, D, G, H and K, captured thirty-six Federal soldiers and killed several more during a skirmish at either Pinckney Island or St. Helena Island on August 21.[88] Company I saw action at Hutson's plantation near Old Pocotaligo on October 22, and Companies C, D and K were ambushed while riding toward the battlefield on a train the same day.[89] Companies F and I were engaged in a skirmish at Coosawhatchie the next day.[90] By late October, the regiment was stationed at Camp Elzey near Hardeeville.[91]

In December 1862, the companies were scattered along the lower South Carolina coast. Companies B and E were at Bluffton. Companies C and D were based at Camp Elzey near Hardeeville and Company F was at Dawson's Bluff. Company G was stationed at Camp Heyward on the Savannah River, H was at Coosawhatchie and I was at Pocotaligo. Finally, Company K was at Camp Jones at Hardeeville.[92]

Companies B and E conducted a scouting mission on Daufuskie Island on January 30, 1863.[93] By late April, the regiment was based at Camp Palmetto near Bluffton.[94] Company I provided infantry support when the Beaufort Volunteer Artillery sank the steamer *George Washington* in the Coosaw River near Beaufort on April 9.[95] Most of the companies were concentrated at McPhersonville by May.[96] A detachment of twenty-eight men skirmished on Pope's Island on the nineteenth.[97] Three companies skirmished near Bluffton on the Combahee River on June 2, and Company E was engaged at Bluffton on the fourth.[98] Twenty-five men of the 11th Regiment, forty of Kirk's Partisan Rangers and twenty-five from the Beaufort Volunteer Artillery participated in an expedition to Barnwell's Island on June 30.[99] Companies began moving to James Island in July. Company C arrived there on July 10, and the rest of the regiment arrived on the twelfth.[100] Several companies were assigned to detached duty during the summer and autumn of 1863; on July 30, five companies were at James Island, and five were at McPhersonville.[101] By August 31, the regiment was at McPhersonville, but on September 7, it was ordered back to the Charleston area.[102] While stationed at the battery at Lowndes Mill, Company C participated in the capture of a Federal telegraph party on September 12, 13 and 14.[103] Company C was based at the Ashepoo and Combahee Rivers from September to December. By September 20 the entire regiment was stationed at James Island.[104]

The 11th Regiment was attached to Hagood's Brigade from the time it was created on September 20, 1863. Two hundred and fifty men from Companies D, H, I and K were sent to garrison Fort Sumter on September 19.[105] Company D was relieved nine days later because its captain, who was second in command at the time, was not considered competent to take charge if the fort's commander, Stephen Elliott, should become incapacitated.[106] Company H was relieved at Fort Sumter on October 2 or 3, and Companies I and K on the seventeenth.[107] Eight companies were stationed at Fort Johnson, and

Companies C and I were at McPhersonville in early November.[108] At year's end seven companies were at James Island, Company C was at Adams Run, Company G was at McPhersonville and Company E was at Hardeeville.[109] Nine companies were at James Island, and Company E was at McPhersonville on January 31, 1864.[110] The regiment, less Company E, left James Island at midnight on February 20 and left Charleston at eight o'clock the next morning for Florida, arriving at Baldwin on the twenty-seventh.[111] The regiment was not present at the battle of Olustee (Ocean Pond) on February 20, but it was engaged at Cedar Creek near Baldwin on March 1.[112] The regiment left Camp Milton in east Florida on April 14, arrived in Charleston on the twenty-first and moved rapidly to Sullivan's Island.[113]

Hagood's Brigade—the 11th, 21st, 25th and 27th Regiments and the 7th Battalion—was ordered to Virginia by way of Wilmington on April 28, 1864, but the 11th Regiment actually left Sullivan's Island on May 1 and arrived in Wilmington on the fourth.[114] Company E, which stayed behind on outpost and scout duty, left Charleston on May 29.[115] Most of the 21st Regiment left James Island by rail for Wilmington on April 28 and arrived there the next day.[116] Company G of the 21st had been on garrison duty at Fort Sumter and left Charleston on May 2. Company A of the 21st left Charleston on May 29.[117] The 27th Regiment, leaving Company G behind, departed James Island for Wilmington on April 29.[118] The 25th Regiment left Charleston on May 3 and arrived at Wilmington the next day.[119] The 7th Battalion also moved to Wilmington about that time.

Seven companies of the 21st Regiment, along with three of the 25th—G, H and I—left Wilmington by rail on May 5 and arrived at Drewry's Bluff about five the next morning. They marched to Walthall Junction, arriving there after dark on the sixth.[120] The remainder of the 21st Regiment arrived by train at Walthall Junction about the same time. The 21st Regiment and Companies G, H and I of the 25th skirmished that evening near Walthall Junction, also called Mrs. Howlett's farm.[121] The rest of the brigade—the 11th and 27th Regiments, seven companies of the 25th Regiment and the 7th Battalion—arrived at Drewry's Bluff by train on the sixth and marched to Walthall Junction, arriving after dark and missing the day's action.[122] Three regiments, the 21st, 25th and 27th, were also engaged at Walthall Junction on May 7.[123] The 7th Battalion and 11th Regiment arrived after the action on the seventh. That day, the 21st Regiment broke and ran under a flank attack; Colonel Graham was wounded, and Lieutenant Colonel Dargan was killed. Companies B and K of the 21st, used as skirmishers on the right of the regiment, were not engaged on the seventh.[124]

Eight companies of the 11th Regiment, eight or nine of the 21st and three—A, H and K—of the 25th were engaged in a reconnaissance action at Swift Creek on May 9.[125] The brigade left for Drewry's Bluff on the tenth and arrived there the next day. It skirmished from May 12 to May 15 in front of the Drewry's Bluff fortifications and was engaged there again on May 16.[126] The brigade moved to Bermuda Hundreds on the seventeenth and eighteenth, skirmishing heavily there from May 18 to May 31. During a series of maneuvers Beauregard bottled up Butler at the Bermuda Hundreds Neck.[127] On May 31, Hagood's Brigade was ordered from the trenches at six in the morning and moved by foot and rail through Richmond to Cold Harbor. It arrived there about one in the morning on June 1. The brigade was engaged at Cold Harbor on June 1, 2, 3, 5 and 6, 1864.[128] Company E of the 11th Regiment and Company G of the 27th finally arrived on June 4, having missed all the action in Virginia up to that time.

Leaving Cold Harbor at eight in the morning on June 13, the men crossed the Chickahominy River and moved to Malvern Hill. The brigade moved to the pontoon bridge over the James River near Drewry's Bluff on the fourteenth and crossed to the south side of the river the next day. It arrived at Petersburg after dark on the fifteenth and occupied the lines later the same night. The brigade saw action at Petersburg on June 16, skirmished under shellfire on the seventeenth and was engaged at Hare's Hill on the eighteenth. Three regiments—the 11th, 21st and 27th—attacked the extreme right of the Union trenches on the south bank of the Appomattox River near Petersburg on June 24. Lieutenant Colonel Nelson of the 7th Battalion was temporarily in command of the skirmish line that day, but his battalion was not engaged. He was killed, and the 27th Regiment was "cut to pieces" during the attack.[129] Hagood's Brigade remained under constant fire and suffered many casualties as it occupied the Petersburg trenches from June 18 to August 20.[130] The brigade withdrew on August 20 and made its famous charge against Warren's Federal army corps, which was numerically superior and well entrenched, along the Weldon Railroad on the twenty first. Hagood took 740 men into the action and returned with only 292 unscathed. The 27th Regiment again suffered heavy casualties, counting only about 40 men remaining after the engagement.[131] The men of the brigade considered this charge their most desperate encounter.[132]

From August 31 to September 2, the 7th Battalion was stationed at the Iron Bridge in Petersburg. The brigade was sent to Dunlop's Park near Swift Creek, north of Petersburg, for rest and recuperation from September 2 to September 15. The 7th Battalion was stationed along the Boydton Plank Road from September 16 to September 18. The brigade returned to the Petersburg trenches on September 28 and was sent the next day to the north side of the James River, where the men built and occupied a new line of works between the New Market and Darbytown Roads. The brigade, except for Companies D, E and G of the 21st Regiment, was held in reserve during the assault on Fort Harrison on September 30 but suffered casualties while in the trenches at Chaffins Farm on October 2.[133] The 25th Regiment was actively engaged that day. Leaving Chaffins Farm for the Darbytown Road on October 6, the brigade was held in reserve there the next day but still suffered casualties from shellfire.[134] The brigade occupied the lines around Richmond in October and November and was engaged below the capital on October 27.[135]

The brigade conducted an armed reconnaissance, which involved some skirmishing around the Federal right flank, on December 10 and marched on the twenty-first to Richmond, where the men boarded trains for Danville. Between the twenty-second and the twenty-sixth, the men of the brigade traveled by rail to Greensboro. Most of them arrived at Wilmington on the twenty-sixth, left by steamer for Fort Fisher the same day and returned to Wilmington on the thirty-first.

In early January 1865, Hagood's Brigade moved to Fort Anderson, about fifteen miles south of Wilmington on the Cape Fear River. The 21st Regiment skirmished on January 13 and 14. On January 14 and 15, the 21st and 25th Regiments moved by steamer from Gander Hall Landing on the Cape Fear River down to Battery Buchanan and back up the peninsula to Fort Fisher. Unable to move into the fort because of Federal naval shellfire, the 7th Battalion and 11th Regiment were sent across the river to Smithville. On January 15, while the 27th was still at Fort Anderson and the 7th Battalion and most of the 11th Regiment were at Smithville, most of the men of the 21st and 25th Regiments were captured during an engagement at Fort Fisher.[136] A few men of the 11th Regiment who were there that day were captured as well.[137] From February 17 to 18, the brigade skirmished below Fort Anderson; on the nineteenth, it abandoned the fort and withdrew to Town Creek, about nine miles below Wilmington on the opposite side of the Cape Fear River. On the twentieth, the brigade was engaged at Town Creek, and that day, most of men of the 25th and the 11th Regiments who had not been captured earlier were captured there. The 7th Battalion was held in reserve during the action.

Hagood's Brigade evacuated Wilmington on February 22 and marched on the twenty-third to Rockfish Creek, where it remained until March 5. It arrived at Kinston, North Carolina, by rail on March 8 and was soon consolidated into a twelve-company regiment, named for its commander, Lieutenant Colonel Rion. Rion's Regiment comprised the 7th Battalion and remnants of the 11th, 21st, 25th and 27th Regiments, an aggregate of about five hundred men. Rion's Regiment skirmished near Kinston from March 8 to March 10 and remained in the lines for two or three more days. It was not engaged at Averasboro on the sixteenth, but it saw action at Bentonville from March 19 to March 21.

Rion's Regiment withdrew to Black Creek on the twenty-second and marched through Smithfield on April 10. Two days later the men marched through Raleigh. From April 13 to April 17, the regiment marched to Chapel Hill, Greensboro and finally Salisbury. Men began leaving in significant numbers as rumors of surrender circulated in mid-April. Generals Johnston and Sherman agreed to articles of a military convention, in effect surrendering Johnston's army, on April 26. The surrender was announced the next day, and officers signed for and received paroles for the men on May 1 and 2. Rion's Regiment surrendered 40 officers and 510 men. The men broke camp on the third and left on foot for Lancaster Court House in South Carolina, where they were given their paroles. Hagood's Brigade (Rion's Regiment) was disbanded there on May 7, 1865.

9.

THE 11TH BATTALION, SOUTH CAROLINA INFANTRY

The 11th Battalion, SCV, also called the Eutaw Battalion, was raised between December 1861 and May 1862 in Charleston in response to the December 7, 1861 legislative act calling for twelve-month volunteers.[1] In December 1861, Charles H. Simonton and John G. Pressley attempted to raise a regiment.[2] Although field officers were to be appointed by the governor, the two men agreed that Simonton would be colonel and Pressley lieutenant colonel. An executive order, however, authorized not a regiment but a battalion, which was to be called the Washington Light Infantry Battalion. The initial plan called for only four companies and a year of state service.[3] Captains Simonton and E.W. Lloyd commanded the first two companies, both of which were from the Washington Light Infantry. The *Charleston Daily Courier* announced on February 22 that the battalion was nearly complete.[4] Captains were elected, and their commissions were dated the same day. The *Courier* announced on March 31 that the four-company Eutaw Battalion, comprising two companies from the Washington Light Infantry and one company each from Orangeburg and Williamsburg, was complete.[5] Additional companies were expected to be added to the battalion.[6] Field officers received their commissions on April 30, 1862, the same day the South Carolina Executive Council approved an expansion allowing the Eutaw Battalion seven companies.[7] By late April three new companies had joined the original four, providing the battalion with its full complement.[8]

Other than the two-company Washington Light Infantry, the battalion's companies were: the Wee Nee Volunteers, the St. Matthews Rifles, the Beauregard Light Infantry, the Edisto Rifles and the Ripley Guards.[9] The Marion Rifles and the Yeadon Light Infantry were added to the battalion by late May, and by mid-June the battalion of nine companies was anticipating one more, which would bring it to regimental strength.[10] The

Clarendon Guards was added on July 13, and the 25[11] Regiment, SCV, was created on July 22, 1862.[11] Regimental status might have seemed a foregone conclusion to the *Courier*, which referred to the battalion as the "Eutaw Regiment" as early as May 9. The *Edgefield Advertiser* followed suit in its June 25 issue, possibly because then the battalion was at near regimental size.[12] The *Official Records*, too, names the 25th Regiment, not the Eutaw Battalion, at the battle of Secessionville on June 16.[13]

The Eutaw Battalion took its name from the flag that had been carried by Colonel William Washington's regiment in the Revolutionary War battle of Eutaw Springs. Colonel Washington's widow, Jane Elliott Washington, committed this flag, a red damask without device, to the trust of the Washington Light Infantry on April 19, 1827. The Washington Light Infantry erected a large monument honoring the Washingtons at Magnolia Cemetery in Charleston on May 5, 1858.

FIELD OFFICERS

Charles Henry Simonton of Charleston became the first and only lieutenant colonel of the Eutaw Battalion when he was nominated on April 30, 1862.[14] The Executive Council approved his nomination the same day.[15] Previously captain of the Washington Light Infantry, Company A, Simonton was appointed colonel of the 25th Regiment at its creation on July 22, 1862. The CSR shows September 12 as the date of his appointment to colonel, with rank from August 14, 1862.

John Gotea Pressley of Williamsburg District was commissioned major of the Eutaw Battalion on April 30, 1862.[16] He was previously captain of the Wee Nee Volunteers, Company E of Hagood's 1st South Carolina Volunteer Regiment. Presumably Pressley commanded the Wee Nee Volunteers in the 11th Battalion for only two or three weeks before he became major. He was appointed lieutenant colonel of the 25th Regiment when it was created on July 22, 1862. The CSR shows the date of his appointment to lieutenant colonel as September 12, with rank from August 14, 1862.

COMPANIES

Since the 11th Battalion is not listed in the CSR, letter designations have not been well preserved.

The Washington Light Infantry, Company A, was probably designated Company A in the 11th Battalion. It was composed of men from Charleston and recruited from the ranks of a company named the Washington Light Infantry in the 1st Regiment Rifles, South Carolina Militia. The Washington Light Infantry militia company provided three companies for service in the War Between the States: Companies A and B of the Eutaw Battalion and Company A, the Washington Light Infantry Volunteers, of the Hampton Legion. After the Washington Light Infantry Volunteers left Charleston to join the Hampton Legion, recruitment was so successful that the remaining militia component of the Washington Light Infantry split into two companies—A and B.[17] Charles H. Simonton was elected captain of the Washington Light Infantry in June 1861.[18] Elected captain of Company A of the Eutaw Battalion on February 22, 1862, he became lieutenant colonel of the battalion on April 30.[19] On February 24 while based at Charleston, the Washington Light Infantry mustered in Confederate service for twelve months as Captain Simonton's Company. First Lieutenant James M. Carson was elected captain on April 30 and retained command in the 25th Regiment.[20] The Washington Light Infantry Company A became Company A of the 25th Regiment in July 1862; Simonton was appointed the regiment's colonel.

The Washington Light Infantry, Company B, was probably designated Company B in the 11th Battalion. It was formed from excess recruitment by the Washington Light Infantry militia company. While based in Charleston, the men of Company B mustered in Confederate service for twelve months on February 24, 1862. Edward William Lloyd was elected captain of Company B of the Eutaw Battalion on February 22, 1862, having served previously as captain of Washington Light Infantry Company B as early as June 1861.[21] Lloyd was re-elected in late April 1862.[22] When this company became Company B of the 25th Regiment in July, Lloyd retained his rank.

The Wee Nee Volunteers, also known as the Williamsburg Company, was probably Company C. It was from Kingstree and had served most recently as Company E in Johnson Hagood's 1st Regiment, SCV.[23] The company mustered out of Hagood's regiment on April 12, 1862, and went home on a two-week furlough two days later.[24] The company left Kingstree on the twenty-eighth to join the 11th Battalion at Secessionville.[25] John Gotea Pressley was promoted to major of the 11th Battalion on April 30, and Thomas Jefferson China, who had helped Pressley raise the company, became captain.[26] When the 11th Battalion merged into the 25th Regiment on July 22, the Wee Nee Volunteers was designated Company C.

The St. Matthews Rifles, or Riflemen, was composed of men from Orangeburg District. Previously called Company D of Hagood's 1st Regiment, SCV, its men had chosen to enlist in the Eutaw Battalion at the end of their initial twelve-month enlistment—about April 11, 1862. Martin Henry Sellers was elected captain of the company on the eleventh and retained command in July, when it became Company F in the 25th Regiment.

The Beauregard Light Infantry, probably Company E, was composed of men from Colleton District and Charleston. Organized in July 1861, the company was attached to the 1st Regiment Rifles, South Carolina Militia, until February 1862 when it joined the Eutaw Battalion.[27] While based in Charleston, its men mustered in Confederate service on February 22, 1862, and re-enlisted two months later for the duration of the war.[28] Peter B. Lalane, who had served as captain in the militia company, was not re-elected when the company joined the Eutaw Battalion.[29] Robert D. White was elected captain on February 22 and retained command in July when the company became Company E of the 25th Regiment.

The Edisto Rifles of Orangeburg was Company A of Hagood's 1st Regiment, SCV, until April 12, 1862, when its term of enlistment expired. William V. Izlar's book, *A Sketch of the War Record of the Edisto Rifles*, says the company actually disbanded at that time. Most of its men, however, immediately re-enlisted for three years, or for the duration of the war, although some re-enlisted in other units.[30] The newly reconstituted Edisto Rifles retained its officers when it was attached to the Eutaw Battalion about mid-April.[31] John Vinyard Glover, who had served as captain in Hagood's regiment, was re-elected when the company mustered in the Eutaw Battalion, and he retained command in the 25th Regiment until he was elected major.[32] The Edisto Rifles became Company G of the 25th Regiment in July 1862.

The Ripley Guards was part of the Eutaw Battalion from April to July 1862.[33] Also called Gordon's Company, Ripley Guards, SCV, the company was raised by Captain William Blackwood Gordon and First Lieutenant Francis James Lesesne in late 1861.[34] Gordon had been elected captain on December 29, 1861, and had been commissioned two days later; Lesesne would be killed at Swift Creek on May 9, 1864. Most of the Guards were from Williamsburg and Clarendon Districts, with a few from Charleston. All enlisted unconditionally in 1862 for the duration of the war.[35] The company performed local guard duty from its post at the Santee Bridge for several months early in 1862 before joining the Eutaw Battalion.[36] The Ripley Guards became Company K of the 25th Regiment.

The Marion Light Infantry, made up of men from Marion District, probably mustered in service on April 15, 1862. William Jasper McKerall was elected captain the same day. The Marion Light Infantry became Company D in the 25th Regiment.

The Yeadon Light Infantry was also called Captain Hammond's Company, and John P. Thomas named it the Gordon Light Infantry.[37] Most of its men were from Charleston and Williamsburg Districts, although some came from Sumter, Orangeburg, Anderson, Newberry, Darlington, Edgefield and Lexington Districts. A few had been in Company I of Hagood's regiment. The company, which was organized in the spring of 1862 as the Yeadon Guards, was authorized to recruit volunteers for early April enlistment.[38] The *Mercury* reported that the Yeadon Light Infantry was actively recruiting as the month drew to a close.[39] The men mustered in for the duration of the war at some point between April 30 and May 20, 1862. Samuel LeRoy Hammond was elected captain on May 20.[40] The Yeadon Light Infantry became Company H of the 25ᵗʰ Regiment.

BRIGADE AFFILIATIONS

The 11ᵗʰ (Eutaw) Battalion spent its entire existence in the Department of South Carolina, Georgia and Florida. Part of a temporary brigade called the "Advanced Forces," it was commanded in June 1862 by then Colonel Johnson Hagood. Other units in the "Advanced Forces" were Hagood's 1ˢᵗ Regiment, SCV, the 46ᵗʰ Georgia Regiment, the 24ᵗʰ Regiment, S.C. Volunteers and McEnnery's Louisiana Battalion.

MAJOR MOVEMENTS AND ENGAGEMENTS

The Washington Light Infantry Companies A and B and the Beauregard Light Infantry were stationed at Cole's Island in early 1862.[41] After the 11ᵗʰ Battalion was organized in late April, the companies began to gather at Secessionville on James Island. The Wee Nee Volunteers, the Edisto Rifles and the St. Matthews Rifles, who were all there by May 1, were soon joined by the two-company Washington Light Infantry and the Beauregard Light Infantry. The Eutaw Battalion was stationed at Camp Eutaw on Goat Island on May 1, and by the ninth, it had moved from Cole's Island and Goat Island to Secessionville.[42] By late May, the Yeadon Light Infantry, the Marion Rifles and the Ripley Guards were also at Secessionville. The men performed picket duty in small boats at Light House Inlet. On June 1, the Edisto Rifles sniped at Federal gunboats in the Stono River, and on the third, the Beauregard Light Infantry was engaged on James Island under the command of Ellison Capers. The Washington Light Infantry Company A, the Wee Nee Volunteers, the St. Matthews Rifles and the Ripley Guards were sent to support Capers, but they arrived after the action ended. Still, the entire battalion endured heavy shellfire that day. The battalion also skirmished on James Island on June 5. Four companies were engaged in a skirmish on James Island on the eighth but were held in support during an engagement at Grimball's plantation two days later. The Eutaw Battalion was engaged on the right flank of the Confederate lines and suffered a few casualties during the battle of Secessionville on June 16. The battalion was referred to as both the 25th and the Eutaw Regiment during that engagement, even though its official designation as such was still a month away.[43] Picket duty near Secessionville occupied the battalion until the end of June, and it moved its camp to Wappoo Cut on July 10 and 11.[44] The battalion might have drawn some garrison duty at Fort Sumter that month as well. On July 13, Colonel Graham of the 21st Regiment, SCV, agreed to allow the Clarendon Guards to withdraw and join the 11th Battalion. On July 22, 1862, the unit previously known as the 11th Battalion became the 25th Regiment, SCV.[45]

10.

THE 21ST REGIMENT, SOUTH CAROLINA VOLUNTEERS

The 21st Regiment, SCV, also known as Graham's regiment, was among those raised in response to the governor's call for volunteers to enlist for twelve months of service in defense of the state. The governor's authorization came from resolutions passed by a special session of the legislature in November and December 1861. The Federal invasion of Port Royal in early November and the subsequent threat to Charleston prompted Governor Pickens to call for twelve thousand volunteers on December 9.[1]

The 21st can be traced to a regiment of the Harlee Legion, South Carolina Militia, organized by William Wallace Harlee in early 1861 and initially called the Pee Dee Legion. Colonel R.F. Graham's regiment, from Marion, was designated the 2nd Regiment in Harlee's Legion in November and December 1861.[2] Harlee's organization, which never actually attained its goal of legion status, was in camp at Georgetown when its term of enlistment expired in January 1862.[3] Although the legion was disbanded at that time, several companies of Graham's regiment re-enlisted for twelve months, thereby creating the nucleus of a new regiment, the 21st SCV.[4] It was organized at Georgetown on November 12, 1861, although this might reflect the organization of Graham's regiment and not the 21st. According to some cards in the CSR, the companies of the regiment mustered in Confederate service for twelve months between January 1 and January 25, 1862; other cards say the men mustered in service on January 1 for three years, or for the duration of the war. Hagood records only that the regiment enlisted in January 1862 for three years, or for the duration of the war.[5] The twelve-month enlistment is probably correct—the May 1, 1862, reorganization would have been unnecessary if the original enlistment had been for three years. The *Mercury* states the 21st was officially organized on January 25, and field officers received their commissions on either the twenty-fifth or the twenty-sixth.[6] Many companies, and probably the entire regiment, re-enlisted for the duration of the war about February 25, 1864.

The regiment originally comprised eleven companies but was reduced to ten when Company C was transferred to the 25th Regiment sometime in July 1862. In March 1865, the 21st was consolidated with the 7th Battalion, South Carolina Infantry and remnants of the 11th, 25th and 27th Regiments to form a new regiment of twelve companies called Rion's Regiment.

FIELD OFFICERS

Robert Fladger Graham of Marion is credited with raising the 21st Regiment. Elected colonel of the 2nd Regiment of the Pee Dee (Harlee's) Legion on November 12, 1861, Graham retained the rank as commander of the 21st.[7] He had also served as a lieutenant in Company K of Maxcy Gregg's 1st (six-month) Regiment from January to July 1861, although the *Mercury* referred to him, incorrectly, as the company's captain.[8] Graham mustered in service on January 1, 1862, and was commissioned colonel of the 21st on January 26, a date also shown in the record as January 25, 1862. He was in command at Morris Island during the first Federal assault on July 10, 1863. Graham received a contusion to the chest and a flesh wound through the left leg near Walthall Junction on May 7, 1864, while attempting to rally the regiment as it fled under a flank attack. He was taken to a hospital in Petersburg to recover.[9] Graham was elected to the South Carolina House of Representatives on October 11, 1864.[10] He was paroled at Greensboro on May 1, 1865.

Alonzo Timothy Dargan, a lawyer from Darlington who mustered in service as a lieutenant in Company B on January 1, 1862, was commissioned lieutenant colonel on January 26, a date also shown in the record as January 25, 1862.[11] Dargan was struck in the chest by a Minié ball and killed instantly near Walthall Junction on May 7, 1864. He fell holding the regimental flag in one hand and his sword in the other, trying to rally the men who had broken and fled under a flank attack.[12] Dargan was regarded as one of the finest officers of his age in the entire service.[13] DuBose, for example, wrote that he "possessed talent and ambition in no ordinary degree. His loss was great to his command; and his final act was an inspiring picture."[14] Johnson Hagood called him "an excellent officer," one who "had the aptitude of a born soldier for all military exercises and on the field of battle exhibited that combination of coolness and dashing courage, which enabled the officer to inspire his men with the conviction of success, and to wield their energies obedient to his will." Hagood also believed that "no better soldier or braver gentleman has laid down his life on [South Carolina's] behalf."[15]

George Williams McIver of Chesterfield, who mustered in as first lieutenant of Company D on January 1, was commissioned major on January 26, a date also shown in the record as January 25, 1862.[16] He was promoted to lieutenant colonel after Dargan was killed. The date of the promotion was June 24, 1864, retroactive to May 8, a date also shown in the record as the sixth, seventh, sixteenth and seventeenth. McIver was slightly wounded in the left shoulder near Petersburg while in command of the regiment either on June 16, 17 or 18, 1864.[17] He was on sick furlough in January and February 1865, and he was paroled at Cheraw on March 5, 1865. Two CSR cards note that a "G.W. McNew," lieutenant colonel of the 21st Regiment, was paroled on May 1 at Greensboro. It is entirely possible that both dates are correct if McIver was paroled in person in Cheraw and as part of the regiment, although in absentia, at Greensboro. Johnson Hagood wrote that McIver was an excellent officer.[18]

John Harleston Read Sr. of Charleston and Georgetown was promoted to major from captain of Company A on June 24, 1864, with rank from May 16 or 17.[19] On October 10, 1864, four days before his forty-ninth birthday, Read retired to the Invalid Corps, citing general impairment of the digestive and nervous systems. He was assigned to the superintendent of the Bureau of Conscription on October 15.

Samuel Hugh Wilds of Darlington was promoted to major from captain of Company B on January 28, 1865, retroactive to October 10, 1864. While in command of the regiment, Captain Wilds was slightly wounded in the upper part of his left thigh during the famous charge of Hagood's Brigade on the Weldon Railroad on August 21, 1864. He was also captured near Town Creek, North Carolina, on February 20, 1865, while commanding a remnant of the 11th Regiment. He was taken to Fort Anderson on the twenty-eighth and to the Old Capitol Prison in Washington on March 1, 1865. Transferred to Fort Delaware on March 24, he was released on July 24, 1865.

COMPANIES

Company A was composed primarily of men from Marion and Georgetown Districts, along with a few from Charleston District. John Harleston Read Sr., elected captain on December 20, 1861, mustered in for twelve months of Confederate service with the men at Georgetown on January 1, 1862. He was probably re-elected at the reorganization in the spring of 1862. The company re-enlisted for the duration of the war about February 25,

1864.[20] Captain Read was promoted to major on June 24, 1864, retroactive to May 16 or 17. First Lieutenant Thomas Ford was promoted to captain at some point between November 26, 1864, and January 15, 1865, with rank from May 17, 1864. Ford was wounded once and captured twice. The first capture came on August 21, 1864, after he was wounded during the charge of Hagood's Brigade on the Weldon Railroad. Taken to the Old Capitol Prison in Washington on the twenty-fourth and to Fort Delaware three days later, Ford was paroled on October 30 and exchanged, along with 3,023 other prisoners of war, on November 15 at Venus Point on the Savannah River. He was captured again on January 15, 1865, at Fort Fisher, North Carolina.[21] He was moved to Fort Columbus in New York Harbor on January 26 and to City Point, Virginia, on February 25. On March 5, 1865, Ford was exchanged at Boulware's Wharf. He was on parole when the regiment surrendered in April.

Company B, The Wilds Rifles, was composed mostly of men from Darlington District, along with one man from Marion and two men from Williamsburg District. Organized in August and September 1861, the company was stationed at Georgetown when the men mustered in for twelve months of Confederate service on January 1, 1862. Samuel Hugh Wilds, who organized the company, was elected its captain on January 1 and was probably re-elected at the reorganization.[22] Wilds, whom the men called "Red Sam" behind his back, was wounded on Morris Island on July 10, 1863, and again on the Weldon Railroad on August 21, 1864.[23] He commanded the regiment at Swift Creek on May 9, 1864, and again during Hagood's attack on the Weldon Railroad on August 21. He was promoted to major on October 10, 1864. First Lieutenant John Chapel "Chap" Clements commanded Company B after Wilds's promotion to major.[24] DuBose writes that Clements was made captain in 1865 but had commanded the company at the rank of first lieutenant.[25] The CSR lists Clements as first lieutenant as late as March 5, 1865, but never as captain. Hagood also states that first lieutenant was his highest rank.[26] Clements lost an eye at Battery Wagner in July 1863, and he was captured at Petersburg on June 24, 1864. He was imprisoned at Point Lookout, Maryland, the Old Capitol Prison in Washington, and at Fort Delaware. Paroled on October 6, he was exchanged at Cox's Wharf on the James River on October 15, 1864. Clements returned to the company only to be captured again at Fort Fisher, North Carolina, on January 15, 1865. Sent first to Fort Columbus in New York Harbor on January 26, he was moved to City Point, Virginia, on February 25 and exchanged at Boulware's Wharf on March 5 at the rank of first lieutenant.

Company C, the Clarendon Guards, was composed almost entirely of men from Clarendon District; two men came from Williamsburg District.

Organized on December 21, 1861, the men mustered in for twelve months of Confederate service on January 1, 1862. Edgar Nelson Plowden was elected captain of Company C on January 1, 1862.[27] Thigpen gives his name as Samuel E.N. Plowden.[28] According to the CSR, he resigned exactly four months later, on May 1. Conflicting with this information, however, is the fact that Plowden signed a document as captain on August 18 that year. The CSR also records that First Lieutenant Y.N. Butler was elected captain on May 1, but in the 25th Regiment, not the 21st.[29] Butler definitely succeeded Plowden as captain of the Clarendon Guards. The exact date of Plowden's resignation and Butler's promotion is unknown; it might have been in May 1862 or even later that summer. Because the 21st originally had eleven companies, this one received special permission on July 13, 1862, to transfer out. Accordingly, the Clarendon Guards joined the 11th Battalion as its 10th company on the twenty-second, thus creating the 25th Regiment, SCV.[30]

Company D, the Cheraw Guards, was composed of men from Chesterfield and Darlington Districts.[31] It mustered in for twelve months of Confederate service at Georgetown on January 10, 1862. Milford G. Tarrh was elected captain on January 1 and mustered in with the men on the tenth. Tarrh was re-elected at the reorganization.[32] He was wounded on July 10, 1863, on Morris Island, and again, this time in the breast, on May 16, 1864, at Drewry's Bluff. Tarrh was hospitalized with neuralgia in December 1864, and he retired to the Invalid Corps on March 4, 1865. Whether he retired because of illness or as a result of a wound is unclear from the record. Tarrh was assigned to the South Carolina reserve forces on March 9, 1865. He was not replaced as captain.

Company E, also composed of men from Chesterfield and Darlington Districts, mustered in for twelve months of Confederate service at Georgetown on January 10, 1862. Benjamin Thomas Davis, who was elected captain on January 1, was commissioned on the tenth. He suffered a mortal wound to the thigh at Bermuda Hundreds on May 28, 1864, and died the same day.[33] His brother, First Lieutenant Alfred W. Davis, commanded the company after Benjamin's death but was never promoted to captain. He retired to the Invalid Corps on January 31, 1865, at the rank of first lieutenant and was appointed as the enrolling officer for Chesterfield District on February 2.

Company F, the Thomas Guards, was composed mostly of men from Marlboro District, with a few from Marion District.[34] It was organized about December 20, 1861, at the courthouse in Bennettsville.[35] The men mustered in for twelve months' Confederate service at Georgetown on January 10, 1862. J. Alexander W. Thomas, pastor of the Baptist Church in Bennettsville, was elected captain on January 1.[36] Many men from his congregation were in Company F and had offered him both the chaplaincy of the regiment and command of the company.[37] Thomas was wounded at Morris Island on July 10, 1863.[38] He was injured again, this time a severe fracture involving the left arm, on May 7, 1864, at Port Walthall Junction.[39] After recovering at the South Carolina Hospital in Petersburg, Virginia, and at another hospital in Florence, South Carolina, Thomas returned to Company F by September or October.[40] He was paroled on May 1, 1865, at Greensboro. He was remembered as a man whose "bravery as a soldier was equal to his eloquence and fervor as a preacher."[41]

Company G, the Williams Guards, was composed of men from Darlington and Chesterfield Districts. Evidence suggests that the company was named for a Mrs. Williams of Society Hill.[42] Like some of the other companies, Company G mustered in for twelve months of Confederate service at Georgetown, but their date of muster— January 16, 1862—was different. E. Canty Stockton was elected captain on January 1, a date also shown in the record as January 13, 1862. When Stockton was appointed a lieutenant in the Confederate States Navy on March 6, he resigned his commission as captain of Company G, effective April 15, also shown as both April 21 and May 1, 1862. Robert Dickinson was promoted from first lieutenant to captain on April 16 and re-elected on May 1. A petition requesting his resignation was circulated in the company during the fall of 1862 because he had difficulty getting along with his subordinate officers. He refused to attend an examination board on October 7 and resigned on December 2. One card in the CSR gives his name as Dickerson, but he signed official documents as Dickinson. First Lieutenant R.W. Reddy was promoted to captain on December 8, a date also shown in the record as the seventh. Reddy was reported missing after the engagement at Battery Wagner on July 10, 1863; there is no evidence that he was captured then.[43] By September he had developed tuberculosis and hepatization of his left lung. Although he retired to the Invalid Corps on August 29, 1864, the record does not document the reason. First Lieutenant J.M. Woodward assumed command of the company in August but was never promoted to captain. Woodward was captured at Morris Island on July 10, 1863, taken to Hilton Head Island on the fourteenth, moved to Fort Columbus in New York Harbor on October 6 and to Johnson's Island, Ohio, three days later. After nearly a year of imprisonment, Woodward was released from Johnson's Island on June 11, 1865, at the rank of first lieutenant. Companies G and I were temporarily consolidated in May 1864.[44]

Company H was composed primarily of men from southwestern Darlington District, although a few came from Sumter and Union Districts.

It mustered in for twelve months of Confederate service at Georgetown on January 25, 1862. John Franklin Abraham Elliott, a minister, raised the company, was elected its captain on January 8 and mustered in with the men on the twenty-fifth.[45] A year later, on January 27, 1863, while the regiment was stationed on Morris Island, the fifty-three-year-old Elliott died after an illness of only thirty-six hours.[46] Memorials called him "a pure patriot, an efficient officer, a zealous minister, a consistent Christian."[47] Elliott was replaced on the twenty-seventh by First Lieutenant Hartwell P. Spain, who was charged the same year with forging a draft of an official document. On June 5, several friends and other supporters signed a letter requesting that the charges be dropped and that Spain be allowed to resign his commission. A simple indiscretion of youth, they reasoned, had caused a young man of hitherto unsullied character to be led astray by others. On August 8, 1863, after Spain had offered assurances that in the future his life would be an atonement for his grievous offense, he was allowed to resign. Second Lieutenant D.G. DuBose was promoted to captain on November 10, with rank from August 12. DuBose was wounded in the left side at Drewry's Bluff on May 16, 1864.[48] He was captured on January 15, 1865, at Fort Fisher, North Carolina. Taken to Fort Columbus in New York Harbor on the twenty-sixth, he was paroled there and transferred to City Point, Virginia, for exchange on February 25. DuBose was exchanged at Boulware's Wharf on March 5, 1865.

Company I was composed mostly of men from Marion and Darlington Districts, although a few hailed from Williamsburg and Georgetown Districts. The men of Company I mustered in for twelve months of Confederate service at Georgetown on January 9, 1862. Evander M. Woodberry, who was elected captain on January 1, mustered in with the men on the ninth, although he resigned on March 1 and died at home soon afterward. Private Richard G. Howard was elected captain the same month. He was captured at Morris Island on July 10, 1863.[49] He was moved to Hilton Head Island four days later and was transferred to Fort Columbus in New York Harbor on October 6 and to Johnson's Island, Ohio, on the ninth.[50] Howard developed tuberculosis and was moved to the Hammond United States Army General Hospital at Point Lookout, Maryland, on April 26, 1864. He was paroled there on the twenty-seventh and exchanged at City Point, Virginia, on April 30, along with 323 other prisoners of war.[51] Companies G and I were temporarily consolidated in May 1864.[52]

Company K, probably called the Timmonsville Minutemen, was composed mostly of men from Darlington District, with a few from Williamsburg, Marlboro, Marion and Richland Districts. It was organized on December 28, 1861, and mustered in for twelve months of Confederate service at Georgetown on January 1, 1862.[53] James W. Owens, elected captain on either January 1 or 8, had been captain of the Timmonsville Minutemen in December 1860. He was seriously wounded in the leg at Battery Stephens near Drewry's Bluff on May 14, 1864, and he died soon thereafter at General Hospital #4 in Richmond.[54] The CSR gives three dates for his death: May 15, May 17 and May 18. Probably quoting an erroneous report in the *Charleston Daily Courier*, Kirkland records that Owens was wounded at Swift Creek on May 9 and died from the wound on May 18 in Richmond.[55] Second Lieutenant Edward B. Green was promoted to captain on May 15, a date also shown in the record as the eighteenth. Only a month later, on June 19, 1864, he was shot through the upper portion of the right thigh, fracturing the femur.[56] Green was captured on January 15, 1865, at Fort Fisher, North Carolina.[57] Taken to Fort Columbus in New York Harbor on the twenty-sixth, he was paroled there and transferred to City Point, Virginia, for exchange on February 25, 1865. Green was exchanged at Boulware's Wharf on March 5, 1865.

Company L, composed of men from Marion District, was organized on January 1, 1862, and probably mustered in Confederate service on January 8. According to the CSR, the company mustered in Confederate service for twelve months on March 18, but the captain's commission is dated January 8. Neal C. McDuffie, who was elected captain on January 1, mustered in service with the men on January 8 but resigned and transferred to the Quartermaster Department on November 26, 1862. He was appointed assistant quartermaster on April 1, 1863, and regimental quartermaster two days later. McDuffie's first name is also spelled variously as Neil and Neill. First Lieutenant Hannibal LeGette was promoted to captain on November 26, 1862, a date also shown in the record as both December 7 and 9. LeGette was severely wounded at Port Walthall Junction on May 7, 1864, when a ball entered below the right nipple and exited in the lower part of his back. He was taken first to a Petersburg Hospital but was soon transferred home to Marion.[58] LeGette died at home on July 2 from the effects of the wound.[59] His name is also shown as both Leggett and Legett, but his signature on official documents is LeGette.[60] First Lieutenant William Bennett Baker, who was promoted to captain as LeGette's replacement on September 20, was wounded slightly and captured on January 15, 1865, at Fort Fisher, North Carolina.[61] On January 26 he was moved to Fort Columbus in New York Harbor where he was paroled and transferred to City Point, Virginia, for exchange on February 25. Baker was exchanged at Boulware's Wharf on March 5, 1865, along with 602 other prisoners of war, including 97 officers.

BRIGADE AFFILIATIONS

The 21st Regiment was assigned to the Department of South Carolina, Georgia and Florida from May 1862 to September 1863.[62] It was attached on September 20, 1863, to Johnson Hagood's Brigade, newly organized at Charleston by special order of P.G.T. Beauregard.[63] At that time Hagood's Brigade consisted of the 7th Battalion, South Carolina Infantry, the Charleston Battalion and the 11th, 21st, and 25th Regiments, SCV. The Charleston Battalion became the 27th Regiment on September 30 and remained with the brigade. In early March 1865, the 7th Battalion was consolidated with remnants of the 11th, 21st, 25th and 27th Regiments to form a new twelve-company regiment under the command of Lieutenant Colonel James H. Rion. This consolidated regiment of about five hundred men was placed in a new brigade commanded by Johnson Hagood. Other major components of Hagood's new brigade were Hedricks's 40th North Carolina Regiment, Taylor's Consolidated 36th North Carolina and 1st North Carolina Battalion of Heavy Artillery. The North Carolina troops were reassigned to other brigades on March 31, 1865, and Rion took command of Hagood's Brigade, which then reverted back to its original composition.

MAJOR MOVEMENTS AND ENGAGEMENTS

The 21st Regiment was stationed at Camp Manigault near Georgetown in early 1862.[64] When the 10th Regiment was ordered to Mount Pleasant on March 25, only the 21st Regiment, Nesbit's Battalion, the 4th Battalion Cavalry, Tucker's Cavalry and Ward's Artillery remained at Georgetown.[65] The 21st was still based there on April 17.[66] By May or June, however, the regiment had been transferred to Morris Island, where it remained until the summer of 1863.[67] Around July 1, 1863, the 21st Regiment constituted the main force of the garrison at Battery Wagner on Morris Island, along with Company E of the 1st South Carolina Infantry, Company I of the 1st South Carolina Artillery and the 7th South Carolina Battalion.[68] These units saw action there on July 10 and July 11.[69] The 21st Regiment suffered heavy casualties there on July 10, when about 350 to 400 of its men were engaged at the south end of the island during a Federal assault.[70] The 21st Regiment withdrew to Battery Wagner on the afternoon of the tenth. The next morning, about 200 men of the 21st were engaged during an assault on Wagner.[71] The regiment remained there until July 13, when it was transferred to Fort Johnson. Next, the regiment began a series of moves between Battery Wagner and Fort Johnson, which lasted until September 8. It was sent back to Wagner on July 20; it returned to Fort Johnson on July 25 and remained there until August 3;[72] it was at Battery Wagner from the third to the ninth; and it was at Fort Johnson from August 9 to August 16.[73] On August 14, twenty sharpshooters from the 21st Regiment were at Wagner,[74] and from August 16 until August 22 or August 24, the entire regiment was back there.[75] From August 24 to September 8 it was occupied with boat picket duty between Morris Island and James Island; and after September 8, its long association with the defense of Morris Island ended.[76]

The 21st Regiment returned to Chisholm's Mills near Charleston on September 8. It was sent to Fort Johnson later that month and left for Camp DuBose near Secessionville in October.[77] The regiment remained at Camp DuBose from October 1863 to April 1864. In the last two months of 1863 and the first two of 1864, nine companies were on James Island and one, Company A, was at the Half Moon Battery in Charleston; all remained at these posts until May 6.[78]

During the siege of Charleston, the 21st Regiment saw eventful service that left it rather disorganized. When Johnson Hagood's Brigade was created in September 1863, the 21st Regiment became part of the brigade for the remainder of the war, even though the brigade did not come together as a unit until the next spring. On February 25, 1864, the 11th and 18th Regiments were detached from Hagood's Brigade and sent to Florida, but the 21st was not part of that move.[79] Instead, it was ordered to John's Island on February 12, 1864.[80] Several companies of the 21st Regiment were assigned to garrison duty at Fort Sumter in early 1864; Company G was sent there on February 16, and it probably remained there until May 1.[81] Company D went there on March 12 and Company L replaced Company E there on April 5.[82]

Most of the 21st Regiment left James Island by rail for Wilmington, North Carolina, on April 28, 1864, arriving there the next day.[83] From the twenty-eighth until the end of the war, the 21st Regiment served with Hagood's Brigade. Its major movements and engagements are discussed in this volume under the 11th Regiment. In early March 1865, Hagood's Brigade was consolidated into a twelve-company regiment. Lieutenant Colonel Rion took command of the new regiment, which went by his name—Rion's Regiment. The regiment comprised the 7th Battalion and remnants of the 11th, 21st, 25th and 27th Regiments, an aggregate of about 500 men. On April 26, Generals Johnston and Sherman agreed on articles of a military convention, which effectively surrendered Johnston's army. The surrender was announced the next day, and officers signed for and received paroles for their men on May 1 and 2. Hagood's Brigade surrendered 40 officers and about 510 men. The men broke camp on May 3 and left by foot for Lancaster Court House, where they received their paroles. The remnants of Hagood's Brigade (Rion's Regiment) were disbanded there on May 7, 1865.

11.

THE 23RD REGIMENT, SOUTH CAROLINA VOLUNTEERS

The 23rd Regiment, SCV, was also called Hatch's regiment, Coast Rangers and Hatch's regiment of rifles.[1] It was among those regiments raised in response to the governor's call for volunteers to enlist for twelve months of service in defense of the state. The governor's authorization came from resolutions passed by a special session of the legislature in November and early December 1861. The Federal invasion of Port Royal in early November and the subsequent threat to Charleston prompted Governor Pickens to call for twelve thousand volunteers on December 9.[2] The nucleus of the 23rd Regiment was Lieutenant Colonel Lewis M. Hatch's Battalion of Coast Rangers, SCV, which had been organized in September and October 1861 for service between Bull's Bay and the Stono River. It comprised seven companies, A to G, the first four of which enlisted for the duration of the war in late September.[3] Companies E, F and G enlisted for twelve months of service in late September and October. According to the *Mercury*, Hatch's original battalion, composed of sixteen- to eighteen-year-old boys, was raised solely for state defense.[4] In November and December the battalion was augmented to full regimental strength by the addition of three companies, H, I and K.[5]

The companies of the 23rd Regiment began to assemble at Charleston in mid-November 1861; field officers were elected on the eleventh. Of the ten companies, four had been raised as local defense troops for the duration of the war under the authority of the secretary of war and six had been raised for twelve months of service under the authority of General Ripley. The regiment was reorganized on April 16, 1862, when the men mustered in Confederate service for three years, or for the duration of the war, and held elections for new officers. None of the original field officers was re-elected. Their replacements received commissions dated May 24, and captains' commissions bore the date of May 9, although all were elected on April 16. In March 1864, many regiments were re-enlisting for the duration of the war because their three-year enlistments, made in the spring of 1862 but dated a year earlier, were about to expire. At that time all but twelve men of the 23rd Regiment either re-enlisted unconditionally for the duration or, if they had already done so in 1861 or 1862, reaffirmed their commitments to serve as long as their services were required.[6]

FIELD OFFICERS

Lewis M. Hatch of Charleston District was elected colonel of the 23rd Regiment on November 11, 1861. Formerly quartermaster general of the South Carolina militia, Hatch also served as an aide-de-camp to General Beauregard in the summer of 1861. He raised the Battalion of Coast Rangers in September 1861, and he commanded it with the rank of lieutenant colonel before it evolved into the 23rd regiment as described above. Under Hatch's command, the 23rd built the observatory and fortifications at Secessionville that became known as the Tower Battery, later renamed Fort Lamar. He also constructed a bridge connecting Secessionville with Fort Johnson with the help of a detachment of the 23rd and without engineering assistance—a feat that inspired the press to dub him "the working colonel."[7] According to the *Mercury*, Hatch's men ridiculed him because they were performing manual labor, not fighting, an attitude that lost him command of the regiment.[8] Thus, although he was described as "able and indefatigable," as well as "an efficient and experienced officer," Hatch was not re-elected at the reorganization and was dropped from the rolls in May 1862.[9] He continued to serve in South Carolina commands for the rest of the war, and his service included an appointment as the state engineer with the Office of South Carolina Adjutant and Inspector General in July 1863.[10]

Allen Jones Green Jr. of Gadsden in Richland District was elected lieutenant colonel of the regiment on November 11, 1861. Earlier, in 1860 and early 1861, he had been captain of the Columbia Flying Artillery, a company that was disbanded in May 1861 but was reorganized shortly afterwards.[11] Green served next for a time as a voluntary aide to J.B. Kershaw. The Columbia Artillery, reorganized under Captain Green's command, became Company B of the 3rd Battalion, South Carolina Light Artillery, which was raised in the summer of 1861 and officially organized in November. No longer connected with the artillery company by September 20, Green accepted an appointment to the post of major of Hatch's Battalion later that month.[12] Defeated for re-election as lieutenant colonel of the 23rd Regiment at the reorganization, he was dropped from the rolls in

May 1862. Green was appointed major in the Bureau of Conscription on September 3, 1863, and in January 1864, he raised six volunteer companies charged with arresting deserters and repelling raiders in South Carolina.[13] Later that year, on April 14, Green was reappointed to the conscript service, still with the rank of major, and was given the command of the Camp of Instruction in Columbia.[14] On August 3, 1864, he was commander of the military post at Columbia and continued to serve in that position until at least January 31, 1865.

Lovick Pierce Miller, captain of Company A from September 23, was elected major of the 23rd Regiment on December 28, 1861. Not re-elected at the reorganization and dropped from the rolls in May 1862, he enlisted as a private in Company G, 16th Battalion, South Carolina Cavalry, on June 29. The 16th Battalion became the 6th Regiment, South Carolina Cavalry, in late 1862, and Miller was commissioned its lieutenant colonel on December 13.

Henry Laurens Benbow of Clarendon District was elected colonel on April 16, 1862.[15] The *Memory Roll* records the date of his election as May 1, and the CSR gives several dates for his commission: April 16, May 9 and May 24.[16] Benbow, captain of Company I before the reorganization, had suffered a flesh wound to the thigh from a bursting shell at Second Manassas on August 30, 1862.[17] An inspection on October 6, 1863, found the 23rd Regiment deficient in discipline with an improperly kept adjutant's office, a very dirty camp and defective ammunition. As its commanding officer, Benbow was held responsible and, after a trial, was suspended for six months.[18] He was severely wounded and was captured at Five Forks on April 1, 1865.[19] The same ball entered the outer part of his left thigh, exited the inner part and then entered and passed completely through his right thigh; he sustained a head wound at the same time. On April 3 he was admitted to the Division Flying Hospital of the 5th Army Corps, Army of the Potomac; on May 1 he was moved on to Lincoln General Hospital in Washington; he was released on June 15. Benbow's tributes were mixed: one reads, "A truer, more gallant spirit is nowhere to be found."[20] But in July 1864, Brigadier General Stephen Elliott wrote, "Benbow is a high-spirited tall gentlemanly man rather weak in health and not a very thorough officer."[21]

John Miller Roberts of Marion District, previously captain of Company H, was elected lieutenant colonel at the reorganization.[22] His commission was dated April 16, 1862. Roberts was wounded in the knee at Second Manassas in August and submitted a letter of resignation on October 14, which was forwarded on the eighteenth. Roberts cited his general health as the reason for resigning, but the *Mercury* reported that his wound was the cause.[23] Roberts's resignation was accepted on November 3, a date also shown in the record as November 30, 1862. The *Memory Roll* recorded, erroneously, that he was elected colonel in recognition of the wound he received at Second Manassas. Roberts died at home in Marion from the effects of the wound on November 5, 1862. Kirkland gives the date of his death as November 4.[24]

John Marshall Whilden of Christ Church Parish in Mount Pleasant, previously captain of Company B, was elected major at the reorganization on April 16, 1862; his commission dated from the same day.[25] Whilden was severely wounded in the back and thigh at Second Manassas on August 30, 1862. Even so, he distinguished himself by picking up the regimental colors and leading the 23rd Regiment in three charges against overwhelming numbers of Federal troops. As he led a fourth charge, with the colors in his hands, Whilden fell mortally wounded.[26] He died on September 6, 1862, at Warrenton, Virginia.[27]

John Millar Kinloch of Charleston, captain of Company A, was promoted to lieutenant colonel, replacing Roberts. He was not, however, promoted immediately upon Roberts's resignation, and his record is unclear. Kinloch passed the examination for promotion to lieutenant colonel in March 1863, and he served as acting lieutenant colonel afterward. The promotion must have been viewed as being fully approved since First Lieutenant William B. Seabrook was promoted to captain of Company A on June 4, 1863. Colonel Benbow finally had to request an official promotion after Kinloch had served as acting lieutenant colonel for about two years. The request, dated December 3, 1864, was granted, and Kinloch was promoted to lieutenant colonel on January 5, 1865, with rank from November 3, 1862, a date also shown in the record as November 6. On leave of absence during January and February 1865, Kinloch was still absent from the regiment as late as February 27. One card in the CSR indicates that he was captured at Bennettsville on March 6. If so, he must have returned afterward since he was paroled with the regiment at Appomattox Court House on April 9, 1865.[28]

Matthew Vassar Bancroft of Charleston was promoted to major from captain of Company C on November 6, 1862, replacing Whilden. While occupying the Petersburg trenches on the night of June 18, 1864, Bancroft was shot in the neck by a sharpshooter.[29] He died in a Petersburg hospital on the twenty-second.[30] Bancroft was regarded as an "accomplished officer."[31]

Henry Hilton Lesesne of Clarendon District was promoted to major from captain of Company I after Bancroft was killed. The still-acting Lieutenant Colonel Kinloch recommended on September 13, 1864, that Lesesne be promoted to major. Lesesne received the promotion on either January 5 or 15, 1865, retroactive to June 22, 1864. Wounded at Petersburg and Fort

Stedman, Lesesne was paroled with the regiment at Appomattox Court House on April 9, 1865.[32]

Edgar O. Murden's record is unclear, although the best evidence indicates he was never confirmed as a field officer in the 23rd Regiment. Murden mustered in as captain of Company D on September 30, 1861, and was re-elected on April 16, 1862. He was seriously wounded in the leg and shoulder at Second Manassas on August 30 and captured while still hospitalized at Warrenton, Virginia.[33] The *Charleston Daily Courier* initially reported Murden killed in action, and Kirkland repeated the error.[34] He was paroled at Warrenton on September 29; the *Mercury* reported on October 9 that the United States Cavalry had paroled Murden.[35] Recovering rapidly in late October, he was at home in South Carolina early in November but still using crutches to walk.[36] The muster roll for January and February 1863 shows Murden still recuperating at home. This much we know, but changes within the ranks of field officers of the 23rd Regiment between the battle of Second Manassas and early 1863 are less clear. The *Charleston Daily Courier* reported on October 27, 1862, that Murden had received a "well-earned promotion" to major.[37] According to the *Memory Roll*, he held the rank of both major and lieutenant colonel, but the former was never confirmed. Krick agrees that Murden held both ranks, but he states that dates of promotion could not be found.[38] No fewer than three cards in the CSR state that he held the rank of major; one of those gives the date of his promotion as April 22, 1863, the same day he resigned as captain. The CSR also contains a card that says Murden was promoted to lieutenant colonel, again giving April 22, 1863, as the date. Additionally the CSR records that Murden resigned as captain of Company D on April 22, 1863, and it offers no definite confirmation that he was ever promoted to major or to a higher rank. It is possible that Murden, while a prisoner of war, was promoted to major on September 6, 1862, when Whilden died. Similarly, it is also possible that, having been freed in a prisoner exchange, Murden was promoted to lieutenant colonel when Roberts resigned on November 3, 1862. Nevertheless, when Kinloch became acting lieutenant colonel and Bancroft was promoted to major on November 6, 1862, Murden, whose own promotion had not been confirmed, reassumed the position of captaincy of Company D. Supporting this theory is a report in the *Mercury* of September 2, 1864, which says Bancroft had been promoted to major replacing Murden. The unusual gap of two months between Whilden's death and Bancroft's promotion as his replacement could be explained if, in the interim, Murden was promoted to the rank but never confirmed. Murden's wound forced him to resign as captain of Company D on April 22, 1863, a date also shown in the record as April 13. He subsequently served as master of the blockade-runner *Victory*, was captured with her on June 21, 1863, and was exchanged on October 18, 1864.[39]

COMPANIES

Company A, the Bee Rifles, the color company of the 23rd Regiment, was named for General Barnard E. Bee, who had been killed at First Manassas.[40] It was organized in early August 1861, and most of its men came from Charleston.[41] Some, however, also came from Chesterfield, Darlington, Kershaw, Lancaster, Lexington, Marion, Marlboro, Richland, Sumter and Williamsburg Districts. The company was designated Company A when it was attached to Hatch's Battalion, although its letter designation in Hatch's regiment before the reorganization is not recorded. The men mustered in service at Charleston for the duration of the war and elected Lovick Pierce Miller as their captain on September 23, 1861. Miller was elected major of Hatch's regiment only three months later, on December 28. John Millar Kinloch was promoted from first lieutenant to captain in early January 1862 and was re-elected on April 16.[42] He was promoted to lieutenant colonel on January 5, 1865, with rank from November 3, a date also shown in the record as November 6, 1862. First Lieutenant William B. Seabrook was promoted to captain on June 4, 1863. This date is consistent with Kinloch's tenure as acting lieutenant colonel but is inconsistent with the fact that Kinloch was not actually promoted to the rank until January 1865. Seabrook resigned on October 13, 1863. He had been unable to perform his duties since December 1862 because of ingrown nails on his big toes, one of which had a fungal infection. In an unusual move, Private John C. Evans was elected captain on March 7, 1864—normally the next senior officer would have been in line for promotion. Evans was captured at Five Forks on April 1, 1865, and taken to Washington's Old Capitol Prison on the fifth. He was moved to Johnson's Island, Ohio, on April 11 and was released on June 18, 1865.

Company B, the Chicora Rifles, the flag company of the 23rd Regiment, was composed of men from Charleston and Beaufort Districts, with a few from Lexington District.[43] It was known as Captain John M. Whilden's Company, as well as both Company A and Company B, when it was part of Hatch's Battalion, Coast Rangers, but it was designated Company C in Hatch's regiment before the reorganization. The men mustered in service for the duration of the war at Long Island (Isle of Palms) on September 25, 1861. John Marshall Whilden, who had raised the company, was elected its captain the same day. He was a graduate of three military schools: the

Yorkville Military Academy, The Arsenal Academy and The Citadel.[44] Whilden had commanded a cannon when cadets from The Citadel fired on the *Star of the West* on January 9, 1861. He had also served as an aide to Micah Jenkins at the battle of First Manassas, where he was wounded.[45] Whilden was elected major of the regiment on April 16, 1862, the same day First Lieutenant Paul Hamilton Seabrook was elected captain. Seabrook's commission, however, was dated May 9, a date also shown in the record as May 24, 1862.[46] He sustained a mortal wound to the head on August 30 at Second Manassas and died on September 6 or 7, 1862.[47] First Lieutenant J. Walker Duffus was promoted to captain on September 7. Severely wounded in the leg, Duffus was captured near Petersburg on June 17, 1864, and died later that day.[48] Thomas L. Swinton was promoted from first lieutenant to captain as his replacement on the seventeenth. Swinton was captured at Five Forks on April 1, 1865, and was taken to the Old Capitol Prison in Washington four days later. He was moved to Johnson's Island, Ohio, on April 9 and was released on June 20, 1865.

Company C, the Johnson Rifles, or Johnson Riflemen, was composed of men from Charleston District.[49] Although there is no direct evidence for it, probably the company was named for Benjamin J. Johnson, lieutenant colonel of the Hampton Legion, who was killed at First Manassas. It was known as both Captain H.W. Butler's Company and Company C when it was in Hatch's Battalion, Coast Rangers, and it was designated Company B in Hatch's regiment before the reorganization. Company C mustered in for the duration of the war at Camp Butler on September 23, 1861. Its first captain, Harry W. Butler, was elected the same day but was not re-elected at the reorganization the following spring.[50] Lieutenant Matthew Vassar Bancroft, a graduate of the Yorkville Military Academy, was elected on April 16, 1862, instead.[51] He was promoted to major on November 6, 1862. The *Mercury* reported on September 2, 1864, that Bancroft had been promoted to major to replace Major Whilden, who was mortally wounded at Second Manassas in August 1862 and died on September 6. This is probably correct, and the delay of two months in Bancroft's promotion to major after Whilden's death is best explained by the unconfirmed promotion of Edgar Murden to major. D.K. O'Brien, who was promoted from first lieutenant to captain on June 13, 1863, resigned on April 10 or 11, 1864, saying he had been trained as a machinist and wanted to enter the Confederate States Navy as an engineer. Colonel Benbow wrote on March 28, 1864: "the service will no doubt benefit by the favorable and immediate consideration of the above [O'Brien's] application. I earnestly recommend its acceptance."[52] Second Lieutenant Thomas P. Ryan, who was promoted to captain on December 29, 1864, was wounded in the upper third of his thigh at some point before

March 27, 1865. He was admitted to the Stuart Hospital in Richmond on March 27 and captured there on April 3. Paroled on May 2, Ryan was still hospitalized on May 28, 1865.

Company D, the Duryea Guards, or Duryea Coast Guard, was composed of men from Charleston.[53] It was named in honor of Colonel Robert S. Duryea, a Charleston lawyer and civic leader, who was charged with directing the South Carolina coastal defenses.[54] Designated both Captain E.O. Murden's Company and Company D while attached to Hatch's Battalion, Coast Rangers, the company's letter designation in Hatch's regiment before the reorganization is not recorded. It mustered in service for the duration of the war at Charleston on September 30, 1861, and elected Edgar O. Murden captain the same day. Murden was re-elected on April 16, 1862. Murden was promoted to major, but the promotion was not confirmed. For a full discussion of Murden's record, see "Field Officers" of the 23rd Regiment (page 140). When Murden resigned as captain of Company D on either April 13 or 22, 1863, First Lieutenant P. Augustus Aveilhe Jr. replaced him as captain, with rank from April 14. Aveilhe had suffered for several years from rheumatism; a head wound sustained at Second Manassas brought on vertigo, which forced him to resign on May 14, a date also shown in the record as the nineteenth, only a month after his promotion.[55] The *Memory Roll* spells his name Avelhie, and one card in the CSR reads Avelhe. E.R. White was promoted from first lieutenant to captain in his place on either May 14 or May 19.[56] White, who had been severely wounded at Sharpsburg, also took a serious wound to the shoulder at the Crater on July 30, 1864.[57] He returned to the company in November or December. White was captured at Five Forks on April 1, 1865, and was taken to the Old Capitol Prison in Washington on the fifth. Four days later he was moved to Johnson's Island, Ohio, and he was released on June 20, 1865.

Company E, the Marion Blues, was also called the Marion Rifles and C.J. Fladger's Company.[58] It was composed of men from Marion District and was known as Captain C.J. Fladger's Company, Coast Rangers, when it was attached to Hatch's Battalion.[59] Its letter designation in Hatch's regiment before the reorganization is not recorded. Company E mustered in service for twelve months at Marion on September 28, 1861. Charles J. Fladger, who was elected captain on October 7, soon tendered his resignation, writing that he had a large family and could serve better at home helping other soldiers' families.[60] Hatch must have agreed, for he wrote on January 11, 1862: "Fladger is no military man. He is a clergyman. In plain English, his company is better off without him than with him. At home, he is a very useful man."[61] The resignation was accepted on January 24, 1862. In an ironic twist, a deserter killed Fladger at his home. Second Lieutenant Jim C. Finklea was elected captain on April 16, 1862, with rank from May 9.[62] Although he, too, tendered his resignation on January 23 and again on February 4, 1863, the resignation was not accepted. Finklea was absent, suffering from general debility and edema, from September to December 1863. He tendered his resignation again on July 17, 1864, this time because of pride, writing, "a junior officer has been placed in command over me and I have endeavored but failed to obtain any redress or satisfaction."[63] Finklea could have been referring to either Lieutenant Colonel Kinloch or Major Bancroft. The CSR uses several dates for Finklea's resignation: July 17, July 26, July 28 and August 1, 1864.

Company F, the Chester Grays, was composed of men from Chester District. It was known as Captain John J. McLure's Company while attached to Hatch's Battalion, but no letter designation in Hatch's regiment before the reorganization is recorded. Company F mustered in service for twelve months on October 17, 1861, and elected John J. McLure its captain, probably the same day. The *Mercury* spells his name MacLure.[64] Although the CSR uses both McLure and McClure, official documents are signed McLure. Although absent from the company in April 1862, McLure was re-elected captain at the reorganization on the sixteenth. Poor health forced McLure to decline the position, and he resigned on July 5, a date also shown in the record as July 14, 1862. First Lieutenant James F. Atkinson replaced him on July 5, a date also shown in the record as the fifteenth.[65] The *Memory Roll* states, incorrectly, that he was elected captain in October. Atkinson resigned on January 12, a date also shown in the record as January 31, 1863, saying he had suffered for several years from tuberculosis. Johnson M. Woods was promoted to captain on March 1, 1863. In February 1864, sixty-three of the sixty-six men in the company re-enlisted for the duration of the war.[66] Woods was severely wounded in the arm near Petersburg on June 16, 1864.[67] He died in the Virginia Hospital at Petersburg on July 22. Julius Mills, who had been major of the 17th Regiment, SCV, until the reorganization, was elected second lieutenant on September 9 and was promoted to captain on September 29, with rank from July 27, 1864. Mills was captured at Five Forks on April 1, 1865, and was taken to the Old Capitol Prison in Washington on the fifth. Four days later he was moved to Johnson's Island, Ohio; he was released on June 19, 1865.

Company G, the Douglass Rifles was named for Archibald H. Douglass, a well-known and public-spirited merchant of Bennettsville, who provided the company's arms and uniforms.[68] The *Charleston Daily Courier* spelled his name Douglas.[69] Made up of men from Marlboro District, it was designated both Captain R.C. Emanuel's Company and Company G when attached to

Hatch's Battalion, but its letter designation in Hatch's regiment before the reorganization is not recorded.[70] Company G mustered in service for twelve months at Secessionville on October 31, 1861. The CSR also uses the date October 17, and the *Mercury* makes it October 25.[71] Robert C. Emanuel was elected captain; his commission is dated December 17. Not re-elected at the reorganization, he was dropped from the rolls. According to the *Memory Roll*, Emanuel was murdered after the war. Second Lieutenant Angus McLean McRae was elected captain on April 16, 1862, effective May 9.[72] Mortally wounded during the battle of Second Manassas on August 30, he died the same day.[73] McRae's replacement, First Lieutenant Salathiel Legett, was promoted on August 30 or 31. Legett suffered damage to the radius, a bone in the forearm, at Second Manassas. As late as August 1863 pieces of dead bone were occasionally removed from the still open wound. Legett resigned on September 12, 1863. The *Memory Roll* spells the name Salatha LeGette, and the CSR uses both Leggett and Legett; official documents, however, are signed Salathiel Legett. First Lieutenant W.W. Covington was probably promoted to captain, but the record is not clear on that point. Covington is listed as first lieutenant on October 17, 1863, and as captain ten days later. He also signed as captain commanding the company in December 1863. Even so, when Covington was captured at Petersburg on June 17, 1864, he was listed at the rank of first lieutenant. The muster rolls for late 1864 and 1865 also show him at that rank. If he received a promotion, it is possible it was never confirmed. We do know that on June 25, after his capture, Covington was taken to Fort Delaware, and that on August 20, 1864, he was taken to Hilton Head Island. We know also that he was one of the "Immortal Six Hundred" Confederate officers intentionally exposed to Confederate cannon fire on Morris Island. Covington was moved to Fort Pulaski, Georgia, October 20 and back to Hilton Head Island on January 1, 1865. He was taken to Fort Delaware on March 12 and was not released until June 17, 1865.

Company H, the Roberts Guards, was composed mostly of men from Marion District; two came from Horry District.[74] Company H was not part of Hatch's Battalion, Coast Rangers, but was one of three new companies added to make the battalion a regiment. Company H mustered in service for twelve months and elected John Miller Roberts captain on November 10, 1861. Miller was elected lieutenant colonel at the reorganization on April 26, 1862. First Lieutenant Solon A. Durham was elected captain on April 26, with rank from May 9.[75] He was slightly wounded the following September 17 at Sharpsburg.[76] Durham was wounded again near Goldsboro, North Carolina, probably in December 1862, and was in a Raleigh hospital later that month.[77] He resigned his commission, accepted an appointment to the conscript department on September 25, 1863, and was detailed as an enrolling officer on October 12. An article in the *Confederate Veteran* states that Durham was appointed major in the Confederate States Army, probably meaning in the conscript or enrolling department, and transferred out of the 23rd Regiment.[78] R.W. Hale was promoted to captain in September or October 1863, but the promotion was never confirmed. He first appears as captain on the muster roll for September/October 1863; his rank is shown as first lieutenant on the roll for November/December 1863, then as captain on the muster roll for January/February 1864 and back to first lieutenant on the roll for March/April 1864. Whatever the explanation for his roller coaster rank, Hale resigned with the rank of first lieutenant on May 22, 1864, without stating a reason. Colonel Benbow wrote on May 26, 1864: "First Lieutenant Hale was examined for promotion to captaincy and was reported upon adversely by the Examining Board, which decision was sustained by the Secretary of War. I would earnestly recommend the acceptance of his resignation as he is totally unfit for his present position and is an encumbrance to the company."[79] Wiley Warren Hamilton, who had been wounded in the right arm at Second Manassas, was promoted from first lieutenant to captain on August 1, 1864.[80] He was captured at Five Forks on April 1, 1865, and moved to the Old Capitol Prison in Washington on the fifth. Six days later Hamilton was transferred to Johnson's Island, Ohio, and was held there until his release on June 18, 1865.

Company I, the Sprott Guards, was organized in July 1861 with men mostly from Clarendon District.[81] A few came from Sumter, Charleston and Marion Districts. The company's name honored Joseph Sprott, a patriotic citizen who equipped the company.[82] Like Company H, this company was not part of Hatch's Battalion but was added to increase the battalion to regimental size. It is unclear whether the men were on active duty or were held in reserve between July and November 10, when they mustered in service for twelve months. Henry Laurens Benbow, the first captain, had served as colonel of the 44th Regiment, South Carolina Militia, and as a private in Company C of the Hampton Legion earlier in 1861.[83] He was elected captain in July 1861, and his commission is dated from November 10, a date also shown in the record as November 15.[84] Benbow was elected colonel at the reorganization on April 16, 1862. According to the *Memory Roll*, he was elected on May 1, but his commission date of April 16 makes that unlikely. First Lieutenant Henry Hilton Lesesne, who helped raise the company, was elected captain as Benbow's replacement on April 16. His commission dates from May 9, a date also shown in the record as May 24, 1862.[85] When Lesesne was promoted to major on January 15, 1865, with rank from June 22, 1864, First Lieutenant William J.R. Cantey was promoted to captain effective June 22. Cantey was killed at Five Forks on April 1, 1865. The *Confederate Military History Series* records, erroneously, that Daniel Judson Bradham was a captain of Company I.[86] He served as a second lieutenant in the company, and he lost an arm at the shoulder at Second Manassas. He tendered his resignation as second lieutenant on January 29, 1863.[87] Bradham served as captain of Company B, 3rd Regiment, Junior Reserves, in late 1864 and 1865.

Company K, the Lee Guard, was organized in November 1861 with men from Sumter District.[88] Like Company H and Company I, it was not part of Hatch's Battalion either; it was the last of three new companies added to the battalion to make it a regiment. The company left Sumter for Charleston via Florence in November.[89] While based in Christ Church Parish, the men mustered in service for twelve months on November 15, 1861. The company performed picket duty on Long Island (Isle of Palms) until it was sent back to Charleston in December to join the 23rd Regiment.[90] Company K completed the regiment's organization. Thomas D. Frierson, who was elected captain on November 15, was not re-elected at the reorganization. First Lieutenant Lucius P. Loring, who was elected on April 16 and whose commission became effective on May 9, replaced him.[91] Suffering from severe dysentery and hemorrhoids, Loring resigned on September 19, a date also shown in the record as October 7, 1862. First Lieutenant David R. McCallum was probably promoted to captain on September 19.[92] He too had health problems, which became so severe he was given a sixty-day furlough in April 1864 for chronic diarrhea and chronic pneumonia. McCallum retired to the Invalid Corps on October 14, a date also shown in the record as October 19, 1864, and served as an enrolling officer in Sumter District in 1865.[93] First Lieutenant John Harrington Cooper, who had received a slight head wound on October 4, 1864, was promoted to captain on October 14.[94] He was captured at Dinwiddie Court House (Five Forks) on April 1, 1865, and was taken to the Old Capitol Prison in Washington four days later. On April 9 Cooper was moved to Johnson's Island, Ohio, and was held there until his release on June 18, 1865.

BRIGADE AFFILIATIONS

The 23rd Regiment was assigned to the Department of South Carolina, Georgia and Florida from December 1861 to July 1862.[95] A new independent brigade under the command of Nathan George "Shanks" Evans was created in June 1862; the 23rd Regiment was attached to this brigade in

July. It was organized on or about June 20, 1862, and was known as the Tramp Brigade because of its ubiquity east of the Mississippi River.[96] Other regiments in the Tramp Brigade were the 17th, 18th and 22nd South Carolina Volunteer Regiments and the Holcombe Legion. The 26th Regiment, SCV, was added in May 1863, and the Macbeth Artillery was attached until late 1863. N.G. Evans commanded the brigade from July 7, 1862, until April 16, 1864. William S. "Live Oak" Walker assumed command on May 20, 1864, but was wounded and captured at Clay's farm the same day. Stephen Elliott Jr. commanded from May 24 until he was badly wounded at the Crater on July 30, and William H. Wallace took over the command from July 30 until the end of the war. The brigade served at various times in the following commands: the Department of South Carolina, Georgia and Florida; the Army of Northern Virginia; the Department of North Carolina and Southern Virginia; the Department of the West; and the Department of Mississippi and East Louisiana.[97]

MAJOR MOVEMENTS AND ENGAGEMENTS

Seven companies of Hatch's Battalion, designated A to G, mustered in service in September and October 1861.[98] Four—A, B, C and D—were based on James Island and performed picket duty on Folly Island shortly after they mustered in service.[99] Company B was stationed at Bull Island and Dewees Island on September 25. Two detachments of Company C left Charleston for other points along the South Carolina coast on the twenty-fifth and twenty-seventh.[100] Company C was stationed at Secessionville in early October, and in late October, it was joined there by Company G.[101] Company E was stationed at Black Island in November and December, and Company F was based at Secessionville in November and December. Company H, not part of Hatch's Battalion at the time, was also stationed at Secessionville in November and December. The battalion added three new companies to become Hatch's regiment in November 1861. After it joined the regiment in December, Company K was sent to Mount Pleasant and camped at Christ Church Parish near the Georgetown Road. The 23rd Regiment was based near Charleston from December 1861 to July 21, 1862. It was at Camp Lee, on the south side of the Ashley River Bridge, from mid-December 1861 to February 1862. Company K remained at Christ Church Parish until April and also served as the provost guard in Charleston in 1862.[102] Most of the regiments that would soon form Evans's Brigade were sent to John's Island and Wadmalaw Island on February 1 and to Camp Simmons near Rantowles on June 17, 1862, but it is unlikely that the 23rd Regiment accompanied the brigade there. The 23rd was sent to Secessionville on James Island in the spring of 1862. Still there in April and May, men of the 23rd constructed the Tower Battery, which became known as Battery Lamar after the battle on June 16, 1862.[103] Evidently some men objected to this assignment and for that reason did not re-elect Colonel Hatch at the reorganization in April. The regiment was united for the first time when it was sent to Morris Island, where it acted as guard for the harbor steamer that traveled between Fort Sumter and James Island.[104] In late May 1862 the 23rd Regiment planted the first gun at the battery on Morris Island, a battery that later would be named Battery Wagner.[105] The regiment returned to James Island on June 2, 1862. The 23rd was stationed at the Wappoo Cut in early July.[106] It was sent to the post east of James Island Creek at Dill's Bluff on the eighth.[107]

N.G. Evans's Brigade, comprising the 17th, 18th, 22nd, 23rd Regiments and the Holcombe Legion, was created about June 20. The 17th, 18th and 23rd Regiments, the Holcombe Legion and the Macbeth Light Artillery were ordered to Virginia on July 17. They left by rail between July 18 and 21. The 18th left on July 18 and arrived in Richmond on the twenty-fourth.[108] The 23rd left on July 19 and arrived in Richmond on the twenty-seventh.[109] The 17th Regiment left for Virginia by rail on July 21 and arrived in Richmond on the twenty-fifth. The rest of the brigade, except for the 22nd Regiment, left for Virginia about July 21 and arrived in Richmond on the twenty-fourth. The 22nd Regiment was not included in this order and remained in South Carolina for a few more weeks.[110]

On July 30, the men marched about seven miles down the Darbytown Road to Camp Mary, named for Lieutenant Colonel McMaster's wife, Mary.[111] The brigade skirmished while on an armed reconnaissance near Malvern Hill on August 6.[112] Leaving camp on August 11, the men marched towards Richmond; they left the capital by rail for Gordonsville on the thirteenth and crossed the Rapidan River at Raccoon Ford on August 21.[113] The 22nd Regiment joined the brigade about that time.[114] The brigade lost about ninety men while acting as infantry support in a largely artillery battle at Rappahannock Station on August 23.[115] The brigade was not present on the first day of the battle of Second Manassas, August 28. It crossed through Thoroughfare Gap on the morning of the twenty-ninth and was under constant fire and lightly engaged during reconnaissance that day. It was heavily engaged late in the afternoon of the thirtieth.[116] The Tramp Brigade provided the Holcombe Legion and three other regiments—the 17th, 18th and 23rd—to the fighting on August 30; the 22nd Regiment was not engaged because it was on detached service.[117] A full 70 percent of men in the 17th were killed or wounded that day.[118] The *Mercury* printed a lengthy list of casualties from the 23rd Regiment from the fighting on August 30.[119] The Holcombe Legion suffered casualties in the fighting on both the twenty-ninth and thirtieth, and mustered only about one hundred men for duty after the battle.[120]

A much-weakened brigade crossed the Potomac River into Maryland at White's Ford on September 5 and arrived at Frederick City on the seventh. The brigade marched through Boonsboro to Hagerstown on September 14 and arrived about four in the afternoon at South Mountain (Boonsboro Gap), where it was heavily engaged until dark. Because of the heavy losses at Second Manassas, Company F of the 23rd Regiment took only one man into the battle at South Mountain on the fourteenth. The brigade was present and most of its regiments were engaged at Sharpsburg on September 17. The 18th Regiment was heavily engaged there; about sixty men of the 17th were on the battlefield but were detached from Evans's Brigade and only partially engaged along the advance line of Longstreet's Division.[121] The men remained on the battlefield on September 18 and crossed the Potomac into Virginia that night. The brigade was in camp at Winchester from September 20 to October 30; it participated in the Grand Review in October. Leaving Winchester for Culpeper by foot on October 30, the men boarded trains bound for North Carolina on November 7 and arrived at Weldon the next day. The brigade passed through Halifax Court House and Tarboro before reaching Kinston on November 13.[122] The 18th Regiment was detached from the brigade and ordered to Greenville, North Carolina, on December 3 to perform picket duty on the Tar River. One company of the 22nd Regiment was captured while on picket duty about two miles from Kinston on the night of December 12.[123] The 17th, 22nd, 23rd, the Holcombe Legion and the Macbeth Artillery saw action at Kinston on December 13 and December 14.[124] The 18th Regiment was not engaged at Kinston and rejoined the brigade there on December 22.

The brigade moved on December 17 by rail to Goldsboro, where it was engaged at the Neuse River Bridge that evening.[125] Ordered back to Kinston on the twenty-fourth, the brigade participated in the defense of the Kinston Railroad until early February 1863. It left Kinston by rail on the evening of the seventh and arrived at Wilmington the next day.[126] The men were sent to Topsail Island for picket duty on February 10, and on the twenty-fifth, they marched to Mansonboro Sound, which was about four miles from Wilmington. The Holcombe Legion returned to Charleston about April 18 in advance of the brigade and was based at the Four Mile House.[127] The Legion was "in fine health and under excellent discipline" at that time.[128] The rest of the brigade left by rail for Charleston on April 25 and arrived there on the twenty-sixth. The men camped between the Four Mile House and the Cooper River for two days before moving to the south side of the Ashley River. The brigade was sent to Secessionville on May 4, and, although it was ordered to John's Island on the ninth, it was not engaged and returned to Secessionville on the evening of the eleventh.[129] Companies F and I of the 23rd Regiment were detached from the regiment in early May. Company I served as heavy artillery at Battery Palmer near the John's Island Ferry for about two weeks.[130]

The 26th Regiment was added to the brigade on May 16, and Evans's entire command was sent by rail to Jackson, Mississippi, the same day. Arriving at the railroad terminus on the twenty-third, the men marched from there to Jackson.[131] The brigade remained in camp along the Pearl River near Jackson until June 22. It was stationed about sixteen miles north of Jackson until the surrender at Vicksburg on July 4. The brigade was within three miles of the Big Black River that day and did not hear about the capitulation until the fifth. The brigade marched back to Jackson two days later.[132] It entered the town on the morning of the ninth and participated in the siege, which lasted until the evening of July 16. Engaged on the sixteenth, the brigade evacuated Jackson that night, withdrawing eastward through Brandon to Forest Station. By July 19, the brigade was described as "almost worn out physically and badly depressed mentally."[133] Still, within a few days, it had moved into a new camp—Camp Sprawls—about thirteen miles from Forest along Caney Creek in Scott County.[134] On August 4, the men boarded a train at Forest Station bound for Meridian; from there, they proceeded by rail and steamboat to Demopolis, Alabama, arriving on the fifth.[135] Another train trip to Selma, followed by a riverboat ride to Montgomery, occupied another day. August 7 found the men en route by train to Columbus, Georgia. The brigade continued to move, still by rail, through Macon and on to Savannah on the eighth and ninth. Although bareheaded, barefoot and in rags by this time, the men marched the next day ten miles down the Skidaway Shell Road to Camp Johnson at the Wormsloe plantation along the Skidaway River on the Isle of Hope.[136] A much-needed two weeks of rest and recuperation followed.

On August 26 the brigade, except for the 22nd Regiment, was sent by rail to Sullivan's Island near Charleston, arriving the next morning. The men went into camp at Mount Pleasant on the twenty-eighth and were occupied with building breastworks all the way from the south tip of Long Island (Isle of Palms) to the Cooper River. By the end of August, five regiments—the 17th, 18th, 23rd, 26th and Holcombe Legion—had been put to work clearing timber for one and a half miles in front of the works, guarding the land approach to Charleston from the north and providing emergency infantry support for Sullivan's Island.[137] The men also performed guard duty on Sullivan's Island every fifth night. The 22nd Regiment remained near Savannah in late August and rejoined the brigade about September 20.[138]

On September 30, the brigade moved to a position seven miles northeast of Mount Pleasant near the breastworks. Company A of the 23rd Regiment reported no men for duty on October 17, Companies B and C reported one and Company D reported two.[139] The 23rd was stationed at Hamlin's farm on the road to Georgetown until early November, when it was ordered to Battery Marshall on Sullivan's Island. It remained there until April 1864.[140] Company F of the 23rd was detached and based at Long Island (Isle of Palms) from November 1863 to February 1864. The 18th Regiment was stationed at Bonneau's Landing during September and early October 1863. On October 10, the 17th and 18th Regiments were ordered to James Island. Arriving at Secessionville on October 12, they performed picket duty in front of Fort Lamar, very near the spot they had evacuated just before leaving for Mississippi the previous summer.[141] Brigade headquarters remained at Mount Pleasant.[142] The 26th Regiment moved from Sullivan's Island to Charleston on October 24 but was ordered back to Mount Pleasant about November 29.[143] The 18th Regiment was ordered back to Mount Pleasant on October 24 and probably arrived there two days later.[144]

Although many of the men of the 17th Regiment were still shoeless and in rags during October and November 1863, they somehow managed to stay healthy.[145] Lieutenant Colonel Alfred Roman, assistant inspector general, wrote on November 6: "The general condition of Evans's Brigade, as regards discipline, military appearance, and efficiency in drill, is far from being satisfactory...The materiel of which the brigade is composed is as good as can be found in any part of the Confederacy. The men are willing to do their duty, to fight for their rights, and to be disciplined to that effect." Roman added that, although the field officers were doing a good job, the company commanders, who showed great want of efficiency, energy and firmness, neglected the men. He also wrote that the 22nd was far behind the other regiments in terms of discipline, soldierly bearing and drill, and the Holcombe Legion showed a lack of discipline, practice and attention to drill, as well as considerable deficiencies in arms and ammunition.[146] At that time, the 26th Regiment suffered from defective discipline and ammunition, a very dirty camp and an imperfectly kept adjutant's office.[147]

The 17th Regiment endured frequent shelling while at James Island.[148] On November 9 about a hundred men from Companies B, E, G and K of the 17th were sent to perform garrison duty at Fort Sumter and repulsed a Federal barge attack on the fort that day.[149] Those four companies suffered a continual barrage of shot and shell until November 22, when they returned to James Island. The regiment was ordered back to Mount Pleasant on the twenty-eighth. The 17th Regiment left James Island on the evening of the thirtieth and arrived at Mount Pleasant at two in the morning on December 1. Several companies of the 26th were detached from the regiment about this time. Company C of the 26th was sent to Venning's Landing from September 1863 to February 1864.[150] Company I of the 26th was sent from Mount Pleasant to Accommodation Wharf in Charleston on October 25 and remained there until April 15, 1864; Company H was also sent to Accommodation Wharf on October 28. Company E of the 26th was detached to serve guard duty at the Charleston Arsenal on January 24, 1864. Between November 1863 and January 1864 the Holcombe Legion was based in the vicinity of Mount Pleasant, Christ Church and Sullivan's Island.[151] The brigade resumed picket duty on the beaches in front of the batteries and rifle pits in the center of Sullivan's Island in December 1863 and January 1864.[152] Company B of the 18th Regiment was sent to Fort Sumter on February 12, and another company of the 18th went to Fort Sumter on February 20.[153] Both companies left the fort on February 21.[154] The rest of the brigade was sent to James Island on February 12, was sent back to Sullivan's Island on the thirteenth and was ordered to Green Pond on February 14, arriving the next day.[155]

The brigade re-enlisted for the duration of the war on February 16; the 17th Regiment's vote was unanimous. From February to April, the regiments served in various locations. The 17th Regiment performed picket duty, built a battery on the Combahee River, worked on a battery at Stock's Causeway and built roads and breastworks until April 13. One company of the 22nd Regiment was sent to Fort Sumter on February 20.[156] Other detachments from the 22nd were at Fort Sumter throughout March and April.[157] The 22nd Regiment was sent to James Island on April 7, and Company C was detached for duty at Fort Sumter the same day. The last detachment of the 22nd left Fort Sumter on April 23.[158] Company C eventually rejoined the regiment at Kinston, North Carolina, on May 3. On February 25 a detachment of the 23rd Regiment was sent to Fort Sumter.[159] About half the men of the 23rd Regiment were sent to Fort Sumter for thirty days on March 1.[160] Another fifty-man detachment of the 23rd was sent to Fort Sumter on March 4 and was relieved on the twelfth.[161] Company G of the 23rd was at Fort Sumter on March 12 and was probably relieved on April 7.[162] The last detachment of the 23rd Regiment left Fort Sumter on April 22.[163]

The 18th Regiment was detached from the Tramp Brigade on February 20 and was sent to Baldwin, Florida, near Lake City.[164] While in Florida, the 18th Regiment was attached to Colonel George P. Harrison's Brigade, along with the 11th Regiment, SCV, the 32nd Georgia Regiment and the 59th Virginia Regiment.[165] The 18th Regiment was not engaged during the battle of Ocean Pond on February 20, but it participated in the pursuit of Federal troops toward Jacksonville and was engaged nearby at Cedar Creek. The 18th Regiment left Camp Milton, Florida, on April 16 or 17, arriving at Savannah on April 20 and Charleston on the twenty-first or twenty-second.[166] The 18th Regiment was ordered to Sullivan's Island, but Brigadier General Roswell Ripley, commander of that military district, objected on the grounds that he lacked confidence in the experience of any regiment in Evans's Brigade.[167] He succeeded in having the 11th Regiment ordered to Sullivan's Island and the 18th to Charleston.[168] The 18th Regiment left Charleston on April 29 and arrived at Wilmington on May 1, leaving on the fifteenth and arriving at Weldon the next day.

The Holcombe Legion was also detached from the Tramp Brigade. It left Charleston for Savannah on February 22, 1864, and arrived there on February 24.[169] From this time until October 17 the legion was detached from the brigade. The legion was soon sent to Oatland Island, Georgia, leaving on April 15 for Savannah.[170] It left Savannah by rail on April 16 for Weldon, North Carolina, arriving there on the twenty-first and arriving at Tarboro the next day. The legion went to Kinston on May 5 and two days later was back at Weldon to guard the Petersburg and Weldon Railroad. Companies I and K were captured on May 7 while defending the railroad at Stony Creek Station, Virginia, and the rest of the legion was engaged with Federal cavalry at Jarratt's Station, near Chester, Virginia, on May 8.[171] On May 10, the legion arrived at the Nottoway Bridge in Sussex County, Virginia, where it continued guarding the same railroad. Two companies guarded the bridge over the Nottoway River eighteen miles south of Petersburg, four were posted at the bridge over Stony Creek two miles farther south and four were at the Nottoway River Bridge five more miles south.[172] The legion stayed in that vicinity throughout the summer. It was engaged with Wilson's Raiders at Sappony Church under the command of Wade Hampton on June 28 and June 29, and it may have been engaged at the Ware House on July 1. The Holcombe Legion was not present with the brigade on July 30 during the battle of the Crater. Leaving Stony Creek on October 15, the Holcombe Legion rejoined the Tramp Brigade in the Petersburg trenches on the seventeenth.

The 17th, 22nd, 23rd and 26th Regiments were sent to Wilmington by rail on April 15, 1864, arriving there the next day.[173] The four regiments left Wilmington on the twenty-second and moved the next day to Tarboro with orders to guard Federal prisoners there. The 17th Regiment arrived just as the Holcombe Legion was preparing an offensive strike.[174] Companies A and F of the 17th Regiment left Tarboro on the twenty-sixth, escorting Federal prisoners captured by General Hoke at Plymouth, North Carolina.

They reached Charleston on April 28. The two companies left Charleston the next day, rejoined the rest of the regiment at Wilmington on April 30 or May 1 and were assigned to provost duty in Wilmington for the next two weeks. On April 23, the 26th Regiment left Weldon, arrived at Kinston the next day and left again by May 3. The 22nd and 26th Regiments arrived at New Bern on May 6 and drove in the enemy pickets there the same day.

The brigade left Wilmington by rail on May 16 and arrived at Petersburg before daylight three days later. Ordered immediately into the rifle pits south of the Appomattox River near Petersburg, the brigade returned to the city after dark the same day.[175] The brigade remained in that theater until the surrender at Appomattox; it was under fire daily for nearly a year, from May 20, 1864, until April 9, 1865. The Tramp Brigade left Petersburg on the evening of May 19 and arrived at Chester Station near Clay's farm about two in the morning on the twentieth. The 17th, 18th, 22nd and 26th Regiments fought together that day at Hewlett's House; the 23rd Regiment was engaged at Clay's farm, also called Ware Bottom Church.[176]

The brigade was engaged in the lines at Bermuda Hundreds from May 21 to June 15. It moved by forced march to Petersburg on June 16, built breastworks all night and was lightly engaged there on the seventeenth and eighteenth.[177] The 22nd Regiment was detached from the brigade but was heavily engaged those two days, and five companies of the 23rd Regiment were also independently engaged on the seventeenth.[178] Lieutenant Colonel Joshua Hilary Hudson of the 26th Regiment wrote in 1903 that "it was an unbroken fight from June 17, 1864, until April 2, 1865 [the day after he was wounded]."[179] From June 18 to June 23, the brigade was in the Petersburg trenches alternating periods of hard fighting with hard work. The brigade left the lines about June 23, but it returned to the trenches on July 4.

On July 30 Federal forces blew up a mine filled with eight thousand pounds of gunpowder directly under the Tramp Brigade's position. During the ensuing battle of the Crater, the regiments of the Tramp Brigade were dispersed as follows: from left to right were the 26th, 17th, 18th, 22nd and 23rd, with Pegram's Battery between the 18th and 22nd Regiments.[180] The Holcombe Legion, detached at the time, did not rejoin the brigade until October 17. The 18th and 22nd Regiments were directly over the mine. Five companies of the 18th were blown up when the mine exploded; 83 men of that regiment were killed or wounded in the explosion and 119 were killed in retaking the crater. Companies E and H of the 22nd Regiment were blown up, and nearly all the men in Companies B, C, G and H were captured.[181] The 22nd listed only 48 men for duty the next day.[182] On the right edge of the crater, three companies of the 23rd Regiment were overwhelmed, and the regiment lost 49 men killed or wounded. To the left of the crater, Company A, the right company of the 17th Regiment, was completely overwhelmed. The 17th and 23rd Regiments managed to hold the gap in the thin Confederate line for four critical hours until Mahone's Division arrived.

With the exception of only a few days, the brigade was in the trenches flanking either side of the crater from September 1, 1864, to March 13, 1865. During that time, the men endured almost constant sharpshooting and desultory shelling. The 22nd and 23rd Regiments and the Holcombe Legion were engaged in a picket battle to recapture rifle pits in front of the crater on October 27.[183] The Holcombe Legion was engaged again south of the crater on November 5. Company D of the 17th Regiment was detached from the regiment in early November and worked every other night on the construction of Battery Harrison. It returned to the trenches on November 9.

The entire brigade left its position on March 13, 1865, and marched about twelve miles to a new position near Five Forks on the right of the Confederate lines.[184] It saw action at Hatcher's Run that day; on the twenty-fourth, the men marched twelve miles back to Petersburg. There, the next day, the brigade launched an attack on Fort Stedman on Hare's Hill. It was also engaged on March 29 near the sawdust pile on the Boydton Plank Road; it remained in the lines at Burgess Mill on the thirtieth and was held in support during the engagement at Dinwiddie Court House on March 31. The brigade was engaged at Five Forks on April 1; only a remnant avoided capture. The remainder were involved in continuous skirmishing from April 1 to April 9 on the retreat to Appomattox Court House. The 23rd Regiment surrendered with about 105 men at Appomattox Court House on April 9, 1865.

12.

THE 25TH REGIMENT, SOUTH CAROLINA VOLUNTEERS

The 25th Regiment, SCV, was called both the Eutaw regiment and Simonton's regiment. It was formed on July 22, 1862, by adding the Clarendon Guards to the nine companies of the 11th (also called the Eutaw) Battalion, South Carolina Infantry. The *Edgefield Advertiser* referred to the Eutaw Battalion as a regiment in late June probably because it was of nearly regimental size already.[1] In addition, the *Official Records* names the 25th Regiment, not the Eutaw Battalion, as a participate in the engagement at Secessionville on June 16, 1862, a month before it was officially organized.[2] The regiment was probably raised under authority of an act passed by the Confederate Congress on February 28, 1862. John P. Thomas wrote, incorrectly, that the men enlisted for the war in October 1862.[3] Field officers were originally appointed on September 12, with rank from August 14, 1862, and, according to the *Mercury*, were re-elected in January 1863.[4] A new state law allowed another election for field officers on May 15, 1863, but the men were satisfied with their leaders, and the new elections were never held.[5] In March 1865, the 25th Regiment was reorganized with the 7th Battalion, South Carolina Infantry and remnants of the 11th, 21st and 27th Regiments, SCV, to form a new twelve-company unit designated Rion's Regiment.

FIELD OFFICERS

Charles Henry Simonton, a prominent Charleston lawyer and lieutenant colonel of the 11th (Eutaw) Battalion, was appointed colonel on July 22, 1862, when the regiment was organized. The CSR gives the appointment date as September 12, effective as of August 14, 1862. Simonton was detached from the regiment from August 1862 to April 1864, spending most of that time as acting brigadier general in command of the Eastern Division forces on James Island. During the eighteen-month period from November 1862 to May 1864, Simonton commanded the 25th Regiment on only three occasions, all of short duration.[6] On May 23, 1864, several prominent South Carolinians recommended Simonton for promotion to brigadier general without success. At his own request, Simonton was relieved from duty at James Island on or about May 28 that year.[7] He rejoined the regiment on June 4 but was soon detached again and served elsewhere until February 1865. He was not present at Fort Fisher but was captured at Town Creek near Wilmington on February 20. Simonton was taken to Fort Anderson at Point Lookout, Maryland, on the twenty-eighth and moved to the Old Capitol Prison in Washington the same day. Transferred to Fort Delaware on March 24, Simonton was released on June 24, 1865. Reportedly, General Beauregard had "great confidence" in Simonton.[8]

John Gotea Pressley, a lawyer from Williamsburg District and major of the 11th (Eutaw) Battalion, was appointed lieutenant colonel of the 25th Regiment on September 12, 1862, with rank from August 14. The CSR also reports the date as July 22, when the regiment was organized. Between August 1862 and May 1864, it was Pressley who actually commanded the 25th Regiment most of the time.[9] He was severely wounded when a rifle bullet struck him in the left arm just below the shoulder at Walthall Junction on May 7, 1864.[10] Surgeons resected the arm at the shoulder joint, and he recovered in a Petersburg Hospital.[11] By July 15 Pressley was at home in Kingstree, still suffering from the effects of the wound.[12] Johnson Hagood wrote that even though he did regain some use of the arm, Pressley was never again fit for field duty.[13] Pressley was still absent as 1864 ended, and his arm was in a sling as late as April 1865.[14] Hagood wrote that the loss of his service was a blow to the brigade. There is no documentation in the CSR that he ever resigned his commission. Johnson Hagood found Pressley "a most excellent and meritorious officer."[15] Izlar wrote: "The regiment lost the services of a brave and intrepid officer when he was so seriously wounded; and one to whom the men had become greatly attached. Although a rigid disciplinarian, he guarded jealously the rights of his men and would brook no imposition on them or interference with them."[16] Although Pressley did not return to the regiment, he did survive the war.

John Vinyard Glover was appointed major of the regiment at its organization on July 22, 1862. The CSR gives the date as September 12, effective August 14, 1862. Glover served previously as captain of the Edisto Rifles, Company A of Hagood's 1st Regiment and probably Company A of the Eutaw Battalion as well. Glover was in command of the regiment on June 4, 1864, when Colonel Simonton returned after a prolonged absence.

As the two men stood in a trench near Cold Harbor that day, Glover was in the act of relinquishing command to the colonel when a Federal sharpshooter hit him in the hand. The bullet took off his little finger either when he was hit or because it had to be amputated.[17] Regardless, the wound, although painful and somewhat disabling, did not seem serious.[18] Glover was taken to a hospital, where his condition deteriorated—an eventuality that was out of proportion to the seriousness of the wound. He told one of the surgeons he had been kicked by a horse while the regiment was at Bermuda Hundreds in late May. Izlar provides more details: during the march from Bermuda Hundreds to Cold Harbor, Glover was riding past a horse that was hitched on the side of the road. The horse kicked him near the ankle.[19] The contusion developed into erysipelas and gangrene, and, as a result, Glover died from the leg injury at the General Hospital at Howard's Grove near Richmond.[20] The date of his death was probably June 20, although the *Mercury* records the nineteenth and the CSR says both June 17 and 19.[21] The *Roll of the Dead* uses the obviously incorrect date of June 11, whereas both Kirkland and Hagood make it June 19.[22] Johnson Hagood wrote that Glover was a most excellent and meritorious officer.[23] He noted that "in civil life [he] had made but little mark and was regarded as habitually indolent." In military life, on the other hand, he believed Glover "demonstrated that he was a born soldier. Alert, vigilant, and efficient in the field, he secured alike the confidence and affection of his men, and the approbation of his superiors." He was "a born soldier" and "one of the most gallant and efficient officers of the brigade."[24] Izlar found him "quite conscientious and brave; one of the finest officers in the brigade."[25] J.G. Pressley wrote that "no regimental commander could have an assistant and associate better qualified or worthy of higher esteem."[26]

Companies

Company A of the 25th Regiment had been the Washington Light Infantry, Company A. Composed of men from Charleston, it was known locally as the Washingtons.[27] The company was also called Company E and the 7th Company in the early days of the 25th Regiment. The company was originally recruited from the ranks of a company called the Washington Light Infantry, which was part of the 1st Regiment Rifles, South Carolina Militia. The Washington Light Infantry actually provided three companies for service: Company A of the Hampton Legion and Companies A and B of the Eutaw Battalion (later the 25th Regiment). After the men of the Washington Light Infantry Volunteers left Charleston to become Company

A of the Hampton Legion, excess recruitment caused the remaining militia component of the Washington Light Infantry to split into two companies designated A and B.[28] Charles H. Simonton was elected captain of both in June 1861.[29] Both companies joined the Eutaw Battalion at its organization in early 1862. While based at Charleston, Company A, designated Captain Simonton's Company, mustered in Confederate service for twelve months on February 24. Simonton was elected captain of Company A of the Eutaw Battalion on February 22, a date also shown in the record as the twenty-fourth, and became lieutenant colonel of the battalion on April 30.[30] The *Mercury* reported in early May 1862, somewhat cryptically, that Simonton had resigned to go to an even higher and more distinguished post, a move that apparently never took place.[31] The Washington Light Infantry, Company A of the Eutaw Battalion, became Company A of the 25th Regiment in July 1862, and Simonton was appointed colonel on July 22.

James Marsh Carson was promoted from first lieutenant to captain on April 30.[32] He had just completed a five-week assignment at Fort Sumter on November 6, 1863, when Stephen Elliott wrote that Carson was "a soldier of no ordinary merit."[33] When Carson's left forearm was fractured in action in May 1864, the *Daily South Carolinian* reported that he would probably lose it.[34] Hagood thought, probably incorrectly, that he was wounded at Swift Creek on May 9.[35] Both J.G. Pressley and the CSR, however, record that it happened at Drewry's Bluff on the fifteenth.[36] The *Charleston Daily Courier* reported that Carson was wounded on May 13, 14 or 15.[37] Carson was wounded again, this time in the head, and taken prisoner at Fort Fisher, North Carolina, on January 15, 1865. The wound was initially thought to be mortal.[38] Taken to the United States Army General Hospital at Fortress Monroe on January 17, he was moved on the thirtieth to the military prison at Camp Hamilton, Virginia. He was sent to Fort Delaware on February 9 and held there until his release on June 19, 1865.[39] Carson was a "brave but impetuous officer."[40]

Company B of the 25th Regiment had been the Washington Light Infantry, Company B, and was also called Company A and the 1st Company in the early days of the 25th Regiment. Most of its men were from Charleston, although a few came from Orangeburg, Barnwell and Williamsburg Districts, and a scattering of others came from Germany, England and Georgia. This company was formed from excess recruitment in the Washington Light Infantry militia company. On February 24, 1862, while based in Charleston, the men of Company B mustered in for twelve months of Confederate service in the Eutaw Battalion. Edward William Lloyd was captain of the Washington Light Infantry Company B by October 1861, possibly even as early as June.[41] He was elected captain of Company B of the Eutaw Battalion on February 22, 1862, a date also shown as the twenty-fourth.[42] The Washington Light Infantry Company B became Company B of the 25th Regiment in July, and Lloyd remained as its captain. Following an operation for a hydrocele on August 22, 1863, Lloyd returned to the company on September 22. Reported absent because of illness on June 25, 1864, Lloyd never returned to the company. He retired to the Invalid Corps on August 22 and was assigned to Captain J. Sowers, the assistant quartermaster at the military station at Florence. Lloyd later served in the Quartermaster Department at Cheraw.[43] Second Lieutenant Joseph S. Hanahan was promoted to captain on November 29, 1864. He was captured at Town Creek, North Carolina, on February 20, 1865, and was taken to Fort Anderson at Point Lookout, Maryland. He was moved on the twenty-eighth to the Old Capitol Prison in Washington, was transferred on March 24 to Fort Delaware and was released on June 17, 1865.

Company C, the Wee Nee Volunteers, was known in the 25th Regiment first as Captain China's Company, then as Company B, then as the 2nd Company and finally Company C. This company's history is one of the most interesting and complicated histories of the entire war. It served originally as Company F in Maxcy Gregg's 1st Regiment, SCV, from January to late April 1861, when it refused to serve in Virginia and was disbanded. Next, it reorganized and mustered in state service as Company D, 10th Regiment, SCV, until late August. In early September 1861, the company reorganized again, this time dividing into two companies; one mustered in Confederate service as Company E, Hagood's 1st Regiment, SCV, and the other remained in state service and was attached to Harlee's Legion, South Carolina Militia. At the reorganization in April 1862, the Wee Nee Volunteers left Hagood's regiment and, on the twelfth, mustered in the new 11th Battalion, SCV, which, in July, merged into the 25th Regiment, SCV.[44] The Wee Nee Volunteers, also known as the Williamsburg Company, was raised in Kingstree in Williamsburg District and was given the American Indian name for the Black River running through Kingstree.[45]

Captain John Gotea Pressley, captain of the company in Hagood's regiment, was promoted to major of the 11th Battalion on April 30, 1862, probably with rank from the twelfth. First Lieutenant Thomas Jefferson China, who helped Pressley raise the company originally, was promoted to captain on April 12, a date also shown in the record as the thirtieth.[46] When the 11th Battalion merged into the 25th Regiment on July 22, the Wee Nee Volunteers became Company C, and China remained its captain. On September 13, 1863, he was given a ten-day leave of absence to recover from a brain concussion caused by a "bashing of the skull" while on duty at Battery Wagner.[47] The Wee Nee Volunteers re-enlisted for the duration of the war on February 16, 1864.[48] China suffered a severe wound in the right side of the groin at Drewry's Bluff on May 16, 1864.[49] He died in Richmond on the eighteenth.[50] First Lieutenant Calhoun Logan, who, on the fourteenth, was also wounded in the right leg at Drewry's Bluff, was promoted to captain as China's replacement on the eighteenth. Logan was captured at Fort Fisher, North Carolina, on January 15, 1865.[51] He was taken to Fort Columbus in New York Harbor on the twenty-sixth, was paroled there and was moved to City Point, Virginia, on February 25. Logan was exchanged at Boulware's Wharf, Virginia, on March 5, 1865, along with 602 other prisoners of war.

Company D, the Marion Light Infantry, was also called Company D and the 3rd Company in the early days of the 25th Regiment. This company, made up of men from Marion District, was part of the 11th (Eutaw) Battalion and probably mustered in service on April 15, 1862. William Jasper McKerall was elected captain the same day. He was slightly wounded at Battery Wagner on either September 4, 5 or 6, 1863.[52] McKerall was captured during Hagood's famous charge on the Weldon Railroad on August 21, 1864.[53] Taken to the Old Capitol Prison in Washington on the twenty-third, he was moved four days later to Fort Delaware and placed on parole. He was sent to Point Lookout, Maryland, on October 6 and was exchanged at Cox's Wharf on the James River on October 15, 1864, with 333 other prisoners of war.[54] Whether or not McKerall returned to the company is unclear, but he was marked absent without leave from December 5, 1864. Johnson Hagood recommended on the thirty-first that McKerall be dropped from the rolls because of his absence; his name was removed on February 3, 1865. The *Memory Roll* spells his name McKerrall, and the *Mercury* spells it McKerrel.[55]

Company E, the Beauregard Light Infantry, was also called Captain White's Company and Company D in the early days of the 25th Regiment. Composed of men from Charleston and Colleton Districts, it was organized in July 1861 and remained part of the First Regiment Rifles, South Carolina Militia, until it joined the Eutaw Battalion in February 1862.[56] The company mustered in for twelve months of Confederate service at Charleston on February 21, 1862, the first company to muster in under the new act.[57] In April 1862, it re-enlisted for the duration of the war.[58] Peter B. Lalane, who was captain when it was a militia company, was not re-elected when the company joined the 11th Battalion.[59] Robert D. White was elected instead on February 21, 1862, and he retained the rank in the 25th Regiment. The Beauregard Light Infantry became Company E of the 25th Regiment in July 1862. White resigned on September 3, giving a cryptic "owing to the present circumstances" as the reason.[60] First Lieutenant Nathaniel "Nat"

Broughton Mazyck replaced him the same day. Mazyck was wounded when the magazine exploded at Fort Sumter on December 11, 1863.[61] He was captured at Town Creek, North Carolina, on February 20, 1865. Taken to Fort Anderson at Point Lookout, Maryland, on the twenty-eighth and to the Old Capitol Prison in Washington the same day, he was moved to Fort Delaware on March 24 and was released on June 17, 1865.

Company F, the St. Matthews Rifles or Riflemen, was also called Captain Seller's Company, Company C and the 5th Company in the early days of the 25th Regiment. One source states the name was the Dantzler Rifles.[62] The company was composed of men from Orangeburg District, most of whom were originally either in Company D or in a few of the other companies of Hagood's 1st South Carolina Volunteer Regiment. At the end of the initial twelve-month enlistment in that regiment, most chose to enlist in the 11th (Eutaw) Battalion, most likely on April 11, 1862. When the Eutaw Battalion merged into the 25th Regiment in July, the St. Matthews Riflemen became Company F of the 25th Regiment. Martin Henry Sellers, the only captain of the company in the Eutaw Battalion, was its first captain in the 25th Regiment.[63] The CSR records his election on April 11, 1862, probably the date the company joined the Eutaw Battalion. Sellers was slightly wounded in the forearm at Walthall Junction on May 7, 1864, and was initially reported killed in action.[64] He suffered a slight wound to the head in the Petersburg trenches on July 7, 1864.[65] Sellers was mortally wounded in Hagood's Charge on the Weldon Railroad on August 21, 1864, and died the same day.[66] Johnson Hagood praised him: "In action he was cool, determined and unflinching, and exhibited a capacity for higher command, which he would assuredly have reached had a kinder fate spared his valuable life. He always did his duty well; had more than once distinguished himself; and had been recommended for promotion to the vacant majority of his regiment. The place of such a man could not be well filled."[67] First Lieutenant Leonidas A. Harper, who was promoted to captain on August 21, had been wounded at Fort Sumter on December 11, 1863, when the powder magazine exploded. During the charge on the Weldon Railroad on August 21, 1864—the day of his promotion—he was wounded again, this time in the left thigh. Suffering from the wound, Harper was still absent from the company at the end of the year; there is no record of his return.

Company G, the Edisto Rifles, was composed of men from Orangeburg, most of whom had served in Company A of Hagood's 1st Regiment until the expiration of their term of enlistment on April 12, 1862. Most had immediately re-enlisted for three years, or for the duration of the war, under the same officers; they mustered in the Eutaw Battalion about April 12.[68] A few Company G men had served in other companies of Hagood's regiment.[69] John Vinyard Glover, who was captain of the company in Hagood's regiment in April 1862, was re-elected when the company joined the Eutaw Battalion, and he retained command until he was elected major of the 25th regiment on July 22.[70] First Lieutenant James Ferdinand Izlar was promoted to captain the same day.[71] Izlar was severely wounded in the thigh at Morris Island some time between September 1 and 7, 1863. He was captured at Fort Fisher on January 15, 1865, and was taken to Fort Columbus on Governors Island in New York Harbor on the twenty-sixth.[72] Paroled at Fort Columbus, Izlar was transferred to City Point, Virginia, on February 25 and was exchanged at Boulware's Wharf, Virginia, on March 5, 1865, with 602 other prisoners of war.[73]

Company H, the Yeadon Light Infantry, was also called Captain Hammond's Company, Company F and the 6th Company in the early days of the 25th Regiment. John P. Thomas wrote, incorrectly, that the company's name was the Gordon Light Infantry.[74] Although most of the men were from Charleston and Williamsburg Districts, a few came from Sumter, Orangeburg, Anderson, Newberry, Darlington, Edgefield and Lexington Districts. Some had served previously in Company I of Hagood's regiment. Organized in the spring of 1862, the company, then called the Yeadon Guards, was authorized to begin recruiting in early April for the duration of the war.[75] The *Mercury* reported at the end of the month that recruitment was actively underway.[76] The company mustered in service for the duration between April 30 and May 20 and was attached to the 11th Battalion about the same time. Samuel LeRoy Hammond was elected captain on May 20, 1862.[77] A year later, in May 1863, Hammond requested appointment as major, lieutenant colonel or colonel in the western army or the Army of Northern Virginia. J.G. Pressley, N.G. Evans and S.R. Gist provided strong recommendations, and Colonel C.H. Simonton added his assessment, calling Hammond "an excellent and indefatigable officer and a bold and daring soldier."[78] Even so, Hammond did not receive the promotion he sought.

Between September 1 and 6, 1863, the final days before the evacuation of Battery Wagner, Hammond was twice stunned by shell concussions and suffered slight contusions to the temple, to one side of his body and to one shoulder.[79] Hammond was killed in action at Swift Creek on May 9, 1864.[80] According to the *Confederate Veteran*, he was killed in a skirmish on May 10.[81] One card in the CSR states he was killed on the twelfth. Izlar wrote that Hammond was a "good officer...[a man] of poetic turn of mind... [who] wrote some very pretty verses under the *nom de plume* of 'Charlie Wildwood.'"[82] An article in the *Charleston Daily Courier* described him as "a young man of genius and talent. He was gifted and eloquent as a poet and speaker, brave and gallant as a soldier and officer, social and gentlemanly as a companion and citizen."[83] William H. Bartless Jr. was promoted from second lieutenant to captain on May 21, 1864.[84] Bartless's father served as major of the 8th Battalion, South Carolina Reserves. Captured at Town Creek, North Carolina, on February 20, 1865, Bartless was taken to Fort Anderson at Point Lookout, Maryland, on the twenty-eighth and was moved to the Old Capitol Prison in Washington the same day. He was transferred to Fort Delaware on March 24 and was released on June 10, 1865.

Company I, the Clarendon Guards, was also called Captain Butler's Company, Company G and the 9th Company in the early days of the 25th Regiment. All but two of its men were from Clarendon District; according to the *Memory Roll* the two others came from Williamsburg District. The company enlisted on December 21, 1861, for twelve months of state service and mustered in Confederate service on January 1, 1862, as Company C of the 21st Regiment, SCV. On July 13, 1862, Colonel Graham of the 21st Regiment agreed to allow the Clarendon Guards to leave the regiment and join the 11th Battalion instead. So it was that when the Clarendon Guards was merged with the nine-company 11th Battalion on July 22, the 25th Regiment, SCV, was created.[85] E.N. Plowden, who was elected captain on January 1, 1862, resigned the following May 1. The fact that Plowden signed a document as captain on August 18, 1862, however, conflicts with that resignation date. According to the CSR, First Lieutenant Y.N. Butler was elected captain on May 1, 1862.[86] The CSR also states that Butler was not a captain in the 21st Regiment but did hold that rank in the 25th Regiment. While Butler did succeed Plowden as captain of the Clarendon Guards, the exact date of Plowden's resignation and Butler's promotion is somewhat murky. It was probably May 1, but it could have been later in the summer of 1862. Butler tendered his own resignation on April 15, 1863, on the grounds that he had been elected sheriff of Clarendon District. When the resignation was rejected, he submitted it again on May 22, this time writing that it was "absolutely necessary" to accept in person his new responsibilities as sheriff.[87] Butler's resignation was accepted on June 11, 1863, and First Lieutenant Joseph Copely Burgess was promoted to captain the same day, a date also shown in the record as June 17.[88] Burgess was slightly wounded at Battery Wagner on September 4, 5 or 6, 1863.[89] Suffering as well from general debility caused by swelling of the lower extremities, he retired to the Invalid Corps on August 29, 1864. First Lieutenant John J. Logan, who had been wounded in the face at Battery Wagner between September 1 and 6, 1863, was promoted to captain on August 29, 1864, replacing Burgess. Logan was wounded again on July 8, 1864. The next year, on January 15, he was wounded in the left shoulder and then captured at Fort Fisher. He was taken to the United States Army General Hospital at Fortress Monroe on the seventeenth, and on January 30, he was sent to the military prison at Camp Hamilton, Virginia. He was moved to Fort Delaware on February 9 and was released on June 17, 1865.

Company K, the Ripley Guards, was also called Company B and the 10th Company in the early days of the 25th Regiment. The Ripley Guards had served in the Eutaw Battalion from April to July 1862.[90] The men originally enlisted unconditionally for the duration of the war in 1862 and saw no need to re-enlist in 1864.[91] Captain William Blackwood Gordon and First Lieutenant Francis James Lesesne raised the company in December 1861.[92] Lesesne was killed at Swift Creek on May 9, 1864. Most of the men came from Williamsburg and Clarendon Districts, but a few were from Charleston. Before the company joined the 25th Regiment, it was called Gordon's Company, Ripley Guards, SCV. Stationed at the Santee Bridge early in 1862, the company was assigned special duty as a local guard for several months before joining the 25th Regiment.[93] Gordon was elected captain on December 29, 1861, and was commissioned on December 31. He was slightly wounded in the left arm at Battery Wagner on September 4, 5 or 6, 1863.[94] He was slightly wounded again around May 18, 1864. Gordon was acting major of the 25th Regiment when Hagood made his famous charge into the Federal salient known as the horseshoe on the Weldon Railroad on August 21, 1864.[95] He was mortally wounded during the charge and fell into the hands of the enemy. Both the CSR and the *Roll of the Dead* state that Gordon died on August 21, but the *Mercury* reported in 1865 that he was wounded and died a few days later.[96] Second Lieutenant Edward R. Lesesne, who had been slightly wounded at Battery Wagner between September 1 and 6, 1863, was promoted to captain on August 21, 1864. He was paroled with the company at Greensboro on May 1, 1865.

BRIGADE AFFILIATIONS

The 25th Regiment was in Colonel Peyton H. Colquitt's Temporary Brigade from July 1862 until about April 4, 1863. The 16th and 24th Regiments, SCV, the 7th South Carolina Battalion and the 46th Georgia Regiment were also in Colquitt's Brigade in early 1863. In April 1863 C.H. Stevens's Brigade comprised the 24th and 25th Regiments; the 2nd Regiment, South Carolina Artillery; the 8th Georgia Battalion; Lucas's Battalion of Regulars; two companies of White's Battalion; five artillery batteries; and three companies of cavalry. In August and September 1863, the 25th Regiment was in Taliaferro's 1st Subdivision of Ripley's 1st South Carolina Military

District of the Department of South Carolina, Georgia and Florida. Next, the 25th was assigned to Johnson Hagood's Brigade, organized at Charleston by special order of P.G.T. Beauregard on September 20, 1863.[97] As of that date Hagood's Brigade comprised the 7th Battalion South Carolina Infantry, the Charleston Battalion and the 11th, 21st and 25th South Carolina Regiments. After September 30 the Charleston Battalion and the Battalion of Sharpshooters were merged into the 27th Regiment. Elements of the 25th Regiment served in the Department of South Carolina, Georgia and Florida from October 1863 to January 1864. In early March 1865 the 7th Battalion was consolidated with remnants of the 11th, 21st, 25th and 27th Regiments to form a new twelve-company regiment under the command of Lieutenant Colonel James H. Rion. This consolidated regiment of about five hundred men was placed in a new brigade commanded by Johnson Hagood. The other major components of Hagood's new brigade were Hedricks's 40th North Carolina Regiment, Taylor's Consolidated 36th North Carolina and the 1st North Carolina Battalion of Heavy Artillery. On March 31, 1865, the North Carolina troops were reassigned to other brigades, and Rion took command of Hagood's Brigade, which reverted back to its original composition.

MAJOR MOVEMENTS AND ENGAGEMENTS

Men of the 11th Battalion were engaged at Secessionville on June 16, 1862, about a month before the battalion became part of the 25th Regiment. The *Official Records*, however, cited the 25th Regiment, not the 11th (Eutaw) Battalion, in that engagement.[98] In July 1862, the 25th Regiment was ordered to detail twenty-four men to serve in Pemberton's Battalion of Sharpshooters. Both officers and men resented the order, and the company captains retaliated by selecting the worst men in their commands.[99] As a result, Pemberton's scheme failed, and the men were incorporated into the 1st Battalion Sharpshooters.

The 25th Regiment was stationed at different points on James Island in the summer and fall of 1862, including Secessionville and Camp Stono.[100] From July 19 to August 31, the regiment performed picket duty at James Island.[101] The right wing of the regiment was sent to Elliott's Cut near the Stono River on August 8, and the left wing followed the next day. At four in the afternoon on October 22, the 25th was ordered to Pocotaligo; the men traveled on the same train with the 46th Georgia Regiment. On the train all night, neither regiment was present during the engagement at Pocotaligo on the twenty-second. The 25th returned to Camp Stono on October 24.

Between November 5 and 7 the regiment moved to Camp Glover, named in memory of the late Colonel T.J. Glover of the 1st Regiment, SCV, near Fort Pemberton on James Island.

In late 1862, Federal troops at New Bern, North Carolina, were threatening the Wilmington and Weldon Railroad. On the night of December 14, the 25th Regiment left Camp Glover by rail for Wilmington, arriving on the sixteenth.[102] At that time, the 24th and 16th Regiments, SCV, the 46th Georgia Regiment, the 7th South Carolina Battalion, Culpeper's Battery and Waties's Battery also went to Wilmington. The 25th Regiment was assigned to Camp Cobb. When nothing had happened by the thirty-first, the regiment returned by rail to Charleston, arriving at Camp Glover on January 1, 1863. The 25th was ordered to Wilmington again on January 9; by the fourteenth, after two days of train travel and more time on the march, the regiment was in camp at the racecourse near Wilmington.[103] The regiment was back at Camp Glover by February 11.

About March 1, the regiment moved to Camp Gadberry near the Presbyterian Church on James Island, where it was assigned picket duty until late April. The 25th was involved in a skirmish at Grimball's place about March 13 and skirmished again on April 6 at Horse Island on the banks of Green Creek. On the thirteenth, it participated in a scouting mission to Long Island.[104] The regiment moved to Secessionville in May. Four companies of the 25th Regiment, along with Abney's Battalion of Sharpshooters, pursued two hundred Federal troops near Legare's house on James Island on May 31, but they were not actively engaged.[105] During the early summer of 1863, one battalion of the regiment was based at Legare's Point, on the east side of James Island, and another on the Stono River, on the west side.[106] The 25th Regiment was in line of battle and under artillery fire on James Island on July 10. It left Secessionville three days later and moved to Camp Pettigrew near Camp Stono. On July 16, the regiment was engaged at the Rivers house on James Island.[107] On the night of August 4, thirty men from Company F attacked and captured a Federal picket post occupying an unfinished Confederate battery at the mouth of Vincent's Creek, also called Schooner Creek, between Morris and James Islands.[108] The regiment was still based at James Island on July 31.[109] Some companies of the 25th Regiment were sent to the besieged Battery Wagner on the night of September 1; others were sent the next night. They all remained there until the evacuation on the night of the sixth, and they all suffered casualties.[110] Izlar described the five days at Battery Wagner as the most "fearful experience of the four years in the war."[111] On September 7, the regiment's 2nd Battalion moved to Legare's on James Island, where it provided infantry support for Battery Haskell on the east side of the island until the thirteenth[112] Hagood's Brigade was created on

September 20, but the various regiments of the brigade did not serve as one unit until April 1864. Companies of the 25th Regiment served as the garrison at Fort Sumter from late September to early May 1864: Company A replaced Company D of the 11th Regiment on September 28 and Company B went in on October 3.[113]

Between October 1 and November 30, the regiment was moved from Camp Gadberry to the Presbyterian Church.[114] Company A was still at Fort Sumter in late October. On October 31 at three in the morning, as a detachment of men, along with their arms and accoutrements, slept in the lower story of the eastern barracks, a Federal shell launched from Morris Island struck and collapsed the upper two stories. Thirteen men, eleven of them from Company A, were killed.[115] On November 1, six companies were at James Island, Companies A and B were at either Sullivan's Island or in Christ Church Parish and Companies C and E were in Charleston.[116] Companies C and D were sent to Fort Sumter from November 2 to November 14.[117] On November 17, while part of the garrison at Fort Moultrie, Company F was engaged with the *U.S.S. Lehigh*. Company E was at Fort Sumter from December 4 to December 6, and Company F was there from December 5 to December 7.[118] Companies E and F suffered casualties when the powder magazine at Fort Sumter exploded on December 11.[119] Company H took its turn on December 30, and a detachment from Company D was there on the thirty-first.[120] The regiment, still stationed at Secessionville in December 1863 and January 1864, remained there all winter.[121] Company H was relieved at Fort Sumter on January 10, 1864.[122] Company I performed garrison duty at Fort Sumter from January 22 until February 2.[123] Company A was there from February 12 to February 24.[124] Company C returned to Fort Sumter on February 24 and was relieved by Company D on March 6.[125] Company E relieved Company D on the twelfth.[126] Company G was sent to Fort Sumter in April and was relieved by Company F on April 5.[127] Company H, the last company to perform service at Fort Sumter, left the fort on May 1.[128]

Between March 11 and April 14, the 25th Regiment moved from Secessionville to the "New Lines" on James Island and set up camp about four to five hundred yards from the Presbyterian Church. The regiment was based at Camp Perrin on James Island in mid-April.[129] Hagood's Brigade was ordered to Wilmington on April 28.[130] On the afternoon of May 1, the 25th Regiment arrived at The Citadel Green in Charleston. It left on the third and arrived at Wilmington the next day.[131] Most of the other regiments in Hagood's Brigade arrived at about the same time. From this time until the end of the war, the 25th Regiment served with Hagood's Brigade. Its major movements and engagements are discussed above under the 11th Regiment.

In early March 1865, Hagood's Brigade was consolidated into a twelve-company regiment with Lieutenant Colonel Rion in command. Rion's Regiment comprised the 7th Battalion and remnants of the 11th, 21st, 25th and 27th Regiments—an aggregate of about 500 men. On April 26, General Johnston and General Sherman reached agreement on articles of a military convention and effectively surrendered Johnston's army. Hagood's Brigade surrendered 40 officers and 510 men. The surrender was announced on April 27, and officers signed for and received paroles for their men on May 1 and May 2. The men broke camp on May 3 and marched for Lancaster Court House, South Carolina, where they were given their paroles. The remnants of Hagood's Brigade (Rion's Regiment) were disbanded there on May 7.

13.

THE 26TH REGIMENT, SOUTH CAROLINA VOLUNTEERS

The 26th Regiment, SCV, was formed by consolidating the seven companies of the 9th Battalion, South Carolina Infantry, and three of Byrd's 6th Battalion, South Carolina Infantry.[1] It was officially created at Church Flats below Charleston on September 9, 1862. Companies B and E, and possibly the entire regiment, re-enlisted for the duration of the war on February 8, 1864.[2]

FIELD OFFICERS

Alexander D. Smith of Bennettsville in Marlboro District had been lieutenant colonel of the 9th Battalion before the organization of the 26th Regiment. He was appointed colonel of the regiment on October 7, 1862, retroactive to September 9.[3] An October 1863 inspection of Evans's Brigade found a variety of shortcomings in the 26th Regiment, among them poor discipline, dirty camp conditions, a poorly run adjutant's office and defective ammunition.[4] On January 1, 1864, a court martial held Smith responsible and suspended him for six months.[5]

Smith was wounded in the shoulder at the crater on July 30, 1864, and was granted a forty-five-day leave on August 1.[6] A.H. Edwards, captain of Company A of the 17th Regiment, wrote that Smith's wound disabled him for the rest of the war.[7] Still absent on October 26, Smith had returned to the regiment by November or December. He received another leave of absence on February 14, 1865, but whether or not this leave was wound-related is unclear. Still at home later that month, he found himself cut off by Sherman's troops.[8] He was unable to return to Virginia and was not present at Appomattox Court House on April 9, 1865. Smith survived the war and died in 1867.[9]

Joshua Hilary Hudson of Bennettsville in Marlboro District, major of the 9th Battalion, was promoted to lieutenant colonel of the 26th Regiment on April 29, 1863, with rank from September 9, 1862.[10] While both Colonel Smith and Major Byrd were appointed to their respective ranks in the 26th Regiment on October 7 with rank from September 9, 1862, Hudson was not promoted until the following spring. In a letter to Adjutant and Inspector General Samuel Cooper on January 5, 1863, Hudson sought clarification of his rank and status by submitting a request for an official assignment as lieutenant colonel of the 26th Regiment. Hudson explained that all parties had agreed fully on the consolidation and that the field officers were to be Smith as colonel, Hudson as lieutenant colonel and Byrd as major. He was, he said, the logical choice because he outranked Byrd, although only by six days, and furthermore, he had served as acting lieutenant colonel from the date of his colleagues' appointments. Evidently Cooper agreed, and official appointment to lieutenant colonel followed in April. The controversy did not end there, however. In January 1865, Hudson wrote that Major Byrd had claimed the right to command him by virtue of superior rank. Still later, in 1903, he wrote in his *Sketches and Reminiscences* that when two battalions merged into a regiment, army regulations entitled the major of the larger battalion to promotion to lieutenant colonel of the new regiment, regardless of the date of either officer's commission to major. Thus, since the 9th Battalion was larger than the 6th, it was he, Hudson, who was entitled to be promoted to lieutenant colonel of the 26th Regiment.

Hudson was wounded at Five Forks on April 1, 1865. A Federal soldier standing just a few paces away shot him through the side just below the left lung. Hudson was carried to Ford's Station on the South Side Railroad and left there to die. He was captured there on the third and he lay on the floor of the station without medical attention for six weeks. He was paroled, and he arrived home in mid-May 1865.[11] There is no parole card for Hudson in the CSR. Brigadier General Stephen Elliott wrote in July 1864: "Hudson reminds me, so far as I have seen him, of the party who set Othello, Cassio, Desdemona, and the rest of them so much together by the ears."[12] Hudson was a judge and a popular speaker after the war.

Stephen Decatur Miller Byrd of Williamsburg District, major of the 6th Battalion, was appointed major of the 26th Regiment on October 7 with rank from September 9, 1862.[13] Hudson's commission preceded Byrd's by about six days; Hudson had been elected major of the 9th Battalion on May 19, 1862, and Byrd had been elected major of the 6th Battalion on May 25, 1862. When the 26th Regiment was created, Hudson was appointed to lieutenant colonel and Byrd was appointed to major. Although he served in an acting capacity, however, Hudson was not appointed immediately, and throughout the remainder of 1862 Byrd claimed to outrank Hudson. Contributing to this problem might have been the fact that Byrd was serving detached from the regiment at McClellanville from September 9, 1862, until at least February 1863. The issue was not resolved until Hudson's appointment finally came through in April. Byrd, who probably knew of his rival's imminent appointment to lieutenant colonel, tendered his resignation on April 4, demonstrating the perceived slight by giving his rank as lieutenant colonel. Byrd wrote that he was resigning because of "a difficulty existing between myself and another person concerning the lieutenant colonelcy of the regiment" and because he was a physician and a member of the South Carolina legislature.[14] Byrd's resignation was accepted on April 16, a date also shown in the record as April 23, 1863. He went home to Scranton, in the part of Williamsburg District that is now Florence County, to practice medicine.[15]

Cornelius D. Rowell of Marion District was promoted to major from captain of Company C on May 1, 1863, replacing Byrd. He was wounded at Petersburg in July 1864, and, having been absent on sick leave for some fifty days, Rowell tendered his resignation on September 15, 1864. He said he had suffered from chronic diarrhea complicated by lung disease for the past thirteen months. The resignation was accepted on October 29, 1864.

Ceth Smith Land of Williamsburg District was promoted to major from captain of Company I on December 21, 1864, retroactive to the ninth.[16] Recommending Land for promotion to major, Colonel A.D. Smith wrote on November 15 that he had demonstrated "marked valor and skill" and displayed "great coolness and intrepidity" in command of his company on the skirmish line at Jackson, Mississippi, in July 1863, at Clay's farm on May 20, 1864, and at the crater on July 30, 1864. He added that Land "manifests the highest order of courage and gallantry."[17] Land had shown conspicuous courage on the field during the battle of the crater, where he was wounded in the face, suffered another injury and was carried from the field.[18] He was promoted to major over the more senior Captain J.A. Evans of Company B for this display of valor and skill as provided in an act passed by the Confederate Congress on April 16, 1862. Land, in fact, was in command of the regiment at Appomattox because Colonel Smith was at home and disabled and Lieutenant Colonel Hudson was a prisoner of war. He was paroled on April 9, 1865, at Appomattox Court House.[19]

COMPANIES

Company A, the Bull Creek Guerillas, was previously Company A of the 9th Battalion. Its men were from Horry District. Samuel Smart, captain of the company in the 9th Battalion, was the first captain in the 26th Regiment.[20] He resigned on January 15, 1863, because of his advanced age and "the effects of active service," which had "unfavorably influenced his health."[21] His replacement, First Lieutenant Henry L. Buck, was promoted on January 15, a date also shown in the record as February 21, 1863. Buck was captured on March 25, 1865, while bearing the regimental flag in advance of Fort Stedman and beyond the lines already captured by Evans's Brigade.[22] Taken to the Old Capitol Prison in Washington on the twenty-seventh, Buck was moved to Fort Delaware on March 30 and held there until his release on June 17, 1865.

Company B was previously Company B in the 9th Battalion. Its men were from Chesterfield District. John A. Evans, captain of the company in the 9th Battalion, was also its captain in the 26th Regiment.[23] Company B re-enlisted for the duration of the war in February 1864.[24] Evans was captured at the battle of the Crater on July 30, 1864, and was taken to the Old Capitol Prison in Washington on August 2. He was moved ten days later to Fort Delaware; in late September the *Mercury* reported that he was still there and in good condition.[25] When Rowell resigned in October, Colonel Smith recommended Captain Land of Company I for promotion to major, although Evans was senior to Land and thus next in line. Smith did not recommend Evans for promotion because Evans was "not distinguished for daring or skill."[26] Captain Evans was released from Fort Delaware on June 17, 1865.

Company C, previously Company A of the 6th Battalion, was composed of men from Marion District. Cornelius D. Rowell served as captain in both the 6th Battalion and the 26th Regiment.[27] Rowell was promoted to major on May 1, 1863; First Lieutenant Henry Michael Lofton succeeded him as captain the same day.[28] Lofton had served as captain of Company I, 10th Regiment, SCV, in 1861. He was on sick leave in a Greenville, South Carolina hospital in November and December 1864, and he was absent without leave after February 21, 1865. He probably never returned to the company. At the time of his parole at Appomattox Court House on April 9, 1865, Lieutenant R.H. Rogers was in command of Company C.[29]

Company D, the Irby Rifles, had been Company C in the 9th Battalion. The *Mercury* spelled the name Erby Rifles.[30] Most of the men were from Marlboro District.[31] The rest came from Robson and Brunswick Counties in North Carolina, from Maryland and even from Ireland and Germany. Alexander D. Smith raised the company and served as its first captain in the 9th Battalion. Later he advanced to lieutenant colonel of the 9th Battalion and colonel of the 26th Regiment. First Lieutenant Washington W. Davis succeeded Smith as captain and remained in command of the company when the 26th Regiment was created.[32] Davis was killed on May 20, 1864, at Clay's farm, Virginia.[33] He was considered a "brave and meritorious officer" whose death was "regretted by all who knew him."[34] Alexander "Alex" E. Bristow was promoted from first lieutenant to captain on May 20, 1864. Elected sheriff of Marlboro District, effective January 26, 1865, Bristow accepted the post and resigned his captain's commission on February 9, 1865. He was replaced the same day by First Lieutenant Harris Covington, who was paroled with the regiment at Appomattox Court House on April 9.[35]

Company E, the Watchesaw Rifles, was previously Company D in the 9th Battalion. Most of its men were from Horry District. The rest came from Beaufort, Darlington, Anderson and Charleston Districts. John James Best, elected captain at the reorganization on May 19, 1862, continued in command when the company joined the 26th Regiment.[36] On May 30, 1863, Best tendered his resignation, writing: "I am induced to take this step from a consciousness of my inefficiency to take command of a company."[37] The resignation was accepted on August 7; he was appointed second lieutenant on September 8. Best was captured at Dinwiddie Court House on April 1, 1865, and was taken to the Old Capitol Prison in Washington on the fifth. He was moved four days later to Johnson's Island, Ohio, and held there until his release on June 18, 1865. On Best's resignation— on August 7, 1863—First Lieutenant Edward Bostick, who had been slightly wounded near Jackson, Mississippi, in May or June 1863, was promoted to captain.[38] Considered an "efficient and well-educated officer," Bostick was recommended to command an African American regiment in March 1865.[39] He was shot through the head and killed near Petersburg on April 1, 1865, although both Kirkland and the *Roll of the Dead* record that Bostick was killed on February 15, 1864, at Petersburg. Several facts support 1865 as the year he died: first, the *Mercury* lists Bostick as captain of Company E in May and again in August 1864.[40] Second, the 26th Regiment was stationed in South Carolina in February 1864; and third, the March 1865 recommendation described above, can be found in Bostick's CSR records.

Company F, probably called the Chesterfield Eagles, was from Chesterfield District. It was previously Company E in the 9th Battalion. D. Smilie, or Smily, Wadsworth was elected captain on May 19, 1862, and continued to command the company when it became part of the 26th Regiment.[41] Wadsworth tendered his resignation on June 21, 1864, without giving a reason, but subsequent events provide a clue: Wadsworth was admitted to General Hospital #4 in Richmond on July 4, 1864, with remitting fever; his resignation was accepted on July 11, and he died at the hospital on July 15 or 16. William P. Kirkley was promoted from second lieutenant to captain on August 4, 1864. He was captured at Dinwiddie Court House on April 1, 1865, and was taken to the Old Capitol Prison in Washington on the fifth. He was moved on the ninth to Johnson's Island, Ohio. Kirkley was released on June 18, 1865.

Company G was previously Company F of the 9th Battalion. Its men were from Darlington and Williamsburg Districts.[42] Daniel W. Carter was elected captain on May 19, 1862.[43] He continued to command the company when it became part of the 26th Regiment.[44] Carter was killed by an exploding shell on August 27, 1864, and was not replaced as captain. Kirkland gives the date of Carter's death as August 19.[45]

Company H, the Chesnut Guards, was previously Company B of the 6th Battalion. Its men were primarily from Sumter and Clarendon Districts; a few came from Williamsburg, Charleston and Darlington Districts. First Lieutenant Robert E. Wheeler was elected captain of Company B at the reorganization on May 24, 1862, and he remained in command when the company became part of the 26th Regiment.[46] When Wheeler was killed at the crater on July 30, 1864, First Lieutenant Reece C. Tomlinson was promoted to captain as his replacement, effective the same day. Tomlinson was captured near Petersburg on March 25, 1865, probably at Fort Stedman, and was moved two days later to the Old Capitol Prison in Washington. He was transferred to Fort Delaware on March 30 and was held there until his release on June 17, 1865.

Company I, the Kickapoo Riflemen, was previously Company C of the 6th Battalion. Its men were mostly from Williamsburg and Clarendon Districts; a few came from Sumter District. First Lieutenant Ceth Smith Land was elected captain of Company C on May 24, 1862, and he continued to command when the company became part of the 26th Regiment.[47] In recognition of his valor and skill he was promoted to major on December 21, effective December 9, 1864. He was slightly wounded twice and was not replaced as captain of Company I.[48]

Company K, the Eutaw Rifles, was previously Company G of the 9th Battalion. Made up of men from Horry and Georgetown Districts, the company was probably known earlier as the Floyd Guerillas. George Reynolds Congdon, who had been wounded at Second Manassas, transferred from Company F of the 1st Regiment when he was elected captain on November 11, 1862. Congdon served as the first captain of Company K in the 26th Regiment.[49] He resigned on June 26, 1863, a date also shown in the record as July 5, and was appointed to the Confederate States Navy on January 9, 1864.[50] He served on the steamer *Pee Dee*. First Lieutenant B. Lewis Beaty was promoted to captain on June 26, a date also shown in the record as July 5, 1863. Wounded in the right arm at Petersburg on March 29, 1865, Beaty was treated at the General Hospital at Danville, Virginia. This fact might explain the absence of a parole card in the CSR.

BRIGADE AFFILIATIONS

The 26th Regiment, assigned to the Department of South Carolina, Georgia and Florida, served in Johnson Hagood's Brigade from its creation until May 1863.[51] On May 16, 1863, it was attached to an Independent Brigade created about June 20, 1862, and was commanded by Nathan George "Shanks" Evans. This force, popularly known as the Tramp Brigade, comprised the 17th, 18th, 22nd and 23rd South Carolina Volunteer Regiments and the Holcombe Legion. The Macbeth Artillery was also part of the brigade until late 1863. Evans was in command from July 7, 1862, until April 16, 1864. His successor, William S. "Live Oak" Walker, assumed command on May 20 but was wounded and captured at Clay's farm the same day. Next came Stephen Elliott Jr. His tenure lasted from May 24 until he was badly wounded at the crater on July 30. The last commander, William H. Wallace, led the brigade from July 30, 1864, until the end of the war. The Tramp Brigade served at various times in the Department of South Carolina, Georgia and Florida, the Army of Northern Virginia, the Department of North Carolina and Southern Virginia, the Department of the West and the Department of Mississippi and East Louisiana.[52]

MAJOR MOVEMENTS AND ENGAGEMENTS

The 9th Battalion was sent from Secessionville to Rantowles Station on the Charleston and Savannah Railroad on September 4, 1862, and to Church Flats about three miles away the next day. The 26th Regiment was officially created on September 9 by the consolidation of the 6th and 9th Battalions.[53] The 9th Battalion was present when the regiment was created, but the 6th remained at McClellanville. The entire regiment did not come together, in fact, until December at the earliest and possibly as late as February 1863. The regiment remained at Church Flats and in the Charleston area until May 1863, but some companies were detached from time to time for other duty.[54] For the most part, the regiment performed picket duty and kept close watch on Federal vessels in the coastal waters. The three companies of the old 6th Battalion, C, H and I, were based at McClellanville and at Fort Warren on the Santee River from September 1862 to February 1863 under the command of Major Byrd.[55] A detachment of Company H drew picket duty at Bulls Bay during that time. The seven companies of the old 9th Battalion based at Church Flats were sent to Pocotaligo by rail on October 22, 1862, but returned two days later without engaging the enemy. Company A was based at Yonges Island in March and April 1863.[56] Company H was based at Battery Hagood and Battery Washington from January to April 1863.

On April 25, 1863, Evans's Brigade, comprising the 17th, 18th, 22nd and 23rd Regiments and the Holcombe Legion, was sent from North Carolina to Charleston, arriving on the twenty-sixth. It was ordered to Secessionville on May 4 and to John's Island on the ninth.[57] The 26th Regiment became part of the brigade on May 16, the same day the brigade left South Carolina by rail for Jackson, Mississippi. The major movements and engagements of the brigade are discussed in this volume under the 23rd Regiment. The 26th Regiment surrendered at Appomattox Court House with about 121 men present on April 9, 1865.

14.

THE 27TH REGIMENT, SOUTH CAROLINA VOLUNTEERS

The 27th Regiment, SCV, also called Gaillard's regiment, was created by a special order from the headquarters of the Department of South Carolina, Georgia and Florida, which merged two infantry battalions. Accordingly, on September 30, 1863, the seven companies of Peter C. Gaillard's 1st (Charleston) Infantry Battalion and the three companies of Joseph Abney's 1st Battalion South Carolina Sharpshooters became the 27th Regiment. It was reduced by one company in mid-1864 when the secretary of war ordered the disbanding of Company K because of certain illegalities in its organization. The 27th, the last infantry regiment created in South Carolina, was reorganized in March 1865, when the 7th Battalion, South Carolina Infantry, and remnants of the 11th, 21st and 25th Regiments, SCV, were brought together in a new twelve-company unit known as Rion's Regiment. Composed mostly of Charlestonians, the 27th was considered an excellent regiment when it was under Colonel Gaillard's command.

FIELD OFFICERS

Peter Charles Gaillard of Charleston served as lieutenant colonel of the 1st (Charleston) Infantry Battalion before its merger into the 27th Regiment. An 1835 graduate of the United States Military Academy at West Point, Gaillard had also served in the United States Army until 1838. He was wounded twice while still in the 1st Battalion, first, slightly in the knee at Secessionville on June 16, 1862, and next, more seriously, at Battery Wagner on August 23, 1863, when he suffered injuries to the leg and also to the left hand, which resulted in amputation just above the wrist.[1] Although Gaillard was still recuperating in Charleston in early October, he argued that the loss of a hand should not preclude continued service in the field.[2]

The authorities must have agreed, for on October 17, Gaillard was promoted to colonel of the newly created 27th Regiment, with rank from October 2, 1863. But the wounded arm, still not completely healed, continued to trouble him, and Gaillard applied for an extension of his leave on November 2, 1863. Nearly six months later, on April 23, 1864, Gaillard, with Johnson Hagood's backing, applied for the vacant seat on the South Carolina military court for the Department of South Carolina, Georgia and Florida created by the death of D.F. Jamison. The application was unsuccessful.

In June 1864, because of his wounds, the surgeons required him to leave the Petersburg trenches.[3] He soon returned to the regiment but was captured—and escaped—during Hagood's charge on the Weldon Railroad on July 21, 1864.[4] He was detached from the 27th Regiment on August 18 and detailed to command the post at Weldon, North Carolina, where he remained until his retirement. On March 6, following a February 6, 1865 appearance before a medical examining board, the fifty-two-year-old Gaillard retired to the Invalid Corps. Although he was certainly overage, Gaillard's retirement could be traced directly to the wound he had suffered at Battery Wagner almost two years earlier. From that point on he was assigned to light duty only. Krick records Gaillard's middle name as Cheves, but the memorial marker at the French Protestant Church in Charleston reads Charles.[5] Johnson Hagood lauded Gaillard's "unbounded influence over his command" and called him "every inch a soldier."[6] He was elected Charleston's first postwar mayor.[7]

Julius Augustus Blake of Charleston had served as major of the 1st (Charleston) Battalion since August 1863.[8] Blake, who had been wounded at Secessionville, was promoted to lieutenant colonel of the 27th Regiment on October 17, with rank from October 2, 1863. He sustained a slight wound to the head at Walthall Junction on May 7, 1864, but he returned to duty on May 10 after a few days in a Petersburg hospital.[9] Blake was captured during the charge on the Weldon Railroad on August 21.[10] Three days later he was sent to the Old Capitol Prison in Washington, and on August 29 he was transferred to Fort Delaware.[11] Blake was paroled on October 30 and was moved to Point Lookout; on October 31, 1864, he was exchanged.[12] He was received, along with 3,023 other prisoners of war, at Venus Point on the Savannah River on November 15 and granted a thirty-day leave.[13] After the exchange Blake became ill and returned home. On December 31 Johnson Hagood, who viewed him as an ineffective and negative officer, asked that Blake be dropped from the rolls as absent without leave.[14] Discharged from the hospital on January 6, 1865, Blake was ordered to report to the 27th Regiment. When he was dropped from the rolls on January 27 for overstaying his leave, Blake appealed the decision on the grounds of a grave injustice.[15] A board of inquiry was formed at Hoke's Division camp near Rockfish, North Carolina, on February 25 to investigate Blake's case. Convened on March 4, the board found that after his exchange Blake was granted leave until December 13, 1864, but that he was in poor health and was admitted to a hospital in Charleston. The board found further that he was discharged from the hospital on January 6 and reported to his command the next day. Concluding that Blake was absent with authority until December 13 and that he rejoined his command as soon as his health and circumstances permitted, the board recommended his reinstatement. The fact that Blake was not replaced as lieutenant colonel supports this recommendation, although Hagood wrote after the war that the decision of the board was never announced.[16] Hagood also continued to insist that Blake failed to gain the confidence of his men and that the regiment was less efficient when Blake commanded in Gaillard's absence.[17]

Joseph Abney of Edgefield District was colonel of the 22nd Regiment, SCV, for the first few months of 1862, but he was not re-elected at the reorganization, possibly because of poor health; he was dropped from the rolls on May 5, 1862. He was appointed major of the 1st Battalion Sharpshooters on June 21, 1862, and a little over a year later, on October 2, 1863, Abney was appointed major of the 27th Regiment. He suffered a wound in the right side at Drewry's Bluff on May 16, 1864, and he probably never returned to the regiment.[18] A sketch in *Recollections and Reminiscences* says Abney was shot through the body and lung at Drewry's Bluff and never fully recovered from the wound.[19] Still absent on December 31, 1864, Abney was a patient in Pettigrew General Hospital #3 in Raleigh on January 30, 1865, undergoing treatment for chronic diarrhea and rheumatism. One card in the CSR says he returned to duty on January 24, but the hospitalization makes this date suspect. Abney retired to the Invalid Corps on March 6, 1865. He was ordered to Edgefield and Barnwell Districts under Brigadier General B.D. Fry to "induce agriculturists to send their produce to government depots for security."[20] According to Hagood, "Abney was a brave man, but his habits were not good, and his virtues were rather passive than active." He also wrote that Abney lacked "sufficient élan and failed to command the [men's] confidence" and that the regiment was far less efficient under Abney's command.[21] Abney's death in 1870 was attributed to his war wound.

COMPANIES

Company A, the Calhoun Guards, or Guard, was previously Company E of the Charleston Battalion.[22] Made up of men from Charleston, its captain,

Francis "Frank" Turquand Miles, MD, commanded the company in both the battalion and 27th Regiment.[23] Miles had been wounded at Secessionville in June 1862. He had also been stunned by a shell at Battery Wagner on August 17, 1863, but he refused to be relieved. Miles tendered his resignation on April 5, 1864; it was accepted on the eighteenth,[24] and Miles's replacement, 1st Lieutenant Barnwell W. Palmer, was promoted to captain the same day.[25] Miles was accepted by the army Medical Board as a surgeon, and subsequently he served in the Medical Department. The first Federal shell fired at dawn on June 16, 1864, exploded in the Petersburg lines, killing both Barnwell Palmer and Captain Hopkins of Company D, along with fifteen or sixteen other men.[26] Johnson Hagood wrote that Palmer "was an efficient officer."[27] First Lieutenant J. Waring Axson, who was promoted to captain on June 16, commanded the company for only eight days after Palmer's death.[28] Axson had been wounded at Secessionville and again, although only slightly in the right knee, at Battery Wagner on August 17, 1863. He suffered a mortal wound in the early stages of the charge of the 11th, 21st and 27th Regiments on June 24, 1864, at Petersburg.[29] He lingered painfully for several hours on the battlefield before he died.[30] Axson was not replaced as captain.[31]

Company B, the Charleston Light Infantry, had also been Company B in the 1st (Charleston) Battalion.[32] On August 14, 1863, Company B of the 1st (Charleston) Battalion was divided into two companies designated B and G. The newly created Company G was also called the Charleston Light Infantry. Company B of the battalion became Company B of the 27th Regiment, and the new Company G became Company K in September 1863. Although most of its men were from Charleston, Spartanburg District and Ireland, a few came from Richland, Colleton, Orangeburg, Newberry, Abbeville and Union Districts. Still others came from Georgia, North Carolina, Maryland and Pennsylvania, as well as England, France and Prussia. Thomas Y. Simons, who was elected captain on February 17, 1862, mustered in Confederate service on March 24 while the company was still in the battalion; he remained in command when the 27th Regiment was formed.[33] Simons was often absent from the company, generally for service as a judge advocate in courts-martial. He tendered his resignation on March 14, 1865, citing both poor health and his recent appointment as judge advocate general for the state of South Carolina. The resignation was approved all the way through Major General McLaws, but evidently Simons remained with the regiment because the record indicates he was paroled on May 1, 1865, at Greensboro.

Company C, the Union Light Infantry Volunteers, was previously Company F in the 1st (Charleston) Battalion. It was also called the "Union

Light Infantry Volunteers and German Fusiliers," reflecting the two militia companies that originally formed its ranks. Most of its men were from Charleston's Scottish population, but some came from York and Spartanburg Districts.[34] First Lieutenant Samuel Lord Jr. was promoted to captain on April 16, effective May 3, 1862, the date the company was attached to the battalion.[35] Lord retained command in the 27th Regiment. He received a thirty-day medical leave on December 13, 1863, for treatment of congestion of the liver. Near the end of his furlough, on January 2, 1864, Lord received an extension to allow him to prepare his resignation. Submitted on January 14, the resignation was accepted on January 26. In the meantime, Confederate States District Attorney James Conner appointed Lord to the post of district attorney pro tem under the terms of an act of the Confederate Congress that allowed such appointments when sitting district attorneys were serving in the field.[36] First Lieutenant George W. Brown was promoted to captain on January 26, 1864. Brown had been wounded at Secessionville on June 16, 1862, and at Battery Wagner on July 18, 1863, when a shell fragment struck the top of his head.[37] He was injured in the face and shoulder by a shell near Petersburg on June 22, 1864, and he died only a few hours later.[38] One report in the *Charleston Daily Courier* states that Brown died on the twenty-third.[39] According to the *Mercury*, he was killed on June 24, but another issue of the *Charleston Daily Courier* reported that Brown was wounded on the twenty-fourth and died the next day.[40] Still another date, June 21, appears in Kirkland's account.[41]

Company D was called the Sumter Guards, the Sumter Guard Volunteers and the Gamecocks, all names honoring South Carolina Revolutionary War General Thomas Sumter.[42] This company of Charleston men was previously Company D in the 1st (Charleston) Battalion.[43] J. Ward Hopkins was promoted to captain on June 16 or 17, 1862, and retained command in the 27th Regiment.[44] He was killed at Petersburg on June 16, 1864, as described earlier under Company A.[45] Evidently, he was highly regarded; Brigadier General Johnson Hagood wrote that "after Colonel Gaillard, [Hopkins] commanded the respect and confidence of the men and his superiors more perhaps than any other officer in [the regiment]. His loss was a calamity to the regiment."[46] First Lieutenant John A. Cay was promoted to captain on June 16, 1864.[47] Cay had suffered a slight wound to the left calf at Battery Wagner on July 18, 1863. He was wounded again, this time in the right thigh, in May 1864. Although Cay was present with the regiment in January 1865, no parole card appears in the CSR.

Company E, also called the Union Light Infantry and German Fusiliers, was previously Company A in the 1st Battalion of Sharpshooters. Its men were from a number of districts: Charleston, Lexington, Newberry,

Orangeburg, Sumter, Spartanburg, Laurens, Barnwell, Edgefield, Pickens, Anderson, Richland and York. Robert Chisolm, who was appointed captain on July 23, with rank from June 22, 1862, retained command in the 27th Regiment.[48] While serving with a detachment of prison guards on James Island on May 7, 1864, Chisolm requested relief to return to the 27th Regiment, which had just been sent to Virginia. He was sick and sent to the rear on June 22 and was still absent on authority of a surgeon's certificate on August 8, 1864.[49] Chisolm was appointed to serve as one of the officers in a court-martial on November 15, 1864. While court was in session, he received conflicting orders, creating a dilemma that ended with his arrest. The president of the court, Lieutenant Colonel Clement G. Wright of the 66th North Carolina Regiment, ordered Chisolm to attend court proceedings on December 10, and at the same time General Hagood ordered him to march with his regiment, which was then moving out, possibly to meet the enemy. Chisolm was unsuccessful in an attempt to clarify matters. He concluded that Wright's authority in this case was paramount and stayed behind. Hagood had Chisolm arrested and charged with conduct prejudicial to good order and military discipline and with conduct unbecoming an officer and a gentleman. Chisolm was tried and acquitted in 1865. No further record for Chisolm appears in the CSR, but his letters indicate he was with the regiment in March or April 1865.[50]

Company F, the Sumter Guards, was previously Company B of the 1st Battalion of Sharpshooters. Although Companies D and F of the 27th Regiment bore the same name, their origins were unrelated. Company F men were from all over the state: they came from Georgetown, Beaufort, Charleston, Edgefield, Marion, Laurens, Clarendon, Sumter, Barnwell, Lexington, Anderson, Darlington, Greenville and Richland Districts. Joseph Blyth Allston, who was appointed captain on June 23, 1862, in the 1st Battalion Sharpshooters, retained command in the 27th Regiment.[51] Some cards in the CSR spell his name Alston, but his signature on official documents is Allston. Allston was wounded at Pocotaligo and again, this time a slight one to the ankle, at Drewry's Bluff on May 16, 1864.[52] The *Confederate Veteran* records, incorrectly, that he was captured at Fort Fisher on January 15, 1865.[53] Allston was captured, but the place was Town Creek, North Carolina, and the date was February 20. He was commanding the regiment at the time. Taken to Fort Anderson at Point Lookout, Maryland, on February 28, he was moved to the Old Capitol Prison in Washington the same day. Allston was transferred to Fort Delaware on March 24 and was released on June 17, 1865. J.G. Pressley considered Allston one of the best officers of both Gaillard's regiment and Hagood's Brigade. Julius D. Huguenin commanded Company F with the rank of first lieutenant. He was also captured at Town Creek on February 20 and was imprisoned at Fort Delaware. On March 25, 1865, although he was in prison at the time, Huguenin was promoted to captain of a company in Rion's Regiment for his skill and valor and was released from prison on June 17, 1865.[54]

Company G, called both the Charleston Sharpshooters and the Palmetto Guard, was previously Company C in the 1st Battalion of Sharpshooters. Its men came primarily from Spartanburg, Orangeburg, Laurens, Union and Charleston Districts, although a few were from Newberry, Marion, Barnwell and Lexington Districts. Henry Buist was appointed captain on June 24, 1862, when the company was in the battalion, and he retained command in the 27th Regiment.[55] About August 26, 1863, the secretary of war authorized raising an artillery company for incorporation into the 20th Regiment. Its colonel requested on October 2 that Buist be appointed captain, and Buist was soon given command of the new company. Buist's Company Light Artillery was supposed to comprise men transferring from other companies in the 20th Regiment and officers and some men from Company G of the 27th. The rolls of Company G, in fact, confirm that a large number of men transferred to Buist's Company by Special Order Number 323 on September 9, 1863. The new company served at Mount Pleasant for its entire seven-month existence. Its creation was later determined illegal, so Buist's Artillery Company was never officially organized. On April 11, 1864, its men, including those from the 27th Regiment, were ordered to return to their former commands. Throughout the month of May, Buist's Company was listed as heavy artillery attached to the 27th Regiment.[56] Company G left Charleston on May 29 and rejoined the 27th in Virginia on June 4. On June 24, Buist was wounded. He and forty other men of Company G were captured on the enemy's works near Petersburg.[57] He was taken to Bermuda Hundreds and on to Fort Monroe, Virginia, the next day. Moved to Point Lookout, Maryland, on the twenty-sixth, he was sent to the Old Capitol Prison in Washington on June 30. A month later, on July 22, Buist was moved to Fort Delaware for another month. He was transported to Hilton Head Island on August 20 and was sent to Morris Island later that month. There, as one of the "Immortal Six Hundred" Confederate officers and prisoners of war, he was intentionally exposed to Confederate cannon fire.[58] On October 3, 1864, Buist was exchanged in Charleston Harbor for Captain J.G. McWilliams of the 57th Illinois Volunteers by order of the secretary of war.[59] Most of the remaining six hundred Confederate officers were transferred to Fort Pulaski on October 21.[60] Buist was absent without leave after December 31. He never served in the field after his capture, and he resigned on February 4, 1865.

Company H, the Irish Volunteers, was previously Company C in the 1st (Charleston) Battalion. The prewar militia company called the Irish

Volunteers raised two companies for Confederate service from within its ranks: Company K of Gregg's 1st Regiment, SCV, and Company C of the 1st (Charleston) Battalion. Both were called the Irish Volunteers, and Company C retained the name when it became Company H of the 27th Regiment. William Hasett Ryan, captain of Company C in the battalion, was killed at Battery Wagner on July 18, 1863; First Lieutenant James M. Mulvaney's promotion to captain took effect the same day.[61] Mulvaney retained command in the 27th Regiment.[62] While "literally upon the enemy's works, waving his cap and cheering on his men," Mulvaney was captured near Petersburg on June 24, 1864.[63] Information in the *Confederate Veteran* that he was captured on May 7, 1864, is incorrect.[64] Taken to Bermuda Hundreds the day he was captured, Mulvaney was moved several times: to Fort Monroe on June 25; to Point Lookout, Maryland, on the twenty-sixth; to Old Capitol Prison in Washington on the twenty-ninth; to Fort Delaware on July 22; and, finally, to Hilton Head Island on August 20. Mulvaney was sent to Morris Island as one of the "Immortal Six Hundred" later that month.[65] He was transferred to Fort Pulaski on October 21, 1864, along with most of the other six hundred officers.[66] Mulvaney took the oath of allegiance while a prisoner of war, a fact that probably explains the lack of a parole card in the CSR.[67]

Company I, the Charleston Riflemen, was previously Company A of the 1st (Charleston) Battalion.[68] Its men were from Charleston. William Dove Walter was promoted from first lieutenant to captain on August 5, a date also shown in the record as October 2, 1863.[69] Julius Blake, who had served as major of the battalion since August 1863, also acted as lieutenant colonel from the creation of the 27th Regiment, although his commission was dated October 2, 1863. Walter's case was similar: he, too, had probably acted as Company I's captain since August 1863, and his commission was probably dated October 2 as well. When the battalion merged into the 27th Regiment, Walter retained command.[70] On sick furlough since June 18, 1864, because of remittent fever, he never returned to the regiment and retired to the Invalid Corps on December 23. Walter was assigned to the South Carolina reserve forces on January 3, 1865, and survived the war.

Company K, the Charleston Light Infantry, was previously Company G in the 1st (Charleston) Battalion. It was created on August 14, 1863, by a special order dividing the battalion's Company B into two companies, designated B and G. Company B became Company B in the 27th Regiment in September 1863; Company G became Company K of the 27th Regiment, made up of men from Charleston and Spartanburg Districts, Ireland and various other parts of the state. William Clarkson, previously first lieutenant in Company B, was appointed captain of Company G on August 14, 1863.[71]

He retained command when the regiment was created in September 1863.[72] Clarkson had been slightly wounded at Battery Wagner on July 18, 1863. The secretary of war determined on April 1, 1864, that Company K had been organized illegally; accordingly, he ordered the company disbanded, a move that left the regiment with only nine companies. Clarkson was still listed as captain of Company K while hospitalized at General Hospital #9 in Richmond on June 2, 1864, and the actual dissolution of the company probably didn't take place until July 11. The officers of Company K were sent back to their original positions in Company B.

BRIGADE AFFILIATIONS

The 27th Regiment, created on September 30, 1863, was attached to Johnson Hagood's new brigade, which itself had been organized by special order of P.G.T. Beauregard only ten days earlier. The Charleston Battalion had been attached to Hagood's Brigade from September 20 to September 30.[73] After September 30, Hagood's Brigade consisted of the 7th Battalion, South Carolina Infantry and the 11th, 21st, 25th and 27th Regiments, SCV. Although all its elements had seen prior service, they had not been brought together into a brigade until this point. In early March 1865, the 7th Battalion was consolidated with remnants of the 11th, 21st, 25th and 27th Regiments to form a new twelve-company regiment under the command of Lieutenant Colonel James H. Rion. This consolidated regiment of about five hundred men was placed in a new brigade commanded by Johnson Hagood. The other major components were Hedricks's 40th North Carolina Regiment and Taylor's Consolidated 36th North Carolina and 1st North Carolina Battalion of Heavy Artillery. The North Carolina troops were reassigned to other brigades on March 31, 1865, and Rion took command of Hagood's Brigade, which reverted back to its original composition.

MAJOR MOVEMENTS AND ENGAGEMENTS

The 1st (Charleston) Battalion was stationed in Charleston as provost guard in late September 1863, having completed a two-week tour of duty at Fort Sumter in mid-September. Six of its seven companies were transferred to Legare's Point on James Island in late September and early October to join the 27th Regiment. Company K, created in August 1863, left Charleston for James Island on October 29. The three companies of the former 1st Battalion Sharpshooters, E, F and G, were stationed in Georgetown and nearby Battery White from early June 1863 to mid-September.[74] They left Georgetown on the twenty-third and arrived at James Island five days later to join the 27th Regiment. All ten companies were stationed on James Island by October 29.[75]

The regiment remained on James Island with its companies taking turns with garrison duty at Fort Sumter until late April 1864.[76] Most of the regiment was stationed at Lighthouse Point guarding the batteries there from late 1863 until April 1864. Company B was detached to Fort Sumter from November 22 to December 5, 1863, and from December 16 to December 27. Company D manned Fort Sumter from November 22 to December 4 and from December 16 to December 29.[77] Company D was sent back several times in 1864: from January 9 to January 21, from February 2 to February 23 and from March 3 to March 24. Company E took its turn on December 17 and served until the thirtieth.[78] Company F was at Fort Sumter from January 1 to January 22, 1864.[79] Company G was sent to Battery Gary in Mount Pleasant from January to early April 1864, and was sent to Battery Rutledge on Sullivan's Island on April 9.[80] Company H went to Fort Sumter on February 2 and was relieved, probably on the twentieth.[81] Company C was sent to Fort Sumter on February 10.[82] Company I was sent on March 6 to relieve Company C and remained there until the twelfth.[83] On the twelfth Company D relieved Company I.[84] Company F relieved Company E on April 5. Company K, the last company of the 27th to serve at Fort Sumter, left on May 1.[85]

Hagood's Brigade was ordered to Virginia on April 28, 1864.[86] The 27th Regiment, probably without Company K, left James Island bound for Wilmington on the twenty-ninth.[87] Most of the regiments in Hagood's Brigade arrived at Wilmington about the same time. From this time until the end of the war, the 27th Regiment served with Hagood's Brigade. Its major movements and engagements are discussed in this volume under the 11th Regiment. In early March 1865, Hagood's Brigade was consolidated into a twelve-company regiment. Lieutenant Colonel Rion took command of the new regiment, which went by his name. Rion's Regiment comprised the 7th Battalion and remnants of the 11th, 21st, 25th and 27th Regiments—an aggregate of about 500 men. On April 26, Generals Johnston and Sherman agreed on articles of a military convention, effectively surrendering Johnston's army. Following the announcement of surrender on the twenty-seventh, officers signed for and received paroles for their men on May 1 and 2. Hagood's Brigade surrendered about 40 officers and 510 men. The men broke camp on May 3 and marched toward Lancaster Court House, South Carolina, where they were given their paroles. The remnants of Hagood's Brigade (Rion's Regiment) were disbanded at Lancaster on May 7.

1. Ellerbe Boggan Crawford Cash of Chesterfield District, a major general in the South Carolina Militia at the start of the war, was elected colonel of the 8th Regiment in March 1861. Not re-elected at the reorganization in May 1862, he was colonel of the 2nd Regiment, South Carolina Reserves in late 1862 and early 1863. In 1880 Cash killed William McCreight Shannon in a duel in present-day Lee County. *Courtesy South Caroliniana Library, University of South Carolina, Columbia.*

2. Thomas Epaphroditus Howle was captain of the Darlington Grays, Company F, 8th Regiment, in 1861 and a new company, M, in the spring of 1862. He was mortally wounded in September 1862 at Sharpsburg and died on the field. *Courtesy Old Darlington District Chapter SCGS and The War Between the States Museum.*

3. James E. Bass became captain of the Darlington Grays, Company F, 8th Regiment, in October 1863. He was wounded at Sharpsburg and Berryville. *Courtesy Old Darlington District Chapter SCGS and The War Between the States Museum.*

4. Arthur Middleton Manigault was colonel of the 10th Regiment and was promoted to brigadier general in April 1863. Wounded in the head at the battle of Franklin, Tennessee, in November 1864 and incapacitated for the rest of the war, he died from lingering effects of the wound in 1886. *Courtesy South Caroliniana Library, University of South Carolina, Columbia.*

5. James Fowler Pressley, a physician from Society Hill and graduate of the Citadel, served as a captain, lieutenant colonel and colonel in the 10th Regiment. Incapacitated by a shoulder wound at the battle of Atlanta in July 1864, he never rejoined the regiment. In October 1864 he was elected to the South Carolina House of Representatives from Williamsburg District and commanded Confederate troops at the battle of Dingle's Mill in April 1865. *Courtesy Old Darlington District Chapter SCGS and The War Between the States Museum.*

6. Benjamin Burgh Smith Jr. was a graduate of the Citadel. He served as major of the 11th Regiment in 1861 and 1862, as major of the 2nd Battalion Sharpshooters later in 1862, as assistant adjutant general to General S.R. Gist and as colonel of the Consolidated 16th and 24th Regiment in 1865. *Courtesy The Citadel Archives & Museum.*

7. Cornelius Irvine Walker, first honor graduate of the Citadel Academy's class of 1861, was assistant adjutant general of Manigault's Brigade and lieutenant colonel of the 10th Regiment. Wounded twice, he survived the war and was very active in post-war veterans' activities. He wrote a historical sketch of the 10th Regiment. *Courtesy The Citadel Archives & Museum.*

8. Josiah S. Bedon was captain of the Summerville Guards, Company C, 11th Regiment, from July 1861 to May 1862. *Courtesy The South Carolina Confederate Relic Room and Museum, Columbia.*

9. Charles Henry Simonton, a prominent Charleston lawyer and lieutenant colonel of the 11th (Eutaw) Battalion in early 1862, was appointed colonel of the 25th Regiment in July 1862. Spending most of the war on detached service, he was captured with the 25th at Town Creek near Wilmington in February 1865. Simonton was released in June 1865. *From* Cyclopedia of Eminent and Representative Men of the Carolinas of the Nineteenth Century, *1892.*

10. Alonzo Timothy Dargan, a lawyer from Darlington, mustered in service as a lieutenant in Company B, 21st Regiment, and was commissioned its lieutenant colonel in January 1862. While trying to rally his men, he was struck in the chest by a Minié ball and killed instantly near Walthall Junction on May 7, 1864. *Courtesy The South Carolina Confederate Relic Room and Museum, Columbia.*

11. John Chapel Clements commanded the Wilds Rifles, Company B, 21st Regiment, even after losing an eye at Battery Wagner in July 1863. First lieutenant, not captain, was his highest rank. Captured at Petersburg in June 1864, he was exchanged that October. Clements returned to the company only to be captured again at Fort Fisher, North Carolina, in January 1865. He was finally exchanged in March. *Courtesy Old Darlington District Chapter SCGS and The War Between the States Museum.*

13. John Franklin Abraham Elliott was captain of Company H, 21st Regiment, from January 1862 until his unexpected death in January 1863. *Courtesy Old Darlington District Chapter SCGS and The War Between the States Museum.*

12. Henry Laurens Benbow of Clarendon District was elected colonel of the 23rd Regiment in April 1862. Suspended for six months in 1863 for deficiencies within the regiment, he was severely wounded, and captured, at Five Forks in April 1865 and released on June 15. *Courtesy Old Darlington District Chapter SCGS and The War Between the States Museum.*

14. Stephen Elliott Jr. started the war as captain of the Beaufort Volunteer Artillery and, always associated with various South Carolina units, rose steadily through the ranks to brigadier general by 1864. *Courtesy The State Printing Company.*

15. John Marshall Whilden was major of the 23rd Regiment. After being severely wounded in the back and thigh at the battle of Second Manassas, he continued to lead the regiment in a series of charges, but fell mortally wounded. Whilden died a week later. *Courtesy The Citadel Archives & Museum.*

16. Angus McLean McRae was elected captain of Company G, 23rd Regiment, in April 1862. Mortally wounded during the battle of Second Manassas on August 30, he died the same day. *Courtesy Elizabeth McRae Hamrick and The South Carolina Confederate Relic Room and Museum, Columbia.*

17. James Ferdinand Izlar (left) was captain of the Edisto Rifles, Company G, 25th Regiment. Captured at Fort Fisher in January 1865 and taken to Fort Columbus in New York Harbor, he was exchanged in March. John Vinyard Glover (right) was also captain of the Edisto Rifles and became major of the 25th Regiment in July 1862. He died in June 1864 from complications of being kicked in the leg by a horse. *Courtesy The State Printing Company.*

18. William Wallace Harlee, a delegate to the Secession Convention, commanded Harlee's Legion, South Carolina Militia, until it was disbanded in early 1862. He was also lieutenant governor and postmaster of South Carolina, and the founder of Florence. *Courtesy of South Caroliniana Library, University of South Carolina, Columbia.*

19. Benjamin Huger Rutledge, previously captain of an independent company called the Charleston Light Dragoons, became the 4th Cavalry Regiment's only colonel. He served on detached duty for long periods of time during the war. *From* Cyclopedia of Eminent and Representative Men of the Carolinas of the Nineteenth Century, *1892.*

20. Samuel Wragg Ferguson, a graduate of West Point, was a captain in the 1st Regiment, South Carolina Infantry (Regulars), briefly in early 1861. He refused an appointment as colonel of the 5th Regiment, South Carolina Cavalry, because he was lieutenant colonel of the 28th Regiment, Mississippi Cavalry, at the time. Ferguson, who was promoted to brigadier general in 1863, was given a command in the western army. *Courtesy the United States Military Academy Archives.*

21. David Gregg McIntosh, a lawyer from Society Hill, was captain of Company D, 1st Regiment (the Pee Dee Rifles), which became the Pee Dee Light Artillery in March 1862. Independent for the next two years, the battery became Company C, 18th Battalion, South Carolina Artillery, in June 1864. McIntosh was promoted to major in March 1863 and given command of an artillery battalion. He was eventually promoted to colonel and named chief of artillery for the Second Corps. *Courtesy South Caroliniana Library, University of South Carolina, Columbia.*

MAJ. JAS. F. HART.

22. James Franklin Hart, a Union lawyer before the war, commanded the Washington Artillery, South Carolina Volunteers, which served with both the Hampton Legion and as an independent battery. Though he lost a leg at Burgess's Mill in October 1864, Hart returned to duty in February 1865 and was promoted to major. *Courtesy The State Printing Company.*

15.

INDEPENDENT INFANTRY ORGANIZATIONS

THE ORDNANCE GUARDS–SOUTH CAROLINA

The Ordnance Guards–South Carolina was commanded by Captain Thomas D. Dotterer. The company was organized on February 22, 1862. Its troops were part of the local defense of Charleston and were employees of foundries and workshops who had been organized under the authority of the governor and Executive Council.[1] The CSR records the following: "We, the undersigned Artizans connected with the various workshops, employed in State Service, hereby agree to form ourselves into a company, for the defense of this city, when so ordered, for the term of 12 months, under the name and style of the 'Ordnance Guards.'"

CAPTAIN RHETT'S COMPANY, SOUTH CAROLINA

Captain Rhett's Company, South Carolina, was also called the Brooks Home Guards and the Brooks Guards. This company of Charlestonians was organized on January 9, 1861. The *Mercury* names John E. Carew as captain in January 1861, but the CSR shows him at the rank of third lieutenant.[2] Andrew Burnet Rhett was captain of the company in early 1861 when it was attached to the 17th Regiment, South Carolina Militia. Most of the Brooks Home Guards were employed on the railroads throughout the war; the company was never in active service.[3] The *Memory Roll* records the following:

> *Note: Gen'l A M Manigault,*
> *Dear Gen'l*
> *This company was never in active service and do not believe they ever fired a gun. It was what was then termed the Home Guards, and was never*

attached to Kershaw's Reg't and in fact the best part of them never did a day's service. Nearly all of them being employed during the whole war on railroads.
very respectfully S.C. Gilbert
Ex Orderly Serg't Brooks Guards and
Ex Lieut. Of Brooks Artillery.

A volunteer detachment of the Brooks Home Guards, called the Brooks Guard Volunteers, was organized in Charleston on May 8, 1861, and was augmented by some recruits from Pickens District. It became Company K of Kershaw's 2nd Regiment, SCV, hence the above-mentioned reference to Kershaw's regiment.[4] Andrew Burnet Rhett, captain of the Brooks Home Guard, was elected captain by the volunteer detachment of the Brooks Guards in late April. Brooks called for more volunteers to go to Virginia.[5] In 1862 Rhett and sixty-one Company K men asked for and received special permission to reorganize after serving only eight months of their twelve-month term of enlistment.[6] They re-enlisted for two years before February 12, 1862, and they formed a new artillery company known as Fickling's Battery or the Brooks Light Artillery.[7]

CAPTAIN JOHN SYMONS'S COMPANY, NAVAL BRIGADE, SOUTH CAROLINA VOLUNTEERS

Captain John Symons's Company, Naval Brigade, SCV, was also called the Sea Fencibles. John Symons was elected captain of the Richardson Guards, previously the Palmetto Fire Company, in January 1861 and served until March 1.[8] In late April, the Richardson Guards was detached from the 17th Militia Regiment to become Company M of Maxcy Gregg's 1st (six-month) Regiment. Meanwhile, Symons and a group of like-minded seafaring men decided to form a new company to establish some sort of coastal observation and defense. The first organizational meeting was held on June 17, 1861.[9] A second followed around July 23.[10] The men elected the fifty-two-year-old Symons as captain at one of these meetings. The men were of limited personal means and could not afford to pay for uniforms and equipment.[11] Even so, Symons and the Sea Fencibles mustered in Confederate service at Charleston on August 6, 1861, for the duration of the war.

THE BUREAU BATTALION, CHARLESTON, SOUTH CAROLINA

The Bureau Battalion, Charleston, South Carolina, commanded by a Major Echols, was probably created on May 5, 1864, for the emergency defense of Charleston.[12] It consisted of about seventy men, most of whom were clerks, miscellaneous employees and detailed men. The battalion was called out to help man the "New Lines" on James Island on July 2, 1864, in response to the Federal assault there.[13] Stationed at James Island until July 11, it was exposed to some artillery fire.

CAPTAIN L.H. CHARBONNIER'S COMPANY, SOUTH CAROLINA MILITIA

Captain L.H. Charbonnier's Company, South Carolina Militia, was also known variously as the Pickens Rifles, the Pickens Guard and the Pickens Cadets.[14] It was organized after the bombardment of Fort Sumter in April 1861 and was attached to the 16th Regiment, South Carolina Militia, as the right file company. The company was attached to the 1st Regiment, South Carolina Reserves, later in 1861 and 1862.[15] It was the only independent boy company in the state in 1861.[16] According to the *Memory Roll*, all the members were fourteen to sixteen years old, but the *Mercury* reported that the members' ages ranged from sixteen to eighteen.[17] The company, originally called the Pickens Cadets, was made up of students at B.R. Carroll's Academy in Charleston; Carroll himself was a private in the company, and S.K. McDonald served as the first captain.[18] Governor Pickens accepted the Pickens Cadets into state service in the spring or early summer of 1861. By August, the members had changed the company's name to the Pickens Rifles simply because the governor armed them with Mississippi Rifles. In August 1861, the *Mercury* referred to the company as both the Pickens Guard and the Pickens Rifles.[19] McDonald resigned as captain either because he was too young or because he was hurt in a camp accident. The CSR does not list him at the rank of captain, probably because he served as second lieutenant after the company entered Confederate service on November 13, 1861. Professor L.H. Charbonnier was elected captain at about the same time.

From enlistment to January 6, 1862, the Pickens Rifles was assigned to Roswell Ripley's military headquarters, where the men performed camp and guard duty. They guarded stores and supplies on the Southern Wharf in Charleston and salvaged stores after the 1861 fire.[20] The company was in Confederate service less than three months—from November 13, 1861, until January 6, 1862. When all the state organizations were merged into the Confederate army in early 1862, the Pickens Rifles lost its distinctive character because its ranks were rapidly decimated when members joined other companies.[21] There is no record of the company's existence after August 21, 1862.

THE CHARLESTON ARSENAL BATTALION, LOCAL DEFENSE TROOPS, SOUTH CAROLINA

The Charleston Arsenal Battalion, Local Defense Troops, South Carolina was composed of employees of the Charleston Arsenal, who were organized into volunteer companies for the defense of the city. Major J.T. Trezevant commanded the battalion. The CSR contains a report of organization dated July 13, 1863, and the *Mercury* of July 15 implies that the battalion had been organized only recently.[22] The battalion consisted of 333 men aged sixteen to sixty. It was divided into five companies of roughly equal size. Thomas B. Ford was captain of Company A, which had 70 men. Captain W. Tweedy commanded the 76 men of Company B, Captain J. Peterson the 66 men of Company C and Robert James served as captain of the 63-man Company D.[23] C.H. Anders commanded the 58 men of Company E.

ESTILL'S COMPANY OF INFANTRY, SOUTH CAROLINA VOLUNTEERS FOR LOCAL DEFENSE

Estill's Company of Infantry, SCV, for Local Defense was also called Captain Estill's Company of South Carolina Infantry Local Defense-Arsenal Company Charleston and The Arsenal Guard, Charleston, South Carolina.[24] Captain Alex D. Estill, assistant superintendent of state gunboat construction at Charleston, commanded the company. The adjutant general authorized its formation from employees of the Ordnance Department of the Canonsboro Arsenal and Workshop in Charleston; accordingly this company was organized on February 18, 1862, for the defense of The Arsenal and the city of Charleston.[25] Estill's Company mustered in Confederate service for a twelve-month term on February 20 and was detailed by order of District Commander General Roswell Ripley, on the same day. This unit was unrelated to Trezevant's Charleston Arsenal Battalion.

THE FIRE COMPANIES OF CHARLESTON

The fire companies of Charleston were organized into several volunteer military corps and incorporated into the 4th Brigade South Carolina Militia in late 1860. This group was probably known as the Fire Battalion. The governor called the 4th Brigade into active service on December 20, 1860. The 4th Brigade, numbering 1,531 men on December 27, served as the backbone of the defenses around Charleston Harbor until April 1861. Along with the small South Carolina Regular Army, the 4th Brigade constituted a large portion of those forces engaged with Fort Sumter on April 12 and April 13. By January 1861, many of the members of the Fire Department of the City of Charleston had volunteered for service in other organizations, leaving the city short of men to fight fires and patrol the streets. The Fire Department was considered so strategic that on January 28, 1861, the General Assembly passed an act requiring members of the Board of Fire Masters, officers of the Fire Department and officers and members of the various Fire Engine and Axe Companies of the City of Charleston to consider themselves subject to the mayor's call to perform armed patrol or guard duty in the city.[26] The Fire Brigade was actually sent to James Island on July 2, 1864, because of Federal activity there.[27]

Firefighters with the Phoenix Fire Company formed their own company, called the Phoenix Rifles, and elected Peter C. Gaillard captain. When Gaillard was elected colonel of the 17th Regiment, South Carolina Militia, in September 1861, the men chose Lewis F. Robertson as their captain.[28] Robertson resigned in January 1862.[29]

The Aetna Fire Company formed a company called the Aetna Rifles, or the Aetna Guard, on December 6, 1860.[30] E.F. Sweegan was elected captain.

The Vigilant Fire Engine Company formed the Vigilant Rifles, or Vigilant Light Infantry, in November 1860.[31] The men elected Samuel Y. Tupper captain. This company left the most nearly complete record. It was present on Morris Island when The Citadel Cadets fired on the *Star of the West* on January 9, 1861.[32] The Vigilant Rifles, however, were relieved of duty and returned to Charleston about January 20.[33] The company was transferred to the Five Gun Battery at Sullivan's Island on February 23, but it was not actively engaged during the bombardment of Fort Sumter in April.[34] The Phoenix Rifles were probably also on Sullivan's Island during this period, since the *Mercury* reported their return to Charleston on April 17.[35] The Vigilant Rifles returned to the city on the twenty-second.[36] In September, the Vigilant Rifles was ordered to Fort Pickens on Battery Island.[37] After April 1861, the Vigilant Rifles was attached to the 1st Regiment South Carolina

Artillery Militia.[38] Perhaps the most noteworthy member of the Vigilant Rifles was Andrew Buist Murray, one of Charleston's most esteemed citizens. A second axeman in the company, he supported many benevolent projects in Charleston after the war, and in his will he bequeathed funds for the Fort Sumter Monument at White Point Garden.

HARLEE'S LEGION, SOUTH CAROLINA MILITIA

Harlee's Legion, South Carolina Militia, was also called the Brigade of State Militia and the Pee Dee Legion. It was commanded by William Wallace Harlee, a prominent South Carolinian and delegate to the secession convention. Evidence suggests that he held a commission as brigadier general, but whether he actually commanded the legion at that rank or as colonel is unclear.[39] In addition to holding dual office as lieutenant governor and postmaster of South Carolina in December 1860, Harlee is also notable as the founder of Florence, which he named for his daughter.

Harlee's Legion was organized in the fall of 1861 in general to guard the South Carolina coast and specifically to guard the Great Pee Dee River and its tributaries.[40] The original plan was that the legion would comprise several regiments.[41] In September, headquarters were established at Marion Court House, and training grounds were laid out at the nearby Methodist Centenary Campground.[42] By late October, the legion comprised two infantry regiments, one infantry battalion and two cavalry companies, but Harlee's goal was a full legion or even a brigade.[43] Over the next month, Chesterfield District contributed one cavalry and two infantry companies; Marlboro District provided two companies—one cavalry and one infantry; Darlington District also provided two; and Marion District contributed Colonel Graham's Infantry Regiment.[44] The latter was designated the 2nd Regiment in the legion, and the other was most likely the 33rd Regiment, South Carolina Militia.[45] The infantry battalion was the Horry Battalion comprising the seven companies of Lieutenant Colonel Ralph Nesbit's Battalion of State Troops.

Captains of the Marion District companies were McDuffie, Ellerbe, Edwards, Scott, Gregg and M. White.[46] Captain Samuel W. Maurice's Wee Nee Volunteers of Williamsburg District was also a company in the 3rd Battalion of the legion.[47] Maurice, previously a first lieutenant in the Wee Nee Volunteers in Maxcy Gregg's regiment, was appointed first lieutenant in the Confederate States Army and ordered to report to Mobile, Alabama, in February 1863.[48] Alexander D. Smith served as captain of a Marlboro District company in the legion. The Williamsburg Light

Dragoons, commanded by either J.C. Wilson or John Watson—also part of Harlee's Legion—was later Company B of the 12th (4th) Cavalry Battalion and Company I of the 4th Regiment, South Carolina Cavalry. S.T. Cooper commanded another company in the legion, the Black River Rangers.[49] The Rangers was probably disbanded along with the legion in early 1862.

The approximately 650 men of the legion were based at Camp Harlee near Georgetown in November and December 1861.[50] Near the end of the year, when Harlee tendered his services to President Davis, friends convinced him to remain in civil service, and the legislature passed an act ordering the legion to disband within a week of December 27, 1861.[51] With its term of enlistment expired, the legion was dissolved in early January 1862.[52] Most of the men promptly re-enlisted in other units for twelve months.[53] Harlee returned to his duties as lieutenant governor and served as a member of the Executive Council. Graham's Infantry Regiment formed the nucleus of the 21st Regiment, SCV, in January 1862, and the 9th Battalion, South Carolina Infantry, created in March 1862, was built around Nesbit's Horry Battalion.

16.

THE 2ND/8TH BATTALION CAVALRY, SOUTH CAROLINA RESERVES

The 2nd Battalion Cavalry, South Carolina Reserves, was also called the 8th Battalion, South Carolina Cavalry.[1] It was organized on May 30, 1862, from seven independent cavalry companies. According to the CSR, the battalion comprised eight companies, A–H, many of whose men had served previously in the 1st Regiment, South Carolina Mounted Militia. In May 1862, the *Mercury* reported that it had enlisted seven companies and was authorized to receive one more.[2] In late August 1862, the battalion merged with three additional companies to form the 3rd Regiment, South Carolina Cavalry. The *Mercury* reported on September 3 that the 3rd Regiment, known briefly as the 2nd, had recently been organized.[3] The numerical confusion was probably caused by the fact that the 2nd and 3rd Cavalry Regiments were organized about the same time.

FIELD OFFICERS

Charles Jones Colcock of Beaufort was elected lieutenant colonel on May 12, 1862.[4] Colcock had served as lieutenant colonel of the 1st Regiment, South Carolina Mounted Militia, from November 1861 to early February 1862. He had also been captain of the Ashley Dragoons from February 22, 1862, until the election.[5] Colcock was elected colonel of the 3rd Regiment, South Carolina Cavalry, on August 21, 1862.

Thomas Hewlett Johnson of Barnwell District was elected major of the 2nd Battalion on May 12, 1862.[6] Captain of the Savannah River Guards from November 1861 to early February 1862, he became lieutenant colonel of the 3rd Regiment in August 1862.

D.J. Barnette was major of the 2nd Battalion, according to the CSR, but this appears unlikely, unless the 2nd Battalion had two majors at the same time. The CSR gives his name as both Barnette and Barnett.

COMPANIES

Companies A, D, E and G are listed below, although the individual letter designations are actually unknown. The only ones known are for Companies B and F and possibly C. The *Mercury* reported on seven companies and their captains on May 19, 1862, but did not identify the companies by letter.[7] The list also omits the Spartan Rangers.

Company B, the Marion Men of Combahee, was a company in the 1st Mounted Militia Regiment until February 1862. Its men were mostly from Colleton District, along with a few from the part of Beaufort District now in Hampton County. It is unclear whether the company existed independently between February and March 19, 1862, but its men did reorganize sometime in March and on the nineteenth, while stationed at Pocotaligo, re-enlisted for three years, or for the duration of the war.[8] Captain Daniel Blake Heyward commanded the company, which was attached to the 2nd (8th) Battalion about May 30 as Company B. It was also briefly designated Company B in the 3rd Regiment before receiving the permanent designation of Company A.

The Spartan Rangers was possibly Company C, but the CSR is probably confusing the 2nd Battalion, South Carolina Cavalry Reserves, an 1862 unit, with the 2nd Battalion, South Carolina Reserves raised in 1864. In January 1861, the *Mercury* reported that Captain Thomas Hall was organizing a company called the Spartan Rangers, but the fate of Hall's Company is unknown.[9] The CSR lists the Spartan Rangers under the 2nd Battalion, South Carolina Cavalry Reserves, as Company L of the 3rd Regiment. On the roster of the 3rd Regiment, however, neither the Spartan Rangers nor any other company appears as Company L. The difficulty probably centers on another company with the same name, this one raised by William T. Wilkins in 1864. Wilkins's Company was definitely Company C, but it was Company C in the 2nd Battalion of South Carolina Reserves.

Thomas H. Johnson commanded Company F, the Savannah River Guard, or Guards, when it was part of the 1st Regiment, Mounted Militia. Most of its men were from Barnwell District. When the regiment disbanded in late January 1862, the Savannah River Guards re-enlisted in Confederate service on the twenty-seventh.[10] On April 2 the company, at the time independent and known only as T.H. Johnson's Company, South Carolina Cavalry, re-enlisted for the duration of the war. Not until May did it become Company F of the 8th Battalion. When Johnson became the battalion's major, A.B. Estes was promoted to captain of Company F. The same company was later designated briefly Company F of the 3rd Regiment and finally as Company K of the 3rd Regiment.

The Ashley Dragoons, or Ashley Rangers, was also called Captain Colcock's Company, South Carolina Cavalry, and its men were probably from Charleston and Beaufort Districts. Organized on February 22, 1862, it mustered in for the duration of the war on March 12.[11] Some of its men had served previously in George Cuthbert Heyward's Company and another company called the May River Troop of the 1st Regiment, South Carolina Mounted Militia, which was disbanded in late January and early February 1862. C.J. Colcock was captain of the independent Ashley Dragoons from February 22 until his election as lieutenant colonel of the 8th Battalion in May.[12] Heyward replaced him as captain of the Ashley Dragoons about that time. The company was subsequently designated Company G of the 3rd Cavalry Regiment for a brief period before becoming the regiment's Company H.

The Barnwell Dragoons from Barnwell District, previously called Lawton's Company, SCV, mustered in for the duration of the war on March 28, 1862.[13] Unlike most of the other companies, Lawton's Company did not serve in the 1st Regiment, South Carolina Mounted Militia. Captain Ben W. Lawton, MD, raised and commanded the company. Briefly designated Company A of the 3rd Cavalry Regiment, Lawton's Company was eventually designated Company D of the 3rd Regiment.

The Calhoun Minute Men or Calhoun Mounted Men was composed of men from Colleton District and the upper part of St. Peter's Parish in Beaufort District.[14] There were also a few men from Barnwell District and from Georgia and Virginia. The company was called Martin's Company, SCV, from February to May 1862, and Martin's Company, 8th Battalion, South Carolina Cavalry, after that. Most of the men had served previously in the Calhoun Minute Men in the 1st Regiment, South Carolina Mounted Militia, and had mustered out of that company on February 15. Some had served in the Hardeeville Guerillas of the same regiment. The men re-enlisted on March 30 for the duration of the war as Captain Martin's Company, South Carolina Cavalry, an independent unit under the command of Captain Alfred M. Martin. Although briefly designated Company F of the 3rd Cavalry Regiment, Martin's Company eventually became Company E of the 3rd Regiment.

The Beaufort District Troop, also called Captain J.H. Howard's Company, was composed mainly of men from Beaufort District, with a few from Barnwell District and some from Texas. Its men had served from November 4, 1861, to March 27, 1862, in the 4th Regiment Cavalry, South Carolina Militia, as volunteers, and most had enlisted then for the duration of the war. Sixty-one-year-old Captain John H. Howard commanded the company.[15] Briefly designated Company D of the 3rd Regiment, it became Company C of the 3rd Regiment. This company shared a common name with Company C of the Hampton Legion (later Company B, 2nd Regiment, South Carolina Cavalry), but the two were otherwise unrelated.

The Colleton Rangers was a company in the 1st Mounted Militia Regiment until that regiment was disbanded in February 1862. Captain Archibald Lawrence Campbell was its commander. The men re-enlisted in Confederate service for the duration of the war on March 26, 1862. The Colleton Rangers remained an independent company until May 20.[16] Briefly designated Company C of the 3rd Cavalry Regiment, the company's final designation was Company B of the 3rd Regiment.

BRIGADE AFFILIATIONS

The 2nd (8th) Battalion served in the Department of South Carolina, Georgia and Florida throughout its three-month existence.[17]

MAJOR MOVEMENTS AND ENGAGEMENTS

The battalion was stationed on the lower South Carolina coast during its three-month existence. The Marion Men of Combahee did experience action at Pocotaligo on May 29, 1862. The company was initially held in reserve, but its men were later deployed as skirmishers, and they participated in the pursuit of Federal troops to Port Royal Ferry after the battle.[18]

17.

THE 3RD REGIMENT, SOUTH CAROLINA CAVALRY

The 3rd Regiment, South Carolina Cavalry, also called Colcock's regiment, was organized in Beaufort District, at either Grahamville or Camp Lay between Hardeeville and Bluffton, about August 19, 1862. Although originally called the 2nd, its designation was soon changed to the 3rd Regiment.[1] This change is best explained by the fact that the 2nd and 3rd Regiments were formed within a few days of each other, one in Virginia and the other in South Carolina. Since the 1st Cavalry Regiment had already been organized, there was probably some confusion as to which of the two new organizations would be designated the 2nd Regiment.

The seven companies of Colcock's 8th (2nd) Battalion, South Carolina Cavalry, merged with three independent cavalry companies to create the 3rd Regiment. An eighth company from the same battalion became the regiment's eleventh company at some point, and a twelfth company was formed in 1863 with men from existing companies. The 3rd Regiment was made up of independent planters and farmers from Barnwell, Beaufort, Colleton and Charleston Districts.[2] It was armed with rifles, and its men frequently fought on foot as infantry.[3]

FIELD OFFICERS

Charles Jones Colcock of Beaufort, Barnwell and Charleston was elected colonel of the 3rd Regiment on August 21, 1862. His appointment, approved on October 7, was retroactive to August 19. Colcock had served as lieutenant colonel of the 8th (2nd) Battalion, South Carolina Cavalry, from May to August 1862.[4] From February to May 1862, he had served as captain of an independent cavalry company, the Ashley Dragoons, and from November 1861 to early February 1862, he served as lieutenant colonel of the 1st Regiment, Mounted Militia. In addition, from 1863 to 1865, Colcock was named acting brigadier general of the 3rd South Carolina Military District, encompassing the territory between the Ashepoo and Savannah Rivers.[5] In mid-March 1865, he issued an order from his headquarters in Sumter—an order that was later countermanded—that said that Governor Magrath had ordered him to remain in "Carolina" to defend the state and organize all the soldiers of the Confederate army who were separated from their commands.[6] As late as April 4, he was serving with his regiment near Charlotte.[7] John L. Black, colonel of the 1st Cavalry Regiment, wrote that Colcock was "a very polished gentleman and an excellent officer."[8]

Thomas Hewlett Johnson of Barnwell District was commissioned lieutenant colonel of the 3rd Regiment on October 7, 1862, with rank from August 19. Johnson, major of the 8th (2nd) Battalion from May to August 1862, had served as captain of the Savannah River Guards from November 1861 to early February 1862.[9]

John Jenkins of Edisto Island and Colleton District, an older brother of Micah Jenkins, was captain of Company I from January or February of 1862 until the 3rd Regiment was created in August. He was promoted to major on October 7, effective August 19, 1862. Jenkins often served in a detached capacity, including a period from May 1863 to August 1864, when he commanded all Confederate forces on John's Island.[10] In April 1865, he was serving in Orangeburg as commander of the Confederate troops there.[11] P.G.T. Beauregard wrote that Jenkins was "a most reliable officer" and "fully entitled to promotion by [his] resolute gallantry."[12]

COMPANIES

Company A, the Marion Men of Combahee, was designated Company B soon after the regiment was created, perhaps even while it was designated the 2nd Regiment. From May to August 1862, it was attached to the 8th (2nd) Battalion as Company B. Before that, from November 1861 to February 1862, it was Captain D.B. Heyward's Company in the 1st Mounted Militia Regiment. Most of its men were from Colleton District, although a few came from that part of Beaufort District now in Hampton County. D. Blake Heyward, who commanded the company as early as the summer of 1861, was re-elected on March 19, 1862. He resigned on December 26 when a Board of Examiners failed to confirm his competency.[13] Asbury M. Lowry succeeded Heyward as captain on February 13, 1863.

Company B, the Colleton Rangers from Colleton District, was designated Company C early, probably while the 3rd was still designated the 2nd

Regiment. From November 1861 to February 1862, it was known as Captain Campbell's Company in the 1ˢᵗ Regiment, Mounted Militia. The men re-enlisted in Confederate service as an independent company for the duration of the war on March 26, 1862.[14] The company was attached to the 8ᵗʰ (2ⁿᵈ) Battalion from May 20 until it mustered in the 3ʳᵈ Regiment in August. Its only captain, Archibald Lawrence Campbell, was commissioned on March 24, 1862.[15] According to the CSR, the Colleton Rangers was attached to the Holcombe Legion at one time.[16]

Company C, the Beaufort District Troop, was Company D earlier in the existence of the 3ʳᵈ Regiment, probably while it was still designated the 2ⁿᵈ. Although most of its men were from Beaufort District, a few came from Barnwell District and some came from as far away as Texas. This company is not the same as Company B of the 2ⁿᵈ Regiment, South Carolina Cavalry, although it bore the same popular name.

Company C was also called Captain John H. Howard's Company, South Carolina Cavalry. Its men had served as volunteers in the 4ᵗʰ Cavalry Regiment, South Carolina Militia, from November 4, 1861, to March 27, 1862, at which time, most of them re-enlisted for the duration of the war. Howard, who was sixty-one at the time, commanded the company.[17] He resigned on May 9, 1864, a date also shown in the record as May 31. The 1ˢᵗ and 2ⁿᵈ Regiments, South Carolina Cavalry, returned to South Carolina from Virginia in April 1864, and there was a strong possibility that the 3ʳᵈ Regiment would be among their replacements in May. Rumors to this effect probably prompted Howard's resignation, since he had written that he was "not disabled yet, but would be unable to take his command to Tennessee or Virginia if ordered to do so."[18] First Lieutenant Thaddeus G. Buckner commanded the company after Howard's resignation. Buckner had suffered a severe wound to his intestines during an engagement near Coosawhatchie on October 22, 1862, and although he was "saved by skillful surgery," he was recuperating at his Gillisonville home until at least December 31, 1864.[19] Even so, he was promoted to captain in absentia on June 9, 1864. Returning to the company sometime in 1865, Buckner was wounded again about February 20, this time in the body; he was furloughed on March 1. Bits of misinformation on Buckner's fate exist: the *Roll of the Dead* records that First Lieutenant T.G. Buckner of the Beaufort District Troop died of wounds received in battle at Pocotaligo. Kirkland, apparently using this entry as his source, wrote that First Lieutenant T.G. Buckner of Company C, the Hampton Legion, died of wounds received on May 29, 1862, at Pocotaligo.[20] But the Hampton Legion was in Virginia on that date. Kirkland had confused Company C of the Hampton Legion with Company C of the 3ʳᵈ Regiment, no doubt because of their common name.

He also assumed, incorrectly, that Buckner was wounded on May 29 instead of October 22, 1862, and he repeated the erroneous conclusion from the *Roll of the Dead* that Buckner died of his wounds. First Lieutenant James McPherson Gregorie commanded the company in Buckner's absence, but he was never promoted to captain.

Company D, the Barnwell Dragoons, was previously called Lawton's Company, SCV. Its men, from Barnwell District, mustered in service for the duration of the war on March 28, 1862.[21] Although not in the 1st Mounted Militia Regiment, this company was part of the 8th (2nd) Battalion. Although the company was designated Company A of the 3rd Regiment briefly, probably while the 3rd was still called the 2nd Regiment, its permanent designation was Company D of the 3rd Regiment. Ben W. Lawton, MD, raised the company and commanded it in both the battalion and the regiment. In early March 1863, Lawton received an appeal from fifty-nine citizens of Lower Barnwell District. It asked him to return home to his medical practice of eighteen years. For that reason, and because he was a state senator, Lawton resigned on March 19. George H. Kirkland replaced him as captain shortly thereafter. Kirkland probably commanded Company H, 2nd Regiment, South Carolina Junior Reserves, in 1864 and 1865.

Company E, the Calhoun Minute Men, or Calhoun Mounted Men, was mostly from Colleton District and the upper part of St. Peter's Parish in Beaufort District, now in Hampton County.[22] A few men came from Barnwell District, Georgia and Virginia as well. Most had served in the Calhoun Minute Men in the 1st Regiment, Mounted Militia, and had mustered out on February 15, 1862. Some had served in the Hardeeville Guerillas of the same regiment. The men re-enlisted in the Calhoun Minute Men on March 30, 1862, for the duration of the war. It was an independent company known as Captain Martin's Company, SCV, and it served in South Carolina in late April.[23] Martin's Company joined the 8th Battalion, South Carolina Cavalry, on May 30. It was briefly designated Company F of the 3rd Regiment, probably while the 3rd was still designated the 2nd, although it received permanent designation as Company E shortly afterward. Alfred M. Martin commanded the company in both the battalion and the regiment.[24] He resigned on June 11, 1863, under an act of the Confederate Congress that exempted from duty certain civil officers, including members of state legislatures. Henry C. Raysor was promoted to captain as Martin's replacement in June.[25]

Company F, the St. Peter's Guards, was composed of men from lower Barnwell and Colleton Districts and from St. Peter's Parish in Beaufort District, now in Hampton County.[26] Previously in the 1st Regiment, Mounted Militia, the men mustered out of service on January 31, 1862. A number re-enlisted for the duration of the war on April 4 as an independent company known as Captain Smart's Company, South Carolina Cavalry. Henry C. Smart mustered in with the men and commanded the company throughout the war.[27] He managed to avoid capture when about thirty-eight of his men were surprised and taken prisoner at South Newport, Georgia, on August 17, 1864.[28] The company was on duty in South Carolina in late April 1862.[29] Unlike most 1st Regiment Mounted Militia companies who chose the 8th Battalion in May and the 3rd Regiment in August 1862, the St. Peter's Guards skipped the battalion entirely. Designated briefly as Company H of the 3rd Regiment, probably while it was still designated the 2nd, the St. Peter's Guards became Company F, 3rd Regiment.

Company G, the German Hussars, was made up of German Charlestonians. The German Hussars, South Carolina Militia, also called Captain Theodore Cordes's Company of Cavalry, South Carolina Militia, was organized about May 18, 1859, as part of the 4th Brigade, South Carolina Militia.[30] Another company called the German Hussars had been in existence since 1830, but the relationship between the two companies is unclear.[31] The Hussars served with the 1st Regiment Rifles in the 4th Brigade in early 1861. Before the April bombardment of Fort Sumter, the Hussars acted as pickets and couriers on Morris Island and at Stevens's Iron Battery. The company was in Colonel W.B. Ryan's Squadron in April.[32] The Hussars remained at Morris Island until at least early May. The men were ordered to patrol Sullivan's Island on November 8, 1861, and they remained there until the following February.[33] Some of Cordes's militiamen enlisted for twelve months in February 1862 and became Captain Cordes's Company, SCV.[34] They re-elected Cordes on March 12.[35] In April, both the *Mercury* and the *Charleston Daily Courier* reported that the men mustered in Confederate service for twelve months on April 5, 1862.[36] These men, the *Mercury* reported, had mustered in on April 5 and were called Captain Theodore Cordes's Company, German Hussars, South Carolina Cavalry.[37] The company was on duty in South Carolina in late April.[38] After the battle of Secessionville in June, the German Hussars were sent to James Island, where they performed picket duty at Battery Island, Grimball's place and other spots along the Stono River. When the 3rd Regiment was formed in August 1862, the German Hussars was initially designated Company I, probably while the 3rd Regiment was still designated the 2nd, but its permanent designation was soon changed to Company G. Forty-eight-year-old Theodore Cordes, first captain of the company in Confederate service, enlisted with the men on April 5. He resigned because of poor health on June 1, a date in the record also shown as June 23, 1864. Charles Fremder was promoted to captain in August, and he commanded the company until the end of the war.[39] (See independent cavalry organizations for more information.)

Company H, the Ashley Dragoons, or Ashley Rangers, was probably from Charleston and Beaufort Districts.[40] Some of its men had previously served in both George Cuthbert Heyward's Company and the May River Troop of the 1st Regiment, Mounted Militia, which disbanded in February 1862. The company was reorganized on February 22 and mustered in service as an independent company for three years, or for the duration of the war, on March 12, 1862.[41] It was on duty in South Carolina in late April.[42] The Dragoons served in the 8th Battalion, South Carolina Cavalry, from May to August and was briefly designated Company G of the 3rd Cavalry Regiment, although this probably happened while the 3rd Regiment was called the 2nd. Its permanent designation was Company H of the 3rd Cavalry Regiment. Heyward, who commanded the company in both battalion and regiment, was paroled at Augusta, Georgia, on May 18, 1865.

Company I, the Rebel Troop, was known briefly as Company K, although probably only for a short period when the 3rd Regiment was designated the 2nd. Most of its men were from the islands of Edisto, Wadmalaw and John's and from the contiguous mainland of Charleston, Colleton and Beaufort Districts; a few were from Orangeburg and Barnwell Districts. The troop was organized in January 1862 as Captain John Jenkins's Independent Company of Mounted Riflemen, and it mustered in Confederate service for the duration of the war on February 17.[43] It was on duty in South Carolina in late April.[44] Jenkins was promoted to major of the 3rd Regiment on October 7, with rank from August 19, 1862. His replacement, John Lawton Seabrook, commanded the company for the rest of the war. Many of the company's men served in the Signal Corps around Charleston Harbor and as detached guides and scouts while the company was based at Adams Run.[45]

Company K, the Savannah River Guards, or Guard, was known as Captain Thomas H. Johnson's Company in the 1st Regiment, Mounted Militia. Most of its men were from Barnwell District, and most had served in the mounted militia regiment. When the regiment disbanded in late January and early February 1862, the men re-enlisted in Johnson's Independent Company for twelve months of Confederate service from January 27.[46] Not long afterward, on April 2, the company reorganized, and the men mustered in for the duration of the war. The company was on duty in South Carolina in late April.[47] When the company joined the 8th Battalion in May, Johnson was promoted to major, and A.B. Estes became captain.[48] That month, the company became Company F of the 8th (2nd) Battalion. Later, it was briefly designated Company F of the 3rd Regiment, probably while the 3rd Regiment was still designated the 2nd; a permanent designation of Estes's Company as Company K of the 3rd Regiment was established soon afterward. Estes resigned on November 12, 1862, citing a chronic spinal condition, chronic dysentery, acute rheumatism and the fact that he owned two plantations with a hundred slaves and had no overseer. First Lieutenant William B. Peeples succeeded Estes as captain the same day.

There was probably no Company L in the 3rd Regiment, although the CSR lists the Spartan Rangers in that slot. The error probably comes from confusing the 2nd Battalion Cavalry Reserves (created in 1862) with the 2nd Battalion Reserves (raised in 1864) and transferring the confusion to the 3rd Regiment. The CSR listing for the 2nd Battalion Cavalry Reserves states the Spartan Rangers became Company L of the 3rd Regiment, but CSR's roster of the 3rd Regiment does not list the Spartan Rangers or any other troop as Company L. The CSR probably misplaced William T. Wilkins's Company, also called the Spartan Rangers, which was raised in 1864 and was designated Company C, 2nd Battalion, South Carolina Reserves, not Company C, 2nd Battalion, South Carolina Cavalry Reserves. In January 1861, the *Mercury* reported that Captain Thomas Hall was organizing a company called the Spartan Rangers, but the fate of Hall's Company is unknown.[49]

Johnson's Section of Horse Artillery was also called Johnson's Mounted Artillery, Colcock's Light Artillery and Colcock's Section Light Artillery.[50] It was an unlettered company attached to the 3rd Cavalry Regiment. Colonel Colcock had sought and received special permission from General Beauregard to create a section of mounted artillery and to equip it with two English Wiard rifled cannon.[51] The result was Special Order No. 18, which was issued on June 13, 1863. Colcock also ordered 1st Lieutenant Richard Johnson of Company K detached from his company to command the artillery section. Although the *Official Records* called Johnson "captain" in April 1864, he was never actually promoted to the rank.[52] Johnson's horse artillery was composed of six men from each company of the 3rd Regiment.[53] It was part of McLaws's Division with the 3rd Regiment in November 1864.[54] On December 28, the battery was placed in Major George L. Buist's battalion, along with batteries commanded by Gilchrist, Mathewes and Melchers. Buist's battalion served in Colonel Edward C. Anderson's brigade with the 15th and 18th Artillery Battalions and some units from Georgia.[55] Still in existence in January 1865, Johnson's section probably surrendered in April, although whether or not it was attached to the 3rd Regiment at the time is unclear.[56]

BRIGADE AFFILIATIONS

The 3rd Regiment, South Carolina Cavalry, served in various military districts, brigades and commands of the Department of South Carolina, Georgia and

Florida during its existence. On November 20, 1864, for example, Company B was in Brigadier General Beverly H. Robertson's Brigade, while the rest of the regiment was in Major General Lafayette McLaws's Division.[57] On March 29, 1865, the 1st, 2nd and 3rd Cavalry Regiments were placed into a new brigade under Brigadier General M.L. Bonham.[58] The 3rd Regiment is not listed in the organization of troops on April 9, 1865.[59]

MAJOR MOVEMENTS AND ENGAGEMENTS

The 3rd Regiment served in South Carolina, Georgia and North Carolina throughout the war. Colcock wrote that it was stationed on the South Carolina coast at Charleston and between Red Bluff near Savannah and Port Royal Ferry, but that it was never all together at any one time.[60] The regiment was organized in Beaufort District between Hardeeville and Bluffton, at either Grahamville or at Camp Lay, in the summer of 1862.[61] Company F was based at the head of Fording Island Road near Bluffton while picketing Red Bluff on the New River, the May River and Port Royal Ferry on the Colleton River. Companies A, C, D, E and K were based at Grahamville, in Beaufort District, to defend the Charleston and Savannah Railroad and to picket the Coosawhatchie River, the western shore of the Broad River and its tributary creeks. Companies B and G were based at McPhersonville to picket the Tullifinny River and the Port Royal Ferry. Company H, based at the John's Island Ferry, picketed the Stono River, and Company I was based at John's Island and James Island. Major John Jenkins commanded both H and I. Company I was present on John's Island during the battle of Secessionville on June 16, 1862, acting as bodyguard to Brigadier General N.G. Evans.[62] Jenkins's Rebel Troop, Nelson's 7th Battalion, the Holcombe Legion and the 17th Regiment participated in an expedition to Jehossee Island on July 7, but they were not engaged.[63] Elements of the regiment saw action at McPhersonville in August and at Pinckney Island on the twenty-first. Company I reconnoitered Edisto Island on both August 7 and October 20.[64]

Companies A, B, C, K and Johnson's Artillery, as well as two companies of the 1st (Abney's) Battalion of Sharpshooters, were engaged at the battle at Coosawhatchie, also called the Second Battle of Pocotaligo, on October 22, 1862.[65] The same companies also saw action at the battle of Yemassee that day. By the end of October, several companies were based near Grahamville: Company B was at the Jacksonborough Ferry, Company G was at James Island and Company I was at Adams Run.[66] Company K was based on James Island in March 1863.[67] Company I was engaged at Seabrook Island on April 11 and Companies A, B and G were at Bluffton on June 4.[68] By June 19, Company I was performing picket duty at Rockville on Wadmalaw Island, and the rest of the regiment was stationed lower down the coast in the 3rd South Carolina Military District.[69]

From June to November 1863, nine companies were based at McPhersonville in the 3rd South Carolina Military District, while Company I remained headquartered at Adams Run in the 2nd District.[70] Companies C, D and H were engaged with a Federal landing party at Bee's Creek in the fall of 1863, and on Christmas Day 1863, Company I, the Rebel Troop, participated in the attack on the USS *Marblehead* in the Stono River near Legareville. Company I was also on John's Island during the brief affair there on the twenty-eighth, although Major Jenkins's report does not indicate whether the men were actually engaged.[71] On December 31, five companies were at Grahamville, four others plus Johnson's Artillery were at Hardeeville and Company I was still at Adams Run.[72] By the end of January 1864, the nine companies were together again at McPhersonville.[73] Company I was engaged at Haulover Cut on John's Island from February 9 to February 10, and it scouted on Wadmalaw Island on the eleventh.[74] Company B was sent to the Georgia coast on February 27, and it remained there until June 24. Company C was ordered to Darien, Georgia, on February 22, and it stayed there until May 12.

In March 1864, the 1st and 2nd Cavalry Regiments were transferred to South Carolina, and M.C. Butler took the 4th, 5th and 6th Regiments to Virginia as replacements. He had originally planned to take the 3rd, 4th and 5th, but Johnson Hagood convinced him to leave the 3rd Regiment behind. Regimental headquarters was at McPhersonville on April 30, although Company I remained based at St. Andrews/Adams Run.[75] Company G was sent to Savannah early that summer at about the same time Companies B, C, D, G and H, and possibly E, were sent to Georgia to guard the Gulf Railroad as far down as the Altamaha River on the Georgia coast. Lieutenant Colonel Johnson commanded the detachment.[76] Although headquarters remained at McPhersonville in July, the regiment's companies were scattered throughout the military district.[77] Company F was ordered to Riceborough, Georgia, on August 10 and to South Newport two days later.[78] At about eleven on the night of August 17, a Federal force of about three hundred men surprised Company F. Between twenty-seven and thirty-eight men were captured, and about twenty escaped.[79]

In the meantime, on July 2, three companies of the 3rd Regiment were ordered back from Savannah to James Island.[80] Elements of the 3rd Regiment, probably including Company I, were engaged on John's

Island for two days, from July 3 to July 5.[81] About a hundred men of the 3rd Regiment also performed picket duty on James Island on the seventh.[82] All ten companies of the regiment, as well as Johnson's Artillery Section, were based at McPhersonville by October 31.[83] That fall, elements of the regiment, including Company G, were sent to north Georgia to check Stoneman's Raid. Companies A, C and H were engaged with the left wing of Sherman's army as they tried to save the Oconee River Bridge in Georgia on November 22.[84] Sent up the line of the Georgia Central Railroad, Company H tangled with Sherman's advance guard at Balls Ferry on the Ogeechee River. Johnson's Artillery Company saw action at Hudson's Ferry near Briar Creek, Georgia, and at Izard's on the Savannah River about the same time.[85] In late November about six thousand Federal troops tried to take the Charleston and Savannah Railroad near Grahamville. Company K was engaged nearby during the skirmish on Boyd's Landing Road at Honey Hill on November 29 and November 30. Companies B and E, along with detachments of Companies C and I, also participated in the battle of Honey Hill. During the five-hour skirmish before the battle there on the thirtieth, Colonel Colcock commanded both Company K and a gun of Kanapaux's Artillery.[86] Although Major General Gustavus W. Smith was in command, Colcock directed the battle following the long skirmish. All the infantry in that battle were Georgia troops. The artillery units were all South Carolinians. Companies B, E and K, along with detachments of Companies C and I of the 3rd Cavalry Regiment, were engaged as infantry.

Just before the fall of Savannah, Companies H and G returned to South Carolina, and Companies B and C soon followed. Three companies, including D and G, fought as infantry in the trenches around Savannah.[87] Johnson's Artillery, Company K and possibly other elements of the 3rd Regiment, were engaged again at the Tullifinny River on December 7 and December 8.[88] Company D was engaged on the eighth. The regiment kept up its watch on the Savannah River ferries and the coast from Savannah to Red Bluff until the city was evacuated; after the evacuation, it performed picket duty from Pocotaligo to the Combahee River.[89] The regiment reunited near Grahamville on December 20 and, along with Kirk's Squadron of Cavalry, guarded the coastal flank during the evacuation of Savannah.[90] In late December, Companies D, I and K were at Pocotaligo; Companies B and H, as well as detachments of Companies D, F and G, were at Coosawhatchie; and Companies C and E were performing picket and courier duty near Grahamville.[91] Johnson's Artillery and some companies of the 3rd Regiment were engaged about that time at Huspa Bridge, four miles from Old Pocotaligo, and Company G participated in several skirmishes with outlying commands of Sherman's army nearby. While resisting Sherman's right wing on the west bank of the Salkehatchie River, Companies B, H and I were almost cut off at Rivers Bridge.[92] This was probably the January 20, 1865 engagement during which the 3ʳᵈ met a Federal regiment near Kadesh Church on the Salkehatchie Road.[93] It had withdrawn to Broxton's Bridge by the twenty-eighth. Men of Company D acted as couriers between Rivers Bridge and Midway at that time, and on February 2, the rest of the regiment performed picket duty in the vicinity of Rivers Bridge.[94] That same day, four companies, including Johnson's Artillery, were engaged at Broxton's Bridge, and the 3ʳᵈ Regiment served as the rear guard across Whippy Swamp.[95] On February 3, Johnson's Artillery and elements of the 3ʳᵈ Regiment were engaged at Rivers Bridge. Ordered to Walterboro for picket duty, the regiment passed through St. George on February 14.[96] Falling back through Summerville to Charleston, elements of the 3ʳᵈ Regiment burned the Ashley River Bridge during the evacuation of Charleston.[97] Companies H and I kept their men between Sherman and the city as he advanced on Orangeburg and Columbia. The same two companies followed Sherman into Columbia and marched through Chester and Yorkville into North Carolina.[98] Company G and the rest of the regiment followed; they went through Columbia, Charlotte and Greensboro, engaging with bummers and raiding parties along the way. The 3ʳᵈ Regiment successfully turned back Colonel Reuben Williams's 546-man raiding party in Florence on March 5, 1865. It withdrew toward Cheraw from Florence with the 1ˢᵗ Cavalry Regiment and Gaillard's Battery and marched through Darlington, Society Hill and Chesterfield Court House to Wadesboro, North Carolina. Companies H and I turned back from Raleigh toward Charlotte to meet Stoneman's Raiders and skirmished with his troops at the Catawba River Bridge.

During the withdrawal into North Carolina, three companies of the 3ʳᵈ Regiment had been left behind near Orangeburg. Colcock was ordered to South Carolina on March 17, but the order was countermanded, and the companies were ordered to join the regiment in North Carolina.[99] On April 4, companies then in Charlotte were ordered to Raleigh.[100] Elements of the 3ʳᵈ Regiment, possibly Company I, joined President Jefferson Davis at Union, where he dined at General Wallace's home on April 28. While there, Davis ordered Colcock to award the regiment a ninety-day furlough. The CSR records that the 3ʳᵈ Regiment surrendered, at least on paper, with the Army of Tennessee on April 26, 1865. Company I was furloughed at Yorkville about thirty miles from Union. Almost all the men of Company G were captured at Salem, North Carolina; those remaining were disbanded at Rock Hill, about forty miles from Union. It appears that some, if not most, of the companies of the 3ʳᵈ Regiment were disbanded in South Carolina, but some may have surrendered at Greensboro.[101] The 3rd Regiment is not listed in the organization of troops on April 9, 1865.[102]

18.

THE 4ᵀᴴ REGIMENT, SOUTH CAROLINA CAVALRY

The 4ᵗʰ Regiment, South Carolina Cavalry, was also called Rutledge's regiment of Cavalry and Rutledge's Cavalry.[1] It was created by consolidating the four companies of Major Stokes's 10ᵗʰ Cavalry Battalion, the four companies of Major Emanuel's 12ᵗʰ Cavalry Battalion and two independent companies commanded by Captains B.H. Rutledge and Thomas Pinckney. In a letter to General Samuel Cooper, dated October 18, 1862, P.G.T. Beauregard suggested that two more cavalry regiments, the 4ᵗʰ and 5ᵗʰ, should be created. Beauregard wrote that the state's cavalry units were unorganized, and he suggested remedies; he also recommended field officers to command the two new regiments. On December 16, 1862, Beauregard created one regiment under the authority of the War Department's Special Order No. 254. It was called Rutledge's regiment for a few weeks, but it soon became the 4ᵗʰ Regiment, South Carolina Cavalry.[2]

FIELD OFFICERS

Benjamin Huger Rutledge of Charleston and Stateburg in Sumter District, the regiment's only colonel, was commissioned on December 16, 1862.[3] According to the CSR, Rutledge was appointed colonel on April 2, 1864, with rank from December 16, 1862. Previously captain of an independent company called the Charleston Light Dragoons, which became Company K of the 4ᵗʰ Regiment in December 1862, Rutledge served on detached duty for long periods of time.

William Stokes of Branchville in Orangeburg District and of Colleton District was commissioned the regiment's only lieutenant colonel effective from December 16, 1862.[4] The CSR records that Stokes was appointed lieutenant colonel on April 2, 1864, with rank from December 16, 1862.

He had previously been major of the 10th (3rd/2nd) Battalion. Stokes was wounded, probably in early July 1864.[5] Taken to the hospital at Huguenot Springs, Virginia, about July 7, he returned to duty about the fourteenth. Stokes was wounded again when a bullet grazed his leg on October 1, 1864.[6] He often commanded the regiment in Rutledge's absence.

William Pledger Emanuel of Georgetown and Marlboro Districts was commissioned major of the 4th Regiment with rank from December 16, 1862.[7] The CSR records that Emanuel was appointed major on April 2, 1864, retroactive to December 16, 1862. He had served previously as major of the 12th Battalion. Colonel John F. Lay, adjutant and inspector general, wrote on February 2, 1863, that Companies F and I, both under Emanuel's command, were good companies in spite of ineffective drilling and poor leadership. Lay added: "It is evident that the command did not prosper under [Emanuel]."[8] On June 21, 1863, Beauregard had Emanuel arrested and charged with neglect in connection with the June 2 Combahee Raid. Emanuel remained under arrest from June to December but was acquitted in early 1864.[9] Taken prisoner at Louisa Court House on June 11, 1864, Emanuel was sent to Fort Delaware on the twenty-third and to Hilton Head Island on August 20. He was moved to Morris Island, where he became one of the "Immortal 600" Confederate officers intentionally exposed to Confederate cannon fire.[10] Emanuel was moved to Fort Pulaski, along with most of the other prisoners, on October 21. He was paroled and exchanged on December 15, 1864, at Charleston Harbor.[11]

COMPANIES

Company A of the 4th Regiment had been both Company A of the 4th Squadron and Company A of the 12th Battalion before the regiment was created in December 1862. Probably members of a company called the Chesterfield Light Dragoons, the men were mostly from Chesterfield District, although many were from Darlington and Lancaster Districts, and a few were from Horry, Marlboro and Kershaw Districts. James C. Craig and Henry McIver raised the company.[12] The men mustered in service for the duration of the war on January 25, 1862, at Georgetown.[13] Craig, who enlisted on December 26, 1861, was the only captain both during the company's independent phase, from January to May 1862, and when it was in the 4th Squadron/12th Battalion. He was also the company's first captain in the 4th Regiment. Craig suffered from heart disease for several months in the first half of 1863 and, as a result, had been unable to discharge his duties for two months before he resigned on June 17. McIver was promoted to captain on June 25.[14] He was severely wounded in the foot and right forearm at Haw's Shop on May 28, 1864. The CSR says it was the right foot, but a sketch in *Recollections and Reminiscences* says the injury was to the left one.[15] Although he was left for dead on the battlefield, McIver was found alive and sent to Jackson Hospital.[16] Still unwell in June, he was transferred on the sixth, probably to the Wayside Hospital in Florence, where he recovered. McIver returned to the company on November 27 but did not regain full use of his right arm.[17] According to a sketch in *Recollections and Reminiscences*, he refused the colonelcy of the 4th Regiment to remain with his company.[18] The CSR, however, does not substantiate this claim. If McIver were ever offered and refused command of the 4th Regiment, it would have had to have happened at the outset since we know Rutledge was the regiment's only colonel. Lieutenant Colonel Stokes wrote of McIver: "I consider him about the best officer of his rank both in the Regiment or the Brigade."[19]

Company B, the Palmetto Rangers, was previously Company A of the 10th (3rd) Battalion.[20] It became Company B of the 4th Regiment in December 1862. Two-thirds of its men were from Chester and one-third from Fairfield District.[21] Osborne Barber, the only captain in the 3rd/10th Battalion, was also the only captain of the Palmetto Rangers in the 4th Regiment.[22] He was paroled at Greensboro on May 2, 1865.[23]

Company C, the Calhoun Troop, previously Company B of the 10th Battalion, became Company C of the 4th Regiment in December 1862. Its men came from Pendleton in Anderson District and from those parts of Pickens District now in Oconee and Pickens Counties, especially from the Fort Hill area.[24] John Caldwell Calhoun, grandson of the vice-president, was unanimously elected captain at the reorganization on May 6, 1862, and was the company's only captain in the 4th Regiment.[25] Probably wounded in November 1864, Calhoun was admitted to General Hospital #4 in Richmond on the twenty-seventh and treated there for a contusion. Although Calhoun later listed John W. Simpson as a captain in Company C, Simpson was actually a private.[26] Calhoun also listed Michael Calvin Dickson as a captain in his company.[27] It is true that Dickson commanded the company from late February to October 1864, and even acted as major, but the highest rank he attained was junior second lieutenant.[28]

Company D was called Company A, St. James Mounted Riflemen. Organized on April 15, 1861, as Thomas Pinckney's Independent Mounted Riflemen, the company mustered in Confederate service for the duration of the war on October 31, 1861. It was part of Company A, the St. James Mounted Riflemen, of Manigault's Battalion from December 1861 until May 1, 1862, when it was divided into two companies: Pinckney's Company A and Whilden's Company B. Manigault's Battalion was disbanded on May

18, and both companies became part of Byrd's 6th Battalion, South Carolina Infantry. Whilden's Company B, St. James Mounted Riflemen, served as an unlettered company in Byrd's Battalion, became independent in September 1862 and was designated Company E of the 5th Regiment, South Carolina Cavalry, on January 18, 1863. Pinckney's Company A, on the other hand, mustered in Byrd's Battalion as Captain Thomas Pinckney's Company A, St. James Mounted Riflemen, in May. When Byrd's 6th Battalion merged into the 26th Regiment, South Carolina Infantry, in October 1862, Pinckney's Company was not on its roster, an indication that it, too, was probably an independent cavalry company from September to December 16, when it was assigned to the 4th Cavalry Regiment as Company D.

Most Company D men were from Georgetown District, although some came from Charleston, Clarendon, Beaufort and Horry Districts. Thomas Pinckney, commissioned captain on April 15, 1861, commanded throughout the company's existence.[29] He was captured at Haw's Shop on May 28, 1864.[30] An issue of the *Confederate Veteran* records, incorrectly, that he was captured at Hanover, Virginia, on May 23, 1864.[31] Pinckney was held first at White House, Virginia, on June 8; he moved next to Point Lookout, Maryland, and on the twenty-third he was transferred to Fort Delaware.[32] Sent to Hilton Head Island on August 20, Pinckney was among the "Immortal 600" Confederate officers deliberately held on Morris Island and exposed to fire from Confederate cannons.[33] Pinckney was returned to Fort Pulaski with most of the other prisoners on October 21, and he was exchanged with the sick and wounded on December 15, 1864, at Charleston Harbor.[34] He rejoined his command at Smithfield, North Carolina, in March 1865.[35] Pinckney's left ankle was fractured when a horse fell on him one day near Smithfield.[36] One issue of the *Confederate Veteran* records that he went home shortly after the accident, but another issue notes both his presence at the surrender on April 26 and his return home afterward.[37]

Company E was previously Company C of the 12th Battalion, South Carolina Cavalry. Organized in late 1861, it served in the Georgetown area in late January 1862, before the men mustered in service for twelve months on February 4. It became Company E of the 4th Regiment in December 1862. Although most of the men were from Marlboro District, some came from Horry, Georgetown, Williamsburg, Marion and Darlington Districts. The first captain, William P. Emanuel, was promoted to major when the 4th Squadron/12th Battalion was organized on May 1, 1862. Henry Edens, who was promoted to captain the same day, was the first captain of the company in the 4th Regiment.[38] Edens resigned on May 7, 1863, claiming that he had suffered from rheumatism almost constantly for the past five years and that, because the pain had recently become so intense and acute, he was unable to discharge his duties.[39] Peter L. Breeden, who was promoted to captain the same day, was slightly wounded in the left leg at Haw's Shop more than a year later, on May 28, 1864.[40] He was sent to General Hospital #4 in Richmond and then to another hospital, probably Wayside in Florence, on June 6, 1864.

Company F was previously Company D of the 12th Battalion, South Carolina Cavalry. The CSR records the name of this company as the E.M. Dragoons. The Dragoons mustered in service as an independent company on February 3, 1862, joined the 4th Squadron/12th Battalion on May 1 and became Company F of the 4th Regiment in December. Most of the men were from Marion District, although some came from Williamsburg, Georgetown and Clarendon Districts. Huger Godbold commanded the company from the time the 12th Battalion was created on May 1, 1862, and retained command in the 4th Regiment.[41] Godbold, who suffered from chronic hepatitis for two years before resigning on June 17, 1863, was replaced by William E. Hewitt, who was promoted to captain the same day. Hewitt was severely wounded when a ball fractured his femur at Haw's Shop on May 28, 1864.[42] He was also wounded in the shoulder and was captured the same day. Taken to the Lincoln General Hospital in Washington, D.C., on June 5, Hewitt suffered a hemorrhage and died there on June 19. The *Mercury* reported, incorrectly, that he was killed at Haw's Shop on May 28.[43] The *Roll of the Dead*, however, recorded the details correctly. A sketch in *Recollections and Reminiscences* states that Hewitt was wounded at Haw's Shop and captured on the battlefield when the regiment fell back. It also notes that he was taken to Lincoln Hospital, but it adds the erroneous information that he died on June 22 or June 23.[44] Lieutenant W.B. Evans, who had been wounded near Cold Harbor on May 30, 1864, was promoted to captain with rank from June 19.

Company G, the Evans Light Dragoons, was previously Company C of the 10th Battalion and became Company G of the 4th Regiment in December 1862. Its men were from Colleton and Orangeburg Districts.[45] William P. Appleby, elected captain of the company on May 6, 1862, retained command afterward in the 4th Regiment. He was the only captain of the Evans Light Dragoons in the 4th Regiment.[46]

Company H, the Catawba Rangers, was previously Company D of the 10th Battalion.[47] It became Company H of the 4th Regiment in December 1862. The men were from Lancaster District.[48] John C. Foster, who was promoted to captain on December 28, continued to command the company until the surrender.[49]

Company I, the Williamsburg Light Dragoons, was previously Company B of the 4th Squadron/12th Battalion and became Company I of the 4th

Regiment in December 1862. Although composed primarily of wealthy men from Williamsburg, Georgetown and Clarendon Districts, a few of its members came from Horry District. Samuel John Snowden, who became the fourth, and last, captain of the company on October 15, 1862, while it was still in the 12th Battalion, retained command when the company mustered in the 4th Regiment.[50]

Company K, the Charleston Light Dragoons, evolved from an exclusive company known as the Charleston Horse Guards, which existed as early as 1733. Its name was changed during the American Revolution. Immediately before the War Between the States, many of its members joined Benjamin Huger Rutledge's militia company, which soon adopted the name Charleston Light Dragoons for itself. In April 1861, Rutledge's Company was attached to Colonel W.B. Ryan's Squadron of the 4th Brigade, South Carolina Militia.[51] It may also have been called the Charleston Light Hussars.[52] Commonly known as the "Drags," the company guarded Sullivan's Island at night in the spring of 1861.[53] It was based at Pocotaligo in November 1861, and it was then at Coosawhatchie until mid-February 1862, when most of the men formed a new company, re-elected Rutledge as captain and volunteered for twelve months of Confederate service.[54] The men mustered in service on March 25 as an independent company called Captain Benjamin H. Rutledge's Company, South Carolina Cavalry, and they re-enlisted for the duration in May.[55] The company was engaged at Pocotaligo on May 29.[56] Stationed at Grahamville and McPhersonville, the men performed picket duty from Bull River to Mackey's Point from March to December 1862. On October 22, they saw action during engagements at both Yemassee and Pocotaligo.[57] In December 1862, the Charleston Light Dragoons became Company K of the 4th Regiment, South Carolina Cavalry.[58] Rutledge commanded the company until he was promoted to colonel of the 4th Regiment on December 16, 1862. R.H. Colcock was promoted to captain the same day, and he commanded the company until the surrender.[59] Colcock became a permanent invalid as a result of his service in the malarial districts of South Carolina. (See independent cavalry organizations for more information on the Charleston Light Dragoons.)

BRIGADE AFFILIATIONS

The 4th Regiment, South Carolina Cavalry, was attached to the Department of South Carolina, Georgia and Florida from December 1862 until April 1864.[60] At that time the 4th Regiment was attached to the Army of Northern Virginia in Wade Hampton's Old Brigade: the 4th, 5th and 6th South Carolina

Cavalry Regiments. After May 1864, M.C. Butler and John Dunovant commanded the brigade, and after the regiment returned to South Carolina in early 1865, three men—W.S. Walker, Evander Law and T.M. Logan—led the brigade, which was attached to Hampton's Cavalry command until the end of the war.[61]

MAJOR MOVEMENTS AND ENGAGEMENTS

Companies A, E, F and I, the four companies of the former 12th Battalion, remained on the Waccamaw Neck north of Georgetown and at nearby Battery White from December 1862 to May 7, 1863, when they left to join the 4th Regiment at Pocotaligo.[62] By late December, the other companies of the regiment were together at Camp Pritchard near Pocotaligo.[63] From the 4th Regiment's organization on December 16, 1862, until the following May, six of its companies were charged with picket duty along the coast near Pocotaligo, Coosawhatchie, Yemassee, McPhersonville and Green Pond. In May, the four companies of the former 12th Battalion joined the six companies.

Company D was at Sullivan's Island on March 13, 1863.[64] Five companies of the 4th Regiment provided artillery support when Confederate batteries sank the steamer *George Washington* in the Coosaw River near Beaufort on April 9.[65] Lieutenant Colonel Stokes, however, does not support that position in his discussion of the engagement in his diary.[66] The former 12th Battalion companies were at Murray's (Murrell's) Inlet when a Federal party landed there briefly on April 27, but they were not engaged.[67] The same group skirmished with seven men from a Federal landing party at Murrell's Inlet on May 4 and marched three days later to Pocotaligo, where they joined the rest of the regiment.[68] They had reached McPhersonville and Green Pond by the nineteenth.[69] The regiment changed its camp from Camp Pritchard to McPhersonville in late May.[70] During June, elements of the regiment conducted picket duty and raids around Bluffton and along the Combahee River. Companies E and F were engaged near Middleton's plantation on the Combahee on the second.[71] Company B was engaged at Bluffton on June 4.[72] The Charleston Light Dragoons were sent to Charleston in August and camped at the Race Course. Some of its men guarded bridges in the city; others served as couriers on Morris Island. The dragoons served as couriers from August 20 until Morris Island was evacuated seventeen days later. For seven months—from September 1863 to April 1864—the company was stationed on the Ashley River near Charleston.[73] The other nine companies remained based at McPhersonville and occasionally at Hardeeville for nearly a year, from June 1863 to April 1864.[74]

About eighty men of Companies F and G saw action near Lowndes's Mill on the Combahee River on September 12, 13 and 14, 1863.[75] Company H was engaged with a Federal raiding party near Cunningham's Bluff on the Combahee on November 24.[76] On March 17, 1864, orders arrived for the regiment to join the Army of Northern Virginia.[77] It was ordered to begin the march to Columbia on April 4.[78] The 4th Regiment arrived in Columbia on April 10; there, the horses were shod. It moved on to Camden in late April and marched through Lancaster Court House on May 4.[79] Company C, the Calhoun Troop, was in the upstate in late April 1864. It left Fort Hill for Columbia on May 4, and on the ninth, it left Columbia for Greensboro, arriving there two days later. The rest of the regiment arrived on the twelfth. Marching twenty to thirty miles each day through North Carolina, the regiment arrived at Clarkesville, Virginia, on May 18 and at Amelia Courthouse on the twenty-second.[80] The regiment joined the 5th and 6th Cavalry Regiments in relieving the 1st and 2nd, which had been sent back to South Carolina.

Companies A, D and G arrived in Richmond on May 23, 1864. Other companies probably arrived on the twenty-fourth and the twenty-sixth.[81] The 4th Regiment skirmished with the enemy almost daily from late May to August 1864. It may have been engaged at Bethesda Church on May 25, although neither Stokes's accounts nor *The Sketch of the Charleston Light Dragoons* mentions such an engagement.[82] The regiment was in camp near Hanover Junction on May 27, and about half its men fought dismounted at Haw's Shop on the twenty-eighth.[83] The other half reported after the battle. According to the above-mentioned *Sketch*, Haw's Shop was the first engagement for the Charleston Light Dragoons in Virginia.[84] Companies C and E skirmished near Cold Harbor on May 29, and on the thirtieth, the entire regiment was heavily engaged near Old Church and Matadequin Creek, where the Charleston Light Dragoons was nearly annihilated; only twelve men reported for duty after that engagement.[85] The regiment marched toward Bottom's Bridge on June 1 but was held in reserve during the engagement there the next day. For the next few days, before the brigade marched to Mechanicsville on June 8, the regiment performed picket duty at White Oak Swamp.

The 4th Regiment left Mechanicsville with the brigade on June 9 and marched toward Gordonsville to intercept General P.H. Sheridan. Arriving at Louisa Court House about midday on June 10, the brigade rested that night at Trevilian Station. The next day, during the first day's action near Trevilian Station, the 4th Regiment was engaged at Louisa Court House; it also saw action at Trevilian Station on the twelfth. The regiment pursued Sheridan on the thirteenth, crossed the North Anna River on June 14 and continued its pursuit until the eighteenth, when the command changed direction and headed for White House on the York River. The regiment was engaged there on both the twentieth and the twenty-first.[86] It was also involved in the action at Nance's Shop (also called Ladd's Store and Samaria Church) on June 24 and again on June 25.[87] The regiment crossed to the south side of the James River on June 26 and arrived at Stony Creek Station on the Weldon Railroad, south of Petersburg, two days later. It was engaged with Wilson's Raiders at Sappony Church on the railroad, about three miles from the station, on the night of June 28 and again the next morning, but it was not engaged at Reams Station on the twenty-ninth.

The regiment mostly performed picket duty, but did participate in some skirmishing during the month of July—at Riddell's Shop on July 5, for example, and at Sappony Church on July 9.[88] It was also engaged at Lee's Mills on the thirtieth. During July, some three hundred to five hundred men of Butler's Brigade, all without horses, were formed into three new companies, which became known as the "Dismounted Battalion of Butler's Brigade" or the "Stud Horse Battalion."[89] Major Henry Farley, previously captain of Companies D and H, 1st Regiment South Carolina Artillery (Regulars), in 1862 and 1863, commanded the unit, whose men fought as infantry until mounts could be obtained. About August 11, the 4th marched toward Culpeper, but turned toward Richmond on the fifteenth. The next day the regiment marched through Richmond to Deep Bottom and was held in reserve at Chaffin's Farm near White Oak Swamp. The regiment was engaged at White Oak Swamp on the eighteenth but suffered no casualties.[90] The men recrossed to the south side of the James River on August 21 and moved to a camp on the Squirrel Level Road, about fourteen miles south of Petersburg. Two days later, on August 23, the regiment saw action again, this time at Gravelly Run, also called Monck's Neck Bridge, near Reams Station on the Weldon Railroad. According to the CSR, the 4th Regiment was not only engaged the next day at the station itself—about eight miles from Petersburg—but was also held in reserve on the twenty-fifth. *Saddle Soldiers* indicates that the brigade was not engaged there, but both D.S. Freeman and the CSR document its presence there on the twenty-fourth.[91] U.R. Brooks implies that Dunovant's Brigade was engaged on August 25 at Reams Station, and Stokes agrees that the 4th Regiment was involved that day as well.[92]

The regiment camped and picketed along the Boydton Plank Road for most of the month of September. During the City Point, or Beef Steak, Raid from September 14 to September 17, only about a hundred men of Dunovant's Brigade participated. To create a diversion during the raid, Butler's Division engaged Federal pickets near Burgess's Mill every morning for three days. The division was also engaged at the same location on September 19. The regiment skirmished along the Vaughn and Squirrel Level Roads from September 27 to September 30, including engagements at both Armstrong's Mill and McDowell's farm on the twenty-ninth. It also saw action at Mrs. Cummings's farm on October 1.[93] The regiment camped at Armstrong's Mill on Hatcher's Run until October 21 or October 22, a few days before another engagement on the twenty-seventh along the Boydton Plank Road near Burgess's Mill on the south side of Hatcher's Run.[94] That battle marked the failure of Grant's last attempt in 1864 to turn Lee's right flank.

The regiment remained at Camp Butler on the Quaker Road below Petersburg throughout the month of November. The dismounted battalion was sent to Stoney Creek Depot, where, on December 1, a Federal force captured about 112 men, half of them from the 4th Regiment.[95] A week later, on December 8, the regiment skirmished near Belfield on the Meherrin River, about twenty miles south of Stony Creek Station on the Weldon Railroad; this engagement was the regiment's last before its return to South Carolina.[96] Butler's Division, comprising the 4th, 5th and 6th Cavalry Regiments and Young's Brigade, was sent back to South Carolina on January 19, 1865, for two reasons: one, to help check Sherman's advance and two, to procure horses. The 4th Regiment, which was camped near Columbia by February 2, participated in the evacuation of the city on the seventeenth.[97] It also skirmished almost daily from February 14 to April 13. The regiment was involved in the attack on Kilpatrick's Camp near Fayetteville on March 10, missed the battle of Averasboro on the sixteenth and was engaged at Bentonville on the twentieth and the twenty-first. Lieutenant Colonel Stokes wrote that while the 4th Regiment might have disbanded, it never surrendered.[98] Then in command of the 4th Regiment, Stokes wrote that he led the regiment out of camp on the evening of April 26 simply to avoid surrender the next day. He personally disbanded the regiment near Asheboro on April 27.[99] Captain Snowden and fifteen to twenty of his men were active near Georgetown in early April; Company I disbanded at Camden later that month.[100] The 4th Regiment was officially included in the surrender of the Army of Tennessee on April 26, 1865.

19.

THE 5ᵀᴴ REGIMENT,
SOUTH CAROLINA CAVALRY

The 5ᵗʰ Regiment, South Carolina Cavalry, was also called both Ferguson's regiment and Dunovant's regiment.[1] It was also known as the "Fighting Fifth."[2] In a letter to General Samuel Cooper, dated October 18, 1862, P.G.T. Beauregard suggested the creation of two new cavalry regiments, adding that the cavalry in South Carolina was not well organized and needed attention; he even suggested field officers for the new units. The 5ᵗʰ Regiment was organized on January 18, 1863, by consolidating the four companies of Morgan's 14ᵗʰ (1ˢᵗ and 2ⁿᵈ) Battalion, South Carolina Cavalry, the four companies of Jeffords's 17ᵗʰ (6ᵗʰ) Battalion, South Carolina Cavalry, and two independent companies under Captain Harlan and Captain Whilden.[3]

FIELD OFFICERS

Samuel Wragg Ferguson of Charleston and Union, a graduate of West Point, was appointed colonel of the 5ᵗʰ Regiment by order of General Beauregard with whom he had served previously as a staff officer.[4] Ferguson was lieutenant colonel of the 28ᵗʰ Regiment, Mississippi Cavalry, at the time of his appointment to colonel of the 5ᵗʰ Regiment. Because he elected to remain with the 28ᵗʰ, however, his commission to colonel was canceled. Lieutenant Colonel Robert Jeffords commanded the 5ᵗʰ Regiment between January and July 1863. Ferguson, who was promoted to brigadier general effective July 23, 1863, was given a command in the western army.

John Gore Dunovant of Chester District, the second colonel of the 5ᵗʰ Regiment, was the first to actually command it. Just when he took over is unclear, but it was probably on July 28, 1863, the day of his promotion. Dunovant had been cashiered for drunkenness the previous

November while serving as colonel of the 1st Regiment, South Carolina Infantry (Regulars). Captain A.B. Mulligan wrote on August 7, 1863: "Col. Dunovant is a brave man with much experience having been in the U.S. Army before the war. He has been unfortunate, having been addicted to drinking but he has entirely reformed it is said and I hope will make a good [Colonel]. We could not be worsted anyhow and I am satisfied."[5]

Dunovant was wounded in the hand by a pistol ball on May 28, 1864, at Haw's Shop, one of the 5th Regiment's first engagements in Virginia. He returned to duty on July 8, his hand still in a sling.[6] President Davis promoted Dunovant to the temporary rank of brigadier general on August 22, 1864, when M.C. Butler was named major general.[7] Dunovant commanded the brigade until his death less than two months later.[8] He was killed on October 1 during the engagement at Mrs. Cummings's farm, also called McDowell's farm, on the Vaughn Road. While leading his men in a charge, Dunovant was shot through the chest.[9] Private C.M. Calhoun of the 6th Regiment wrote that after he was shot, Dunovant's foot became caught in his stirrup, and his horse dragged the mangled corpse a considerable distance into the Federal lines.[10] Butler, who personally witnessed the event, wrote that Dunovant was on horseback and his men were on foot during the charge. After the first wound to the chest, Dunovant suffered another when his head struck a root or a log as his horse dragged him. Butler concluded that the first wound was fatal.[11] Lieutenant Colonel Stokes of the 4th Regiment wrote: "The death of General Dunovant is a great loss to the Brigade and is deeply regretted by both officers and men."[12] U.R. Brooks called him a "brave, generous, and chivalrous man."[13] M.C. Butler wrote that Dunovant was "a gallant and distinguished officer."[14] His brother, Richard G.M. Dunovant, served as colonel of the 12th Regiment, South Carolina Infantry.

Robert Josiah Jeffords of Christ Church Parish in Charleston District, previously major in command of the 17th Battalion, was promoted to lieutenant colonel at the organization of the regiment in January 1863. Because the regiment lacked a colonel, Jeffords was in command until Dunovant took over in July. He was slightly wounded in the leg at Charles City Court House on May 24, 1864, and he was severely wounded in the left thigh at Cold Harbor only six days later.[15] It was believed the wound to the thigh was serious enough to prevent his return to duty.[16] He was sent to Jackson Hospital in Richmond on May 31 and was given a thirty-day furlough on June 14. Jeffords did return to command the regiment as the senior field officer in September, although the *Mercury* reported that month, erroneously, that he had been promoted to colonel when Dunovant became brigadier general.[17] Jeffords was shot through the heart and killed while leading his men at Burgess's Mill near the

White Oak Road on October 27, 1864.[18] Wade Hampton Manning of the Charleston Light Dragoons wrote that Jeffords was shot in the head.[19] His death cast a deep gloom over the 5th Regiment.[20] The *Mercury* reported in October that Jeffords, had he survived, probably would have been promoted to brigadier general to replace Dunovant.[21] He was described as a "gallant officer" and a "dashing and fearless officer."[22]

Joseph Hargrove Morgan, MD, of Orangeburg District, previously major of the 14th Battalion, became major of the 5th Regiment at its organization on January 18, 1863. He had been severely wounded in the right ankle at Pocotaligo on May 2, 1862. Mulligan wrote on August 14, 1864, that Morgan "is an old man and is lame and cannot get about on foot and we do nearly all of our fighting on foot."[23] Morgan was wounded again, this time in the left heel, at Gravelly Run on August 23, 1864. He was sent to the hospital the next day, and the foot was amputated, rendering him incapacitated for further service.[24] Although he was unfit for duty, Morgan continued as major of the 5th Regiment until the end of the war.[25] A note in the CSR states that Morgan was a "fit subject for retirement, [but] no application was made." Lieutenant Colonel Stokes of the 4th Regiment records that Morgan had stated he would return within three months of his amputation.[26] "I can," he said "kick like hell with the stump yet."[27] Morgan's desire to return to the regiment probably explains his reluctance to resign.

Zimmerman Davis of Charleston and Fairfield District was captain of Company D until March 15, 1865.[28] He was serving as the assistant adjutant inspector general of Butler's Brigade on July 10, 1864. The 5th Regiment had been without a field officer since Jeffords's death on October 27, 1864. A.B. Mulligan, not Davis, was senior captain in the regiment at the time, and Morgan, who was recovering from a wound, was the only field officer. If Morgan had resigned or had been promoted, the next promotion to field officer grade would normally have gone to Mulligan. Davis, however, confessing to certain personal ambitions—one of which was his wish to advance to colonel if Morgan failed to return to duty—wrote to Mulligan on December 29 and asked him to waive his right to the promotion.[29] Davis also believed, or so he wrote, that Mulligan appeared not to desire advancement. In a response dated January 12, 1865, Mulligan said he felt it was his duty to accept a promotion if it was offered.[30] Even so, Davis was promoted from captain to colonel on March 15, retroactive to October 27, 1864. The promotion was probably offered to Davis because both Morgan and Mulligan had been severely wounded and were not expected to return to active duty for some time. It is also possible that the promotion was not made by proper authority. Davis was slightly wounded at Lynches Creek on February 24, 1865, but he remained with the regiment.[31] On the night before the surrender, Davis marched most of the regiment, about 150 men, to a point about sixty miles south of Greensboro, near the South Carolina line, disbanded them there on April 27 and sent them home with their arms.[32] He was paroled at Augusta, Georgia, on May 25, 1865.

John C. Edwards was promoted from captain of Company A to lieutenant colonel on March 15, 1865, with rank from October 27, 1864, because all the field officers of the 5th Regiment had been either killed or incapacitated. Although he fought with the regiment until it was disbanded on April 27, Edwards's promotion was not official since it was not properly authorized.[33]

COMPANIES

Company A was probably the St. Matthews Troop.[34] It was previously designated Company B of the 14th Battalion, South Carolina Cavalry, and was composed of men from St. Matthews Parish and the Elloree section of Orangeburg District.[35] John Cubbage Edwards, who was commissioned captain on December 24, 1861, was the company's only commander in the 14th (2nd) Battalion, a rank he retained when the company became part of the 5th Regiment. He was detached from the regiment and placed in command of the dismounted battalion, or those men in the brigade who did not have horses, from September to December 1864. Edwards was promoted to lieutenant colonel on March 15, 1865, retroactive to October 26, 1864.[36] The *Memory Roll* notes that the promotion was not official because the proper authority did not make it. The CSR records the supporting fact that Brevet Second Lieutenant T.A. Jeffords commanded the company after Edwards assumed field-grade rank, even though he was never actually promoted to captain. At the same time, the CSR also states that Edwards held the rank of lieutenant colonel in the 5th Regiment. Possibly the promotion was never confirmed because it came so late in the war.

Company B, the Dixie Rangers, was previously Company C in the 17th (6th) Battalion. Although most of its men were from Charleston and Beaufort Districts, some came from Abbeville, Barnwell and Marlboro Districts. Alfred Birmingham Mulligan, captain in both the battalion and the regiment, spent several thousand dollars of his own money to equip the company. He also commanded the regiment after Morgan was disabled on August 23, 1864. On October 27, while serving with the dismounted men of Butler's Brigade, Mulligan was severely wounded in the right hand at the battle of Burgess's Mill.[37] A bullet passed through the palm, leaving the hand virtually useless. Surgeons recommended amputation because Mulligan's fingers were left crumpled, but he refused the operation. Mulligan did not return to the company, and at the end of the war, he still suffered from the effects the wound. He never regained full use of his right hand.[38]

Company C, the Beech Hill Rangers, was previously Company D of the 17th (6th) Battalion. Its men were from Colleton District.[39] Wheeler G. Smith, captain of the company in the 17th Battalion, retained the rank in the 5th Regiment.[40] Chronic gastritis and derangement of the nervous system forced the forty-four-year-old Smith to resign on March 15, 1864. His successor was Lieutenant G.W. Raysor, according to the *Memory Roll*, but the CSR does not record Raysor's promotion to captain. Both the *Roll of the Dead* and Kirkland state that William D. Marvin, who was killed at Gravelly Run on August 23, 1864, was captain of Company C.[41] According to the CSR, Marvin's rank was corporal.

Company D, the South Carolina Rangers, or Carolina Rangers, had been Company A of the 17th Battalion. Most of its men were from Charleston, Beaufort and Colleton Districts, but a few came from Orangeburg, Edgefield, Greenville, Fairfield and Marion Districts. Zimmerman Davis, who became captain on April 12, 1862, commanded the company in the battalion and retained command in the 5th Regiment.[42] The Rangers re-enlisted for the duration of the war on March 5, 1864.[43] Davis was promoted to colonel of the regiment on March 15, 1865, effective from October 27, 1864. First Lieutenant George Tupper, who had been wounded on the Vaughn Road on October 1, 1864, replaced Davis on March 15, although the CSR does not verify his promotion. Tupper was paroled at Greensboro.

Company E was called the St. James Mounted Riflemen, Company B. A predecessor company of almost identical name, the St. James Santee Mounted Riflemen, was organized on April 15, 1861, as Thomas Pinckney's Independent Mounted Riflemen and mustered in Confederate service for the duration on October 31. From December 1861 to May 1862, Pinckney's Company was officially Company A, Manigault's Battalion, SCV. While it was stationed at Camp Palmer on the South Santee River on May 1, Company A was divided into two companies: Pinckney's Company A and Captain Whilden's Company B. When Manigault's Battalion was disbanded on May 18, both companies became part of Byrd's 6th Battalion, South Carolina Infantry. Company B was composed of men from Charleston, Georgetown, Clarendon and Beaufort Districts, and it had a few men from Orangeburg and Horry Districts. It served for a time as an unlettered company in Byrd's Battalion. When Byrd's 6th Battalion merged into the 26th Regiment, South Carolina Infantry, in October 1862, neither company followed. Company B became independent about October 30 and was designated Company E of the 5th Regiment, South Carolina Cavalry, on January 18, 1863. Its captain, Louis A. Whilden, commanded from May 1, 1862, until he was severely wounded in the thigh at Drewry's Bluff in mid-May 1864.[44] Admitted to a Richmond hospital on May 23, most likely Chimborazo Hospital #1, Whilden died of the wound on August 4, 1864, a date also shown in the record as the fifth.[45] His middle name is shown as both Augustus and Angstree.[46] Joseph L. Inglesby commanded the company with the rank of lieutenant after Whilden's death. On March 18, 1864, the men of Company E, who had already enlisted for the duration of the war, reaffirmed their commitment to the cause in a company letter.

Meanwhile, Pinckney's Company A had served as Company A, Byrd's Battalion, and was called Captain Thomas Pinckney's Company A, St. James Mounted Riflemen. It was probably an independent cavalry company from October until December 16, 1862, when it was assigned to the 4th Cavalry Regiment as Company D.

Company F, the Lexington Light Dragoons, was previously Company C of the 14th Battalion.[47] Its men were from the Dutch Fork section of Lexington District.[48] Augustus Henry Caughman, who was elected captain at the reorganization on May 13, 1862, retained command when the company became part of the 5th Regiment on January 21, 1863. Caughman was wounded at Fayetteville, North Carolina, in March 1865.

Company G, the Willington Rangers, was previously Company B of the 17th Battalion. The company was named in honor of Aaron S. Willington, Esq., founder of the *Charleston Daily Courier* and its senior proprietor until his death in February 1862.[49] Most Company G men were from Charleston District, but a few came from Beaufort and Richland Districts. B. Warren McTureous commanded the company in both the battalion and the regiment.[50] McTureous served throughout the war and never surrendered.

Company H, the Santee Guerillas, or Santee Rangers, was previously Company A of the 14th Battalion. Most of its men were from Sumter District, although some came from Clarendon District. Richard M. Skinner commanded in both the battalion and the regiment.[51] When Skinner was killed at Nance's Shop on June 24, 1864, Edward Manly Bradham was promoted to captain as his replacement the same day.

Company I was previously Company D of the 14th Battalion. Most of its men were from Orangeburg District and Springfield in western Barnwell District, but a few were from Lexington and Edgefield Districts.[52] Thomas W. Tyler, a first lieutenant in the battalion, was promoted to captain of Company I on February 4, a date also shown in the record as February 5, 1863. At Trevilian Station on June 12, 1864, Tyler sustained wounds to the great and second toes of his right foot.[53] He had not returned to duty by the end of 1864, and he may never have rejoined the company.

Company K, the Mountain Rangers, was an independent cavalry company known as Captain Harlan's Company, SCV, before it was attached to the 5th Regiment in January 1863.[54] It had existed for at least two months before mustering in service at Columbia on December 30, 1862. Most Company K men were from Union and Spartanburg Districts, although a few came from York, Newberry, Greenville, Richland, Fairfield, Laurens and Chester Districts. Joseph Gist Harlan, whose captain's commission dated from November 1, 1862, was hospitalized on October 10, 1864, probably after a horse fell on him. Disabled by the injury, he retired to the Invalid Corps on February 24, 1865. He was assigned to a position at Union soon afterward.[55] Lieutenant Farr Humphrey Bates assumed command of the company, but he was never promoted to captain.

BRIGADE AFFILIATIONS

The 5th Regiment was attached to various subdivisions and military districts in the Department of South Carolina, Georgia and Florida from January 1863 until May 1864.[56] Its companies, which often served in a detached capacity, were occasionally assigned to the Department of North Carolina during that period.[57] The 4th, 5th and 6th Regiments were attached on May 28, 1864, to M.C. Butler's Brigade in the Army of Northern Virginia. Later brigade commanders were John Dunovant, W.S. Walker, Evander Law and T.M. Logan. After its return to South Carolina in early 1865, the regiment was attached to Hampton's Cavalry command. It remained there until the end of the war.[58]

MAJOR MOVEMENTS AND ENGAGEMENTS

From the regiment's organization on January 18, 1863, until May 1864, its companies performed picket and courier duty at various locations in the North Carolina and South Carolina coastal area. Examples abound: Company A was stationed at McPhersonville in Beaufort District during the first half of 1863, but Company B's experience was more varied. It performed routine picket duty along the Ashepoo and Combahee Rivers in March 1863, and it was based at Camp Morgan below Green Pond later that month.[59] One of the six to arrive in Charleston on April 28, Company B and two others were on James Island by May 10; the rest were still at Green Pond. Company B was sent back into Charleston to guard commissary stores there.[60] It was based in St. Andrews Parish on

July 7, 1863, when orders came to march to Kenansville, North Carolina. On November 24, Company B moved twenty-four miles to Richlands in Onslow County.[61] Company B was sent to Brock's Schoolhouse in the same county on December 20. Company B marched again to Richlands on April 2, 1864, and left for Virginia from Magnolia, North Carolina, on May 6. It rejoined the regiment on the thirteenth.[62]

Company C was based at Green Pond in Colleton District from January to April 1863, and Company D was based there from December 1862 to February 1863. In March 1863, Company D was sent to St. Andrews Parish. From there, it began a whole series of scouting expeditions: on the eighth a small detachment reconnoitered on St. Helena Island, and from March 13 to 20, the company conducted expeditions to both Hutchinson and Fenwick Islands; it returned to St. Helena Island on April 6. Company D, along with the Beaufort Volunteer Artillery, attacked a Federal gunboat in the Ashepoo River at the mouth of the St. Helena Sound on April 20. On the twenty-seventh it marched to Charleston, and then it marched back to Green Pond the next day.

Company E marched to Charleston from Camp Gibbes in Christ Church Parish on November 25, 1862, and to Adams Run on December 18. Company F was stationed at McPhersonville and Pocotaligo in Beaufort District in January 1863. In March Companies A, B, C, D, F, H and I were stationed in the 3rd South Carolina Military District.[63] Company E's bases that month were Sullivan's Island and Christ Church Parish.[64] Company F moved north to McClellanville on April 29. Company G was stationed at James Island for a little over two years, from January 3, 1862, to February 1864.[65] Company H was based at Pocotaligo from January 2, 1863, until it was sent to Charleston in March; Company I, based at Pocotaligo on January 31, was ordered to McClellanville on April 29, 1863. By June 23, Companies F and I were at Georgetown and three others were at Charleston.[66] Company H was sent to Mount Pleasant on June 30, and Company I moved to Adams Run in October. Company K, based in Charleston in March and April, was sent to Pocotaligo on April 28, 1863. Ordered to Kenansville, North Carolina, in July, Company K moved to Wilmington in November, and it remained there until April 1864.

Detachments of Companies A, C and G participated in the engagement near Grimball's Landing on James Island on July 16, 1863.[67] Elements of the regiment were also engaged at the same landing on the thirtieth.[68] Company D's men served as couriers on Morris Island and at Battery Wagner in July and August.[69] On August 20, Company K of the 4th Cavalry Regiment replaced Company D of the 5th Regiment on Morris Island. Company F moved to Dill's Bluff on James Island on August 2. Three companies were at James Island, two at Charleston, two at Georgetown and one, Company E, was at Sullivan's Island on July 30, 1863.[70] From August until the end of 1863, a full four companies of the regiment were usually at James Island. Company E remained at Sullivan's Island until December, when it moved to St. Andrews Parish. Company H remained in Charleston, and Company D was there as well until it was ordered to McPhersonville in November. Company I returned to Georgetown until December, when it joined Company H in Charleston.[71]

In January 1864, four companies of the 5th were stationed at Camp Suber on James Island.[72] Company D was at Adams Run, Company H was at Charleston and Companies E and I were at St. Andrews Parish. Company K, on detached service in North Carolina, was engaged at Shepherdsville about February 2, 1864.[73] Its men, composing the only South Carolina unit present, fought alongside a mixed group of infantry and artillery units from North Carolina and Virginia. The entire regiment was ordered to Virginia on March 17.[74] The period from April 2, when the 5th departed James Island by horseback, until all the men, horses and equipment were together again in Virginia in mid-May, was a time of challenge for the South Carolinians.[75] Through late April and early May, the regiment made its way to Virginia. There it joined two other cavalry regiments, the 4th and 6th, as relief for the 1st and 2nd, which had been ordered back to South Carolina. The newcomers, armed with Enfield rifles, initiated the concept of cavalry units functioning and fighting as mounted infantry.

The 5th Regiment arrived in Virginia about ten days before its horses, and it was stationed initially on the James River between Petersburg and Richmond.[76] It was engaged in skirmishes almost daily from May to August. The four-day period from May 10 to May 14 was one of almost ceaseless activity for the horseless cavalrymen: the regiment was engaged at Chester Station on May 10, at Swift Creek on the twelfth and it skirmished on the thirteenth and fourteenth before its mounts arrived. Recrossing the James, the men were engaged again at Drewry's Bluff on May 15 to May 16 and at Atkinson's farm on the seventeenth.[77] The 5th Regiment fought as infantry at Charles City Court House on May 24 and at Bethesda Church on the twenty-fifth. It was with the Army of Northern Virginia at Hanover Junction on May 26, it was at Atlee's Station on the twenty-eighth and all but a hundred of its men fought at Haw's Shop, or Price's farm, on May 28.[78] The regiment was engaged at Totopotomoi Creek near Atlee's Station on May 29 and at Matadequin Creek, near Cold Harbor, the next day.[79] Although it was held in reserve at Bottom's Bridge on June 2, it was probably part of the engagement near Cold Harbor on June 3.[80] The regiment guarded the extreme right of the Confederate lines that day, and for the next few days it performed picket duty at White Oak Swamp.

On June 8, the brigade marched to Mechanicsville. The 5th Regiment left Mechanicsville with the brigade the next day and headed toward Gordonsville to intercept General P.H. Sheridan. Arriving at Louisa Court House about midday on the tenth, the brigade rested that night at Trevilian Station. The 5th fought at Louisa Court House during the first day's action near Trevilian Station on June 11, and it fought at the station the next day. It continued to pursue Sheridan on June 13, it crossed the North Anna River on the fourteenth and it kept up the pressure until the command changed direction on the eighteenth. It then headed for White House on the York River, where it engaged the enemy on the twentieth and twenty-first.[81] On June 24 the regiment fought at Nance's Shop before crossing to the south side of the James River on the twenty-sixth. Arriving at Stony Creek Station on the Weldon Railroad below Petersburg on June 28, the regiment was engaged with Wilson's Raiders at Sappony Church about three miles from the station that night and the next morning. The 5th Regiment did not participate in the action at Reams Station on June 29. July brought mostly picket duty and occasional skirmishes like those at Nance's Shop on the seventh and Sappony Church on the ninth, but the regiment did participate in a larger engagement at Reams Station on the twenty-third and again on July 30 at Lee's Mills. That same month at Stony Creek, Virginia, some three to five hundred men of Butler's Brigade, all without horses, were formed into three new companies, which became known as the "Dismounted Battalion of Butler's Brigade" or the "Stud Horse Battalion."[82] Commanded by Major Henry Farley, the men fought as infantry until mounts could be obtained.

The regiment left its camp at Malones Crossing about August 11 and headed toward Richmond. It marched through the city on the sixteenth and moved on to Deep Bottom and an engagement at White Tavern on August 16 to August 17. The next day, the regiment fought again on the Darbytown Road. It marched back to the south side of the James on August 21 and made camp on the Squirrel Level Road, about fourteen miles south of Petersburg.[83] More fighting followed on August 23 at Gravelly Run, also called Monck's Neck Bridge, near Reams Station on the Weldon Railroad.[84] The 5th Regiment may also have seen action at Reams Station on August 25, although the record is unclear. *Saddle Soldiers* said the brigade was not involved at all, but D.S. Freeman wrote that it was engaged there on the twenty-fourth.[85] Mulligan wrote that the regiment was in camp near Gravelly Run on August 24.[86] U.R. Brooks implies that Dunovant's Brigade was engaged on August 25 at Reams Station.[87]

The regiment camped and picketed along the Boydton Plank Road for most of September. About a hundred men from Dunovant's Brigade, a few of them from the 5th Regiment, took part in the City Point, or Beef Steak, Raid, from September 14 to September 17. Assigned the task of creating a diversion, Butler's Division engaged Federal pickets near Burgess's Mill on three successive mornings—from September 14 to September 16. The division also saw action near the mill on the nineteenth. Following another clash at Reams Station on September 23, the 5th Regiment skirmished along the Vaughn and Squirrel Level Roads from September 27 to September, 30, and it was engaged at Wyatt's farm on September 29.[88] The 5th Regiment also saw action at Mrs. Cummings's farm on the Vaughn Road on October 1.[89] It fought again on the twenty-seventh on the Boydton Plank Road near Burgess's Mill during Grant's last attempt that year to turn Lee's right flank.[90]

Those men from the 4th, 5th and 6th Regiments without serviceable horses had been sent to Stony Creek about twenty miles from the brigade. On December 1, a Federal force overran the detachment at Stony Creek Depot and captured 112, including 29 from the 5th Regiment.[91] The regiment was engaged on December 7 near the Weldon Railroad and again on the eighth at Hicksford on the Meherrin River about twenty miles south of Stony Creek Station.[92] In late December 1864, a portion of the 5th and 6th Regiments under the command of Captain McTureous left Virginia hurriedly, and without their horses, headed for the South Carolina coast. They were engaged at Heyward's place near the end of the war.[93] M.C. Butler's Division, comprising the 4th, 5th and 6th Regiments and Young's Brigade, was sent back to South Carolina on January 19, 1865, to both help check Sherman's advance and procure horses.[94] The 5th skirmished that day. By February 14, one of its squadrons was stationed at Appleby's Bridge on the Orangeburg Road.[95] The regiment skirmished nearly every day during this period; the record documents a full two months of nearly ceaseless activity, from February 14 to April 13, and casualty lists for the 5th Regiment appeared regularly in the *Edgefield Advertiser.* The regiment suffered losses on four days in February, on eight days in March and on one day in April—the tenth.[96]

The regiment participated in the evacuation of Columbia on February 17, and it skirmished at Killian's Mill north of Columbia, the next day. It was engaged at Kellytown, or Lynches Creek, on February 24 and also in the attack on Kilpatrick's camp near Fayetteville on March 10. The brigade did not engage at Averasboro on the sixteenth, but the period from March 19 to March 22 was marked by daily skirmishes. The regiment fought at Bentonville on March 20 and March 21 before marching to Raleigh and on to

Greensboro. From April 17 to April 18, the 5[97] Regiment served as escort for General Johnston as he made his way to the site of surrender negotiations.[97] Most of the men of the 5th Regiment never actually surrendered. On April 26, some, notably those in Captain George Tupper's Company D, did surrender and received paroles, but most were led in another direction. On the night before the surrender, Colonel Zimmerman Davis marched the majority of the regiment, about 150 men, to a point about sixty miles south of Greensboro near the South Carolina line, disbanded them there on April 27 and sent them home.[98] The 5th Regiment was officially included in the surrender of the Army of Tennessee on April 26, 1865.

20.

THE 12ᵀᴴ BATTALION, SOUTH CAROLINA CAVALRY

The 12th Battalion, South Carolina Cavalry, was also called the 4th Squadron, Emanuel's Squadron and Emanuel's Independent Battalion.[1] Organized about May 1, 1862, its men mustered in service in the field as the 4th Squadron, South Carolina Cavalry, with four companies designated A to D. The adjutant and inspector general soon changed the name officially to the 12th Battalion. On December 16, after seven months of battalion status, the four companies of the 12th joined with four companies of the 10th Battalion and two independent companies under Captains B.H. Rutledge and Thomas Pinckney to form the 4th Regiment, South Carolina Cavalry.

Professor William Rivers wrote that the 12th had been incorrectly identified as the 4th Battalion, South Carolina Cavalry, but John Peyre Thomas, in his 1899 work, definitely names it the "4th Battalion."[2] Only a little documentation that might resolve the difference of opinion exists, although two reports in the *Official Records* do shed some light on the issue. One, written by Major Emanuel on August 15, 1862, lists him as the commanding officer of the "4th South Carolina Cavalry."[3] Unfortunately, the report does not identify the command further as a squadron or a battalion, and thus, it does not clarify the issue. The other, submitted by Colonel A.M. Manigault of the 10th Regiment, South Carolina Infantry, was written on April 5, about a month before the 12th Battalion was created. It refers to the 4th Battalion as a state organization under the command of Major J.C. Wilson.[4]

It is possible that the organization existed as a state organization as early as January 18, 1862, and was known as the 4th Battalion from that time to May 1. Supporting this theory is the fact that all four companies of the 12th Battalion mustered in service in January or early February, although there is no direct evidence that any one of the four was in the

4th Battalion. It is equally possible that the 12th Battalion's companies were all independent from January to May 1, 1862, and Wilson's 4th Battalion comprised other companies. Manigault's report documenting the existence of the 4th Battalion as a state organization commanded by Major Wilson must be considered reliable evidence.[5] Wilson, who was commissioned major on January 18, 1862, served as captain of Company B in the 12th Battalion after May 1, but he never held the rank of major in the 12th Battalion.[6] Furthermore, he is not mentioned in the CSR as commanding the 4th Battalion, the 12th Battalion or any other unit. Whether Wilson's 4th Battalion and Emanuel's 12th Battalion were one and the same remains unknown. The most likely explanation is that the four companies of Wilson's 4th Battalion were in state service but were then reorganized and mustered in Confederate service as Emanuel's 12th Battalion on May 1, 1862. Unfortunately, no direct evidence supports this theory.

FIELD OFFICER

William Pledger Emanuel of Marlboro, Charleston and Georgetown Districts, commanded the 12th Battalion as major and the only field officer.[7] Previously captain of Company C, he was promoted to major on May 1, 1862. He was commissioned major of the 4th Regiment, South Carolina Cavalry, on April 2, 1864, with rank from December 16, 1862.

COMPANIES

Company A of the 4th Squadron was also designated Company A in the 12th Battalion. It was probably called the Chesterfield Light Dragoons. Most of its men were from Chesterfield District, although some came from Darlington and Lancaster Districts, and a few came from Horry, Marlboro and Kershaw Districts. James C. Craig and Henry McIver raised the company, which mustered in service for the duration of the war on January 25, 1862, at Georgetown.[8] Craig had enlisted earlier, on December 26, 1861; the company was called Captain James Craig's Company, SCV, from January 1862 until it joined the 4th Squadron on May 1. Craig was re-appointed at that time, the only captain in the 4th Squadron/12th Battalion and the first captain when his company became Company A of the 4th Regiment, South Carolina Cavalry, in December 1862.

Company B of the 4th Squadron, the Williamsburg Light Dragoons, was also designated Company B in the 12th Battalion. It was composed of wealthy men mostly from Williamsburg, Georgetown and Clarendon Districts, along with a few from Horry District. The company had been a militia unit commanded by Captain J.C. Wilson; most of its men had volunteered for twelve months of state service in Harlee's Legion of Militia in January 1861, and they had stayed until it was disbanded about January 1, 1862. Wilson's service with the company appears to have ended at that time, although, as documented earlier, he shows up again in April as major commanding the 4th Battalion, a state organization.[9] The Williamsburg Light Dragoons mustered in service for twelve months at Georgetown on February 3, and it served in the vicinity for many months in 1862.[10] John Watson was elected captain, also on the third. From February 3 to May 1, the company, called Captain John Watson's Company, SCV, retained its independent status, although the CSR says it was attached to the 21st Infantry Regiment at some point in early 1862. Watson was not re-elected at the reorganization; his replacement, George P. Nelson, was elected on May 1, but poor health forced his resignation on October 15, less than six months later. Samuel John Snowden became the fourth captain on the fifteenth, and he retained command in the 4th Regiment.[11] The Williamsburg Light Dragoons became Company I of the 4th Regiment in December 1862.

Company C of the 4th Squadron was also Company C of the 12th Battalion. It was organized in late 1861, and its officers enlisted on January 12, 1862. The company mustered in for twelve months' service on February 4 at Georgetown. Most of its men were from Marlboro District, although some came from Horry, Georgetown, Williamsburg, Marion and Darlington Districts. From February 1862 until it joined the 4th Squadron/12th Battalion on May 1, 1862, the company was known by the name of its first captain, William Pledger Emanuel. Emanuel was promoted to major, and Henry Edens was promoted to captain at the same time. Edens retained his rank when the company became Company E of the 4th Regiment on December 16, 1862.

Company D of the 4th Squadron was also designated Company D in the 12th Battalion. The CSR records its name as the E.M. Dragoons. Most of its men were from Marion District, but some came from Williamsburg, Georgetown and Clarendon Districts. David E. Monroe, who raised the company, was its first captain.[12] The men mustered in at Georgetown on February 3, 1862, for twelve months' service. The company was known as Captain D. Monroe's Company, SCV, until May 1. Monroe was not re-elected at the reorganization on May 1, and Huger Godbold was elected captain at that time. He retained command when Company D became Company F of the 4th Regiment in December 1862.

On August 31, 1862, Joshua Ward's Artillery Company, the Waccamaw Light Artillery, mustered in as a company of Major Emanuel's 4th Squadron of Cavalry, subsequently designated the 12th Battalion, South Carolina Cavalry. Ward's Company had been temporarily attached to the 10th Regiment, South Carolina Infantry, when it mustered in service at an earlier date.

BRIGADE AFFILIATIONS

The battalion was attached to the Department of South Carolina, Georgia and Florida.[13]

MAJOR MOVEMENTS AND ENGAGEMENTS

Major J.C. Wilson's 4th Battalion served in the Georgetown area in early 1862 and was still there on April 5.[14] Emanuel's 12th Battalion also served in the Georgetown area for the six months it existed, patrolling the area between the town and the Little River Inlet on the North Carolina border.[15] Its camp at Murrell's Inlet was the scene of one small engagement.[16] Elements of Company A were based at Camp Marion near Georgetown in May and June, at Dr. Magill's summer place in July and August and at the mouth of Murrell's Inlet from February to November 1862. Companies B, C and D were stationed at Camp Marion near Georgetown from May to October 1862. On August 14, about half of Company D, a small detachment from Company C and Ward's Battery were engaged with the *Pocahontas* and another Federal gunboat near Mrs. Sparkman's plantation on the Black River, about twenty miles above Georgetown.[17] The battalion also performed picket duty on Pawleys Island. On April 23, 1863, the battalion was ordered to move to Pocotaligo to join the rest of the new 4th Cavalry Regiment.[18] It began the move on May 7.[19]

21.

THE 17ᵀᴴ BATTALION, SOUTH CAROLINA CAVALRY

The 17ᵗʰ Battalion, South Carolina Cavalry, was originally called the 6ᵗʰ Battalion, South Carolina Cavalry, and Jeffords's Squadron; Professor W.J. Rivers called it the 5ᵗʰ Battalion.[1] Exactly when the squadron existed is unclear from the record, but most likely it was only for a few weeks before the creation of the battalion.[2] Jeffords's Squadron probably comprised only Companies A and B. The battalion was organized by late March 1862, when its four companies, designated A to D, mustered in Confederate service.[3] Although briefly designated the 6ᵗʰ Battalion from that point until the reorganization the next month, the adjutant and inspector general officially named it the 17ᵗʰ Battalion, South Carolina Cavalry, on April 12. Documents in the *Official Records* continued to call it the 6ᵗʰ Battalion during June, July and September.[4] On January 18, 1863, the 17ᵗʰ and 14ᵗʰ Battalions were consolidated with two independent companies to form the 5ᵗʰ Regiment, South Carolina Cavalry.

FIELD OFFICER

Robert Josiah Jeffords of Christ Church Parish in Charleston District, elected major of the battalion on April 12, 1862, was its only commander.[5] He defeated Captain Thomas W. Easterling, previously captain of a militia company called the Marion Troop, by 234 to 112 votes.[6] Previously captain of Company A, Jeffords was promoted to lieutenant colonel of the 5ᵗʰ Regiment, South Carolina Cavalry, on January 18, 1863.

COMPANIES

Company A, the South Carolina Rangers, or Carolina Rangers, was composed of men who had served since November 6, 1860, in Captain Robert Josiah Jeffords's Company, South Carolina Militia. Most were from Charleston, Beaufort and Colleton Districts, although a few came from Orangeburg, Edgefield, Greenville, Fairfield and Marion Districts. The company was reorganized on June 17, 1861, in Charleston; its men would serve as partisan volunteers for local defense, and Jeffords would continue as captain.[7] It was attached to the 1st Regiment, South Carolina Mounted Militia.[8] When that unit was disbanded in February 1862, the men re-enlisted for twelve months of Confederate service on February 17 as an independent company still under Jeffords's command.[9] A few men in the "new" company had served previously in the Beech Hill Rangers and the Marion Troop of the 1st Mounted Militia Regiment. The Beech Hill Rangers had been in Jeffords's Squadron before the creation of the 6th/17th Battalion. The company re-enlisted for three years, or for the duration of the war, as Company A of the 17th Battalion on April 12, 1862.[10] Jeffords was elected major of the 17th Battalion at that time, and Zimmerman Davis succeeded Jeffords as captain the same day. The Rangers became Company D of the 5th Regiment in January 1863, and the men re-enlisted yet again on March 5, 1864.[11]

Company B, the Willington Rangers, was known as Captain W.L. Disher's Company, South Carolina Cavalry, before it joined the 17th Battalion. Raised in February 1862, its name honored Aaron S. Willington, Esq., founder of the *Charleston Daily Courier* and its senior proprietor until his death in February 1862.[12] William L. Disher was unanimously elected captain on February 13, 1862, and other officers were elected three days later.[13] While based at Charleston, the men mustered in for twelve months of Confederate service on February 20.[14] By March, they were stationed at Camp Yeadon on Disher's Cooper River farm.[15] The company was attached to Jeffords's Squadron before it joined the 17th Battalion, probably only for a few weeks, for by late March it had become part of the 6th/17th Battalion. By April 11, 1862, the company had enlisted for the duration of the war.[16] Most of its men were from Charleston District, but a few came from Beaufort and Richland Districts. In April, Disher asked the governor and Executive Council to transfer his company from Jeffords's command and assign it to duty elsewhere. The request was denied, perhaps because Disher gave no reason.[17] Disher resigned that year and became a conductor on the railroad. In a likely reference to Disher, Captain Mulligan of Company C wrote that the battalion's senior captain had been defeated in a secret election held in July 1862.[18] B. Warren McTureous, promoted to captain on July 15, commanded the company in the 5th Regiment.[19] The Willington Rangers became the regiment's Company G on January 18, 1863.

Company C, the Dixie Rangers, was called Captain A.B. Mulligan's Company, South Carolina Cavalry, before it joined the 17th Battalion. Raised in January and February 1862, it mustered in state service for twelve months on February 16.[20] On March 20 at Charleston, all but two of its men mustered in Confederate service for the duration of the war.[21] Most of the Rangers were from Charleston and Beaufort Districts, but some came from Abbeville, Barnwell and Marlboro Districts. Alfred Birmingham Mulligan, a Charleston merchant, spent several thousand dollars of his own money to raise and equip the company. He had served previously in the state militia and had held the rank of captain as quartermaster for General John E. Tobin's 2nd Brigade.[22] Unanimously elected captain on February 16, 1862, Mulligan enlisted in Confederate service with the men on March 20.[23] He commanded the company in the 17th Battalion and retained command in the 5th Regiment. Mulligan admitted he was not popular with either Major Jeffords or some of his men.[24] The Rangers left Rantowles on the Charleston and Savannah Railroad on May 19, 1862, to join the 17th Battalion in Charleston and became Company B of the 5th Regiment in January 1863.[25]

Company D, the Beech Hill Rangers, consisted of some men who had served previously in Captain W.G. Smith's Company of the 1st Regiment, South Carolina Mounted Militia, also called the Beech Hill Rangers. On April 2, 1862, while the company was based at Chehaw, South Carolina, some of Smith's militiamen re-enlisted in Company D, 17th Battalion, for twelve months of Confederate service as local defense troops.[26] By the eleventh, the company had enlisted for the duration of the war.[27] The men were from Colleton District.[28] Wheeler G. Smith, who served as captain in both the militia and the battalion, was re-elected on May 15, 1862.[29] He retained command when the company became Company C of the 5th Regiment on January 18, 1863.

BRIGADE AFFILIATIONS

For the ten months of its existence, the 6th/17th Battalion served along the South Carolina coast in the Department of South Carolina, Georgia and Florida.

Major Movements and Engagements

From November 1861 until the following April, Company A was stationed on the peninsula between the Combahee and Ashepoo Rivers. Company B, based at Simpsonville in March and April 1862, was attached to Gist's Brigade about April 24 and was sent to Cole's Island and Secessionville.[30] Company C was based at Camp Gist about five miles below Charleston in late February 1862, and it moved to Camp Deveaux near Green Pond on May 19.[31] Although three companies of the 17th Battalion were ordered to Old Pocotaligo on May 29, they actually arrived the next day, missing the battle completely.[32] About 100 men from Companies A, C and D participated in a reconnaissance on Hutchinson Island on June 12 and June 13.[33] Company C moved about a quarter of a mile to Camp Smith in June.[34] Jeffords led 130 men from the battalion on an expedition to Fenwick and Hutchinson Islands on July 7 and July 8, and Company A was placed on picket duty in Charleston and at Morris and James Islands about the same time. The battalion was stationed at McPhersonville in August and at Chisolmville later that month.[35] It was sent to Green Pond in Colleton District on October 1, and it remained there through November and December. Companies A, B and D were present but not engaged at the Salkehatchie Bridge near Coosawhatchie on October 22.[36] Company C was occupied with picket duty at the Combahee Ferry and Coffer Hope in December 1862.[37] On December 8, 1862, General Beauregard ordered one company to be converted to horse artillery for service with the battalion, although whether or not the order was executed is unclear.[38] In January 1863, the battalion merged into the 5th Regiment, South Carolina Cavalry.

22.

INDEPENDENT CAVALRY
ORGANIZATIONS

THE NORTH SANTEE MOUNTED RIFLES

The North Santee Mounted Rifles was also called Captain A.W. Cordes's Company, South Carolina Cavalry. A.W. Cordes was captain, although Arthur M. Manigault, its first captain, had been elected in December 1860. Part of this company was attached to the 10th Regiment, South Carolina Infantry, in September and October 1861. In late 1861 and early 1862, the company was based in the 1st South Carolina Military District, which extended from the South Santee River to the North Carolina line.[1] Although its fate is unknown, it was probably disbanded in late 1861 or early 1862.

THE RIPLEY RANGERS

The Ripley Rangers, also called Captain A.D. Sparks's Company, South Carolina Cavalry, was composed mostly of men from Lexington, Marion and Marlboro Districts, along with a few from Sumter, Chesterfield, Darlington, Anderson and Union Districts.[2] It was organized as an infantry company on April 3, 1862, when the men mustered in service for the duration of the war and elected Alexander D. Sparks captain.[3] For a discussion of Sparks's military career, see Company E, 19th Battalion, South Carolina Cavalry. Attached to the 20th Regiment, SCV, as Company L that month, the company was detached a year later on April 30, 1863. The *Memory Roll* states, incorrectly, that the company was discharged in 1863 at Mount Pleasant and its men scattered to other commands. According to the CSR, after its detachment from the 20th Regiment, the company was converted to cavalry and known officially as Captain A.D. Sparks's Company, South Carolina Cavalry. It served in the vicinity of Sullivan's Island and Christ Church Parish from the summer of 1863 until November 1864.[4]

The Ripley Rangers was attached to Brigadier General Roswell Ripley's Brigade on November 20, 1864.[5] Exactly a month later, it became Company E of the 19th Battalion, South Carolina Cavalry.

CAPTAIN TUCKER'S COMPANY, SOUTH CAROLINA CAVALRY—THE MARION MEN OF WINYAH

Captain John H. Tucker's Company, South Carolina Cavalry, was also known as the Marion Men of Winyah. Another company called the Marion Light Troop, commanded by Captain Blythe Alston, existed as early as the summer of 1860, but whether it was the predecessor of the Marion Men of Winyah is unclear.[6] Most of Tucker's men were from Georgetown, Williamsburg, Horry and Darlington Districts, but a few came from Charleston, Sumter, Marion, Spartanburg and Marlboro Districts. John Hyrne Tucker, MD, was elected captain on May 5, 1861.

On April 6, 1863, after two years as an independent company, the Marion Men of Winyah was expanded into a two-company squadron. Called both Tucker's Squadron and Tucker's Cavalry, it operated as a single unit until the spring of 1864. William Lewis Wallace, MD, a sergeant in the original company, was elected captain of Company B on May 11, 1863; Tucker retained command of Company A. On March 18, 1864, the two companies were attached to the new 7th Cavalry Regiment. Company A retained its designation and its captain, and Wallace's Company B became Company F.

Major Movements and Engagements

Tucker's Company guarded the coast from the Pee Dee to the Santee River in early 1861. Later that year and in early 1862, the company was based in the 1st South Carolina Military District, which extended from the South Santee River to the North Carolina line.[7] On December 24, 1861, after the *Prince of Wales* was grounded, a detachment was engaged with Federal boat crews at the North Inlet near Georgetown.[8] When the 10th Infantry Regiment was sent to Charleston and the outer Georgetown defenses were dismantled, it was ordered on April 5, 1862, to remain at Georgetown.[9] The company was in camp on Pawleys Island in Georgetown District during part of April, and from May 1 to July 17, its base was nearby Camp Mayrant, from which it mounted patrols along the Waccamaw River. The company's pickets were engaged with Federal gunboats on the Waccamaw on May 29.[10] On July 21, when fifty or sixty Federal troops came ashore at Pawleys Island to destroy the saltworks there, thirteen of Tucker's men drove them off.[11] The company moved to another base on the Santee River later that month; in September it was at Camp Alston near Georgetown, and the next month it was at a camp on the Black River. From November 1862 until the following February, it provided cavalry support at Battery White, which was on Mayrant's Bluff overlooking Winyah Bay near Georgetown.

The company was stationed with Ward's Battery at Fraser's Point about ten miles from Winyah Bay during March 1863, and it was still there the next month, when it became Tucker's Squadron. Ordered to Camp Jackson west of Winyah Bay in May, it remained there until February 1864.[12] General Trapier ordered Tucker detached from his regular duties and placed in command of all cavalry forces west of Winyah Bay during September and October. The squadron returned to Battery White in November and moved to Georgetown for guard duty on February 2, 1864. Returning to Camp Jackson on the twenty-second, it moved to Camp Holly on the twenty-ninth. The men were involved in a skirmish the next day a few miles below Battery White.

The two companies were ordered to Virginia on March 17 as an independent squadron but were attached to the new 7th Cavalry Regiment on the eighteenth instead.[13] The Marion Men of Winyah left the Georgetown area on or about April 18, passed through North Carolina in early May and arrived in Richmond on May 26, 1864. Its major movements and engagements from this point to the end of the war are discussed under the 7th Regiment, South Carolina Cavalry.

Captain Theodore Cordes's Company, German Hussars, South Carolina Cavalry

The German Hussars was also called Captain Theodore Cordes's Company of Cavalry, South Carolina Militia. Although a company called the German Hussars had been in existence since 1830, this particular unit of German Charlestonians was organized about May 18, 1859, as part of the 4th Brigade of Militia.[14] It remained attached to the brigade and served with the 1st Regiment Rifles, also part of the 4th. Before the bombardment of Fort Sumter in April 1861, the Hussars acted as pickets and couriers on Morris Island and at Stevens's Iron Battery. The company was in Colonel W.B. Ryan's Squadron that month.[15] After Fort Sumter, the Hussars remained at Morris Island until at least early May. The men were ordered to patrol Sullivan's Island on November 8, 1861, and they remained there until the following February.[16] In February 1862, some of the militiamen volunteered for the duration of the war and became Captain Cordes's Company, South

Carolina Volunteers.[17] The *Mercury* reported that men who had mustered in on April 5 for twelve months of Confederate service were called Captain Theodore Cordes's Company, German Hussars, South Carolina Cavalry.[18] It is unlikely that the men enlisted for the duration of the war in February and re-enlisted for twelve months in April. After the battle of Secessionville in June 1862, the German Hussars was sent to James Island where it performed picket duty at Battery Island, Grimball's place and other spots along the Stono River. When the 3rd Regiment, South Carolina Cavalry, was formed in the summer of 1862, the German Hussars was initially designated Company I, but that was changed later to Company G.

CAPTAIN MANNING J. KIRK'S COMPANY, SOUTH CAROLINA PARTISAN RANGERS

Captain Manning J. Kirk's Company, South Carolina Partisan Rangers was also called Kirk's Partisan Rangers. Many of its men had served previously in a Kirk company called the May River Troop, which was part of the 1st Regiment, South Carolina Mounted Militia. The Partisan Rangers was organized on July 11, 1862; President Davis appointed Kirk its captain the same day. Although the men of the Rangers had enlisted for the duration of the war, they all re-enlisted on February 17, 1864.[19] Almost immediately, Kirk's Company was divided into two—A and B—and was designated Kirk's Squadron, South Carolina Partisan Rangers. Although Kirk continued to command both Company A and the squadron, S.T. Walker was elected captain of Company B on March 7, 1864. The men of Company A were from Beaufort District, and those in Company B were from Beaufort, Barnwell, Colleton, Union and Charleston Districts. On December 20, 1864, both companies became part of the 19th Battalion, South Carolina Cavalry; Company A kept its alphabetical designation, and Company B became Company C. Both Kirk and Walker retained their company commands in the 19th Battalion. Three South Carolina organizations were raised as partisan rangers: Brooks's Company H, 7th Battalion, Kirk's Cavalry Company and H.K. Aiken's Cavalry Battalion.[20]

Major Movements and Engagements

Kirk's Company was stationed at McPhersonville in July and August 1862. A detachment of fifty-five rangers captured two Union officers and six of their men during a scouting expedition to Chisolm Island on October 19. The company also saw action at both Yemassee and Pocotaligo on

October 22.[21] Kirk's Company was stationed at Pocotaligo from October to the following February. Forty of its men, along with detachments from the Beaufort Volunteer Artillery and the 11th Infantry Regiment, took part in a raid on Barnwell's Island on July 30, 1863.[22] The company's base was returned to McPhersonville from May 1863 to January 1864.[23] The newly created squadron, based at Pocotaligo in February 1864, remained there during March and April before moving to McPhersonville for the next two months.[24] It was engaged on John's Island between July 2 and July 11.[25] The squadron marched to Georgetown on the nineteenth and was based at Battery White on the western side of Winyah Bay. It remained there until November as part of Brigadier General Trapier's Brigade.[26] Ordered to Mount Pleasant on November 23, the squadron left Georgetown two days later.[27] On the twenty-ninth, it was ordered to Pocotaligo.[28] The squadron fought at the Tullifinny River, probably during the three-day period, December 7 to December 9. On the twentieth, it was at Grahamville, where, along with the 3rd Cavalry Regiment, it was assigned to guard the coastal flank during the evacuation of Savannah.[29] The squadron became part of the 19th Battalion the same day. It was at Pocotaligo from December 26 to December 28, and it marched to Charleston on January 5, 1865.[30] On February 16, the squadron was at Andersonville, South Carolina, observing Federal reconnaissance vessels at Seewee Bay.[31] The squadron, by this time Companies A and C of the 19th Battalion, supported the Marion Artillery as it withdrew after an engagement with Federal barges at Seewee Bay on February 16. The 19th Battalion participated in the Carolinas campaign until the end of the war, but it remains unclear whether or not Kirk's Squadron withdrew into North Carolina in March and April 1865.

The Charleston Light Dragoons

Captain Benjamin Huger Rutledge's Company, South Carolina Militia, was called the Charleston Light Dragoons. It counted its lineage from an exclusive company known as the Charleston Horse Guards, which existed as early as 1733 and changed its name to the Charleston Light Dragoons during the Revolutionary War. Immediately before the War Between the States, many of its members joined Rutledge's militia company, which adopted its new name. In April 1861, Rutledge's Company was attached to Colonel W.B. Ryan's Squadron of the 4th Brigade South Carolina Militia.[32] This company may also have been called the Charleston Light Hussars.[33]

The Charleston Light Dragoons, commonly known as the "Drags," guarded the eastern third of Sullivan's Island during April and May 1861.[34]

Relieved on May 19, the company moved next to Pocotaligo, where it was based in November, and then to Coosawhatchie, remaining there until February 1862.[35] On February 13, most of its men formed a new company, re-elected Rutledge as captain and volunteered for twelve months of Confederate service.[36] They mustered in on March 25 as an independent company called Captain Benjamin H. Rutledge's Company, South Carolina Cavalry.[37] The men re-enlisted for the duration of the war in May.[38]

The Charleston Light Dragoons was engaged at Pocotaligo on May 29, 1862.[39] From March to November 1862, while stationed at Grahamville and McPhersonville, it performed picket duty from the Bull River to Mackey's Point.[40] On October 22, the Dragoons fought at both Yemassee and Pocotaligo.[41] The Charleston Light Dragoons became Company K of the 4th Regiment, South Carolina Cavalry, in December 1862.[42] Rutledge was promoted to colonel of the 4th Regiment when it was organized on December 16, 1862.

CAPTAIN KEATING SIMONS'S CAVALRY COMPANY, THE ETIWAN RANGERS, SCV

Captain Keating Simons's Cavalry Company, the Etiwan Rangers, SCV, existed as early as September 1861 as part of Martin's 1st Regiment, South Carolina Mounted Militia.[43] Keating Simons Sr. commanded the company, which was raised for local defense and special service in Charleston District. Most of its members were overseers, who were to be paid only if called out.[44] The company was stationed at Heyward's Landing on James Island from January 3 to February 4, 1862.[45] It was probably disbanded then.

CAPTAIN W.L. TRENHOLM'S COMPANY—THE RUTLEDGE MOUNTED RIFLEMEN

Captain W.L. Trenholm's Company was also called the Rutledge Mounted Riflemen, South Carolina Militia. It was organized in Charleston on November 9, 1860, and was commanded by Captain Clelam K. Huger.[46] The company was part of the 4th Brigade, South Carolina Militia, and its men came from Charleston, St. John's Parish and the nearby islands.[47] It was ordered to Fort Johnson on January 9, 1861, a day famous for the attack on the *Star of the West*. The General Assembly officially authorized the company's organization on January 28.[48] Its men were soon stationed as pickets at Wappoo Cut and the Stono Inlet. The company mustered in state service in April and served with the 1st Artillery Regiment, South Carolina Militia.[49] Relieved from duty at Wappoo Cut on April 30, the company was sent back to Charleston.[50]

Brigadier General Roswell Ripley called the company into Confederate service on September 9.[51] William Lee Trenholm, son of George A. Trenholm, secretary of the treasury, Confederate States of America, in 1864 and 1865, was elected captain the same day.[52] Ripley attached the company to the 1st Artillery Regiment, South Carolina Militia, in September.[53] Some of the men were stationed at Morris Island and the rest were at Sullivan's Island in late September.[54] By October 22, all the men were at Sullivan's Island.[55] After about three months, the company was relieved of duty, an action that was based on an 1841 South Carolina Militia law.[56] The *Memory Roll* says that it was mustered out of service on December 2, and that it remained disorganized until February 22, 1862. Trenholm and his men continued to serve without pay, and they worked to build the company to numbers that would be acceptable for the creation of a new company. Their intention was to muster in Confederate service.[57] According to the *Mercury*, the company was on duty with the 1st Artillery Regiment, South Carolina Militia, as late as February 17, 1862.[58]

During January and early February, Captain Trenholm recruited many of the original members of the Rutledge Mounted Riflemen militia company into a new company, also called the Rutledge Mounted Riflemen. This new company mustered in Confederate service for twelve months on February 22, 1862, while it was based at Pocotaligo. It served continuously on the coast for the next twenty-five months. On the afternoon of May 29, 1862, it was engaged at Old Pocotaligo, providing the advance guard in pursuit of the enemy all the way to Gardner's Corner, and it was engaged again, though unsuccessfully, the next morning. The company also provided support for the Beaufort Volunteer Artillery when it destroyed Federal flats at Port Royal Ferry on June 6.[59] In August, the company was authorized to raise a section of flying artillery.[60]

Based at McPhersonville in late September, the company fought at Pocotaligo on October 22.[61] At some point between December 7 and December 11, following another move from Pocotaligo back to McPhersonville on November 3, the company was officially designated a horse artillery company—the "Rutledge Mounted Riflemen and Horse Artillery Company."[62] It was armed with two twelve-pounder howitzers.

In 1863, the Rutledge Mounted Riflemen and Horse Artillery increased its numbers to 171 officers and men, and by May 28, it had been divided into two companies: Company A, the horse artillery component, and Company B, the cavalry unit. The new two-company squadron was called Trenholm's

Squadron.[63] Trenholm was elected captain of Company A, and J.J. Magee was elected captain of Company B on May 23 or May 24.[64]

The squadron was ordered to Green Pond to intercept a Federal raid up the Combahee River on June 2, but it did not meet the enemy.[65] The new squadron was based at McPhersonville from May 1863 to late January 1864, and it was at Coosawhatchie from February to early April.[66] Magee led a reconnaissance of Morgan and Pine Islands near Beaufort on November 23 and November 24.[67] A few months later, on March 11, 1864, he led 120 men in a failed boat attack on the Federal outpost headquarters on the Broad River.[68]

Trenholm's Squadron was ordered to Virginia on March 17, 1864, but several weeks passed before the squadron actually moved.[69] Meanwhile, on March 18, the 7th Cavalry Regiment was created. Ordered to march to Columbia on April 4, the two companies left Pocotaligo and Coosawhatchie on the seventh.[70] Trenholm's Company did not take its artillery on the march. At this point, Company A of the squadron became Company B, and Company B became Company G of the 7th Regiment. The men marched via Columbia through Charlotte on April 30.[71] They moved through Hillsboro to Clarksville and Burkeville, both in Virginia, arriving at Blacks and Whites on the South Side Railroad, about forty miles southwest of Petersburg, on May 15. The men camped at Seven Pines on May 19 and May 20. The squadron performed scout and picket duty along the Chickahominy River until it joined up with the 7th Regiment on the twenty-seventh. Since the squadron had left its artillery in South Carolina, the company's name was changed back to the Rutledge Mounted Riflemen at the time of its assignment to the 7th Regiment. (For additional information, refer to the 7th Regiment, South Carolina Cavalry.)

CAPTAIN JOHN B.L. WALPOLE'S COMPANY, SOUTH CAROLINA CAVALRY—THE STONO SCOUTS

Captain John Basnett Legare Walpole's Company, South Carolina Cavalry, was also called the Stono Scouts, or Stono Rangers.[72] Walpole's was an independent company from late 1861 to late 1864. His men were from Charleston and Colleton Districts, and they served for that entire time on John's Island. On November 10, 1861, Adjutant and Inspector General States Rights Gist called out the Stono Scouts to serve as vedettes and pickets between the inlets of the North Edisto and Stono Rivers. Although the company was disbanded on January 7, 1862, it was reorganized the next day, by order of General Roswell Ripley, to supply men to serve as scouts and guides along the coast, primarily in the John's Island area, "for as long as necessary."[73] The *Mercury* in April 1862, reported that the Stono Scouts was attached to John Black's 1st Battalion, South Carolina Cavalry, a temporary measure since the company was not a permanent part of either the 1st Battalion or its successor, the 1st Regiment. By the early summer of 1862, its men were armed with revolving Colt rifles, which they supplied themselves. The Scouts participated in the capture of the *Isaac P. Smith* on the Stono River on January 30, 1863.[74] Throughout most of that year, company headquarters remained at Adams Run, but the Scouts themselves performed picket duty on John's Island near Haulover Cut and Legareville.[75]

On Christmas Day, Walpole's Scouts participated in the attack on the USS *Marblehead* on the Stono River near Legareville.[76] The Scouts acted as guides, scouts and couriers during the engagements on John's Island from February 9 to February 12.[77] On April 24, 1864, Brigadier General Henry A. Wise, commanding the Scouts' military district, objected to an order disbanding the company.[78] This was most likely Special Order No. 77 in which the secretary of war disbanded all companies organized after April 16, 1862. No further documentation exists, but the Stono Scouts remained in service. The company participated as scouts and couriers during the engagements at John's Island from July 2 to July 10, 1864, and it volunteered to burn Legareville on John's Island on August 20; sixteen members of the Stono Scouts actually placed the torch to their own homes.[79] By November 20, the company was attached to Brigadier General Beverly H. Robertson's Brigade, where it remained until at least January 31, 1865.[80] The last Confederate troops to evacuate the city of Charleston in February 1865, the Stono Scouts left on the eighteenth, as Federal troops were entering the city, and withdrew into North Carolina. On April 9, Walpole's men were serving as escorts and scouts at the headquarters of Lieutenant General William J. Hardee's corps.[81] According to the *Confederate Military History Series*, the Stono Scouts disbanded as a unit at Smithfield.[82] The CSR says the company was paroled at Greensboro on May 1, 1865.

23.

THE 18TH BATTALION, SOUTH CAROLINA ARTILLERY

The 18th Battalion, South Carolina Artillery, was also called the 18th Heavy Artillery Battalion. Organized with three companies in the spring or summer of 1862, it was reorganized three times. Its four incarnations resulted in a complicated assortment of company names and letter designations. In chronological order, the battalion was known as: (1) Alston's Light Artillery Battalion, (2) the Charleston, South Carolina Siege Train, also called the South Carolina Siege Train and the Siege Train Artillery Battalion, (3) Manigault's Battalion, South Carolina Artillery and (4) Manigault's Battalion, reorganized in 1865.[1]

The first, Alston's Light Artillery Battalion was organized with two companies—the Horry Light Artillery and the McQueen Light Artillery—some time between mid-April and mid-July 1862. It added a third company, the Palmetto Guard Artillery, about July 1862. The *Mercury* referred to the organization as the Alston Artillery as late as early November 1862.[2] About December 4 that year, the battalion was reorganized, and its name was changed to the South Carolina Siege Train. There was no change in the number of companies, but the three were given different letter designations. Although some evidence suggests that the battalion was called by Manigault's name as early as December 1862, Alston was definitely in command until May 1863, and Manigault was not promoted to major until June 8, with rank from May 27, 1863. The battalion adopted Manigault's name after he assumed command. The second reorganization of the battalion, in May 1863, also retained the same three companies, this time with the same letter designations. On August 31, 1863, Company C of the 12th Georgia Battalion was added, but it was not assigned a letter designation—an indication that its association with Manigault's Battalion was probably of short duration.[3] When the McQueen Light Artillery (Company C) was sent to Virginia in May 1864, the Pee Dee Light Artillery took its place as Company C in

Manigault's Battalion. A fourth new company, the Louisiana Battery, was added and designated Company D in December 1863. When Manigault's Battalion reorganized for the third and final time in February 1865, Company A became Company B and Company B became Company D; Company C, the Pee Dee Artillery, and Company D, the Louisiana Battery, were transferred out of the battalion. At the same time, three existing artillery batteries—Company B of the German Artillery, Mathewes's Artillery and Gilchrist's Independent Artillery Company—were added as Companies A, C and E, respectively. The CSR refers to each company of Manigault's Battalion before and after its final reorganization as the "first" and "second" company, respectively. At about the time it reorganized in 1865, the battalion was converted to infantry and withdrew with the rest of the Confederate forces into North Carolina. The name *Siege Train* was derived from the fact that the unit operated cannon that were of heavier caliber than the weapons of the field artillery but that were lighter and somewhat more maneuverable than those of the seacoast artillery.[4]

FIELD OFFICERS

Charles Alston Jr., the first commander of the battalion, initially held the rank of captain but was promoted to major on November 13, 1862.[5] He resigned on May 27, 1863, writing: "I am reluctantly impelled to this state by urgent reasons which now render it a matter of duty [to resign]."[6]

Edward Manigault, brother of Brigadier General Arthur Manigault, was promoted to major on June 8, 1863, with rank from May 23, when he assumed personal command of the battalion. From December 1861 to May 1862, Manigault had served as major in command of another Manigault's Battalion, this one a mixed organization. When he was not re-elected at the general reorganization in May 1862, his battalion was disbanded.[7] The *Mercury* considered Manigault one of the three best South Carolina officers displaced by the elections at the reorganization.[8] His service record is unclear for the thirteen months from May 1862 to June 1863, when he assumed command of the Siege Train. He was struck in the back by a Minié ball on February 10, 1865, during the action at Grimball's Causeway on James Island and, initially, was declared killed in action.[9] In fact, he was taken prisoner and held briefly in a temporary Federal hospital on Dixon's Island.[10] On February 11, he was moved to Folly Island, and on February 14, he was placed on board the *Canonicas* bound for Hilton Head Island. Manigault was admitted to the United States Army General Hospital for Prisoners of War at Beaufort on February 15. Released from the hospital on May 9, he was paroled the next day.[11]

William Alexander Walker, lieutenant colonel of the 1st Regiment, South Carolina Cavalry, may have commanded the 18th Battalion after Manigault was wounded in February 1865.

COMPANIES

Company A of Alston's Battalion, the Horry Light Artillery, was also called the Alston Light Artillery; Captain Alston's Company, Light Artillery, SCV; and Smith's Battery.[12] Organized on April 14, 1862, the battery mustered in service on May 1 at Charleston for the duration of the war. It probably operated as an independent artillery unit for a short time. Although composed mostly of men from Horry District, a few of its members came from Charleston, Georgetown and Marion Districts. One of the two original companies in Alston's Battalion, it was designated Company A at some point between mid-April and mid-July 1862. Afterward it was officially known successively by several names, among them Captain Alston's Company, Light Artillery, SCV; Company A, Alston's Battalion, Light Artillery; "first" Company B in the South Carolina Siege Train; "first" Company B in Manigault's Battalion, South Carolina Artillery; and "second" Company D in Manigault's "reorganized" Battalion in 1865, the name under which it was paroled.

Charles Alston Jr., the company's first captain, who enlisted on April 15, 1862, was promoted to major in command of the battalion on November 13. Samuel Porcher Smith, a graduate of The Citadel's class of 1862, succeeded him as captain on May 19, 1863.[13] Wounded in the face at Averasboro, he was admitted to the General Hospital #3 at Greensboro on March 19.[14] Smith received a furlough on April 7, 1865. Whether he was paroled with the battalion at Greensboro later in April remains unclear, but we do know he survived the war.

Company B of Alston's Battalion, the McQueen Light Artillery, was also called Gregg's Battery and Captain Stanley's Company, Artillery. It was also known as the Third Howitzers.[15] Organized on April 14, 1862, it mustered in service on May 1 at Charleston for the duration of the war. The second of the two original companies of Alston's Battalion, it was designated Company B at some point between April 14 and mid-July 1862.[16] Most of the men were from Marion District, but a few came from Darlington, Chesterfield, Union, Williamsburg and Charleston Districts. Official names for the McQueen Light Artillery were, successively, Captain Stanley's Company, South Carolina Artillery; Company B, Alston's Battalion, South Carolina Artillery; "first" Company C in the South Carolina Siege Train; and "first"

Company C in Manigault's Battalion. On May 1, 1864, the battery was relieved as Company C of Manigault's Battalion and officially became an independent company, called Captain Gregg's Company, South Carolina Artillery; it was assigned to William J. Pegram's Battalion, which was in Virginia at the time.[17] Two weeks later, on May 16, the McQueen Artillery left the 18th Battalion on James Island for a four-day furlough to be followed by the move to Virginia.[18] The Pee Dee Artillery replaced the McQueen Light Artillery as Company C in Manigault's Battalion the next month.

Mathew B. Stanley, who enlisted as captain on April 15, 1862, was the first captain of the McQueen Light Artillery.[19] He had probably served as captain of Company K in Maxcy Gregg's 1st (six-month) Regiment in early 1861. General Beauregard suspended him from duty on February 20, 1863, ordering him to appear before a board of examiners or resign. Stanley refused to be examined and resigned on May 14, 1863. First Lieutenant Thomas E. Gregg, who commanded the company until the end of the war, replaced him the same day.[20]

Company C of Alston's Battalion, the Palmetto Guard Artillery, was also known as the Palmetto Guards and the Buist Light Artillery. It was added to the original two companies of Alston's Battalion in the summer of 1862. Its roots lay in the Palmetto Guard, a large prewar company in Charleston's 17th Militia Regiment. On January 9, after entering state service on December 27, 1860, the company was sent to Morris Island; it participated in the bombardment of Fort Sumter three months later. It was part of the garrison at the fort in late April and was divided into two groups in early May. Half the men volunteered for Confederate service as the Palmetto Guard Volunteers, and they left for Virginia on May 9 to join J.B. Kershaw's 2nd Volunteer Regiment as Company I.[21] The other half, 130 men, remained as a militia unit in Charleston under the command of Ensign George Lamb Buist; they then served as field artillery near Coosawhatchie from the fall of 1861 to late April 1862.[22]

During February 1862, the Palmetto Guard was soliciting volunteers for twelve months of service in the Siege Train.[23] On February 28, while they were based at Pocotaligo, these volunteers enlisted in the Confederate States Provisional Army. After re-enlisting in April for three years, or for the duration of the war, the same group formed the Palmetto Guard Artillery.[24] The Palmetto Guard Artillery was sent to Battery Island at the mouth of the Stono River on May 1, and when Cole's Island was evacuated later that month, it was ordered to James Island for two months. Although the company was ordered to Virginia in July, the order was countermanded for some reason. At about the time the battery was awaiting further orders from temporary locations at the Charleston Race Course and the Magnolia

Cemetery breastworks, it was designated Company C of the 18th Battalion and was sent to garrison Fort Pemberton.[25] The Palmetto Guard Artillery was successively designated Company C, Alston's Battalion; Company A in the Siege Train; "first" Company A in Manigault's Battalion; and "second" Company B, when Manigault's Battalion was reorganized in 1865. It was finally paroled as "second" Company B, 18th Battalion. Its men were mostly from Charleston, Colleton and Barnwell Districts and from New Orleans, along with a few from Abbeville, Beaufort, Richland, Spartanburg and York Districts. George Lamb Buist, commissioned captain on February 18, 1862, was promoted to major of artillery in the Confederate States Army about ten months later, on December 15. He left the 18th Artillery Battalion to take command of the Georgia Siege Train.[26] The CSR gives several dates for the promotion to major: December 15 and December 29, 1862, and January 15, 1863. Benjamin C. Webb succeeded Buist as captain of the Palmetto Artillery on December 15, 1862, a date also shown in the records as January 20, 1863.[27] Fighting at Legareville on Christmas Day 1863, Webb was slightly stunned when a shell exploded nearby. He commanded the 18th Battalion after Manigault was wounded in February 1865. Webb was paroled with the battalion on April 28, 1865, near Greensboro.

When the "first" Company C of Manigault's Battalion, the McQueen Light Artillery, left for Virginia on May 16, 1864, its replacement was the Pee Dee Artillery, which assumed the letter designation as well; thus it became the second company to carry the designation "first" Company C in the 18th Battalion. On June 17 following the actual exchange, which took place on June 4, 1864, the Pee Dee Artillery joined the battalion at Secessionville.[28] The Pee Dee Light Artillery, also called McIntosh's Battery and Captain Zimmerman's Company, South Carolina Artillery, had enlisted originally as the Pee Dee Rifles, Company D, of Maxcy Gregg's 1st Regiment, SCV, on July 21, 1861. That summer, the determination was made that Gregg's regiment had too many companies. Consequently, in March 1862, the Pee Dee Rifles converted to artillery, changing its name to the Pee Dee Light Artillery or McIntosh's Battery. Also detached from Gregg's regiment in March, it served as an independent artillery company for about two years. The men re-elected David Gregg McIntosh as captain in July; he was promoted to major on March 2, 1863.[29] When the Pee Dee Light Artillery was ordered back to South Carolina on May 5, 1864, in exchange for the McQueen Light Artillery, it was designated the "second" Company C of Manigault's Battalion, effective on June 4. In January 1865, the company was ordered to Pocotaligo as a light artillery battery to resist Sherman's advance. Officially detached from Manigault's

Battalion between January and mid-February 1865, it was replaced by Mathewes's Artillery. The Pee Dee Artillery was paroled as Zimmerman's South Carolina Battery in Basil C. Manly's Artillery Battalion. Most of its men were from Darlington District, but a few came from Charleston, Newberry, Sumter, Marion, Marlboro, Laurens, Chesterfield, York, Anderson and Fairfield Districts. William E. Zimmerman, promoted from first lieutenant to captain on June 30, 1864, commanded the Pee Dee Light Artillery when it was Company C of Manigault's Battalion. (Refer to Company D, 1st Regiment, SCV, and to the Pee Dee Light Artillery under independent artillery organizations.)

Alston's Battalion had no Company D. Company D of Manigault's Battalion was Bridges's Louisiana Battery, also called the Beauregard Louisiana Artillery. The Louisiana Battery was created by special order on December 13, 1863. Composed of Louisiana men from Companies A and B of the 18th Battalion, who were transferred into Company D on or about January 1, 1864, the Louisiana Battery had become Company D of the 18th Battalion by February 12. In 1865, it was transferred to Basil C. Manly's Artillery Battalion; it was paroled at Greensboro as Bridges's Louisiana Battery in April 1865. Its only commander, William M. Bridges, previously first lieutenant in the 1st Regiment, Louisiana Artillery, was appointed captain on December 13, 1863.[30]

The Horry Artillery was designated Company D when Manigault's Battalion was reorganized for the final time in 1865.

Company A of Manigault's "reorganized" Battalion in 1865—the "second" Company A—was the German Artillery, Company B. It was added to Manigault's Battalion shortly after the evacuation of Charleston on February 17, 1865, and was formerly Captain Franz Melchers's Independent Company, South Carolina Artillery. It was paroled as the "second" Company A of Manigault's Battalion. (Refer to the German Artillery Battalion and to the 1st Regiment Artillery, South Carolina Militia, for further discussion.)

Company C of Manigault's "reorganized" Battalion in 1865, the "second" Company C, was formerly John Raven Mathewes's Independent Company, South Carolina Heavy Artillery. It was made up of men from Colleton District.[31] This was the third company to carry the designation of Company C in the 18th Battalion: the first was the McQueen Artillery, and the second was the Pee Dee Light Artillery. Mathewes's Artillery was converted to infantry and was attached to Manigault's Battalion on February 17 or February 18, 1865. It was finally paroled as the "second" Company C of Manigault's Battalion.

Company E of Manigault's "reorganized" Battalion in 1865, the only Company E, was the Gist Guard, or Gilchrist's Independent Company,

South Carolina Heavy Artillery. Added to Manigault's Battalion in February 1865, shortly after the evacuation of Charleston, its men were mostly from Charleston, Colleton and Spartanburg Districts, although a few came from Berkeley, Union, Anderson, Laurens, Barnwell, Greenville, Orangeburg and Richland Districts and from Augusta, Georgia. Theodore Gaillard Boag, promoted to captain about February 18, 1865, commanded the company when it was in Manigault's Battalion. It was paroled in April as the "second" Company E of Manigault's Battalion.

BRIGADE AFFILIATIONS

From its creation until early 1865, the 18th Battalion served in several subdivisions and military districts of the Department of South Carolina, Georgia and Florida.

On November 20, 1864, the Palmetto Guard was placed in Beverly H. Robertson's Brigade; the battalion's other companies were in Taliaferro's Brigade.[32] This appears to have been a temporary arrangement. The battalion became part of Colonel Edward C. Anderson's Brigade on December 28, 1864, along with the 15th Battalion, South Carolina Artillery; Major George L. Buist's Battalion consisting of Gilchrist, Matthews, Melchers and Johnson's Batteries; and some Georgia units.[33]

By January 31, 1865, Company D of the South Carolina Siege Train was attached to Stephen Elliott's Brigade, along with two companies of the 2nd Artillery Regiment, the Battalion of State Cadets, eight companies of the 1st Cavalry Regiment, three companies of the 1st South Carolina Artillery and some Georgia units.[34] The remainder of the Siege Train was not brigaded in January 1865.

On April 9, 1865, the entire 18th Battalion was attached to Elliott's Brigade, along with the 2nd Regiment, South Carolina Artillery; the 22nd Battalion, Georgia Artillery; and the 27th Battalion, Georgia Artillery.[35]

MAJOR MOVEMENTS AND ENGAGEMENTS

The 18th Battalion was stationed in the Department of South Carolina, Georgia and Florida and served primarily on James Island. The Horry Light Artillery marched from Marion Court House to James Island on June 19, 1862. It was stationed at Charleston from July 26, 1862, to April 1863. The Palmetto Guard Artillery, stationed at Legare's place in March and April 1862, was engaged at Battery Island on May 16. It was based at

Fort Pemberton in May and June. From July 1862 to the following January, the Palmetto Guard was encamped at the Washington Race Course in Charleston and served along the breastworks just above Magnolia Cemetery.[36] The McQueen Light Artillery was stationed on James Island from April 15 to July 1, 1862, when it was ordered to Charleston. It was based next at Camp Hampstead until April 15, 1863.[37] The battalion's headquarters was at the Charleston Race Course in January 1863. Companies A, B and C—the Palmetto Guard Artillery, Horry Artillery and McQueen Artillery—were engaged during the capture of the USS *Isaac P. Smith* in the Stono River on January 30.[38]

The Palmetto Guard was converted to light artillery and transferred back to James Island in February.[39] It was based at Simon's Bluff, in St. Andrews Parish, in early March. Battalion headquarters was still in the city of Charleston on March 13.[40] The Palmetto Guard Artillery, and possibly other elements of the 18th Battalion, saw action at Grimball's Landing about March 13. In April, both the Horry and the McQueen Light Artillery Batteries were sent to St. Andrews Parish. The Horry Battery was back at James Island in May and, except for brief periods, remained at various locations on the island until February 1865. The McQueen Artillery was also sent to James Island in May 1863, and it stayed there, except for a tour of duty at Battery Wagner and Charleston, until it went to Virginia in May or early June 1864.[41]

Company A, the Palmetto Guard Artillery, and probably Companies B and C, were sent back to Charleston during May and June 1863. Company C, the McQueen Artillery, returned to James Island in late June or early July and was placed at Artillery Crossroads. On the morning of July 10, Companies A and B of the Siege Train moved from Charleston to the McLeod house on James Island in response to the Federal attack on the south end of Morris Island earlier that morning.[42] On garrison duty at Battery Haskell, Company A was able to observe the siege of Battery Wagner from its vantage point at Legare's Point, nearly a mile away. The Palmetto Guard was engaged with the Federal gunboat *Pawnee* on the Stono River on July 16.[43]

The McQueen Artillery, transferred from the west lines of James Island to Battery Wagner on July 20, returned to James Island after August 1 but was sent back to Wagner on August 15 or August 16.[44] It remained there until at least August 21.[45] A detachment of the Siege Train was relieved by a detachment of the Horry Light Artillery at Battery Wagner on August 6.[46] It was still there on September 6, having suffered casualties at Wagner in August and September, although it is unclear if its service was continuous.[47] From August 17 to August 30, from Battery Haskell, the Palmetto Guard

Artillery shelled Federal forces at the south end of Morris Island and at the Swamp Angel Battery.

The Palmetto Guard was stationed at Battery Leroy on the Stono River from August 21 to September 18. An officer and a fifteen-man detachment from the Palmetto Guard served at Battery Wagner from August 21 to August 26, returning to James Island on the twenty-seventh.[48] One section of the Horry Light Artillery arrived at Battery Tatom at the Point of Pines on James Island on August 25. A few days later, on September 2, Battery Haskell resumed firing on Federal forces at Morris Island and at the Swamp Angel Battery and continued until Battery Wagner was evacuated on the night of September 6. After this, targets shifted to other Federal positions on Morris and Black Islands.

The Siege Train was also based on James Island in late September and October 1863.[49] By early November, the Palmetto Guard had occupied Battery Haskell, and the Horry Light Artillery had occupied Batteries Tatom and Ryan in the island's eastern division.[50] Both companies were serving as heavy artillery. The McQueen Light Artillery was based in the western division, and it was also serving as a heavy artillery unit.[51]

On December 6, the Palmetto Guard and Horry Light Artillery were transferred from Legare's Point to Dr. Lebby's house, southwest of the Wappoo Bridges on the road to Fort Pemberton. The men camped at nearby Heyward's place along Wappoo Creek. The McQueen Light Artillery remained in its camp at the James Island Creek Bridge. Early in the morning of December 23, the Palmetto and Horry Batteries were sent to Church Flats on John's Island, where, two days later, they were engaged with the USS *Marblehead* near Legareville.[52]

The battalion remained at its base on James Island throughout December and January.[53] Captain Bridges reported for duty with the Siege Train on February 11, 1864, and the Louisianans in Companies A and B were assigned to his new Company D on the thirteenth.[54] The Palmetto Guard, sent by rail to Lake City, Florida, on February 27, arrived a week after the battle of Olustee, or Ocean Pond.[55] Ordered next to the town of Madison, the battery moved on to Baldwin about nine miles from Jacksonville in March. Returning to South Carolina, also by rail, the Palmetto Guard rejoined the 18th Battalion on James Island on April 30. Meanwhile, Bridges's Louisiana Battery left James Island on February 28 by rail for Green Pond, near the Ashepoo River. It was based at Stock's Causeway from March to June 13, 1864, when it returned to Secessionville.[56] On April 11, the Horry and the McQueen Batteries changed their camps to Artillery Crossroads, roughly in the middle of James Island, a choice location from which to perform picket duty, launch work details and man nearby batteries, especially Battery Pringle. The Horry Light Artillery remained until July 31, or, perhaps, longer.[57]

On May 16, the McQueen Artillery was permanently detached from the 18th Battalion and departed James Island for a four-day furlough before moving to Virginia.[58] Although it was nearby, the Louisiana Battery was not engaged during the battle of Chapman's Fort on May 26 when Company A, 3rd Artillery Battalion, sank the transport USS *Boston*.[59] Ordered on June 10 to perform picket duty at Combahee Point and along the Ashepoo River, the Palmetto Guard remained in that area until the end of October, or, perhaps, longer.[60] The Palmetto Guard was engaged with boats near Buckingham Ferry on August 30.[61] Bridges's Battery was sent to Secessionville on June 14; the Pee Dee Artillery arrived on the seventeenth to replace the McQueen Light Artillery, and it moved its base to Secessionville. Skirmishers from the Siege Train, acting as infantry support for a section of Company A of the 1st Regiment, South Carolina Artillery, were engaged on the east end of James Island on July 2. The Pee Dee and Louisiana Batteries were stationed at Battery Ryan as heavy artillery from July to December 1864.[62] The Palmetto Guard, based on the Charleston and Savannah Railroad, south of Green Pond, in the fall of 1864, missed the engagements on the Tullifinny River in December. In December 1864, the only two original companies of the 18th Battalion remaining, the Horry Artillery and the Palmetto Guard Artillery, were converted to infantry when the battalion was sent to James Island to perform picket duty on its southwestern edge.

The Palmetto Guard participated in an infantry skirmish at Grimball's Causeway near the Stono River on February 10, 1865.[63] On February 17, 1865, the battalion, then comprising the Horry, Palmetto Guard and Mathewes's Batteries and under the overall command of Captain B.C. Webb, evacuated James Island. The German Artillery Company B and the Gist Guard were added to the battalion shortly afterward. The battalion arrived at Cheraw on February 27, remained there until about March 2 and crossed the Cape Fear River at Fayetteville about a week later.[64] The battalion was engaged at Averasboro, North Carolina, on March 16 and at Bentonville three days later. Bridges's and Zimmerman's Batteries, both of which had been detached and were serving at the time in Basil Manly's Artillery Battalion, were at the front in North Carolina on April 10.[65] The 18th Battalion surrendered with the Army of Tennessee on April 26, 1865.

24.

INDEPENDENT ARTILLERY ORGANIZATIONS

THE BEAUFORT VOLUNTEER ARTILLERY

The Beaufort Volunteer Artillery was also called the Beaufort Volunteer Artillery, SCV; Captain Stephen Elliott's Company, Artillery; Captain Stuart's Company, Artillery; Stuart's Battery; and the Beaufort Light Artillery. Although it was created in 1802, its origin was a 1776 artillery company that had served in the Revolutionary War.[1] Made up mostly of men from Beaufort and Charleston, a few of its members came from Bluffton in Beaufort District, from Colleton and Barnwell Districts and from Savannah, Georgia. The Beaufort Volunteer Artillery became Company A of Heyward's 11th Volunteer Regiment in May 1861. According to the *Memory Roll*, Hal M. Stuart, first a lieutenant and later captain of the company, believed the association with the 11th Regiment was a mistake. The battery was reorganized in March 1862, and it became an independent command in early May, soon after the 11th Regiment itself was reorganized. As a result, the 11th Regiment was left with only nine companies; it never again used letter designation of Company A. At that time, the Beaufort Volunteer Artillery became known as Elliott's Company, South Carolina Artillery Volunteers. The secretary of war officially and permanently detached the battery from the 11th Regiment about September 20, 1863.[2] Its men re-enlisted for the duration of the war on February 9, 1864.[3]

Field Officers

Stephen Elliott Jr. of Beaufort, who raised and equipped the Beaufort Volunteer Artillery, was its first captain. He commanded the battery both in the 11th Regiment and for nearly a year after the company became an independent artillery battery. He was wounded in the leg by a shell fragment during the bombardment of Fort Beauregard on November 7, 1861. Following two years of consistent praise from his superiors, Elliott was promoted to major of artillery on April 30, 1863; only six months later, on November 21, he was elevated to lieutenant colonel with rank from September 9. He was slightly wounded in the head by a piece of rock when the magazine exploded at Fort Sumter on December 11, 1863.[4] Always notable in the fort's defense, Elliott served as its commander for several months before April 20, 1864, the date he was appointed colonel of the Infantry Battalion of the Holcombe Legion. Only a month later, on May 24, he was promoted to brigadier general of N.G. Evans's old brigade. Severely wounded at the crater on July 30, Elliott commanded another brigade at Averasboro and Bentonville, where he was severely wounded a second time.[5] On February 21, 1866, less than a year after the war ended, Elliott died from the multiple effects of his wounds.

Hal M. Stuart succeeded Elliott as captain of the Beaufort Volunteer Artillery on May 20, 1863.[6] He was paroled at Greensboro at the end of the war.

Major Movements and Engagements

The Beaufort Volunteer Artillery served at various locations in the Department of South Carolina, Georgia and Florida from early 1861 to March 1865. In July 1861, while it was Company A in the 11th Infantry Regiment, the battery was stationed at Bay Point overlooking Port Royal Harbor. Engaged at Fort Beauregard during the battle of Port Royal on November 7, it also participated in the expedition to Port Royal Island on December 6, 1861.[7] By May 18, 1862, following its detachment from the 11th Regiment that month, the Beaufort Volunteer Artillery was stationed near McPhersonville. One of its sections was engaged at Old Pocotaligo on the twenty-ninth, and the next day the battery moved to Port Royal Ferry, where it shelled retreating Federal troops. On the night of June 6, about twenty Beaufort Volunteer Artillery men, along with Company I of the 11th Regiment and the Rutledge Mounted Riflemen, were engaged again at Port Royal Ferry.[8] The Beaufort Volunteer Artillery was occupied with picket duty around Port Royal Ferry and McPhersonville through June 1862, and the men remained in the area for the next five months. One of its sections was engaged at Port Royal Ferry again on July 4.[9] Sixteen Beaufort Volunteer Artillery men and a detachment of the 11th Regiment saw action at Pinckney Island on August 21. There, most of a company of the 3rd New Hampshire Regiment were either killed or captured.[10] The *Yorkville Enquirer* placed this engagement at St. Helena Island, and the *Camden Confederate* added the information that forty-five men from the Beaufort

Volunteer Artillery and eighty from the 11th Regiment participated.[11] The Beaufort Volunteer Artillery was involved in the skirmish at Coosawhatchie, called Old Pocotaligo, on October 22 and at Pocotaligo the next day.[12] The Beaufort Volunteer Artillery moved to nearby Camp Beaufort on November 11, 1862, and stayed there until February 1863.

A four-gun section of the Beaufort Volunteer Artillery was sent to Chisolm Island where, on April 9, 1863, it and Nelson's Virginia Battery burned and sank the armed steamer *George Washington* in the Coosaw River near Beaufort.[13] The battery moved back to McPhersonville on May 3, and it remained in the general vicinity until December 1864.[14] Twenty-five of its men, along with another twenty-five of the 11th Regiment and forty of Kirk's Partizan Rangers, participated in an expedition to Barnwell's Island on July 30, 1863.[15] On November 2, the battery moved to Camp Beaufort, near Pocotaligo, and remained there until May 1864. It returned to McPhersonville on the twenty-seventh. The battery was attached to General McLaws's Division on November 20.[16] One of its guns was engaged at the battle of Honey Hill on November 30, but the battery arrived too late for the engagement at the Tullifinny River on December 6.[17] The Beaufort Volunteer Artillery was at Coosawhatchie in late December.[18]

On December 28, Stuart was given command of a new battalion. It was denominated the 5th, and it comprised three units—the Beaufort Volunteer Artillery, Wagner's Battery and Gaillard's Battery.[19] Stuart's 5th Battalion was short-lived, and the Beaufort Volunteer Artillery was soon transferred to Robertson's Battalion.[20] It saw action at Rivers Bridge on February 2, 1865, and Broxton's Bridge on the third. By March 31, it had been placed in Major A.B. Rhett's Battalion, along with LeGardeur's Battery.[21] Engaged at Averasboro on March 16, the battery surrendered with the Army of Tennessee on April 26, 1865.[22]

THE CHESTERFIELD LIGHT ARTILLERY

The Chesterfield Light Artillery was also called Coit's Company Light Artillery, SCV, and, later, Captain James I. Kelly's Company–Chesterfield Artillery–South Carolina Light Artillery, and Captain James I. Kelly's Battery–Chesterfield Light Artillery. It mustered in service on August 25, 1861, and six weeks later, on October 11, while stationed at Camp Butler near Montmorenci in Barnwell District, its men enlisted for the duration of the war. It is possible that the men mustered in state service in August and in Confederate service in October, or they might have enlisted for twelve months at first and then re-enlisted for the duration of the war in October.

Most of the men came from Chesterfield and Marlboro Districts, but a few were from Darlington District.

Officers

James Campbell Coit mustered in service as captain on August 25, 1861. He was promoted to major of artillery in Branch's Battalion on September 12, 1863, and had risen to the rank of lieutenant colonel by 1865.[23]

James I. Kelly succeeded Coit in late 1863. He is first listed as captain on the muster roll for November/December 1863. Kelly commanded the company until the end of the war and was paroled at Greensboro on May 1, 1865.

Brigade Affiliations

The Chesterfield Artillery was attached to the Department of South Carolina, Georgia and Florida from November 1861 to the following July, when it was transferred to the Department of North Carolina. It served successively in the Departments of North Carolina, South Carolina and Southern Virginia and Richmond until October 1864. On June 1863, the Chesterfield Artillery was in James R. Branch's Battalion, later called J.C. Coit's Battalion. From October 1864, one of its sections served in the Army of Northern Virginia, and two remained in the Department of North Carolina and Southern Virginia. The Chesterfield Artillery was listed with unattached troops in the Army of Tennessee about April 9, 1865.[24]

Major Movements and Engagements

The Chesterfield Artillery assembled in Columbia and was sent to Camp Butler on September 10, 1861.[25] It was ordered to Florence in late October or early November and to Pig Point, Virginia, on November 15. Its first engagement fell on February 6, 1862.[26] The battery was transferred from Norfolk to Petersburg on May 10, and it was stationed at Fort Clifton from May to October 1862. The battery saw action at Kelly's Store on January 25 and January 30, 1863, and its men participated in the Suffolk campaign during April and May.[27] The battery returned to the Petersburg vicinity, where it remained until August. Soon afterward, on September 12, it was sent to Drewry's Bluff. The battery was stationed at Kinston, North Carolina, for thirteen months, from January 1864 to February 1865.

The Chesterfield Artillery saw action at the Deserted House, Battery Huger, Swift Creek and Drewry's Bluff from time to time between November 1861 and January 1865. One section was detached for participation in the

Petersburg siege from June 1864 to February 1865, was engaged at Chaffins Farm on May 1 and at Petersburg from June 16 to June 18. For four months, from September to December 1864, the detached section—a lieutenant and forty men—served in the Petersburg trenches. The lieutenant and twenty-five of the men were transferred briefly to Goldsboro, North Carolina, in January or February 1865, but they had been sent back to Petersburg by the end of February.[28] The detached section was probably reunited with the other two in February 1865. The Chesterfield Artillery participated in the Carolinas campaign in 1865 and surrendered at Durham Station on April 26.[29]

CAPTAIN FICKLING'S COMPANY, SOUTH CAROLINA ARTILLERY

Captain Fickling's Company, South Carolina Artillery was also called Fickling's Battery–Brooks Light Artillery, South Carolina; Brooks Guard Battery Artillery; Rhett's Company; and Rhett-Fickling's Battery. Its origins lay in a company called the Brooks Guards, or Brooks Home Guards, organized on January 9, 1861, with John E. Carew as its captain.[30] The Brooks Home Guards never saw active service; most of its members were employed as railroad workers throughout the war.[31] In late April 1861, however, a volunteer detachment of the Brooks Home Guards elected Andrew Burnet Rhett captain and called for volunteers to serve in Virginia.[32] The detachment of volunteers, augmented by recruits from Pickens District, was organized in Charleston on May 8, and it became known as the Brooks Guard Volunteers. Rhett was commissioned captain on May 12, the same day the company left for Virginia as Company K of the 2nd Regiment, SCV. Its men mustered in Confederate service on May 23.[33]

Rhett and sixty-one Company K men requested and received special permission to reorganize as an artillery company after serving only eight months of their initial twelve-month enlistment.[34] While based at Manassas, the men re-enlisted for two years and three months on January 28, 1862. They had returned to Charleston early in 1862; one source states that re-enlistment took place there. Having re-elected Rhett as its captain, the new artillery company became known as Rhett's Battery, or the Brooks Light Artillery.[35] The *Mercury* reported in July that a few months earlier, the Brooks Light Artillery had reorganized for the duration of the war.[36] The *Confederate Military History Series* also says the men enlisted for three years in the spring of 1862, probably indicating a total of three years from April 1861.[37] The last re-enlistment, this time for the duration of the war, followed on December 28, 1863, at Bean's Station, Tennessee.[38]

Most of the company's men were from Charleston District, but a few came from Beaufort, Colleton, Pickens and Richland Districts as well as from Savannah, Georgia. It was initially intended as Company A of W.B. Fitzgerald's 1st Confederate States Light Artillery, but since that regiment never completed its organization, the battery served, instead, in several artillery battalions in the Army of Northern Virginia. Wounded at Mechanicsville, Rhett was frequently absent as the war went on.[39] In February 1863, he was on furlough for the purpose of creating a new company. On February 11, the *Mercury* reported that he had recently been promoted to major, although the CSR does not confirm this information.[40] The *Charleston Daily Courier* reported on the twelfth that Rhett's promotion was based on the recommendation of Major Hilary P. Jones, who cited Rhett's "signal gallantry and good management of his guns in the battles of Mechanicsville and Gaines Farm."[41] It is true that Rhett was offered command of a four-battery battalion in Hood's Division in February, but he chose to remain in the Charleston area.[42] Having left the company by June 1863, Rhett did command a battalion of artillery near the end of the war.[43]

William W. Fickling, who was promoted to captain on June 29, 1863, was slightly wounded a few days later at Gettysburg. He was captured at Sayler's Creek, Virginia, on April 6, 1865. Taken to the Old Capitol Prison in Washington on April 14, he was moved three days later to Johnson's Island, Ohio, and was released on July 18, 1865.[44]

Battalion Affiliations

The Brooks Light Artillery served initially in Hill's Reserve Battalion, the 4th Battalion Reserve Artillery, at the Seven Days Battles. Afterward it was part of Stephen D. Lee's 2nd Reserve Battalion and E.P. Alexander's Battalion, both light artillery. Finally, it was attached to Frank F. Huger's Battalion, Light Artillery, composed of batteries from various states. Most of Huger's batteries subsequently became independent. All the above-mentioned battalions were part of Longstreet's corps.

Major Movements and Engagements

The new Brooks Light Artillery remained in Charleston until March 23, 1862, when it left to return to Virginia.[45] There, until May 26, it was based at Camp Lee, a camp of instruction near Richmond.[46] The company saw action at Seven Pines on the thirty-first.[47] It was also engaged at Mechanicsville on June 26, at Beaver Dam Creek (Gaines's Mill) on the twenty-seventh, and it was engaged again on June 30, when Jackson crossed the White Oak Swamp. Both the *Mercury* and the *Charleston Daily Courier* reported casualties on June 28, June 29 and June 30.[48] The battery was engaged at Rappahannock Station on August 23, at Warrenton Springs on August 26, and at Second Manassas on August 30.

During the Maryland campaign, the battery saw action on September 15 and September 16, and it fought in the battle at Sharpsburg on the seventeenth.[49] It was also engaged for three days at Fredericksburg in December. During the Chancellorsville campaign in 1863, the battery saw action again at Fredericksburg on June 2.[50] Moving to Chesterfield on June 3, the battery fought on July 2 at Gettysburg. There, its casualties totaled thirty-eight men killed or wounded.

The Brooks Light Artillery was the only South Carolina battery to accompany Longstreet's corps to Georgia on September 1, 1863, arriving by train on the seventeenth. Although not engaged at Chickamauga, the battery did participate in the siege of Chattanooga. It also fought at Bean's Station and Knoxville during that campaign. Returning to Virginia with Longstreet's corps in the spring of 1864, the battery fought again at the Wilderness in early May and at Spotsylvania Court House on May 8, 9, 11 and 18. During the Overland campaign, the Brooks Light Artillery saw action on the North Anna River on May 23, along the route on May 30 to 31 and at Cold Harbor on June 3. It was also engaged at Port Walthall on June 18 or June 19, at Bermuda Hundred and at the Howlett House. The battery fought in the Petersburg trenches from June 18 until the withdrawal in April 1865. The Brooks Light Artillery saw action for the last time at Sayler's Creek on April 6 and surrendered at Appomattox on April 9, 1865.

THE CALHOUN ARTILLERY

Captain William M. Murray commanded the Calhoun Artillery.[51] Other officers were Lieutenants J.A. Baynard and John Jenkins.[52] A volunteer unit organized in the spring of 1861, the battery was made up of men from Edisto, Fenwick's and Musselboro Islands. They built forts on the North and South Edisto Rivers and garrisoned the one on the North Edisto from April 26 to June 19, 1861.[53] The men furnished their own arms, ammunition and food.[54] Relieved from duty on the seaboard in mid-June, the battery was disbanded about June 19.[55] The St. Paul's Rifles took over garrison duty when the Calhoun Artillery was relieved.[56] During its brief existence, the battery was attached to the 11th Regiment, SCV, as Company B. The St. Paul's Rifles replaced it.

BEAUREGARD'S BATTERY—SOUTH CAROLINA ARTILLERY

Beauregard's Battery—South Carolina Artillery was originally called Captain T.B. Ferguson's Company, Light Artillery and T.B. Ferguson's Battery. It was also known as Captain Beauregard's Company Light Artillery and Beauregard's—formerly Captain T.B. Ferguson's Company—Mounted (Light) Artillery. It was raised at Charleston in April 1862.[57] The *Mercury* referred to the company as Ferguson's Battery (regulars) in November 1864.[58] One entry in the *Official Records* calls it Preston's Battery.[59]

Officers

Thomas Barker Ferguson was the company's first captain. He was a Citadel cadet who had participated in the firing on the *Star of the West* on January 9, 1861.[60] A Federal sharpshooter's bullet struck him in the chest and damaged his lungs during the battle at Wright's farm near Jackson, Mississippi, on July 14, 1863.[61] Perhaps because of the wound, Ferguson had probably left the battery before R.T. Beauregard replaced him in December 1863. Ferguson was promoted to major of artillery on August 2, 1864, with rank from June 15. He should not be confused with the Thomas B. Ferguson who was major of the 6th Regiment, South Carolina Cavalry.

Rene Toutant Beauregard, the general's son, was promoted to captain on April 23, 1864, retroactive to December 21, 1863.[62]

Brigade Affiliations

Beauregard-Ferguson's Battery was assigned to the Department of South Carolina, Georgia and Florida from May 1862 to May 1863.[63] After that, it became part of States Rights Gist's Brigade in the Department of Mississippi and East Louisiana.[64] Gist's Brigade was attached to Major General W.H.T. Walker's Division. Also in Gist's Brigade were the 16th and 24th South Carolina Infantry Regiments, the 46th Georgia Regiment and the 8th Georgia Battalion. The battery was detached from the brigade in late August or early September 1863, but it remained part of the artillery component of Walker's Division.[65] It was reassigned to Gist's Brigade in Walker's Division on September 23, 1863.[66] From October 1863, the battery was assigned to various artillery battalions in the Army of Tennessee. By October 31 it had become attached to A.T. Palmer's Battalion in Longstreet's corps.[67] On November 20, the battery was part of Robert Martin's Artillery Battalion in Walker's Division, Hardee's corps.[68] Although it remained in Martin's Battalion through April 1864, at the earliest, by September, the battery had been assigned to Robert Cobb's Battalion of Light Artillery in Cheatham's corps of the Army of Tennessee.[69]

Major Movements and Engagements

Ferguson's Battery was stationed at Charleston from April to July 1, 1862, when it was transferred to Summerville. By September, it had moved to Sullivan's Island, where it stayed until about mid-January 1863.[70] Based at Camp Helena near Mount Pleasant until early May, most of the men left Charleston between the fourth and the sixth en route to Mississippi with States Rights Gist's Brigade.[71] By the thirteenth, they were on a train near Jackson, and the next day they saw action at nearby Wright's farm. The battery may have been engaged in support of the 16th Regiment, SCV, at Forest, Mississippi, later that month.[72] On May 25 it was located four miles from Canton, to the north of Jackson.[73] Another detachment of the battery left South Carolina for Mississippi about May 26.[74] After serving under Gist's command in the Jackson area near Mount Vernon during May and June, the battery moved on to Rome, Georgia, later that summer.

On September 12, Ferguson's Battery provided the nucleus of a proposed new company, one that would be commanded by a Captain Calhoun and serve as the second company in Ferguson's Battery.[75] There is no record that Calhoun succeeded in this endeavor. The men left Rome for Catoosa Station near Ringgold on September 18, and they arrived the next day; the battery was held in reserve during the battle of Chickamauga.[76] Detached from Gist's Brigade in October, Ferguson's Battery was engaged at the north end of Missionary Ridge on November 25. Confederate troops were forced to retreat into Georgia as a result of that battle. The next day, Federal troops captured three of the battery's four cannon at Graysville, near Ringgold.[77] The last cannon became disabled and was tossed into a river, so the *Yorkville Enquirer* was correct when it reported that the battery lost all four of its cannon, although most of its men and horses escaped.[78] A number of troops from three companies of the 16th Volunteer Regiment were captured as they attempted to guard the battery's guns at Graysville.

By the end of March, following camp at Dalton, Georgia, from December 1863 through the first four months of 1864, the battery had been re-equipped as light artillery.[79] It saw action at McGinnis's Ferry on the Oostenaula River on May 14, and although the brigade was held in reserve, the battery was probably also engaged at Resaca, Georgia, the next day. The battery was not engaged at Tanner's Ferry on May 16, but it fought again at Calhoun on the seventeenth.[80] The entire brigade was held in reserve and not engaged at New Hope Church on May 25. The battery saw action at Dallas on June

4 and at Pine Mountain on the seventeenth. Both brigade and battery were engaged at Kennesaw Mountain on June 20, 24 and 27. The battery fought at Marietta on July 2, at Peachtree Creek, near Atlanta, on the twentieth and at Atlanta on July 22. It was also engaged at Ezra Church on the twenty-eighth and again on August 15. The battery was not engaged at Jonesboro on August 31, but it did participate in action there the next day. By October 10, it was at Cedartown in northwest Georgia. The battery was probably engaged at Mill Creek Gap, Georgia, on October 13.[81] From Mill Creek, the men marched through Gadsden, Alabama, and on to Decatur.[82] Beauregard's Battery fought again at Franklin, Tennessee, on November 30, and all four of its guns were captured at Nashville on December 16, 1864.[83]

THE GERMAN ARTILLERY BATTALION, SOUTH CAROLINA

The German Artillery Battalion, SCV, was composed of two companies, A and B. A group of young Germans organized a battery in 1841 to join General Sam Houston in Texas.[84] When Houston was elected president there and hostilities ended, the German Artillery had not completed its organization. It continued with its organization, maintained its integrity and by the late 1850s was part of the 1st Regiment Artillery, South Carolina Militia. In 1859, the German Artillery expanded into a two-company militia battalion. A group of volunteers from the German Artillery mustered in Confederate service on August 22, 1861, for five years. This group became known as the German Volunteers of Charleston and was designated Company H of the Hampton Legion Infantry Battalion. By November, it had been converted to artillery and designated Company B of the Hampton Legion Artillery Battalion. Meanwhile, many men remained in Companies A and B of the original militia battalion. When the men enlisted in Confederate service on February 12, 1862, their unit became known as the German Battalion, SCV. According to the CSR, the two companies mustered in Confederate service for twelve months at Fort Chapman on April 1; the *Mercury* records the muster date as June 5. The companies often served separately, and by late 1864 or early 1865, the battalion had been broken up: Company A became an independent company, and Company B became Company A of Manigault's 18th Battalion, South Carolina Artillery.

Companies

Company A, was called Captain Didrich Werner's Company when it was part of the 1st Militia Regiment. Later in the war, it was called Captain F.W.

Wagner's Company Light Artillery, South Carolina Volunteers. Carsten Norhden was elected captain of the company on August 17, 1860.[85] On July 23, 1861, he died at his home in Charleston from an illness contracted after exposure to the elements on Morris Island.[86] Didrich Werner succeeded Norhden as captain in the summer or autumn of 1861; although his commission was dated July 3, 1862, this date reflects his enlistment in Confederate, not state, service. Werner suffered a wound to the mouth at the battle of Port Royal on November 7, 1861.[87] He resigned on March 24, 1863, citing inability "to perform military duties in consequence of injuries received whilst in service."[88] Werner's successor, F.W. Wagner, was promoted to captain on March 9, 1863, and he commanded the company for the rest of the war. He was paroled at Greensboro on May 1, 1865. Most of the company's men were from Charleston, but some came from Aiken in Barnwell District and from Anderson, Pickens, Lexington and Orangeburg Districts.

Company B was previously called Harmes's Company, 1st Militia Regiment and the German Flying Artillery.[89] Later in the war it was known as Captain F. Melchers's Company–Company B, German Artillery, South Carolina Artillery, and Melchers's Company Light Artillery.[90] From 1859 until he resigned on June 5, 1862, Captain Henry Harmes commanded Company B while it was in the militia artillery battalion.[91] The *Confederate Military History Series* says Company B enlisted in Confederate service on February 12, 1862, but both the CSR and the *Charleston Daily Courier* say the date was April 1.[92] According to the *Mercury*, most of the men of Company B enlisted in Confederate service about June 5 as Captain Franz Melchers's Company, South Carolina Artillery.[93] Melchers, who was promoted from first lieutenant to captain about the same time, commanded the company until the end of the war.[94] The men of Company B were mostly from Charleston, but some were from Aiken in Barnwell District and from Darlington and Georgetown Districts. In February 1865, this company became Company A of Edward Manigault's 18th Battalion, South Carolina Artillery.

Brigade Affiliations

Both companies served in the Department of South Carolina, Georgia and Florida from their organization until the end of the war.

On December 28, 1864, Company A was attached to a new battalion—the 5th—under the command of Captain H.M. Stuart of the Beaufort Volunteer Artillery.[95] Also in Stuart's Battalion were the Beaufort Volunteer Artillery and Gaillard's Battery. Company A was part of Robertson's Brigade by January 31, 1865.[96]

Company B was briefly attached to Lucas's 15[97] Battalion in June 1863.[97] In mid-November 1864 and January 1865, it was part of Brigadier General Trapier's Brigade.[98] The battery was placed in Major George L. Buist's Battalion on December 28, along with batteries under Gilchrist, Mathewes and Johnson. Buist's Battalion was in Colonel Edward C. Anderson's Brigade with the 15th and 18th Battalions, South Carolina Artillery, and some Georgia units.[99] Company B was paroled as Company A of the 18th Battalion.

Major Movements and Engagements

Many of the companies of the 1st Regiment Artillery, South Carolina Militia, enlisted in Confederate service in the spring or early summer of 1862. The two German artillery companies appear to have mustered in Confederate service in either February, April or June 1862.

COMPANY A

Company A camped along Meeting Street in Charleston in March 1862. From April 1, 1862, to March 1863, it was stationed at various sites in the 4th South Carolina Military District, including Fishburn's Causeway, Laurel Hill at St. Stephen's Santee, along the South Santee River and in McClellanville.[100] By March 13, 1863, the company had moved to Sullivan's Island and Christ Church Parish.[101] Both companies were based in the vicinity of Georgetown in June and July.[102] Company A served at Mount Pleasant for a year, from July 1863 to July 1864, and functioned as a light artillery battery on Sullivan's Island during part of that time.[103] From July 2 to 11, it was at James Island as part of the artillery reserve.[104] Later that month, the battery was sent to Liberty County, Georgia, where one section was at Riceboro in September and October.[105] Company A also served at Toogoodoo, Savannah and Doctor Town, Georgia, and at Tar Bluff and Gravel Hill, South Carolina. It was attached to Major General McLaws's Division on November 20.[106] The company evacuated Savannah on December 20 and marched through Hardeeville; by December 28, it was at Pocotaligo.[107] Early in 1865, Company A saw action at Pocotaligo in an engagement with Federal gunboats. Withdrawing into North Carolina, the battery was at Hillsborough on April 10, 1865.[108] Both companies surrendered at Durham Station on the twenty-sixth.

COMPANY B

Company B was serving along the coast as early as December 1861.[109] Between February and April 11, 1862, it was at Chapman's Fort on the Ashepoo River and at the Combahee Ferry Battery. Later that month, the company was transferred to Fort Pemberton on James Island along the Stono River, where it saw action with the Federal fleet on the twenty-sixth. Company B was also engaged during the battle of Secessionville on June 16. It was assigned garrison duty at the battery at Lawton's place on James Island on September 5.

From January to early May 1863, Company B garrisoned Battery Glover on James Island as part of T.L. Clingman's Brigade.[110] It observed the capture of the *Isaac P. Smith* in January. Leaving Battery Glover on May 8, the company arrived at Battery White on Winyah Bay near Georgetown on the twelfth. Both companies were based in the vicinity of Georgetown in June and July 1863, and Company B remained there until February 20, 1865.[111] About that time, Company B evacuated Battery White and withdrew through Kingstree to Cheraw. United with Johnston's army at Smithfield, North Carolina, it was assigned to Major Manigault's 18th Battalion, South Carolina Artillery, as Company A. Both companies surrendered at Durham Station on April 26, 1865.

CAPTAIN BACHMAN'S COMPANY, SOUTH CAROLINA ARTILLERY–GERMAN LIGHT ARTILLERY

Captain Bachman's Company, South Carolina Artillery–German Light Artillery, was also called the German Light Artillery, the German Flying Artillery, the Charleston German Artillery and Captain William K. Bachman's Battery. From the fall of 1861 to the following spring, it was simply called the German Volunteers and was officially designated Company B of the Hampton Legion Artillery Battalion.[112] A number of young Germans in Charleston had formed a military company in 1841 with the intention of joining General Sam Houston in Texas. Instead, Houston was elected president of Texas, and hostilities ended before the company could carry out its plans. Even so, the German Artillery completed its organization, maintained its integrity and, in 1859, expanded to a two-company battalion attached to the First Regiment of Artillery, South Carolina Militia. Early in 1861, a number of Charlestonians of German extraction volunteered in a new company for Confederate service. This company, designated the German Volunteers of Charleston, was one of three raised from Charleston's German Artillery Battalion. Many of the men in the German Volunteers had served previously in the battalion, but others had no previous military experience.[113] On August 22, 1861, when they mustered in the Hampton Legion at the Half Moon Battery, a Revolutionary War relic near Union Station, they were based at Camp Hampstead in Charleston.[114] Because the term of service was for five years, the *Mercury* evidently referred to the company as the "German Volunteers for the War."[115] William Kunhardt Bachman, who also enlisted on August 22, was the company's only captain.[116]

On February 16, 1864, Bachman wrote that although his company volunteered to serve unconditionally for the duration of the war, "not a man in the company owed allegiance to the Confederate States of America—every man being a foreigner and unnaturalized."[117] Although recruited as an artillery battery, the German Volunteers became Company H of the Hampton Legion Infantry Battalion.[118] The company left Charleston for Virginia by rail on September 10, 1861.[119]

Soon afterward, the German Volunteers joined the Hampton Legion at Freestone Point. On November 1, the company was equipped with two Blakely cannons and redesignated Company B of the newly created Artillery Battalion, Hampton Legion. Stephen D. Lee wrote: "A good infantry company [the German Volunteers] has just been converted into artillery."[120] The Hampton Legion did not reorganize as a legion in the spring of 1862; instead its infantry, cavalry and artillery battalions were assigned to other organizations. The German Artillery was mustered out of the Hampton Legion on June 22 and became an independent battery known as Captain Bachman's Company, the German Light Artillery. Originally, most of the German Artillery's men came from Charleston; later, however, the company attracted conscripts from other districts: Greenville, Beaufort, Colleton, Pickens, Richland, Chesterfield, Lexington, Edgefield, Spartanburg, Union, Kershaw, Clarendon, Lancaster, Barnwell, Anderson and Marion were all represented. Even though they had originally enlisted for the duration, the German Volunteers re-enlisted for the war in February 1864.[121] Bachman was given command of a three-battery battalion on December 28, 1864.[122] Lieutenant James Simons Jr. commanded the company when Bachman was absent. Bachman was paroled as captain on May 1, 1865, at Greensboro.

Brigade Affiliations

The German Artillery was attached to Walker's Artillery Battalion in June 1862. Some time after June 22, it became part of Pender's Brigade; later, on July 28, the battery was transferred to Hood's Brigade. Still later, until after the battle of Gettysburg, it served in Toombs's Brigade of Hood's Division, along with Garden's South Carolina Battery, and it was attached successively to artillery battalions commanded by B.W. Frobel, M.W. Henry and J.C. Haskell. From October 1863 to the end of the war, the German Artillery served in the Department of South Carolina, Georgia and Florida. On November 20, 1864, the battery was part of McLaws's Division.[123] The next month, on December 28, it was placed in the newly created 3rd Battalion with Kanapaux and DePass's Batteries, and Bachman was named battalion commander.[124] By January 31, 1865, both the German Artillery and DePass's Battery were part of Mercer's Brigade.[125]

Major Movements and Engagements

The German Artillery, which left Charleston on September 10, 1861, camped at the Rocketts, a western suburb of Richmond, until September 23. It united with the Hampton Legion at Freestone Point on the twenty-third or the twenty-fourth. On the twenty-fifth, both the German Artillery and the Washington Artillery were engaged there with the *Seminole*, a Federal steam man-of-war, and a side-wheel steamer, *Jacob Bell*, although the German artillery probably acted as infantry during the engagement. The legion returned to its camp the next day. In early November, the Blakely cannons arrived via Savannah, Georgia, and the German Artillery converted back to an artillery battery. This action created the Artillery Battalion, Hampton Legion. One section of the Washington Artillery and one section of the German Artillery arrived at Cockpit Point, or the Cockpit, on the Potomac River on November 13. Employing their Blakelys for the first time at the Cockpit, the two sections were engaged there on the fourteenth with Federal land batteries. The Artillery Battalion joined the Infantry Battalion at Occoquan Bay, the site of winter quarters for both, on December 1. On the twelfth, two rifled guns of the Washington Artillery engaged two tugs taking soundings in the Occoquan Bay. The legion withdrew from winter quarters on March 8 and marched towards Fredericksburg. After the Chickahominy campaign, during which the battery was engaged at Seven Pines on May 31, the unit was detached from the legion. One of its sections saw action on June 26, 1862, at Mechanicsville.[126] On June 27, while it was attached to the Maryland Artillery, the battery was engaged at Gaines's Mill.[127] Whether it saw action at Frayser's Farm is unclear.

The German Artillery rejoined A.P. Hill's Division on the New Market Road on July 10, 1862. About August 7, it left Richmond and marched to meet General T.J. Jackson's corps. The battery was engaged in a skirmish with enemy pickets on August 24, the same day it joined Jackson. The

German Artillery fought at Second Manassas on August 29 and August 30, 1862; it was engaged again in September—at Boonesboro Gap on the fourteenth and at Sharpsburg three days later. Sources differ as to its involvement at Fredericksburg on December 13.[128]

Ordered to Suffolk, Virginia, the battery saw action there in early 1863, but it soon returned to Fredericksburg, where, in May, it was engaged during the Chancellorsville campaign. The German Artillery fought at Gettysburg on July 2, accompanying infantrymen from Hood's Division as they charged Round Top, and it fought again the next day when it repulsed General Farnsworth's charge. The battery recrossed the Potomac into Virginia on July 14, and during August, it was stationed at Fredericksburg. It did not go to Tennessee with Longstreet's corps in September, but instead it drew a temporary assignment to Hill's 3rd Corps at Gordonsville, Virginia.

Because the German Artillery had lost so many men at Gettysburg, commanders decided it should return to South Carolina where aggressive recruitment might restore its numbers.[129] In mid-October 1863, the *Mercury* reported that the battery had recently returned to Charleston.[130] It was stationed at Pocotaligo later the same month, and by November 1, it was in Greenville, where it remained until the twentieth, when it left for Branchville for the rest of the month. The battery was ordered back to Charleston on December 2 and to Pocotaligo on the third. It was involved in a skirmish at Port Royal Ferry on March 11, 1864.[131] The battery remained in the vicinity of Pocotaligo and McPhersonville until it was ordered back to Charleston in late October.[132] It assisted in the defense of Savannah in November or December, and it was engaged at the Tullifinny River from December 7 to December 8.[133] The battery moved to Pocotaligo on December 17, then moved closer to Charleston on the twentieth, and then, in March 1865, withdrew into North Carolina. While serving temporarily with Wade Hampton's cavalry command, the battery saw action at Fayetteville; it was also with the army at Averasboro and Bentonville, according to Lieutenant Simons, although whether or not it actually fought there remains unclear.[134] It was with the army in North Carolina on April 10 and was included in the surrender on April 26.[135] The German Artillery was detached, however, and was ordered to escort General James Conner, who was attempting to join his command in Camden, South Carolina. Although the battery's ultimate goal was to move to the trans-Mississippi Department and continue the struggle from there, its men determined the war was lost and the battery was disbanded and furloughed at Camden.[136] The German Artillery was paroled at Augusta, Georgia, in May.[137]

CAPTAIN GILCHRIST'S COMPANY—THE GIST GUARD—SOUTH CAROLINA HEAVY ARTILLERY

Captain Gilchrist's Company—the Gist Guard—South Carolina Heavy Artillery, was also called Captain Robert C. Gilchrist's Company, South Carolina Heavy Artillery; the Gist Guard Light Artillery; and Captain Boag's Company E, Manigault's 18th Battalion. The battery was originally called Captain Charles E. Chichester's Company Heavy Artillery. A prewar company, the Gist Guard of Charleston raised two companies for Confederate service from its own ranks. One, organized in July 1861 and called the "Zouave Volunteers for the War," became Company H of the Hampton Legion Infantry Battalion in July 1862. The other, the "Gist Guard Light Artillery," had been raised by mid-January 1862.[138] Its name honored States Rights Gist, who was adjutant general of South Carolina at the time.[139] The battery mustered in Confederate service for three years, or for the duration of the war, on April 2, 1862, while based at Charleston.[140] It served as both light and heavy artillery during the war. Most of the men were from Charleston, Colleton and Spartanburg Districts, but a few came from Union, Anderson, Laurens, Barnwell, Greenville, Orangeburg and Richland Districts and from Augusta, Georgia.

Officers

Charles Edward Chichester, of Charleston, was the battery's founder and first captain.[141] He had served as captain of the Chichester Zouaves in the 1st Regiment Rifles, South Carolina Militia, in early 1861, and his commission dated from September 12, 1861, nearly seven months before the battery's muster date.[142] Chichester's health was affected by nearly constant exposure at Battery Wagner and Battery Gregg on Morris Island between September 1862 and August 1863.[143] On July 25, 1863, Chichester had requested and received permission to return to Battery Wagner, even though the Gist Guard was not on duty there at the time.[144] He served as acting chief of artillery at Wagner from July 25 to July 30.[145] In early August 1863, L.M. Keitt, commanding officer at Morris Island, recommended Chichester's promotion to major and recommended him as chief of ordnance for Morris Island.[146] On the twenty-first, he was still there, although exhaustion left him barely able to walk.[147] In late August, Chichester was moved to St. George's Station to recuperate.[148] He requested a leave of absence on April 4, 1864, saying he was unfit for duty because of a functional kidney disease and neuralgia of the sacrolumbar spine. Chichester resigned on September 7 on the grounds that his physical afflictions prevented any hope of returning to duty.[149] He was regarded as "a brave and gallant officer."[150]

Robert Cogdell Gilchrist, who had received a scalp wound at Battery Wagner in July 1863, was promoted to captain on September 11, 1864, and to major on February 18, 1865. He was paroled on May 1 at Greensboro as assistant adjutant general of General Hardee's staff.

Theodore Gaillard Boag, who was promoted to captain on February 18, 1865, probably helped to raise the company in February 1862. He suffered a wound to the face at Battery Wagner on July 12, 1863.[151] Boag commanded the company until the end of the war and was paroled at Greensboro in 1865.

Brigade Affiliations

The Gist Guard Artillery was an independent organization even though it was temporarily attached to various South Carolina artillery battalions on several occasions.[152] It served in the Department of South Carolina, Georgia and Florida until the last three months of the war.[153] Following temporary service with the 15th Battalion, South Carolina Artillery, in June 1863, the battery was attached to Brigadier General Roswell Ripley's Brigade on November 20, 1864.[154] The next month, on December 28, it was placed in Major George L. Buist's Battalion, along with batteries commanded by Mathewes, Melchers and Johnson. The battalion itself was part of Colonel Edward C. Anderson's Brigade, as were the 15th and 18th Battalions, South Carolina Artillery, and some Georgia units.[155] On January 31, 1865, the Gist Guard was not brigaded.[156] In February, however, it was attached to Manigault's 18th Battalion, South Carolina Artillery, as Company E, and it was paroled by that designation.

Major Movements and Engagements

The Gist Guard Artillery served primarily in the Charleston area throughout the war. It was stationed at Legare's place on Oak Island from January 15 to April 30, 1862, and was engaged with three Federal gunboats at Battery Island on May 1.[157] It saw action again, along with the Palmetto Guards of the 18th Battalion, at Battery Island on May 16. While stationed at Legare's house on James Island, the battery was engaged with three Federal gunboats, this time in the Folly River on June 1.[158] During withdrawal later the same night, the Guard lost three of its cannon. The battery was engaged at Secessionville on June 16 and remained there during July and August. It was transferred to Morris Island about September 1 to become part of the permanent garrison of Battery Wagner. The Gist Guard remained on the island almost continuously until its evacuation on September 6, 1863.[159] It saw action at Wagner in January 1863, again on March 13 and yet again on April 7, when Federal ironclads attacked Fort Sumter.[160] Engaged inside Battery Wagner during the first infantry assault from July 10 to 11, the Guard was relieved on the fifteenth.[161] It was sent from Sullivan's Island back to Battery Wagner on July 19 and to Fort Johnson on James Island on the twenty-fifth.[162] It was on Morris Island again on July 30, but it was soon relieved.[163] It returned to Wagner on August 5.[164] Although the record is unclear as to whether there was a period of continuous service, the battery was still based at Wagner on August 11. It was relieved there on the night of August 17.[165] By August 24, it was again on Morris Island, this time at Battery Gregg, where it fought that day as part of Lucas's Battalion. It remained there until at least August 27. It was at James Island by the last day of the month.[166] The record is clear that the Gist Guard Artillery was present at either Wagner or Gregg for twenty-nine of the fifty-seven days of consecutive bombardment in July and August 1863; its only relief was duty at Battery Bee, near Fort Johnson, and at Battery Simkins on James Island. The Guard was also on Morris Island when it was evacuated on September 6, but it was back at James Island by late September.[167]

During November and December 1863, the Gist Guard Artillery was based at the Blakely Gun Battery at Fraser's Wharf and the Half Moon Battery, both in Charleston. It remained at the Blakely Battery until May or June 1864.[168] By June 26, the battery was on garrison duty at Fort Sumter where it served for most of July.[169] From late July to December, its base was Fort Moultrie on Sullivan's Island.[170] After assisting with the defense of Savannah in December, the battery returned to South Carolina. Evacuating Charleston in February 1865, it withdrew with the army into North Carolina. The Gist Guard fought at Bentonville on March 19 and surrendered on April 26, 1865.

CAPTAIN GREGG'S COMPANY, THE MCQUEEN LIGHT ARTILLERY, SOUTH CAROLINA ARTILLERY

Captain Gregg's Company, the McQueen Light Artillery, South Carolina Artillery, was also called Captain Thomas E. Gregg's Artillery. Organized on April 14, 1862, as one of the two original companies of Alston's Battalion, it was designated Company B at some point between April 14 and mid-July.[171] Most of its men were from Marion District, but a few came from Darlington, Chesterfield, Union, Williamsburg and Charleston Districts. Designated Company C in the South Carolina Siege Train, the McQueen

Light Artillery was the "first" Company C in Manigault's 18th Battalion, a slot from which it was relieved on May 1, 1864, when it was assigned instead to Pegram's Battalion Artillery, Army of Northern Virginia.[172] The Pee Dee Artillery, depleted in men and horses and needing to recruit, replaced the McQueen Light Artillery as Company C in Manigault's Battalion.

Officers

Mathew B. Stanley was the first captain of the McQueen Light Artillery.[173] Suspended by General Beauregard on February 20, 1863, he resigned three months later on May 14.

Thomas E. Gregg, who succeeded Stanley on May 14, 1863, commanded the company until the end of the war.[174]

Major Movements and Engagements

The service of the McQueen Light Artillery before its departure for Virginia on May 1864, is discussed under the section on the 18th Battalion, South Carolina Artillery. Following an engagement at Turkey Ridge near Cold Harbor on June 3, it served in the Petersburg trenches and fought at Battery Number 5, Davis's farm and Hatcher's Run.[175] The battery served as the right flanking battery for the Army of Northern Virginia for the last eight months of the war. It saw action near the Appomattox River on both July 22 and July 30, 1864.[176] According to Welburn, the battery manned two mortars that fired into the crater during that battle on July 30.[177] The battery was engaged again on August 19.[178] It also fought at Fort Harrison, on the Squirrel Level Road, and at Jones's Farm before the end of September. The battery was engaged at Pegram's Farm on October 1 and on the Harman Road the next day. It also saw action on both October 27 and October 28.[179] The *Marion Star* reported that the battery participated in eight engagements between May and November 16, 1864.[180] It fought at Five Forks on April 1 and Petersburg on April 2, 1865. Serving as the artillery of the rear guard during the first week of April, the McQueen Light Artillery surrendered at Appomattox on April 9, 1865.[181]

CAPTAIN KANAPAUX'S COMPANY, THE LAFAYETTE ARTILLERY, SOUTH CAROLINA LIGHT ARTILLERY

Captain J.T. Kanapaux's Company, the Lafayette Artillery, South Carolina Light Artillery, was also called Kanapaux's Battery—Lafayette Light

Artillery—South Carolina and the Lafayette Light Artillery. The Kanapaux Light Artillery, a different company, was commanded by C.E. Kanapaux and designated Company D of the 3rd Battalion, South Carolina Artillery.[182] The origins of J.T. Kanapaux's Company lie in a prewar company known as the Fusiliers Française, made up of French-born Charlestonians. Originally an infantry company, it was converted to artillery about 1840.[183] A number of its members had served in a militia company called the Lafayette Artillery, which was commanded by Captain J.J. Pope Jr. This unit of heavy artillery was attached to the 1st Regiment Artillery, South Carolina Militia, in 1860 as part of Charleston's local defense forces. At some point, probably in early 1862, Pope raised the Lafayette Light Artillery for the duration of the war, but for some reason, he was not elected its captain.[184] John T. Kanapaux was unanimously elected captain on February 26. He mustered in service on March 13, 1862.[185] His brother, C.E. Kanapaux, was captain of Company D, 3rd Battalion, South Carolina Artillery.[186] J.T. Kanapaux, who commanded the battery until the end of the war, was paroled at Greensboro on May 1, 1865.

The battery mustered in Confederate service on March 13, 1862, while it was stationed at Charleston.[187] It is possible that it signed on for only twelve months at first and re-enlisted for three years shortly afterward.[188] Both the *Mercury* and *Charleston Daily Courier*, however, reported that the company enlisted originally for three years.[189] On February 13, 1864, the Lafayette Artillery re-enlisted for the duration of the war.[190] Its men were from Charleston, Beaufort and York Districts.

Brigade Affiliations

The Lafayette Artillery served in the Department of South Carolina, Georgia and Florida from its creation until February 1865. It was attached to Major General Lafayette McLaws's Division on November 20, 1864.[191] The next month, on December 28, the battery was placed in a newly created battalion, the 3rd, along with DePass and Bachman's Batteries.[192] The Lafayette Artillery served for a time in Robertson's Brigade in 1865 and was attached to Lieutenant General Stephen D. Lee's corps of the Army of Tennessee in March and April.[193]

Major Movements and Engagements

The Lafayette Artillery served along the coast between Charleston and Savannah from March 1862 to February 1865. It was stationed at Camp O'Connor near Charleston from March 13 until it was ordered to James Island on May 1, 1862. The battery was transferred to the McPhersonville/Pocotaligo area on October 13. A detachment was engaged at the Coosawhatchie Bridge on October 22 and remained nearby at Camp Walker during November.[194] With only a few exceptions, the battery was based at Coosawhatchie from November 1862 to October 1864.[195] It participated in a demonstration at Boyd's Landing on February 19 and February 20, 1863, and two of its guns were engaged on John's Island on February 10, 1864. The battery fought at Honey Hill on November 30, with one gun engaged in the skirmish and another involved in the battle. On December 26, the battery was stationed at Bee's Creek, with a detachment at Dawson's Bluff.[196] By the twenty-eighth, one section was at Grahamville and another was at Pocotaligo.[197] On January 13, 1865, sections were at Bee's Creek and Honey Hill.[198] The battery saw action at Binnaker's Bridge on the Edisto River, probably on February 9, and at Columbia a few days later.[199] The Lafayette Artillery was engaged at Bentonville and surrendered with the Army of Tennessee on April 26, 1865.[200]

THE MARION ARTILLERY

The Marion Artillery was also called Captain Edward L. Parker's Company, South Carolina Light Artillery; the Marion Light Artillery, South Carolina Volunteers; the Marion Artillery, 1st Artillery Regiment, South Carolina Militia; Parker's Company; and Captain Parker's Company, Light Artillery. Its roots lay in a militia company that was originally composed of Charlestonians and was incorporated in 1843.[201] John Gadsden King served as captain in 1860 and during the first half of 1861, when the battery was still a militia unit.[202] King resigned in mid-July, and in October, he became captain of Company F, 1st Regiment, South Carolina Artillery (Regulars).[203] Arthur M. Huger was elected captain in July 1861.[204] When Huger was elected major of the 1st Regiment Artillery, South Carolina Militia, about September 5, he was succeeded, on the twelfth, by Edward L. Parker thus the name Captain Edward Parker's Company—the Marion Artillery; 1st Regiment, South Carolina Militia Artillery.

The company was reorganized about the same time Parker took command, adding some men from Georgetown and Kershaw Districts and a few from Greenville, Richland, Clarendon, Sumter, Abbeville and Pickens Districts. In 1864, the *Mercury* reported, probably incorrectly, that the men had re-enlisted in September 1861 for the duration of the war.[205] A comparison of the rolls, however, shows that most Marion Artillerymen signed up on

June 6, 1862, for the duration of the war as members of an independent company called Captain Edward L. Parker's Company, Marion Artillery, SCV. Parker, who commanded the company throughout the remainder of the war, was given command of a new three-battery battalion, designated the 2nd, in late December 1864.[206]

Brigade Affiliations

The Marion Artillery served in the Department of South Carolina, Georgia and Florida from the time it entered Confederate service in June 1862 to February 1865. It was attached to Brigadier General Beverly H. Robertson's Brigade on November 20, 1864.[207] On December 28, the battery was placed in Parker's newly created 2nd Battalion, along with Wheaton and Le Gardeur's Batteries.[208] By January 31, 1865, it was part of A.M. Rhett's Brigade, along with the 1st Regiment, South Carolina Artillery; the 1st Regiment, South Carolina Infantry (Regulars); the 19th Battalion, South Carolina Cavalry; the 1st Regiment, South Carolina Militia; the 19th Regiment, South Carolina Militia; and some Georgia units.[209] It was also attached to Major A.B. Rhett's Artillery Battalion in the Army of Tennessee in April 1865.[210]

Major Movements and Engagements

The Marion Light Artillery was engaged at Edisto Island on March 29, 1862, and although it participated in an expedition to John's Island on May 22, it saw no action there.[211] From June 1862, when it became independent, until February 1865, the Marion Light Artillery was stationed in the John's /James/Edisto Island sector.[212] On June 21, it was engaged with Federal gunboats at Simmons's Bluff on Yonge's Island, and it was based there from July to October 1862. The battery moved on November 8 to Camp Echo near Yonge's Island and Adams Run. It skirmished at Grimball's place on James Island on or about March 13, 1863. Although the men moved to John's Island on May 10, they returned to Camp Echo after four days. During the Federal feint on the Charleston-Savannah Railroad near Jacksonboro on July 10, 1863, one of the battery's sections engaged three Federal vessels, an armed steamer, the *John Adams*, and two smaller boats, the transport *Enoch Dean* and a small tug, the *Governor Milton*, at Willtown Bluff on the South Edisto River.[213] The *Governor Milton* was destroyed. The battery arrived at Battery Wagner on July 10 and fought there two days later.[214] It was engaged again at Grimball's place on James Island on July 16, this time with Federal rifled guns.[215] On picket duty from July 16 to August 1, the battery once again dueled with Federal gunboats on the Folly River and saw action at Grimball's Landing on July 30.[216] A section was ordered to Battery Wagner on August 1, and the other followed on the twenty-first. Although at least one section was still at Morris Island on August 25, the entire battery was back on James Island by the thirty-first.[217]

Picket and garrison duty at Fort Johnson occupied the battery during September and October 1863, and by November 1, it was serving as light artillery in the western division on James Island.[218] It alternated between Adams Run, John's Island and the "west lines" on James Island from December 1863 to February 1865. One of its sections was engaged with the *Marblehead* at Legareville on December 25, 1863.[219] By December 31, the battery was based at St. Andrews Parish.[220] In late 1863 or early 1864, one section was sent to Church Flats, and the other section drew picket duty on the Mathews plantation on John's Island.[221] Both sections encamped at Church Flats in February.[222] The Marion Light Artillery participated in a three-day engagement near Haulover Cut and Bugbee Bridge on John's Island from February 9 to February 11, 1864.[223] The first section fought all three days, and the second section on the last two; both were back at Church Flats by the thirteenth.[224]

The battery remained at its St. Andrews Parish base throughout the spring, summer and autumn of 1864.[225] Both its sections skirmished near Legareville on John's Island on April 21. While the first section remained at the Church Flats Bridge on June 2, the second was ordered to the Presbyterian parsonage. The battery helped turn back a Federal advance on John's Island in early July. The first section, on John's Island by July 3, skirmished at Huntscum's Corner on the fifth and near Grimball's Waterloo place on the sixth. The next day it was engaged at Gervais's Field, and on the ninth, it fought again, this time at Burden's Causeway.[226] From July 2 to July 11, the second section guarded the Church Flats Bridge. The two sections alternated as pickets on John's Island and along the Stono River in September and October 1864. One was based at Church Flats as heavy artillery during November and December, and the other was at the Episcopalian parsonage. During this period one detachment was ordered to perform picket duty as infantry at Grimball's place on the Stono River, and the other drew the same duty at Seabrook Island. The battery saw action with Federal reconnaissance barges at Andersonville, near Seewee Bay, at some point between February 12 and February 16, 1865.[227] Engaged for the last time at Averasboro, the Marion Light Artillery surrendered on April 26, 1865.[228]

CAPTAIN MATHEWES'S COMPANY, SOUTH CAROLINA HEAVY ARTILLERY

Captain Mathewes's Company, South Carolina Heavy Artillery, was also called Mathewes's Battery; Mathewes's Independent Company; the Mathewes Artillery; and F.N. Bonneau's Company Artillery, SCV, Confederate States Provisional Army.[229] It was an independent battery raised in late 1861, and it was made up of men from Colleton District, who probably mustered in service on October 1, 1861.[230] Effective February 17 or February 18, 1865, it was converted to infantry and attached to Manigault's 18th Battalion. Mathewes's Artillery, paroled as Company C of Manigault's 18th Battalion, was the third company to carry the designation. Its first captain, Frank N. Bonneau, resigned on February 11, 1863, writing: "By profession a sailor, I can be of more service to the country upon my own element than in the army and await acceptance of resignation to accept another appointment."[231] John Raven Mathewes succeeded Bonneau as captain in February 1863.

Brigade Affiliations

Mathewes's Artillery was assigned to the Department of South Carolina, Georgia and Florida from 1861 to February 1865. In June 1863, it was attached, temporarily, to Lucas's Battalion.[232] On November 20, 1864, the battery was placed in Brigadier General Beverly H. Robertson's Brigade.[233] Assigned to Major George L. Buist's Battalion on December 28, it served with other batteries commanded by Gilchrist, Melchers and Johnson. Buist's Battalion was part of Colonel Edward C. Anderson's Brigade, along with the 15th and 18th Artillery Battalions and some Georgia units.[234] Mathewes's Artillery was attached to B.H. Robertson's Brigade on January 31, 1865.[235]

Major Movements and Engagements

Mathewes's Artillery served in the Charleston area of the Department of South Carolina, Georgia and Florida from October 1861 to February 1865. From October 1, 1861, to April 30, 1862, it was stationed in and around Charleston Harbor, but in November, it moved to a base at Bear Island at the mouth of the Ashepoo River.[236] For about two months in late 1861 and early 1862, the battery's station was on board the *Rattlesnake*, a lightship that had been converted to a gunboat.[237] Mathewes's Artillery was stationed on a "floating battery," possibly the *Rattlesnake*, moored in a creek near Dixon's Island on the Stono River when it was engaged with a Federal gunboat on May 25.[238] It saw action at Secessionville on June 16, and from July 1862 to the summer of 1863, it was stationed at Battery Wagner on Morris Island.[239] While serving as part of the garrison at Wagner on April 7, 1863, it was engaged with gunboats during the ironclads' attack on Fort Sumter.[240] Mathewes's Artillery probably participated in most, if not all, the engagements at Morris Island in January 1863, and it also saw action there on March 13. As part of the garrison, it was engaged during the first infantry assault on Battery Wagner from July 10 to July 11, and it was engaged there again on the eighteenth. The battery suffered one casualty at Morris Island on July 20. About that time, it began rotating with other artillery batteries at Wagner. Leaving for Sullivan's Island about July 20 or July 21, the battery returned to Wagner on the twenty-third. It suffered two casualties there on the twenty-fifth.[241] By July 30, it was back at Sullivan's Island, but it returned to Wagner on August 5.[242] The battery remained on Morris Island through the end of August.[243]

While Mathewes's Artillery, the 20th Volunteer Regiment and the 23rd Georgia Regiment were evacuating Morris Island on the steamer *Sumter* on the night of August 30, Confederate batteries at Fort Sumter and Sullivan's Island fired on and sank the boat.[244] Rescued, the men of Mathewes's Artillery spent August 31 at Fort Sumter and moved to James Island that night.[245] From September to December 1863, the battery was stationed at Fort Johnson on James Island, and it may have served at Battery Cheves then.[246] Leaving Fort Johnson on December 29, the men moved to Green Pond; by December 31, the battery was based at Chapman's Fort on the Ashepoo River. From January to April 30, 1864, the battery was based at Godfrey's farm in the vicinity of Adams Run.[247] Although nearby, the battery was held in reserve and not engaged at the battle of Chapman's Fort on May 26.[248] From August to December 1864, the men were based at the Pineberry Battery near a community of the same name.[249] Mathewes's Artillery was attached to Manigault's 18th Battalion as Company C about February 17 or February 18, 1865. It saw action at Averasboro and Bentonville and surrendered on April 26, 1865.[250]

CAPTAIN CHRISTOPHER GAILLARD'S COMPANY—SANTEE LIGHT ARTILLERY

Captain Christopher Gaillard's Company, Light Artillery, SCV, was also called Gaillard's Light Artillery and the Santee Light Artillery. Its roots lay in the first Company G, called the Coast Guards, of the 10th Infantry Regiment, which was made up of men from Charleston District. According to the CSR, they came from Christ Church and St. Thomas Parishes, both in Charleston District, but a sketch in *Recollections and Reminiscences* says they came from St. John's Berkley, also located in Charleston District.[251] The Coast Guards did not enter Confederate service with the 10th Regiment in August 1861, and it disbanded on September 6. On October 30 at McClellanville, many of its men mustered in Confederate service for the duration of the war, but they mustered for local defense only.[252] The new company formed in this way became Company B in Edward Manigault's Battalion, which was raised for local defense in December 1861 by special permission from the War Department. Retaining its popular name, Santee Light Artillery, Company B served as the artillery component of the battalion at McClellanville until June 1862.[253] Christopher "Kit" Gaillard was elected captain on October 15; his commission was dated October 30, 1861. Gaillard was the company's only captain, and he was paroled at Greensboro on April 30, 1865.

Manigault's Battalion was disbanded about May 18, 1862; its three infantry companies became the 6th, or Byrd's Battalion. Several others were also attached temporarily to Byrd's Battalion. The Santee Light Artillery, which became independent in May 1862, was among those attached to Byrd's Battalion, although it was there temporarily as an unlettered company. The CSR points out that the Santee Light Artillery was mustered in service as part of Byrd's Battalion on October 31, 1862, but was not officially recognized as part of that organization. It may even have served as an infantry company during this period. The 10th and 19th Regiments, SCV, captured four cannon at the battle of Murfreesboro on December 31, 1862.[254] One source describes the guns as three-inch rifled, steel cannon. Another states simply that they were Napoleons.[255] Yet another records them as two Wiards and two Parrotts.[256] Whatever their variety, the cannon were engraved with the names of four men—two men from the 10th and two from the 19th Regiment—who displayed conspicuous bravery during the battle.[257] The former were Captains John R. Nettles of Company H and John S. Palmer of Company K. The latter were Colonel A.J. Lythgoe and Second Lieutenant John T. Norris of Company A. As for the cannon, they were shipped to South Carolina for further use; two were assigned to the Santee Light Artillery in March 1863.[258] From the end of 1862 to the close of the war, the Santee Light Artillery continued to function as an independent artillery battery. Although made up mostly of men from rural Charleston District, some of the battery's members came from Williamsburg District, and a few were from Richland, Barnwell, Clarendon and Marion Districts.

Brigade Affiliations

The battery was in the Department of South Carolina, Georgia and Florida from its creation until February 1865. On November 20, 1864, it was attached to Trapier's Brigade.[259] The battery was assigned to H.M. Stuart's newly created 5th Battalion, along with Stuart and Wagner's Batteries, on December 28, 1864.[260]

Major Movements and Engagements

The Santee Light Artillery served on the South Carolina coast from its creation until February 1865.[261] In June 1862, one of its sections was moved up the Santee River to build an earthwork battery.[262] The resulting fortification was probably Battery Warren, where the company's steel rifled cannon, donated by Plowden C.J. Weston, was based.[263] One of the battery's sections was engaged with Federal gunboats at the Blake plantation on the South Santee River on June 26.[264] The next day, the steel cannon exchanged shots with the same gunboats at El Dorado on the same river. From July to October, Battery Palmer served as the company's base. During November and December, one section was stationed at Andersonville, overlooking Seewee Bay, in Christ Church Parish, and the other was based at Battery Warren. During March 1863, the battery was stationed on Sullivan's Island and in Christ Church Parish.[265] April and May found one section at Battery Warren and the other at Andersonville.[266] The battery moved to Mount Pleasant on May 18, and on June 3, the men were sent to Gadsden Green in Charleston. Ordered back to Mount Pleasant on the twenty-third, the men turned up again at Battery Warren three days later.[267] On July 7, one section was sent to Collins Bridge on Blake's plantation, located about two miles from the South Santee Battery, and the full battery was in Georgetown and its vicinity from July to November 1863.[268]

In late December 1863 and January 1864, two sections were stationed near Georgetown, and one section was in the vicinity of Sullivan's Island and Christ Church Parish.[269] One gun was sent to McClellanville on March 7, and it was engaged there with Federal troop barges on the twenty-fifth.[270] It remained at McClellanville until November 23. From April to late November 1864, the rest of the battery stayed in and around Georgetown.[271] The entire battery was ordered back to Mount Pleasant on November 23.[272] It was ordered next to John's Island, which it evacuated in February 1865. The Santee Light Artillery withdrew through Adams Run, Summerville and St. Stephens into North Carolina. By April 10, it was at Hillsboro.[273] On the twenty-second, after marching to Greensboro, the men were ordered back about fifteen miles to haul up the cannon of the Inglis Light Artillery, whose men had left for home the night before. Fifty-two refused to comply with the order, mounted the battery's horses and left for home.[274] Gaillard was paroled at Greensboro on April 30; the rest of the battery was disbanded or paroled at the same time.

CAPTAIN GEORGE H. WALTER'S COMPANY—THE WASHINGTON ARTILLERY—SOUTH CAROLINA LIGHT ARTILLERY

Captain George H. Walter's Company, South Carolina Light Artillery, was also called Walter's Battery—the Washington Artillery; Walter's Company—the Washington Artillery; Walter's Light Battery; and the Washington Artillery. Its roots lay in the Washington Artillery, which had been organized as a Charleston militia company in 1844 and had served in the Palmetto Regiment during the Mexican War.[275] The company was attached to the 1st Artillery Regiment of the 4th Militia Brigade when the regiment was called to active duty on December 27, 1860. When Virginia seceded from the Union, Captain George H. Walter, who had commanded the company since July 6, 1860, advised his men not to volunteer for Confederate service.[276] Even so, eighteen ignored his advice and formed the nucleus of the Washington Artillery Volunteers, which became the artillery arm of the Hampton Legion in May 1861.[277] After the group left to join the legion, most of those who remained in the militia unit continued to serve as light artillery in and around Charleston.[278] Although the idea of attaching the Washington Artillery to the Holcombe Legion came up in December 1861, it was rejected on the grounds that the battery was a state organization and the men might not be willing to volunteer for Confederate service.[279] As it turned out, most of the company's members—124 men—mustered in Confederate service on February 28, 1862, for twelve months as Captain Walter's Company, South Carolina Light Artillery, also called the Washington Artillery.[280] The *Charleston Daily Courier* gives the date as March 3, 1862.[281] The company re-enlisted for three years, or for the duration of the war, later that spring. Both the *Mercury* and the *Charleston Daily Courier* reported in 1864 that the men mustered in service originally for three years, or for the duration of the war.[282] In March 1864, the men affirmed that unlike many other companies that had signed up "for three years or the duration of the war" in the spring of 1862, they did not feel the need to re-enlist because they had enlisted for the duration.[283] So it was that two companies—the Washington Artillery Volunteers of the Hampton Legion and Walter's Company, also known as the Washington Artillery—arose from the ranks of the longstanding Washington Artillery to take their places with the forces of the Confederate States Army. Members of the original militia company came from Charleston; those in Walter's Battery were from Barnwell, Georgetown, Colleton, Winnsboro and Orangeburg Districts and from Augusta, Georgia. George H. Walter, the company's only captain, was given command of a new three-battery artillery battalion on December 28, 1864.[284] He was paroled at Greensboro in 1865.

Brigade Affiliations

The Washington Artillery served in the Department of South Carolina, Georgia and Florida from its creation to February 1865. It was attached to B.H. Robertson's Brigade on November 20, 1864.[285] A month later, on December 28, the battery was placed in George H. Walter's new 1st Battalion, along with Schulz and Kanapaux's Batteries.[286] It was attached to B.H. Robertson's Brigade on January 31, 1865.[287] Upon reorganization of Johnston's army on April 9, the Washington Artillery was assigned to Major Basil C. Manly's Battalion of Artillery.[288]

Major Movements and Engagements

The Washington Artillery mustered in Confederate service on February 28, 1862, and served along the South Carolina coast for about three years.[289] The Washington Artillery and its regiment, 1st Militia, occupied Fort Moultrie on December 27, 1860.[290] The battery participated in the repulse of the *Star of the West* on January 9, 1861.[291] Later that month, it took charge of a light ship stationed in the mouth of the Wappoo Cut, an act that prevented the flow of reinforcements to Fort Sumter through the Cut. Within a few weeks, the battery was sent to Morris Island to serve at C.H. Stevens's Iron Battery, and on March 8, it accidentally fired on Fort Sumter. The battery was ordered to Fort Beauregard on Sullivan's Island on March 20, and in early April, it was sent to Battery Island to prevent a landing there. The island served as the company's base during the bombardment of Fort Sumter on April 12 and April 13.[292]

In late June, a two-gun section of the Washington Light Artillery was sent to Bull Island to prevent the enemy's landing there; it returned to Charleston in late July. The battery was stationed at Wappoo Cut in November.[293] It served primarily as heavy artillery until November 7, when it was fully equipped as light artillery and ordered to St. Andrews Parish to protect Charleston's "back door." During late 1861 and early 1862, the battery served successively at Simons's Landing, Church Flats and Adams Run. Its center of operations became Adams Run. It was based there when the men mustered in Confederate service in February 1862.[294]

On March 29, a section of the Washington Artillery and the Holcombe Legion mounted an expedition to attack Federal forces on Edisto Island. The section remained on Jehossee Island and did not engage the enemy.[295] A month later, on April 29, the Washington Artillery fired on the gunboat *Haile* in the Dawho River on its return from destroying the Pineberry Battery. On May 30, the company moved to King's plantation on the Toogoodoo River.[296] That summer it carried out picket duty at Bennett's Point (Bear Island) along the Ashepoo River.[297] The battery returned to Adams Run on June 4, but it left three days later on an expedition to Legareville on John's Island. It was not engaged there,[298] and it was back at Adams Run by July 25. The Washington Artillery moved to John's Island on May 9, 1863, in anticipation of an attack on Seabrook Island. The attack never came, and the battery returned to Adams Run the same day. One section went back to John's Island on the tenth for picket duty with Major John Jenkins; on June 17, it was engaged with Federal gunboats near Seabrook Island. Later in June, that section was stationed near the Haulover Cut on John's Island.[299] The other section was based at Anderson's place near Jacksonboro in May and June, and it had returned to John's Island by July or August.[300]

The Washington Artillery saw action with an armed steamer, the *John Adams*, and two smaller boats, the transport *Enoch Dean* and the small tug *Governor Milton*, on July 10, 1863. The engagement took place at Willtown Bluff on the South Edisto, or Pon Pon, River during the Federal feint on the Charleston to Savannah Railroad.[301] The *Governor Milton* was destroyed, and the bridge over the river was saved.[302] With only a few exceptions, the battery was stationed in and around Adams Run from July 1863 to February 1865.[303] Lieutenant W.G. Whilden's section engaged the enemy on John's Island on November 15, 1863, and returned to Adams Run afterward.[304]

The battery was based at Camp Hagood, near Green Pond, in November and December 1863, and it was at Camp "Stonewall" Jackson near Jacksonboro from January to April 1864.[305] It fought on John's Island again in March. The battery was back at Adams Run from May 1864 to September; although one section was present at Chapman's Fort on the Ashepoo River on May 26, it may not have been actively engaged. On July 7, however, it was engaged on John's Island at Gervais Field and Waterloo Place and, two days later, at Burden's Causeway.[306] One of its sections was sent by rail to Fort Walker at Pocotaligo on December 12, but it saw no action there. Ordered to Mackey's Point on the twentieth, it was sent back to

Green Pond within a few days. The same section was sent to Chisholmville on the twenty-fifth and back to Adams Run four days later.

Following about a month of picket duty opposite Jehossee Island, some of the men were engaged with the *Pawnee, Sonoma* and *Daffodil* in Toogoodoo Creek on February 9.[307] Shortly after midnight on the seventeenth, the battery burned its camp and began a march to Summerville, arriving the next day. The men left Summerville on the twentieth and marched through Bonneau to St. Stephens, where they boarded railroad cars. The train took them through Kingstree, Effingham, Darlington and Society Hill before they arrived at Cheraw on the twenty-seventh. They left Cheraw on March 2 and crossed into North Carolina. Moving via Rockingham, Bostick's, Carthage and Manchester, the battery arrived at Fayetteville on March 10 and at Averasboro on March 12. Posted at McNeill's Ferry during the battle of Averasboro, the battery was charged with preventing a Federal flanking movement. It arrived at Smithfield on March 17, only to be held in reserve during the battle of Bentonville. On the march again, the men moved through Raleigh, Chapel Hill and Durham, arriving at Hillsboro on March 24. The company remained there for about two weeks before marching toward Salisbury.[308] Moving through Raleigh on April 20, the battery marched on to Salem. Receiving orders to relieve General Lee at Richmond, the men set out again. They got as far as Greensboro, where news of Lee's surrender reached them. Moving on to Bush Hill, the battery was included in the surrender on April 26, 1865, and paroled shortly thereafter.[309]

CAPTAIN HART'S COMPANY OF HORSE ARTILLERY, THE WASHINGTON ARTILLERY

Captain Hart's Company of Horse Artillery, or the Washington Artillery, SCV, was also called Hart's Battery, the Washington Light Artillery, Lee's Battery of Hampton's Horse Artillery and Halsey's Battery. It was finally paroled as Halsey's Company, Stuart's Horse Artillery.[310] The organization's roots lay in a Charleston militia company called the Washington Artillery, which had been organized in 1844 and had served during the Mexican War as Company F in the Palmetto Regiment.[311] The company was attached to the 1st Regiment Artillery, South Carolina Militia, when it was called to active duty on December 27, 1860. The Washington Artillery fired on the *Star of the West* about two weeks later, on January 9, 1861.[312] While under Captain George H. Walter's command, the battery served at Fort Moultrie on Morris Island; it was stationed at Sullivan's Island during the engagement with Fort Sumter in April. Virginia seceded from the Union a few days later, and the seat of war soon shifted there. Against Walter's advice, eighteen men from the Washington Artillery Militia volunteered for Confederate service. They formed the nucleus of a new company, called the Washington Artillery Volunteers, which was attached to the Hampton Legion that summer.[313] The original militia battery continued to exist, finally mustering in Confederate service on February 28, 1862, as Captain Walter's Company, South Carolina Light Artillery, although it was still popularly known as the Washington Artillery.[314] So it was that a prewar militia company provided two discrete artillery batteries for Confederate service, both bearing the name "Washington Artillery."

The eighteen Washington Artillery militiamen, who became the core of the hundred-man Washington Artillery Volunteers, were all from Charleston. Many of the other men came from Barnwell, Georgetown, Colleton, Fairfield and Orangeburg Districts and from Augusta, Georgia. Some came from Anderson, Union, Greenville, Beaufort, Richland, Newberry, Pickens, Marion, Lexington and Sumter Districts and from Virginia. The company was fully recruited by mid-May and was accepted into the Hampton Legion on the eighteenth as the Washington Artillery Volunteers.[315] Later that month, the men briefly considered changing their company's name to the Palmetto Battery.[316]

The company left Charleston for Columbia on June 11 and mustered in Confederate service there on the fifteenth.[317] It left Columbia on June 24 and had arrived at the Rocketts, near Richmond, by July 1. The Washington Artillery Volunteers joined the Hampton Legion at Bacon Race Church on July 31. The legion picked up its second artillery battery when its infantry, Company H, the German Volunteers, converted in September. The two batteries thus became a battalion, and the Washington Artillery assumed the designation Company A of the Hampton Legion's Artillery Battalion.

Stephen Dill Lee was elected captain of the Washington Artillery on June 7, 1861.[318] The command had been proffered to Arthur M. Manigault, William C. Heyward, J.B. Villepigue, John Pegram and James F. Hart, among other West Point graduates, but all had refused.[319] Lee, when asked, however, accepted; by November he had been promoted to major and given command of the Hampton Legion's Artillery Battalion.[320] Lee left the Hampton Legion at the reorganization in the spring of 1862. James Franklin Hart, a Union lawyer before the war, had been offered command of the battery just after the bombardment of Fort Sumter; he turned down the captaincy but accepted the rank of first lieutenant. Hart was promoted to captain on November 27, 1861, replacing Lee at the post.[321]

The command was at Yorktown during the reorganization in the spring of 1862. Hart was re-elected captain, and the battery unanimously re-enlisted for three years in early March.[322] When the Hampton Legion was dissolved in July 1862, the Washington Artillery became an independent command known as Hart's Battery. The secretary of war selected it for conversion to flying, or horse, artillery, so it could operate with the 1st Cavalry Brigade of the Army of Northern Virginia.[323] The conversion was effected in August. Hart's Battery, to a man, re-enlisted for the duration of the war on January 18, 1864.[324]

Although he was so severely wounded on October 27, 1864, at Burgess's Mill that his right leg had to be amputated on the field, Hart returned to duty in February 1865.[325] He was promoted to major on March 1, 1865, effective February 1. Edwin Lindsey Halsey was promoted to captain on March 20, 1865, although he had actually served as such since the previous October 27.[326] Halsey, a gallant leader, was paroled at Greensboro on May 1, 1865.[327]

Brigade Affiliations

The Washington Artillery Volunteers was attached to the Artillery Battalion of the Hampton Legion until July 1862. Afterward, until January 1865, it was attached successively to battalions commanded by John Pelham, R.F. Beckham and James Breathead, and to R.P. Chew's Horse Artillery of the Army of Northern Virginia. In January 1865, before it joined Hart's Battalion, it was part of B.C. Manly's Battalion in the Army of Tennessee. The battery served with South Carolina cavalry brigades under Wade Hampton in 1862 and 1863 and under M.C. Butler in 1864. On April 9, 1865, it was attached to Major General M.C. Butler's Division of Hampton's Cavalry corps.[328]

Major Movements and Engagements

Hart's Battery of Horse Artillery, SCV, saw action in no fewer than 143 battles and skirmishes.

The Washington Artillery left Charleston on June 11 to join the rest of the Hampton Legion in Columbia.[329] On June 26, it left Columbia by rail for Richmond.[330] By July 1, the battery had arrived at Camp Chimborazo at the Rocketts, a western suburb of Richmond. The Washington Artillery was not present at the first battle of Manassas because it had not yet received its ordnance from the Tredegar Foundry in Richmond. By July 30, the Washington Artillery had joined the Infantry and Cavalry Battalions at Bacon Race Church, about nine miles from Manassas. The Washington Artillery remained there until at least September 1. The entire legion left

Bacon Race Church on September 20 and was together at Dumfries, Virginia, where it performed picket duty between that place and the Potomac River. The Washington Artillery built gun pits and placed its guns there on the Potomac River from September 20 to September 24. On the twenty-fifth, both the Washington Artillery and the German Artillery were engaged there with the *Seminole*, a Federal steam man-of-war, and the side-wheel steamer *Jacob Bell*. The legion returned to its camp the next day. On October 20, the Washington Artillery returned to Bacon Race Church. One section of the Washington Artillery and one section of the German Artillery arrived at Cockpit Point, or the Cockpit, on the Potomac River on November 13. The two sections were engaged there with Federal land batteries on the fourteenth.

The Artillery Battalion joined the Infantry Battalion at Occoquan Bay, the site of winter quarters for both, on December 1. On the twelfth, two rifled guns of the Washington Artillery and one rifled-gun section of the German Artillery engaged two tugs that were taking soundings in the Occoquan Bay. On January 1, 1862, all three sections of the Washington Artillery were based at Occoquan and at Wolfe Run Shoals. On February 22, two rifled guns of the Washington Artillery were engaged with two Federal gunboats on the Occoquan Bay. The legion withdrew from its camp at the junction of the Occoquan and Potomac Rivers on March 8 and marched towards Fredericksburg, arriving there on the tenth.[331] The legion withdrew from Fredericksburg on April 8 and arrived at Ashland on the tenth.[332] Leaving Ashland on the fourteenth, the men arrived in the vicinity of Yorktown on April 18. There, only camp duty awaited them. The Hampton Legion's original term of service expired on June 12; the legion was dissolved, either then or shortly thereafter, certainly no later than June 27. The two artillery batteries fought with the Infantry Battalion in Wade Hampton's new brigade until late June, when they were attached to the Army of Northern Virginia. Men of the Washington Artillery, at Yorktown during the reorganization, re-enlisted for three years. The Washington Artillery was engaged in rear guard action at Williamsburg in early May. After withdrawing from Yorktown with the army, the Washington Artillery was engaged in several skirmishes, including those at Myers's farm, the White House, West Point, and Garnett's Farm. The Artillery Battalion arrived at Richmond by late May. The Washington Artillery was engaged at Mechanicsville on June 26 and at both Golden's farm and Savage's Station on the twenty-ninth. It also saw action at Malvern Hill on July 1.

After the Seven Days Battles, the three branches of the Hampton Legion were separated. The company, now known as Hart's Battery, was engaged in a rear guard action at Malvern Hill on August 18, 1862. The battery was not present at the battle of Second Manassas because it was in the process of being converted to horse artillery. After transformation to horse artillery, six horses drew the battery's gun caissons and all the men were mounted.[333] Rejoining the Army of Northern Virginia on September 2, the battery, that day, saw action during the pursuit of the Federal army. Hart's was the first Confederate artillery battery to cross the Potomac in September.

It was engaged at Monocacy and Frederick on September 12, near Middleton on the thirteenth and at Cotoctin Mountain on the fourteenth. Low on ammunition at the battle of Sharpsburg on September 17, the men were able to fire only a few rounds. The brigade skirmished daily from the fifth to the nineteenth, and the battery was probably engaged during the delaying action at Williamsport on September 19 and September 20. One section of the battery participated in the Chambersburg Raid from October 9 to October 10 and engaged the enemy at the Potomac River crossing on the twelfth. The battery faced daily skirmishes over the next six weeks, among them Barber's Crossroads on November 5, Gaines's Cross Roads on the sixth, Little Washington, Sperryville, sites along the Hazel River, Ellis's Ferry, Martinsburg, Middletown, White Ferry, Amissville and Rapidan Station.[334] The battery did not participate in the Dumfries/Occoquan raids in December, but it did fight at Fredericksburg on December 13, and it set up camp at Stevensburg, where it rested for about six weeks. About February 1, 1863, the battery was ordered to the Shenandoah Valley to obtain horses. At Gordonsville in early March 1863, the battery saw action during the pursuit of General Kilpatrick. It also helped delay the Federal advance for about a week in early April before rejoining Wade Hampton's Cavalry. The battery was not present during the battle of Chancellorsville in May.

The battery was included in the Grand Review held on June 8, 1863; the next day it fought on the Beverly Ford Road and also at Stevensburg, during the first battle of Brandy Station.[335] Barely avoiding capture that day, it was rescued just in time by the 1st Regiment, South Carolina Cavalry, and the Cobb Legion.[336] On June 16, the battery began a march north as the guard for the right flank of the Army of Northern Virginia. Skirmishes followed at Warrenton on June 17 and at Rector's Cross Roads, near Middleburg, on the nineteenth. Two days later at Upperville, the battery lost one of its Blakely cannon when a limber chest was struck and exploded, dismounting the cannon.[337] This was the only gun the battery lost during the war, although every piece but one was disabled at Upperville. That day, the battery also lost many of its horses.

Hart's Battery, temporarily detached from Stuart's command about June 30, was assigned for a while to Longstreet's corps after repairing its guns. The battery arrived at Gettysburg on July 1, and it fought there as part of the special command under John Logan Black, colonel of the 1st Regiment, South Carolina Cavalry. The next day it held its position on the right wing and, for most of the day, resisted a Federal flank attack. It also participated in a desultory skirmish on the Confederate right on July 3. It retreated with the army on the evening of July 4, acting as rear guard, and was engaged at Williamsport in the "wagoners' fight" on July 6. After Williamsport, the battery was under the temporary command of Fitzhugh Lee. Crossing the Potomac at Falling Waters on July 13, it skirmished almost daily for the next two weeks in and around Martinsburg. While covering the rear of the Army of Northern Virginia, the battery was engaged at the second battle of Brandy Station on August 1. The next month brought a lull—Hart's Battery skirmished only once or twice.

Following an engagement at Raccoon Ford on the Rapidan River from September 11 to 12, the battery moved to Lee's left and, among other skirmishes, saw action later that month at Jack's Shop on the Warrenton Turnpike. October brought a skirmish at Warrenton, the third battle of Brandy Station (Fleetwood Heights) and another skirmish at Mount Auburn near Catlett's Station on the thirteenth and fourteenth. By late October, the battery was in camp near Culpeper Court House. Following a skirmish on November 10 at Stevensburg, the battery moved south of the Rapidan River. It participated in the Mine Run campaign from November 26 to December 2, and it was engaged at Parker's Store on November 29 and, in its last engagement that year, at Mine Run near Germana Ford on December 2. A respite in winter quarters at Hamilton's Crossing ended in January, when the battery moved back to the railroad near Panola Station.[338] The men voluntarily and unanimously re-enlisted for the duration of the war in early 1864.[339] On March 1, one gun helped to foil Kilpatrick's Raid as it supported Wade Hampton's night attack on Kilpatrick's camp near Atlee's Station. In late April, the battery moved forward and bivouacked near Hamilton's Crossing on the Rappahannock River. It was engaged, but only lightly, at the Wilderness from May 5 to May 6, but it saw action at Mitchell's Station on the ninth. Afterward, one of the battery's sections was sent to Richmond, and another, commanded by Lieutenant Halsey, was sent to Yellow Tavern. Halsey's men saw action at Yellow Tavern on May 10 and at Spotsylvania two days later. The two sections reunited at Hanover Junction.

The battery was engaged at Haw's Shop on May 28, and it intercepted a cavalry raid at Ashland on June 1. It fought against Sheridan's cavalry at Louisa Court House on June 11 and at Trevilian Station on June 11 and June 12. The battery helped pursue Sheridan and fought at White House on the York River on the twentieth and at Samaria Church on June 24.

Transferred to the south side of the James River, it participated in a number of skirmishes during the summer of 1864—it repelled Wilson's Raiders at Sappony Church, entered into a scrap on the Petersburg and Weldon Railroad about three miles from Stony Creek Station on June 28 and had another fight at Reams Station on August 25. Late that month, the battery was sent to the Shenandoah Valley to reinforce Jubal Early, but it had returned to Petersburg by early September. Two of its cannon participated in the Cattle Raid at City Point from September 14 to September 17.[340] From September 14 to September 30, the battery was stationed on the right of the Confederate lines near Petersburg. It saw action at McDowell's farm, near Hatcher's Run, on September 29 and more action near Armstrong's Mills on October 1. The battery was engaged almost daily in October. Among those engagements were incidents on the twenty-seventh at Stony Creek and Burgess Mill on the Boydton Plank Road.[341] Ordered to North Carolina in December, the battery engaged the enemy at Hicksford on the Meherrin River near Weldon on December 8.

March 1, 1865, found the battery at Salisbury.[342] It skirmished at Moccasin Creek on April 10 or April 12, fought at Bentonville and fought again near Greensboro on April 24, just two days before the surrender. On April 26, 1865, before it surrendered with the Army of Tennessee, Hart's Battery fired the Confederate artillery's last shot.

CAPTAIN ZIMMERMAN'S COMPANY, THE PEE DEE ARTILLERY, SOUTH CAROLINA ARTILLERY

Captain Zimmerman's Company, the Pee Dee Artillery, South Carolina Artillery, was also called the Pee Dee Light Artillery; Captain McIntosh's Battery; Captain McIntosh's Company Light Artillery; and Captain Brunson's Company, South Carolina Light Artillery. Its history is complicated. Frederick Fraser Warley organized the Darlington Guards in Darlington District on June 28, 1859.[343] On January 3, 1861, that company became Company B in Colonel Maxcy Gregg's 1st Regiment, SCV, a six-month regiment.[344] After the bombardment of Fort Sumter in April, Gregg called for volunteers from his regiment to serve in Virginia, but Warley and many others in the Darlington Guards refused to go. David Gregg McIntosh, a lawyer from Society Hill in Darlington District and first lieutenant in the company, agreed to the plan and led a small contingent of the Darlington Guards to Virginia.[345] The *Mercury* reported that the Darlington Guards, meaning McIntosh's contingent, was on Gregg's regimental roster in May 1861.[346] In the meantime, in April, Warley had led home to Darlington the men who refused to serve in Virginia.[347] These men reorganized on June 24, and they elected Warley their captain. Although precisely what became of Warley's new company is unknown, it was most likely the Inglis Light Artillery, discussed elsewhere in this narrative.[348] In any event, by May 29, 1862, Warley was captain of the Inglis Light Artillery, which became Company D of the 2nd Regiment, South Carolina Artillery.[349] Gregg's regiment was also reorganized after its initial term of enlistment expired in early July 1861, and McIntosh's Darlington Guards, too, disbanded and ceased to exist at about the same time. On July 21, 1861, McIntosh organized a new company, primarily from men who had served in the Darlington Guards, this one called the Pee Dee Rifles. Its men mustered in Confederate service for the duration of the war as Company D of Gregg's new regiment, also called the 1st Regiment, SCV.[350] Since Gregg's new regiment had twelve companies, instead of the usual ten that were allowed a standard regiment, the Pee Dee Rifles was converted to a light artillery battery in March 1862, and it changed its name to the Pee Dee Light Artillery. It was detached from Gregg's regiment that month, and it served as an independent battery until May 1864. The men of the Pee Dee Artillery re-elected McIntosh captain in July 1862. Why such an election needed to be held remains unclear unless it was to satisfy requirements of the general reorganization held earlier that year.[351] On February 15, 1864, the Congress of the Confederate States passed a joint resolution thanking the Pee Dee Artillery for its re-enlistment for the duration of the war.[352] In early 1864, it was common practice for companies that had originally enlisted for the duration of the war in 1861 or 1862 to "re-enlist." Such re-enlistment evidently reaffirmed the original enlistment and presented a show of solidarity with comrades in arms who were required to re-enlist because their enlistments had expired.

On May 5, 1864, the Pee Dee Light Artillery was ordered back to South Carolina in exchange for the McQueen Light Artillery and was designated Company C of Manigault's 18th Battalion, South Carolina Artillery. The actual exchange apparently took place on June 4. The "first" Company C of the battalion, the McQueen Light Artillery, was sent to Virginia about the same time; oddly enough, the Pee Dee Artillery thus became the second company to carry the designation, "first" Company C of Manigault's Battalion. Detached from Manigault's Battalion about February 17 or February 18, 1865, the Pee Dee Artillery was replaced by Mathewes's Artillery, and it was paroled as Zimmerman's South Carolina Battery in Manly's Artillery Battalion.

Most of the men of the Pee Dee Light Artillery were from Darlington District, although some came from Charleston, Newberry, Sumter, Marion,

Marlboro, Laurens, Chesterfield, York, Anderson and Fairfield Districts. David Gregory McIntosh, captain of Company D in Gregg's 1st Regiment, SCV, retained command of the Pee Dee Artillery when it became an independent battery in March 1862. He was wounded at the battle of Second Manassas on August 30 the same year. General T.J. Jackson recommended him for promotion to lieutenant colonel after the battle of Fredericksburg.[353] McIntosh was promoted to major on March 2, 1863, and was given command of an artillery battalion made up of three batteries from Virginia and one from Alabama. Sergeant Brunson wrote that McIntosh was promoted for his "coolness and courage" at Fredericksburg.[354] McIntosh was wounded in the body about August 18, 1864, and spent a week in the hospital. He was eventually promoted to colonel and was named chief of artillery for the 2nd Corps near the end of the war.[355] First Lieutenant Ervin Brown Brunson succeeded McIntosh as captain of the Pee Dee Artillery on March 2, 1863. He was wounded at Gettysburg that July.[356] In January 1864, Brunson was elected to a four-year term as clerk of court for Darlington District. Arraigned and tried before a military court of the 3rd Corps, Army of Northern Virginia, in February 1864, he was charged with embezzling money meant for payment to men under his command and with conduct unbecoming an officer and a gentleman.[357] The court found him guilty on both counts and cashiered him. Further, the court ordered that his crime, name, place of abode and sentence be published in the Charlottesville newspapers and in South Carolina. Finally, the court required that Brunson be duly enrolled in military service; he enlisted as a private in Purcell's Battery of Virginia Artillery. Governor M.L. Bonham requested a discharge so Brunson might fulfill his duties as clerk of court; he was discharged on June 30, 1864. First Lieutenant William E. Zimmerman was promoted to captain on June 30, 1864. Wounded at Gaines Cross Roads in the summer of 1863, Zimmerman was paroled at Goldsboro, North Carolina.

Brigade Affiliations

The Pee Dee Artillery was detached from the 1st Regiment, SCV, and was assigned to Maxcy Gregg's Brigade in March 1862. It served in R.L. Walker's Battalion from early July 1862 to January 1863, when it was transferred to W.J. Pegram's Battalion of the Army of Northern Virginia. In June 1864, the Pee Dee Artillery was reassigned to Manigault's 18th Battalion in the Department of South Carolina, Georgia and Florida.[358] In late February 1865, it was attached to Kemper's Battalion of Reserve Artillery, and by April 9, the battery was attached to Major Basil C. Manly's Battalion in the Army of Tennessee.[359]

Major Movements and Engagements

The Pee Dee Artillery was in camp at Suffolk, Virginia, with Gregg's regiment until February 1862; it was detached from the regiment in March. After drilling for about a month, the battery was sent to Goldsboro, North Carolina, but remained for only a few days. Later, in April, it was transferred to a camp near Massaponax Church, about seven miles from Fredericksburg. In May, the Pee Dee Artillery was sent to Richmond; it was shelled but not actively engaged at the battle of Seven Pines. After firing the opening gun, the battery was heavily engaged at Mechanicsville on June 26, lightly engaged at Gaines's Mill the next day and under fire but not actively involved at Frayser's Farm and Malvern Hill.[360] After resting for a few weeks, the battery marched through Richmond on its way to Culpeper. Not engaged at Cedar Run on August 9, it fought at Warrenton Springs on the Rappahannock River in August. At the battle of Second Manassas, the battery was exposed to heavy rifle fire on the evening of August 28 and heavily engaged on the twenty-ninth.[361] It fought again at Ox Hill on September 1. Placed in position on Bolivar Heights above Harpers Ferry on September 14, the battery was engaged there the next day and again on the seventeenth at Sharpsburg. There, the men entered the battle on the left of the division and faced Federal infantry without their own infantry support. A.C. Haskell wrote that McIntosh's Battery rushed forward and was captured before it had time to unlimber.[362] Three of the battery's cannons and its flag were abandoned in the face of the enemy but were soon recovered by the 12th Regiment, SCV, and Toombs's Brigade.[363] The battery remained on the battlefield on September 18 and recrossed the Potomac into Virginia that night.

After Sharpsburg, the battery went into a rest camp near Bunker Hill. Leaving camp on November 22, the men reached Fredericksburg on December 3.[364] On the twelfth, the battery took up its position at nearby Hamilton's Crossing; it sustained heavy losses the next day.[365] Ordered to Moss Neck on January 15, 1863, the battery set up its winter quarters at Camp Taylor near Milford Station. There picket duty occupied the men until spring.[366] The Pee Dee Artillery marched toward Chancellorsville on April 29, and from May 1 to May 4, before it returned to Camp Taylor for about two weeks, it was engaged there with heavy loss. On June 15, the battery left the camp and began its march toward Pennsylvania, where it fought at Gettysburg all three days, from July 1 to July 3. Withdrawing on the fourth, it reached Hagerstown, Maryland, four days later. In either July or August, the Pee Dee Artillery was engaged with Federal cavalry at Gaines Cross Roads, and that autumn it saw action again at Verdiersville, Bristoe Station and Rixeyville near Culpeper Court House. The battery spent the winter at Camp Taylor, near Gordonsville. Only a lack of horses prevented it from participating in the battle of the Wilderness. During the 1864 Overland campaign, the Pee Dee Artillery was engaged at Spotsylvania Court House on May 11, at the North Anna River on the twenty-third, at Hanover Junction and at Cold Harbor, its last battle in Virginia, on June 3. By the spring, the battery was greatly reduced in numbers and needed new recruits; consequently, it was ordered to South Carolina in early May to become Company C of the 18th Battalion. Leaving its artillery equipage in Virginia, the battery transferred to South Carolina on June 4. Back in Charleston by mid-June, the Pee Dee Artillery was sent to Battery Ryan on James Island, where it served as heavy artillery until December.[367] In January 1865, the battery was sent to Pocotaligo to help resist Sherman's advance, and on February 14, it moved to the Salkehatchie River. Re-equipped as a light artillery battery, it was engaged at the battle of Rivers Bridge on the Salkehatchie River from February 2 to February 3. In March the battery withdrew into North Carolina as part of Kemper's Battalion of Reserve Artillery. It surrendered at Greensboro on April 26, 1865, and disbanded at Hillsboro.[368]

CAPTAIN MAYHAM WARD'S BATTERY, THE WACCAMAW LIGHT ARTILLERY

Captain Mayham Ward's Battery, the Waccamaw Light Artillery, was also called Captain Joshua Ward's Company, South Carolina Light Artillery. It was organized in December 1860, shortly after South Carolina seceded from the Union. Mustering in state service on January 20, 1861, the company served with the 33rd Militia Regiment from Horry District in April.[369] In what appears to have been a legal technicality, the state legislature authorized the formation and incorporation of the Waccamaw Light Artillery in January 1862, and the *Mercury* announced that the battery was accepted into the 33rd Regiment for fourteen years.[370]

The Waccamaw Light Artillery was stationed at Waccamaw in Georgetown District when it mustered in Confederate service for the duration of the war on January 20, 1862.[371] Its men came from the lower Waccamaw River in Horry and Georgetown Districts. The battery was temporarily attached to the 10th Regiment, which drew its men from Georgetown and Horry Districts. The Waccamaw Light Artillery was detached from the 10th Regiment about March 25, when General Pemberton ordered Colonel Manigault to dismantle the defensive works at Georgetown and march his regiment to Charleston.[372] The Waccamaw Light Artillery remained in and around Georgetown. On August 31, it officially became a company in Major Emanuel's 4th Cavalry Squadron, subsequently the 12th Cavalry Battalion, although it was not assigned a letter designation. The battalion was in existence only four months at the time. On December 16, 1862, it was merged with the four companies of Major Stokes's 10th Cavalry Battalion and with independent companies commanded by Captains B.H. Rutledge and Thomas Pinckney to create the 4th Regiment, South Carolina Cavalry. There is no evidence that the Waccamaw Light Artillery was ever attached to the 4th Regiment, a fact that lends credence to the idea that it functioned as an independent organization from late 1862 to the end of the war.

The first known captain of the Waccamaw Light Artillery was T.W. Daggett, who was commanding in April 1861[373] and probably led the battery until January 1862. He later commanded another company that participated in resisting Potter's Raid along the Black River in April 1865.[374] Joshua Ward was elected captain of the battery on January 20, 1862, and resigned on July 18, 1864, because chronic liver problems gave him repeated attacks of fever and chills, which rendered him unfit for service. Ward added that he wished to go to Europe for a change of scene or climate. His physician attested that Ward suffered from malarial poisoning and an organic derangement of the liver. Mayham Ward succeeded him as captain on August 6, 1864, and commanded the company until the end of the war.

Brigade Affiliations

The Waccamaw Light Artillery served in the Department of South Carolina, Georgia and Florida throughout its existence. By November 20, 1864, the battery was attached to Trapier's Brigade, where it remained until at least January 31, 1865, or perhaps even later.[375]

Major Movements and Engagements

The Waccamaw Light Artillery performed various duties along the South Carolina coast from December 1860 to January 1862. In mid-April 1861, while serving with the 33rd Militia Regiment, it was posted between North Island, near Georgetown, and Murray's (Murrell's) Inlet.[376] On April 11, 1861, a detachment was based at Fort Randall on the Little River at the North Carolina line, along with Company L of the 7th Volunteer Regiment.[377] At the same time, Fort Ward at Murray's (Murrell's) Inlet was occupied by another detachment of the Waccamaw Light Artillery.[378] During much of the time between January 1862 and December 1864, the company was stationed at Battery White, overlooking Winyah Bay. From January 20 to March 25, 1862, it served with the 10th Volunteer Regiment in the

Georgetown area, particularly at Cat Island. When the 10th left Georgetown for Charleston in late March and early April, the Waccamaw Light Artillery remained at Georgetown. Stationed at nearby Camp Ward in May and June, it was moved to Camp Laurel for July and August. According to the *Mercury*, the battery was stationed in the Georgetown vicinity on the Black River in August.[379] On the fourteenth, one of its sections, along with the 12th Battalion (4th Squadron), South Carolina Cavalry, engaged the Federal gunboat *Pocahontas* at Mrs. Sparkman's plantation on the Black River, about twenty miles above Georgetown.[380]

From September 1, 1862, to December 1864, the company was stationed at Battery White.[381] Between August and December 1862, it served with the 12th Battalion in the Georgetown area.[382] On February 3, 1863, one of its sections was based at Fraser's (Frazer's) Point near Georgetown.[383] The battery remained in and around Georgetown for the rest of that year and for nearly all of 1864.[384] It guarded Federal prisoners of war at Florence from September 19 to sometime in October 1864, and it may also have spent some time in the Charleston area in late 1864 or early 1865. The Waccamaw Light Artillery surrendered in North Carolina on April 26, 1865.

Appendix 1.

INFANTRY COMPANIES WITH UNKNOWN REGIMENTAL OR BATTALION AFFILIATIONS

1. The Southern Guards was a company of Wofford College students organized on February 22, 1860. According to one source, the captain was Talliaferro Simpson; another source names T.B. Anderson.[1] Anderson is not listed in the CSR, probably because the company was never in Confederate service.

2. The Charleston Guard, commanded by Captain Myer Jacobs, was composed of alarm men and those otherwise exempted from service.[2] Myer is not listed in the CSR, probably because the company was never in Confederate service.

3. The Snow Hill Guards was a company from Newberry District.[3]

4. The Magrath Guard, a company of Irishmen probably from Charleston, was commanded by a Captain Farrelly.[4] Henry S. Farley was captain of Companies D and H of the 1st Regiment, South Carolina Artillery Regulars, but no Captain Farrelly appears in the CSR.

5. The Hudson Street Guard, a company of "armed juveniles," probably took its name from Hudson Street in Charleston.[5]

6. The Gasper Guards was a company of boys, probably of school age, commanded by Master Algernon Alston.[6] Alston is not listed in the CSR.

7. The Southern Boys was a company commanded by Captain Sam Thomas.[7] Thomas is not listed in the CSR.

8. The University Riflemen, from Greenville, was made up of Furman University students. It existed in January 1861, and it may have become the Brooks Troop, Company B of the Hampton Legion.[8]

9. The Marion Men was commanded by Captain G.B. Lartigue.[9] In July 1861, the *Mercury* announced that Lartigue was unable to complete the organization of the company.[10] He is not listed as a captain in the CSR.

10. The Sumter Cadets was a company of "juveniles."[11]

11. The Hope Guard, a Charleston company, was probably raised from the Hope Fire Engine Company.[12] Company H of the 13th Regiment, SCV, was a Lexington District company also known as the Hope Guards.
12. The Confederate Guards was a home guard company from Williston in Barnwell District.[13]
13. The Citizen Guards was a Chesterfield District company commanded by a Captain Tawh.[14] Tawh is not listed as a captain in the CSR.
14. The Home Guard of Union District was commanded by Captain F. Scaife.[15] This was probably Ferdinand D. Scaife who, in November 1861, became captain of Company A of the 18th Regiment, SCV, and later became its lieutenant colonel.
15. The Carolina Greys was a Charleston company commanded by Captain F. Marion Ronan.[16] Ronan was a lieutenant in the 16th Regiment, South Carolina Militia, but the record is unclear on whether or not the Carolina Greys was a company in that regiment.
16. Captain William Greene was attempting to raise the Manigault Guards in Georgetown in late December 1861.[17] The result of that effort is unknown.
17. Captains O'Connell, Stewart and Pulliam were from Pickens District.[18]
18. The Keitt Guard was commanded by Captain H. Smith Bass.[19] Bass is not listed in the CSR.
19. John W. Carr, a private in the St. George's Volunteers, served later in the 18th Regiment, SCV.[20] Carr was disabled in December 1861. He is not listed in the CSR.
20. Captain Samuel Y. Tupper commanded a "force" of exempt men and others who provided auxiliary services to the army in the defense of Charleston in June 1864.[21] Tupper had been captain of the Vigilant Rifles, part of the 4th Brigade, South Carolina Militia, in 1861. Later that year, he served in the 1st Regiment, S.C. Artillery Militia. Tupper enlisted on July 11, 1863, as captain of Company H of the 1st Regiment, Charleston Guard, South Carolina. An order dated May 29, 1864, authorized him to raise a company of volunteers from those citizens exempt from immediate military duty for service at batteries in Charleston. Another order, this one dated September 23, detached Tupper for duty as an agent of the state commissioners assisting in the removal of noncombatants from Charleston.
21. Captain James K. Mackett of the 1st Battalion was exchanged on October 15, 1864. He was not listed in the CSR.
22. The Foreign Legion was organized on January 18, 1865, to maintain good order in Charleston. It was commanded by Captain Nicholas

Scherhammer, previously captain of Beat #1 of the 16th Regiment, South Carolina Militia.[22]

23. Captain W.R. Holmes commanded the Burke Sharpshooters.[23] Holmes is not listed in the CSR.

24. A company of boys called the Davis Guards was raised at the military school in Anderson. The boys were taught by Major B.F. Sloan and Captain Joseph Adams, who probably commanded the company.[24]

25. James Long was captain of Company A of Perryman's Battalion. Either the company or battalion was from Pickens District and was named the Mountain Rangers, but the battalion cannot be definitely identified. The Mountain Rangers served from July 1864 to May 1865 and was disbanded at Greenville. Another captain in this company was George A. Rankin. Pension records show that Long's Company was designated D of the 1st or 8th Reserves in May 1864, or possibly A or B of the 1st Regiment, South Carolina State Troops. Possibly the same James Long was captain of both Company D, 4th Regiment, SCV, and Company A, 13th Battalion, SCV, in 1862 and was colonel of the 42nd Regiment, Militia.

26. Two companies of "Old Men's Home Guards" from the Oconee section of Pickens District were commanded by Captains C.F. Seeba and E.P. Verner.[25]

27. Gregg Light Infantry, probably a militia company in Columbia in 1863, was commanded by William J. Taylor.[26]

28. The Mountain Guards, men exempt from military service, was raised on January 5, 1861, to protect homes and families and quell insurrection.[27] It was commanded by Captain J.J. Quinn. Another company, G of the 18th Regiment, SCV, may have had the same name.

29. The Bethel Guards, a company of exempt men, was organized about January 17, 1861, to protect homes and families in an emergency.[28] Its captain was J.J. Wilson. Thomas and Silverman wrote that the Bethel Guards was Company B of the 5th Regiment, SCV.[29]

30. The Walhalla Riflemen was a Pickens District company in January 1861. Captain __ Hershel may have commanded the company at first, but Jonathan M. Hencken was captain in June 1861.[30] Although the men desired to muster in Orr's Rifles that month, there is no record of the company either there or in Moore's (2nd) Rifles.

31. A company of exempt men was organized in January 1861 in the northwest part of York District; it was commanded by Captain John B. Mintz.[31]

32. A company of exempt men was organized in January 1861 in the Kings Mountain part of York District; its commander was Captain M.R. Bird.[32]

33. The Bull Swamp Guards, organized in Orangeburg District in January 1861, was commanded by Captain L.W. Dash.[33]
34. The Broad River Light Infantry was organized in February 1861 and was commanded by Captain John S. Crosby.[34]
35. The Rich Hill Guards existed in February 1861.[35]
36. The Home Guards of Yorkville, organized in April 1861, was commanded by Captain Asbury Coward.[36]
37. In May 1861, Captain John B. Jackson organized a new company in York.[37]
38. The Carolina Home Guards was raised in February 1861 by W.T. Field and R.C. Clayton. It was probably from Pickens District.[38]
39. The Mountain Creek Home Guards, organized on May 4, 1861, at Kirksey's Cross Roads in Edgefield District, was commanded by W.H. Holloway.[39] Holloway raised another company in the summer of 1861, which became part of Company G, Gregg's 1st Regiment, SCV.
40. A company of Home Guards, organized in Edgefield District on June 1, 1861, was commanded by G.D. Huiet.[40]
41. The Pleasant Lane Home Guards, organized in Edgefield District in June 1861, was commanded by Luke Culbreath.[41]
42. The Greenville Riflemen was organized in June 1861 from an artillery company unable to procure a battery of field artillery.[42] Whether or not this company was related to Company M of Maxcy Gregg's regiment is unknown.
43. A cavalry company of the Home Guards of Edgefield District was organized in June 1861; its captain was Lewis Jones.[43]
44. A company called the Confederate Stars was organized in Columbia in July 1861. Its members were boys who were five to thirteen years old.[44]
45. The Lanham Guards, organized in August 1861, was commanded by T.W. Lanham.[45]
46. The Dean Guards was a mounted infantry company organized in the Pine Grove section of Edgefield District in July 1863 for domestic defense. Theodore Dean was its captain.[46]
47. The Chichester Guards, organized in July 1864 for local defense in Edgefield District, was commanded by E.J. Dawson. It consisted of about fifty managers and operatives at Bath Paper Mills and Southern Porcelain Company and was named in honor of the owner of the Bath Paper Mills.[47]
48. A Home Defense Company, organized on March 16, 1865, in Edgefield, was commanded by E.H. Youngblood. It was made up of about seventy men, most of them either exempt from service or in the 2nd Class militia.[48]

49. The Golden's Creek Company, organized on June 1, 1861, for home defense, was commanded by William Hunter.[49] This company was probably from the Golden's Creek area northeast of Columbia.

50. The Pendleton Home Guard, organized in June 1861, was commanded by F.A. Hoke.[50]

51. The Anderson's Mills Home Guard, commanded by A.G. Field, was organized in July 1861.[51]

52. The Village Creek Home Guard, organized in July 1861, was commanded by Patterson Orr. Members were required to be older than twelve.[52]

53. The Mile Creek Home Guard, commanded by Levi N. Robins, was organized in July 1861.[53]

54. The Claremont Vigilance and Military Volunteer Committee elected Major John C. Miller as president in July 1861.[54]

55. The Snow Creek Vigilant Committee elected J.A. Elrod as president in July 1861.[55]

56. The Pumpkin Town Home Guard was organized in July 1861; G.W. Keith was its captain. It was also called the Mountain Rangers.[56]

57. The Battleground Home Guard, organized at Gill's Creek in May 1861, was commanded by Dr. D.A. Belk.[57]

58. The Independent Blair Guards, a home guard company organized in the lower part of Lancaster District in May 1862, was commanded by T.R. Clyburn.[58]

59. A Home Guard company commanded by John D. Andrews was organized in Lancaster District in May 1862.[59]

60. The Pleasant Hill Guard, organized in May 1861, was commanded by J.E. Rutledge.[60]

61. The Wild Cat Vigilant Company, commanded by J. Funderburk, was organized in May 1861.[61]

62. A Home Guard Company was organized in Lancaster District in May 1861; W.W. Baskin was its captain.[62]

63. The Lynches Creek Home Guards was organized in September 1861 in the lower part of Lancaster District; its commander was the Reverend N. Faile.[63]

64. The Greenville Home Guard was organized in January 1861. C.J. Elford was its captain.[64]

65. A Home Guard Company of Mounted Riflemen, also called the Greenville Home Guards–State Troops, was organized on July 1, 1863, in Greenville District. T.S. Arthur was its captain.[65] In its sole engagement, it forced General I.N. Palmer's Federal raiding column, which was in pursuit of President Davis, from its direct route.

66. A Home Guard Company of Infantry, organized in Greenville District on July 1, 1863, was commanded by G.E. Elford.[66]
67. The Hanging Rock Home Guards was organized in April 1862 in Lancaster District.[67]
68. The Brooks Boys, named for Preston Brooks, was organized in February 1861 from the Upper Battalion of the 2nd Regiment, South Carolina Militia, from Pickens District. Warren R. Marshall was its captain.[68]
69. The Anderson Home Guard, organized in February 1861, was commanded by a Captain Cox.[69]
70. W.P. McKellar was captain of a Greenwood company in September 1861.[70]
71. Captain Alfred J. Frederick commanded a company of South Carolina Militia in January 1865.[71]
72. The Home Guard of Charleston was commanded by Captain G.S. Hacker in May 1861.[72]
73. The City Guard of Charleston was a three-company battalion commanded by Captain H.S. Bass in May 1861.[73]
74. The Palmetto Reserve Guards #6 elected T.W. Holwell as captain on August 25, 1861. This company was composed of harbor pilots, shipmasters and others exempt from military duty.[74]
75. The Yeadon Blues was raised by G.E. Steedman in the summer of 1862 and named in honor of Richard Yeadon, senior editor of the *Charleston Daily Courier*. It was also called the "boys from Aiken."[75] G.E. Steedman's name does not appear in the CSR as captain or lieutenant of any company.
76. The Georgetown Reserves was commanded by Captain David Henry Smith.[76]
77. Willis Wilkinson Shackelford was captain of the Georgetown Home Guard.[77]
78. Captain J.H. Simons's Company, South Carolina Infantry, was commanded by J. Hume Simons. It enlisted in Confederate service for the duration of the war on May 14, 1862, at Charleston; Simons was elected at about the same time. The term of service dated from April 15. It might have been called the Miles Grenadiers.[78]
79. The Chesterfield Eagles, commanded by Neill F. Graham, was probably raised in Chesterfield for special state defense. Graham was captain of Company E of the 9th Battalion, but whether or not the two companies were the same is unclear.
80. The St. Paul's Home Guards was stationed at Adams Run and was charged with local defense. The St. Paul's Rifles, probably the same company, took over garrison duty from the Calhoun Artillery when

it was disbanded in June 1861. A Captain Smith commanded the St. Paul's Rifles.[79]

81. Captain Dougherty's Reserve Corps was commanded by Captain John Dougherty.

82. The Edgefield Reserves, commanded by Captain Joseph Abney, volunteered for twelve months of state service. Upon its organization, the company, in early December 1861, requested service with other Edgefield Companies; whether that request was honored is unknown. A company called the Edgefield Riflemen, however, commanded by Joseph Abney, became Company A of the 22nd Regiment at its organization in May 1862.

83. The Walhalla State Guards from Pickens District was commanded by Captain James O'Connell. See Company D, 22nd Regiment, SCV.

84. The Signal Corps was commanded by Captain Joseph Manigault and Captain C.G. Memminger.

85. The Port Royal Guards was commanded by Lieutenant Randolph Peyton.[80]

86. The Independent Men of Waxhaws, a militia company from Lancaster, was commanded by R.M. Sims.[81]

87. William Shivers commanded the Rebel Guards, a local defense company.[82]

88. Captain H.A. Shaw commanded an Edgefield District company that existed as early as April 1864. It served as a ferry guard at Vienna, South Carolina, before moving to Waynesboro, Georgia, to observe Sherman's troops. It was sent next to Beaufort and then served along the courier line between Augusta and Columbia until February 1865. The company was discharged at Trenton, South Carolina, in April 1865.

89. E.J. Dennis commanded a company of scouts in Charleston District in 1865.

90. Peter Sudduth, or Suddeth, was captain of a company of home guards, also described as a company of reserves, raised in 1864 from Spartanburg and Greenville Districts. The men performed bridge duty and were discharged at Columbia in April 1865.

91. The "Boy Cavalry" was in the 2nd Reserves and was commanded by B.B. McCoy.

92. In late 1864 and 1865, a Captain McMurphy commanded a home guard company of sixteen-year-olds from the part of Beaufort District that is now Hampton County.

93. John Lovell, or Lowell, commanded a home guard company of sixteen-year-olds from Horry District in late 1864 and 1865.

94. E.H. Peeples commanded a company of "old men" in one of the reserve organizations in late 1864 and 1865.
95. George Camp commanded an independent company organized at New Prospect. It performed patrol duty for three to four months.

Appendix 2

CAVALRY ORGANIZATIONS WITH UNKNOWN REGIMENTAL OR BATTALION AFFILIATIONS

1. The Horry Hussars from northern Horry District are not mentioned in the CSR.

2. Patterson's Rangers is mentioned in *Saddle Soldiers* as one of the few active cavalry organizations left to guard the South Carolina coast in March 1864, when most of the other organizations were transferred to Virginia. The possibility exists, however, that it was neither a South Carolina unit nor part of a militia or reserve force.[1] No Captain Patterson appears in either the CSR for South Carolina cavalry units or the *Official Records* for March 1864.

3. The Spartan Rangers, commanded by Captain Thomas Hall, was in the process of organizing in January 1861.[2] It may have failed to organize completely, or, instead, it could have been a militia unit since Hall's name does not appear in the CSR. Alternatively, the company may have been the predecessor of Company L, 3rd Regiment, South Carolina Cavalry. A company called the Seneca Rangers, commanded by Captain Thomas Hall, existed in early 1861.[3] It volunteered for service in the 4th Militia Regiment on January 3, 1861.[4] Whether or not the Spartan Rangers and the Seneca Rangers were the same company remains unclear.

4. A Home Guard of Cavalry in St. Paul's Parish at Adams Run existed in January 1861.[5] Since Hawkins S. King, its captain, is not listed in the CSR, the company was probably a militia unit.

5. The Newberry Chargers from Newberry District existed in February 1861.[6] No further information on this company appears in the record.

6. The Columbia Mounted Rifles was on duty in Charleston in April 1861.[7]

7. In June 1861, a Captain Lucas commanded a company of juveniles called the Lone Star Dragoons; it was probably a militia unit.[8]

8. The Ashepoo Guerillas, probably a militia company, was commanded by Charles Witsell, MD, in October 1861.[9]

9. The Black River Troop, commanded by W.J.N. Hammett, is listed in the index to the *Southern Historical Society Papers*, and Hammett's name appears as a sergeant in the Hampton Legion in the CSR. Hammett commanded the Black River Troop in the fall of 1860.[10]

10. The cavalry of the Western Battalion of the Sumter District South Carolina Militia, organized on July 25, 1863, elected South Carolina Senator F. J. Moses Jr. as its captain.[11] The Claremont Troop, probably the same unit, was a Sumter District militia company also called the Sumter Cavalry, South Carolina Militia. It was organized for home defense in November 1863 and was also commanded by Moses.[12] It is unlikely that this company and the Claremont Cavalry, Company A of the Holcombe Legion Cavalry Battalion, later Company I of the 7th Cavalry Regiment, were the same.

11. Captain Edward Avery commanded a company of boys under the age of eighteen in July 1863.[13] The company mustered in state service that month. When Avery's requests for active field service were denied, the company disbanded on January 1, 1864.[14] Avery is not listed in the CSR.

12. The Spartan Troop of Spartan Village was created by the General Assembly on January 28, 1861, and was attached to the Upper Battalion of the 9th Regiment, 5th Brigade, South Carolina Cavalry Militia.[15]

13. The South Carolina Executive Council authorized the creation of a company called the Combahee Rangers and accepted it for police duty and state service on May 26, 1862. Its captain was T.J. Allen.[16]

14. The Richland Rangers, which existed before the war, was commanded by Colonel R. Anderson, probably Richard Anderson who was elected lieutenant colonel of the 15th Infantry Regiment in September 1861. Its men tendered their services to the governor in January 1861, and they also offered themselves to the Confederacy. Although the company existed in April 1861 and was in Columbia the following October, any further activity is unknown.[17] It probably disbanded in the fall of 1861.

15. The Anderson Troop, commanded by Captain John W. Guyton, volunteered for service in the 4th Militia Regiment on January 3, 1861.[18]

16. The Mountain Cavalry, commanded by Captain Miles M. Norton, was in the 1st Regiment (probably the 1st Regiment, South Carolina Militia) in January 1861. Norton was later captain of Company E, Orr's Rifles.[19]

17. The Saluda Rangers, also called the Saluda Sentinels, existed in January 1861. Its captain was A.D. Bates.[20]

18. The Jefferson Nullifiers, which existed in February 1861, was commanded by Captain John F. Talbert.[21] The company, probably from Edgefield District, was disbanded at some point before September 4.[22] Governor Pickens ordered the company to return its arms by September 30. In 1862 and 1863, Talbert commanded Company F, 5th Regiment Reserves.

19. The Little River Rangers, commanded by Captain James L. Boyd, existed as a Home Defense Company in June 1861.[23]

20. The Salem Mounted Men, a Home Guard Company in Sumter District, commanded by Captain William Harris, existed in August and September 1863.[24]

21. Farmer's Rangers was commanded by Claus Volmer, who was elected captain on January 16, 1865.[25] Volmer served as first sergeant in the German Hussars when it was part of the South Carolina Militia earlier in the war.

22. Companies existing in Abbeville in April 1861 were: the Abbeville Light Infantry under Captain James C. Calhoun, the Mounted Minute Men under Captain J. Wardlaw Perrin, the Abbeville Squadron and the Southern Rights Dragoons.[26]

Appendix 3

ARTILLERY ORGANIZATIONS WITH UNKNOWN REGIMENTAL OR BATTALION AFFILIATIONS

1. Wood's Battery was based on the Black River. Whether it was a militia battery, a South Carolina battery called by an unrecognized name or, possibly, not a South Carolina battery at all, remains unclear.
2. There may have been a Captain Daniell or Daniell's Battery.
3. The McDuffie Artillery was probably a prewar militia organization from Newberry.
4. Moore's Battery was at Coosawhatchie in November 1861. We do not know if it was a militia battery, a South Carolina battery called by an unrecognized name or if it was not a South Carolina battery at all.
5. Thomas's Battery was engaged briefly at Columbia on February 15, 1865. It is described as "a small two-gun battery armed with obsolescent six pounders, which guarded the Congaree River Bridge at the foot of Gervais Street."[1] It was almost certainly manned by The Arsenal Cadets under the command of John Peyre Thomas.[2]
6. Nelson's Battery was engaged at Pocotaligo on October 22, 1862.[3] A Lieutenant Massie commanded the Nelson Light Artillery in January 1864.[4] It was probably a battery from Virginia.
7. Crenshaw's Battery was probably not a South Carolina battery.
8. The Camden Artillery Company was commanded by Captain A.W. Thames in June 1861.[5] Once again, it may have been a militia battery, a South Carolina battery called by an unrecognized name or one that was never accepted into service and was disbanded.
9. The Fairfield Artillery was commanded by Captain S.M. Smart, who was elected captain on September 14, 1861.[6] Whether this battery was a militia battery, a South Carolina battery called by an unrecognized name or a company that was never accepted into service and was disbanded is unclear.

10. From the fall of 1861 to December 1861, the Star Battery existed as a forty-man detachment of the 5th Regiment, South Carolina Infantry. It had two cannon detached from the Calhoun Artillery, probably indicating that it was Company A, Calhoun's Company, of the 1st Battalion, South Carolina Artillery (Regulars). The Star Battery was commanded by Lieutenant F.G. Latham of Company G.[7]

11. The Georgetown Artillery, also called Henning's Battery and the Georgetown Artillery Company, was commanded by Captain James G. Henning. This was a militia battery composed of older men of the community, many of whom had sons in Company A—the Georgetown Rifle Guards of the 10th Regiment, SCV. The General Assembly incorporated the battery on January 28, 1861.[8] That summer it participated in a brief expedition up the Waccamaw River with Company A of the 10th Regiment.[9] Although available for service, the battery had not been called up by late 1861 and early 1862.[10]

Appendix 4

COMPANY NICKNAMES

1ST REGIMENT, INFANTRY (REGULARS) AFTER MAY 1861

Company D, the Calhoun Light Infantry, Company K, Rivers's Battery

THE 1ST REGIMENT, SOUTH CAROLINA VOLUNTEERS (HAGOOD'S)

Following are the companies that mustered in Confederate service on August 22, 1861:
Company A, the Edisto Rifles
Company B, the Jamison Guards
Company C, the Glover Guards
Company D, the St. Matthews Rifles or the Keitt Guards
Company E, the Allen Guards, later the Wee Nee Volunteers
Company G, the Johnson Guards
Company I, the Republican Blues, later the Pickens Sentinels and the Buford's Bridge Guards
Company K, the Bamberg Guards

Following are the companies of Hagood's regiment created at the reorganization on April 12, 1862:
Company A, the Bamberg Guards
Company C, the Buford's Bridge Guards
Company D, the Waxhaw Guards
Company F, the Dixie Guards
Company H, the Winsmuth Guards

The 1st Regiment, South Carolina Volunteers (Six Months) and the 1st Regiment, South Carolina Infantry, Provisional Army (Gregg's)

Gregg's 1st (six-month) Regiment was made up of the following companies:
Company A, the Richland Rifles, the Richland Volunteer Rifle Company, the Richland Volunteer Rifles, the Richland Riflemen
Company B, the Darlington Guards
Company C, the Edgefield Rifles, the Edgefield Riflemen
Company D, the Abbeville Volunteers, the Abbeville Minute Men
Company E, the Union Volunteers, the Union District Volunteers
Company F, the Wee Nee Volunteers
Company G, the Hamburg Volunteers, the Hamburg Company, the Hamburg Minute Men
Company H, the Cherokee Pond Volunteers, the Cherokee Pond Guards, the Meriwether Guards
Company I, the Monticello Guards, the Fairfield Volunteers, the Monticello Volunteers
Company K, the Marion Volunteers
Company L, the Rhett Guards
Company M, the Richardson Guard
Company N, the DeKalb Rifle Guards, the DeKalb Rifles, the DeKalb Guards, the Camden Rifle Guards
Company O, the Saluda Guard

Gregg's regiment, after the reorganization in the summer of 1861, was made up of the following companies:
Company A, the Gregg Guards
Company B, the Rhett Guards
Company C, the Richland Rifles, the Richland Volunteer Rifle Company
Company D, the Pee Dee Rifles
Company E, the Marion Rifles, the Marion Volunteers
Company F, the Horry Rebels, Horry Rifles
Company G, the Butler Sentinels, the Edgefield Company
Company H, Haskell's Rifle Corps, the Models
Company I, the Richardson Guards
Company K, the Irish Volunteers, the Irish Volunteers For The War
Company L, the Carolina Light Infantry Volunteers, the Carolina Light Infantry for the War, the Boy Company
Company M, the Furman Guards

THE 1ˢᵀ REGIMENT, SOUTH CAROLINA RIFLES (ORR'S)

Company A, the Keowee Riflemen, the Keowee Rifles, the Keowee
    Volunteers, the Keowee Volunteer Company
Company B, the McDuffie Rifles, the McDuffie Guards
Company C, the Mountain Boys, the Pickens Boys
Company D, Orr's Rifles
Company E, the Oconee Riflemen, Oconee Rifles, the Mountain Cavalry,
    the Pickens Mountain Cavalry
Company F, the Blue Ridge Riflemen, the Blue Ridge Volunteers
Company G, the Marshall Riflemen, the Marshall Rifles, the Abbeville
    Riflemen
Company H, the PeeDee Guards
Company K, the Marshall Guards
Company L, the Calhoun Guards

THE 1ˢᵀ REGIMENT, CHARLESTON (SOUTH CAROLINA) GUARDS

Company H, the Vigilant Rifles

THE 1ˢᵀ (CHARLESTON) BATTALION, INFANTRY

Company A, the Charleston Riflemen
Company B, the Charleston Light Infantry
Company C, the Irish Volunteers
Company D, the Sumter Guards, the Sumter Guard Volunteers,
    the Gamecocks
Company E, the Calhoun Guards or Guard
Company F, the Union Light Infantry Volunteers, the Union Light Infantry
    Volunteers and German Fusiliers
Company G, the Charleston Light Infantry

THE 1ˢᵀ BATTALION, SOUTH CAROLINA SHARPSHOOTERS

Company A, the Union Light Infantry and German Fusiliers
Company B, the Sumter Guards
Company C, the Charleston Sharpshooters, the Palmetto Guards

THE 2ND REGIMENT, SOUTH CAROLINA VOLUNTEERS

Following are the six companies that refused to go to Virginia in May 1861:
The Claremont Rifles
The DeKalb Rifle Guards, the DeKalb Rifles, the DeKalb Guards
The Lancaster Grays, the Lancaster Greys
The Richland Guards
The Salem Company, the Chicora Guards
The States Rights Guards, the Fork Troop

The following ten companies made up the 2nd Regiment after it entered Confederate service in April 1861:
Company A, the Governor's Guards
Company B, the Butler Guards
Company C, the Columbia Grays, the Richland Grays, the Columbia Greys
Company D, the Sumter Volunteers
Company E, the Camden Volunteers, the Camden Light Infantry, the Kershaw Guards
Company F, the Secession Guards, Perryman's Company, the Abbeville Volunteers, the Abbeville Guards
Company G, the Flat Rock Guards
Company H, the Lancaster Invincibles, the Lancaster Volunteers, the Lancaster Guards
Company I, the Palmetto Guard or Guards
Company K, the Brooks Guard Volunteers, the Brooks Guards, Brooks Home Guards

THE 3RD REGIMENT, SOUTH CAROLINA VOLUNTEERS

Company A, the State Guards, the State Guards Rifle Company, the Laurens Guards, the Garlington Rifles
Company B, the Williams Guard
Company C, the Pickens Guards, the Yahoo
Company D, the Cross Anchor Volunteers, the Cross Anchors
Company E, the Quitman Rifles, the Quitman Guard, the Quitman Riflemen, the Quitmans
Company F, the Wadsworth Guards, the Wadsworth Volunteers
Company G, the Briers, the Briars, the Laurens Briers, the Liars Briers

Company H, the Brooks Guards, the Brooks Palmetto Guards, the Dutch, the Dutch Fork Boys
Company I, the Musgrove Volunteers, the Musgrove Guards, the Clinton Company, the Clinton Divers
Company K, the Blackstock Volunteers, the Blackstock Company
No letter designation, the Helena Guard
No letter designation, Company Raiborn, Company Rabun

THE 3ᴿᴰ BATTALION, SOUTH CAROLINA INFANTRY

Company B, the Williams Company
Company E, the Hunter Guards
Company F, the Harper Rifles
Company G, the Aiken Guards

THE 4ᵀᴴ REGIMENT, SOUTH CAROLINA VOLUNTEERS

Company A, the Butler Guards, Hoke's Rifle Company
Company B, the Palmetto Riflemen, the Palmetto Rifles, Whitner's Rifle Company
Company C, Dean's Infantry Company
Company D, the Piercetown Guards, Long's Infantry Company
Company E, the Calhoun Mountaineers, the Calhoun Guards, Kilpatrick's Infantry Company
Company F, the Tyger Volunteers, Poole's Infantry Company
Company G, the Saluda Volunteers, Hawthorne's Infantry Company
Company H, the Twelve Mile Volunteers
Company I, the Pickens Guards, Hollingsworth's Infantry Company
Company J, the Confederate Guards, Ashmore's Infantry Company
Company K, the Fort Hill Guards, Shanklin's Company

THE 5ᵀᴴ REGIMENT, SOUTH CAROLINA VOLUNTEERS

The following companies of the 5ᵗʰ Regiment existed from early March 1861 until the regiment was reorganized and mustered in Confederate service on June 4, 1861:
Company A, the Johnson Rifles, Johnson Riflemen
Company B, the Pea Ridge Volunteers
Company C, the Batesville Volunteers

APPENDIX 4

Company D, the Pacolet Guards
Company E, the Jasper Light Infantry
Company F, the Lawson's Fork Volunteers
Company G, the Kings Mountain Guard
Company H, the Catawba Light Infantry
Company I, the Morgan Light Infantry, the Morgan Rifles
Company J, the Whyte Guards, the "Wild Geese"
Company K, the Tyger Volunteers, Tyger River Volunteers, the Goshen Hill Volunteers
Company L, the Spartan Rifles

Following are the companies of the 5th Regiment existing from June 4, 1861, to April 13, 1862:
Company A, the Johnson Rifles or Riflemen
Company B, the Kings Mountain Guards
Company C, the Lawson's Fork Volunteers
Company D, the Tyger River Volunteers, Tyger Volunteers, the Goshen Hill Volunteers
Company E, the Pea Ridge Volunteers
Company F, the Morgan Light Infantry, Morgan Rifles
Company G, the Pacolet Guards, the Limestone Spring Company
Company H, the Catawba Light Infantry
Company I, the Jasper Light Infantry
Company K, the Spartan Rifles
The Star Battery

Following are those companies of the 5th Regiment existing from April 23, 1862, to the end of the war:
Company A, the Lancaster Greys, the Lancaster Grays
Company B, the Catawba Light Infantry
Company C, the Limestone Southern Rights Guards
Company D, the Tyger River Volunteers, Tyger Volunteers, the Goshen Hill Volunteers
Company E, the Turkey Creek Grays
Company F, the Kings Mountain Guards
Company H, the Pea Ridge Volunteers
Company K, the Lawson's Fork Volunteers

THE 6ᵀᴴ REGIMENT, SOUTH CAROLINA VOLUNTEERS

The following companies were originally attached to the 6ᵗʰ Regiment from its inception on February 8, 1861, until it mustered in Confederate service in June:
The Boyce Guards
The Buckhead Guards
The Calhoun Guards
The Catawba Guards
The Cedar Creek Rifle Company, the Cedar Creek Rifles
The Chester Blues
The Chester Guards
The Fairfield Fencibles
The Little River Guards
The Monticello Guards, the Fairfield Volunteers
The Pickens Guards

Following are the ten companies of the 6ᵗʰ Regiment after they mustered in Confederate service in June and July 1861:
Company A, the Calhoun Guard or Guards
Company B, the Catawba Guards, the Catawba Light Infantry
Company C, the Buckhead Guards
Company D, the Boyce Guards
Company E, the Chester Guards
Company F, the Chester Blues
Company G, the Pickens Guards
Company H, the York Volunteers, the York Guards, the York Guard
Company I, the Limestone Springs Infantry, the Limestone Light Infantry, the Limestone Guards
Company K, the Carolina Mountaineers

Following are the companies created at the reorganization in the spring of 1862:
Company A, the Catawba Guards, Catawba Light Infantry
Company B, the Alston Riflemen
Company F, the Chester Blues
Company G, the Boyce Guards
Company H, the Buckhead Guards
Company I, the Chester Guards
Company K, the Dixie Guards

MANIGAULT'S BATTALION SOUTH CAROLINA VOLUNTEERS

Company A, the St. James Santee Mounted Riflemen, the Mounted Rifles Company, Captain Thomas Pinckney's Company, Thomas Pinckney's Independent Mounted Riflemen

Company B, the Santee Light Artillery, Gaillard's Company of Light Artillery

Company C, the Trenholm Rifles, the Infantry Company–Trenholm Rifles, the Palmer Rifles

Company D, the Infantry Company–Chesnut Guards

Company E, the Kickapoo Riflemen

THE 6TH BATTALION SOUTH CAROLINA INFANTRY

Company B, the Chesnut Guards
Company C, the Kickapoo Riflemen
Santee Light Artillery
St. James Santee Mounted Riflemen

THE 7TH REGIMENT, SOUTH CAROLINA VOLUNTEERS

Following are the companies of the 7th Regiment from its enlistment in state service in April 1861 until the reorganization in May 1862:

Company A, the Secession Guards, Perryman's Company, the Abbeville Volunteers, the Abbeville Guards

Company B, the Southern Guards, the Cokesbury Minutemen

Company D, Hester's Company

Company E, the Mount Willing Guards

Company F, the Davies Guard, Davies Guards, the Graniteville Riflemen

Company G, the Brooks Greys

Company H, the Ninety Six Rifles

Company I, the Red Hill Guard

Company K, the Ruffin Guards

Company L, the Horry Volunteers, the Horry Guards, the All Saints Riflemen, the All Saints Rifles

Following are the companies of the 7ᵗʰ Regiment after the reorganization in May 1862:
Company A, the Ninety Six Riflemen
Company B, the Southern Guards, Cokesbury Minutemen
Company E, the Mount Willing Guards
Company F, the Davies Guards
Company G, the Brooks Greys
Company H, the Ninety Six Rifles
Company I, the Red Hill Guard
Company K, the Ruffin Guards
Company L, the Horry Volunteers
Company M, the Saluda Riflemen

THE 7ᵀᴴ BATTALION, SOUTH CAROLINA INFANTRY

Company A, the Lucas Guards
Company B, the Lyles Rifles
Company C, the McCullough Rifles
Company D, the Kershaw Grays or Greys
Company F, the Lucas Rifles
Company G, the Moffatt Rifles
Company H, the Joe Johnston Rifles, the Johnston Rifles, the Partisan
 Rangers, the Brooks Infantry Partisan Rifles

THE 8ᵀᴴ REGIMENT, SOUTH CAROLINA VOLUNTEERS

Company A, the Darlington Rifleman
Company B, the Chesterfield Rifles
Company C, the Chesterfield Guards
Company D, the Jackson Guards
Company E, the Timmonsville Minute Men
Company F, the Darlington Grays
Company G, the Marlboro Guards, the Marlborough Guards
Company H, the Jeffries Creek Company, the Jeffries Volunteers
Company I, the Marion Guards
Company K, the McQueen Guards
Company L, the Spartan Band

THE 9ᵀᴴ REGIMENT, SOUTH CAROLINA VOLUNTEERS

Company A, the Lancaster Greys
Company B, the States Right Guards, the Fork Troop
Company C, the Clarendon Blues
Company D, the Chicora Guards, the Salem Company
Company E, the Kershaw Troop
Company F, the Sumter Grays
Company G, the Hartsville Light Infantry
Company H, the Blanding Blues
Company I, the Cowpens Guards or Guard, the Cowpens Cavalry
Company K, the Pickens Sentinels
Unlettered, the Clarendon Volunteers, Clarendon Riflemen,
    Clarendon Rifles

THE 9ᵀᴴ BATTALION, SOUTH CAROLINA INFANTRY

Company A, the Bull Creek Guerillas, the Bull Creek Rangers
Company C, the Irby Rifles
Company D, the Watchesaw Rifles, the Wachitaw Rifles
Company E, the Chesterfield Eagles
Company G, the Eutaw Rifles, the Floyd Guerillas

THE 10ᵀᴴ REGIMENT, SOUTH CAROLINA VOLUNTEERS

Companies attached to the 10ᵗʰ Regiment in early 1861:
Original Company D, the Wee Nee Volunteers, the Williamsburg Company
Original Company G, the Coast Guards
Original Company I, the Carver's Bay Palmetto Rifle Guards, the Carver's
    Bay Sharpshooters
Joshua Ward's Artillery Company, Mayham Ward's Company, South
    Carolina Light Artillery
The North Santee Mounted Rifles
The Sampit Rangers

Following are the twelve companies of the 10ᵗʰ Regiment after it mustered in Confederate service in August 1861:
Company A, the Georgetown Rifle Guards
Company B, the Brooks Guards, Brooks Rifle Guards

Company C, the Lake Swamp Volunteers
Company D, the Marion Volunteers
Company E, the Black Mingo Rifle Guards, Black Mingo Riflemen
Company F, the Pee Dee Rangers
Company G, the Horry Rough and Readys
Company H, the Liberty Volunteers
Company I, the Swamp Fox Guards
Company K, the Eutaw Volunteers
Company L, the Liberty Guards
Company M, the Horry Dixie Boys, the Horry Volunteers

THE 11ᵀᴴ REGIMENT, SOUTH CAROLINA VOLUNTEERS

Company A, the Beaufort Volunteer Artillery
Company B, the Calhoun Artillery, the St. Paul's Rifles
Company C, the Summerville Guards
Company D, the Whippy Swamp Guard
Company E, the Hamilton Guards or Guard
Company F, the Republican Blues, the Yemassee Volunteers
Company G, the Butler Guards, Butler Rifles
Company H, the St. George Volunteers, St. George's Volunteers
Company I, the Colleton Rifles
Company K, the Eutaw Volunteers
Bellinger's Company–the Colleton Guard, Colleton Rifles
Sheridan's Company–the Round O Guards

THE 11ᵀᴴ BATTALION, SOUTH CAROLINA INFANTRY

The Beauregard Light Infantry
The Edisto Rifles
The Marion Light Infantry
The Ripley Guards, Gordon's Company
The St. Matthews Rifles, or Riflemen
The Washington Light Infantry, Company A
The Washington Light Infantry, Company B
The Wee Nee Volunteers, the Williamsburg Company
The Yeadon Light Infantry

THE 12TH REGIMENT, SOUTH CAROLINA VOLUNTEERS

Company A, the Palmer Guards
Company B, the Campbell Rifles, the Sevier Rifles, the Rock Hill
  Campbell Riflemen
Company C, the Cedar Creek Rifles
Company D, the Richland Guards
Company E, the Blair Guards
Company F, the Means Light Infantry, the Long Run Company, the
  Monticello Guards
Company G, the Bonham Rifles Volunteers, the Bonham Rifles, the
  Confederate Guards
Company H, the Indian Land Guards
Company I, the Lancaster Hornets
Company K, the Grisham Rifles
Unlettered, the Lancaster Guards

THE 13TH REGIMENT, SOUTH CAROLINA VOLUNTEERS

Company A, the Martin Guards
Company B, the Brockman Guards
Company C, the Forest Rifles, the Forest Guards
Company D, the Newberry Riflemen
Company E, the Cherokee Guards
Company F, the Pacolet Volunteers, Pacolet Guards
Company G, the DeKalb Guards
Company H, the Hope Guards
Company I, the Iron District Volunteers
Company K, the Johnson Rifles, Johnson Riflemen

THE 14TH REGIMENT, SOUTH CAROLINA VOLUNTEERS

Company A, the Lynch Creek Guards
Company B, the Dearing Guards
Company C, Company Raiborn
Company D, the Edgefield Rifles, the Confederate Light Guards
Company E, the Enoree Mosquitoes, the Enoree Rifles
Company F, the Carolina Bees, the South Carolina Bees
Company G, the McGowan Greys, Captain Jay's Company

Company H, Ryan's Guards, the Ryan Guard
Company I, the McCalla Rifles
Company K, the Meeting Street Saludas

THE 15TH REGIMENT, SOUTH CAROLINA VOLUNTEERS

Company A, the Columbia Rifles
Company B, the Gist Guards
Company C, the Lexington Rifles, the Lexington Guards
Company D, the Kershaw Guards
Company E, the Monticello Guards
Company F, the Thicketty Rifles
Company G, the Williamsburg Riflemen
Company H, the Mount Tabor Company, the Pinckney Guards
Company I, the Dutch Fork Guards
Company K, the Dorn Volunteers, the Dorn Invincibles, the
    Independent Guards

THE 16TH REGIMENT, SOUTH CAROLINA VOLUNTEERS

Company A, the Mountain Rebels, the Reedy Rifles
Company C, the Croft Mountain Rangers
Company D, the Elford Guards
Company E, the McCullough Lions
Company K, the Goodlett Guard, the Buttermilk Rangers, the
    Greenville Guard

THE 17TH REGIMENT, SOUTH CAROLINA VOLUNTEERS

Company C, the Defenders of Right, the Broad River Light Infantry
Company D, the Palmetto Rifles, the Palmettoes
Company E, the Indian Land Tigers, the Indian Land Rifles, the
    York Rangers
Company F, the Carolina Rifles
Company I, the Lancaster Tigers
Company K, the Lacy Guards

THE 18ᵀᴴ REGIMENT, SOUTH CAROLINA VOLUNTEERS

Company A, the Unionville Rifles
Company B, the Union District Volunteers, the York Rangers
Company C, the Cross Keys Company
Company G, the Mountain Guards
Company H, the Bethel Rifles
Company I, the Darlington Rifles
Company K, the Broad River Guards

THE 19ᵀᴴ REGIMENT, SOUTH CAROLINA VOLUNTEERS

Company B, the Lamar Guards
Company C, the Dorn Guards

THE 20ᵀᴴ REGIMENT, SOUTH CAROLINA VOLUNTEERS

Company C, the Evans Guards
Company D, the Bull Swamp Guards
Company F, the Kinard Phalanx
Company G, the Spring Hill Volunteers
Company I, the Edisto Guards
Company K, the Lexington Volunteer Rifle Company, the Lexington Riflemen Company L, the Ripley Rangers
Company M, Keitt's Company Mounted Riflemen, the Mounted Riflemen
Company N, the Peterkin Rangers
Company O, Venning's Company
Buist's Company Light Artillery

THE 21ˢᵀ REGIMENT, SOUTH CAROLINA VOLUNTEERS

Company B, The Wilds Rifles
Company C, the Clarendon Guards
Company D, the Cheraw Guards
Company F, the Thomas Guards
Company G, the Williams Guards
Company K, the Timmonsville Minutemen

THE 22ND REGIMENT, SOUTH CAROLINA VOLUNTEERS

Company A, the Edgefield Riflemen, the Edgefield Reserves, the Edgefield Blues, the Confederate Light Guards
Company B, the Cedar Hill Guards
Company C, the Chapel Guards
Company D, the Hopewell Guards
Company E, the Lancaster Guards
Company F, the Hagood Guards

THE 23RD REGIMENT, SOUTH CAROLINA VOLUNTEERS

Company A, the Bee Rifles
Company B, the Chicora Rifles
Company C, the Johnson Rifles or Riflemen
Company D, the Duryea Guards, Duryea Coast Guard
Company E, the Marion Blues, the Marion Rifles
Company F, the Chester Grays
Company G, the Douglass Rifles
Company H, the Roberts Guards
Company I, the Sprott Guards
Company K, the Lee Guard

THE 24TH REGIMENT, SOUTH CAROLINA VOLUNTEERS

Company A, the Marion Rifles
Company B, the Pee Dee Rifles
Company C, M.T. Appleby's Company
Company D, the Evans Guard
Company E, the Colleton Guard
Company F, Hill's Company
Company G, Pearson's Company
Company H, Thomas's Company
Company I, the Edgefield Light Infantry, the Edgefield Guard
Company K, Tompkins's Company

The 25th Regiment, South Carolina Volunteers

Company A, the Washington Light Infantry, Company A
Company B, the Washington Light Infantry, Company B
Company C, the Wee Nee Volunteers
Company D, the Marion Light Infantry
Company E, the Beauregard Light Infantry
Company F, the St. Matthews Rifles or Riflemen
Company G, the Edisto Rifles
Company H, the Yeadon Light Infantry
Company I, the Clarendon Guards
Company K, the Ripley Guards

The 26th Regiment, South Carolina Volunteers

Company A, the Bull Creek Guerillas
Company D, the Irby Rifles
Company E, the Watchesaw Rifles
Company F, the Chesterfield Eagles
Company H, the Chesnut Guards
Company I, the Kickapoo Riflemen
Company K, the Eutaw Rifles, the Floyd Guerillas

The 27th Regiment, South Carolina Volunteers

Company A, the Calhoun Guards or Guard
Company B, the Charleston Light Infantry
Company C, the Union Light Infantry Volunteers
Company D, the Sumter Guards, the Sumter Guard Volunteers,
    the Gamecocks
Company E, the Union Light Infantry and German Fusiliers
Company F, the Sumter Guards
Company G, the Charleston Sharpshooters, the Palmetto Guard
Company H, the Irish Volunteers
Company I, the Charleston Riflemen
Company K, the Charleston Light Infantry

THE HAMPTON LEGION

Infantry Battalion

Company A, the Washington Light Infantry, the Washington Light
   Infantry Volunteers
Company B, the Watson Guards
Company C, the Manning Guards or Guard
Company D, the Gist Rifles, the Gist Guards, the Gist Riflemen
Company E, the Bozeman Guards
Company F, the Davis Guards
Company G, the Claremont Rifles
Company H, the German Artillery Volunteers, the South Carolina Zouaves

Cavalry Battalion

Company A, the Edgefield Hussars, the Edgefield Huzzars, the
   Edgefield Dragoons
Company B, the Brooks Troop, the Brooks Guards, the Brooks Dragoons,
   the University Riflemen
Company C, the Beaufort District Troop, the Beaufort Dragoons
Company D, the Congaree Troop, the Congaree Mounted Riflemen,
   Congaree Mounted Rifles, the Congaree Mounted Infantry, the Richland
   Light Dragoons

Artillery Battalion

Battery A, the Washington Artillery Volunteers, the Washington Mounted
   Artillery, the Washington Artillery for Confederate service, Lee's Battery,
   Hampton Horse Artillery
Company B, the German Artillery, the German Light Artillery, the
   German Flying Artillery, the German Volunteers, Hampton Legion,
   Bachman's Battery

THE HOLCOMBE LEGION

Infantry Battalion

Company A, Smith's Riflemen, the Palmetto Riflemen
Company B, the Batesville Volunteers
Company C, the Morgan Rifles
Company D, the Stevens Guards

Company E, the Spartan Guards
Company F, the Ripley Rifles
Company H, the Frog Level Scouts
Company I, the Fort Prince Guards
Company K, the Lucas Guards
Unlettered, the Stevens Light Infantry

Cavalry Battalion

Company A, the Claremont Cavalry
Company B, the Congaree Mounted Guard, the Congaree Mounted Riflemen, the Congaree Cavaliers
Company C, the Newberry Rangers, the Palmetto Light Dragoons
Company D, the McKissick Rangers, McKissick's Rangers
Company E, the Kirkwood Rangers, the Kirkwood Cavalry, the Kirkwood South Carolina Cavalry, The Kirkwoods, the Camden Rangers

THE PALMETTO SHARPSHOOTERS

Company A, the Johnson Rifles
Company B, the Calhoun Mountaineers
Company C, the Palmetto Riflemen
Company D, the Morgan Light Infantry
Company E, the Darlington Sentinels
Company F, the Pickens Sentinels
Company G, the Jasper Light Infantry
Company H, the Cowpens Guards
Company I, the Pickens Guards
Company K, the Spartan Rifles
Company L, the Confederate Guards
Company M, the Pacolet Guards

THE BATTALION OF SOUTH CAROLINA STATE CADETS, LOCAL DEFENSE TROOPS

Company A, The Citadel Cadets
Company B, The Arsenal Cadets

THE SOUTH CAROLINA COLLEGE CADETS

The South Carolina College Cadets, the College Cadets, the Third Cadet
  Company, the Stevens Light Infantry

CAPTAIN RHETT'S COMPANY, SOUTH CAROLINA

Captain Rhett's Company, the Brooks Home Guards, the Brooks Guards

CAPTAIN JOHN SYMONS'S COMPANY, NAVAL BRIGADE, SOUTH CAROLINA VOLUNTEERS

The Sea Fencibles

HARLEE'S LEGION, SOUTH CAROLINA MILITIA

The Black River Rangers
The Williamsburg Light Dragoons

CAPTAIN L.H. CHARBONNIER'S COMPANY, SOUTH CAROLINA MILITIA

The Pickens Rifles, the Pickens Guard, the Pickens Cadets

SHIVER'S COMPANY–LOCAL DEFENSE TROOPS, SOUTH CAROLINA

The Rebel Guards

THE FIRE COMPANIES OF CHARLESTON

The Aetna Fire Company, the Aetna Rifles, the Aetna Guard
The Phoenix Fire Company, the Phoenix Rifles
The Vigilant Fire Engine Company, the Vigilant Rifles, Vigilant
  Light Infantry

THE (COLUMBIA) VOLUNTEER BATTALION

The Cedar Creek Riflemen
The Columbia Artillery
The Emmett Guards
The Governor's Guards
The Richland Volunteer Rifle Company

1ST REGIMENT CHARLESTON RESERVES, SOUTH CAROLINA MILITIA

Company A, the Hibernian Guard
Company B, the Charleston Home Guard
Company C, the Pickens Rifles

THE 7TH REGIMENT RESERVES (90 DAYS 1862–1863)

Company B, the Rocky Creek Troop

THE 9TH REGIMENT RESERVES (90 DAYS 1862–1863)

Company K, the Yemassee Volunteers

THE 2ND BATTALION SOUTH CAROLINA RESERVES

Company C, the Spartan Rangers, the Spartanburg Rangers, the Spartan Rangers Independent Cavalry-Reserves
Company H, Captain Kay's Detachment, South Carolina Mounted Reserves the Palmetto Mounted Infantry

THE 8TH BATTALION SOUTH CAROLINA RESERVES

Company B, the Confederate Reserve Corps of Colleton District

2ND REGIMENT, JUNIOR RESERVES, SOUTH CAROLINA STATE TROOPS

Company B, the Saluda Company

3RD REGIMENT, JUNIOR RESERVES, SOUTH CAROLINA STATE TROOPS

Company K, the Bonham Guards

4TH REGIMENT, JUNIOR RESERVES, SOUTH CAROLINA STATE TROOPS

Company B, the Union Laddies

SOUTH CAROLINA MILITIA UNITS-CAVALRY

The 1st Regiment, South Carolina Mounted Militia
The Allendale Mounted Guard
The Beaufort District Guerillas, the Coosawhatchie Guerillas
The Beech Hill Rangers
The Bluffton Troop, the May River Troop
The Calhoun Minute Men
The Charleston Mounted Guard
The Colleton Rangers
The Dorchester Guerillas
The Etiwan Rangers
The Grey Riders of St. Bartholomew Parish, the Colleton Grey Riders, the Walterboro Home Guard
The Hardeeville Guerillas
The Marion Men of Combahee
The Marion Troop, the Marion Rangers, the Marion Scouts
The May River Troop, the Bluffton Troop
The Palmetto Hussars
The Palmetto Rangers
The Parish Mounted Rangers, the Parish Rangers
The Pickens Rangers
The Red Oak Rangers

The Salkehatchie Guerillas, the Saltketcher Guerillas
The Savannah River Guards
The South Carolina Rangers
The St. Helena Mounted Rifles, St. Helena Volunteer Mounted Riflemen
The St. Paul Home Guard, St. Paul Mounted Men
The St. Paul Rangers
The St. Peter's Guards

THE 4TH REGIMENT, SOUTH CAROLINA MILITIA

The Beaufort District Troop, Beaufort Troop
The Charleston Light Dragoons
The Combahee Troop, the Combahee Rangers
The German Hussars
The Hammond Huzzars, or Hussars, the Evans Light Dragoons
The Marion Troop
The McDonald Troop
The Palmetto Troop
The Wassamassaw Troop

THE 1ST REGIMENT ARTILLERY, SOUTH CAROLINA MILITIA

Company A of the German Artillery Battalion
Company B of the German Artillery, the German Flying Artillery
The Lafayette Artillery
The Marion Artillery
The Rutledge Mounted Riflemen
The Vigilant Fire Engine Company, the Vigilant Rifles, Vigilant
    Light Infantry
The Washington Artillery of Charleston

THE 1ST REGIMENT RIFLES, SOUTH CAROLINA MILITIA

The Beauregard Light Infantry
The Carolina Light Infantry
The Chichester Zouaves, the Charleston Zouave Cadets, the Zouave Cadets

The German Riflemen
The Jamison (or Jamieson) Riflemen
The Meagher Guards, the Emerald Light Infantry
The Moultrie Guard or Guards
The Palmetto Riflemen
The Pickens Rifles
The Sarsfield Light Infantry
The Washington Light Infantry, the Washingtons

THE 1ST REGIMENT, SOUTH CAROLINA MILITIA

Piney Mountain Company
The Saluda Battalion
The Tyger Battalion

THE 5TH REGIMENT, SOUTH CAROLINA MILITIA

The Pickensville Silver Greys

THE 7TH REGIMENT, SOUTH CAROLINA MILITIA

The Edgefield Riflemen

THE 13TH REGIMENT, SOUTH CAROLINA MILITIA

The Colleton Rifle Corps, the Colleton Rifle Company
The Palmetto Volunteers
The St. Paul's Rifles

THE 15TH REGIMENT, SOUTH CAROLINA MILITIA

The Lexington Rifle Company

THE 16TH REGIMENT, SOUTH CAROLINA MILITIA

The Jackson Guard
The Marion Rifles
The Pickens Rifles, Pickens Guards

THE 17TH REGIMENT, SOUTH CAROLINA MILITIA

The Brooks Guards or Brooks Home Guards
The Cadet Rifles or Riflemen
The Calhoun Guards or Guard
The Charleston Riflemen
The Emmet Volunteers
The German Fusiliers
The Highland Guards
The Irish Volunteers
The Jasper Greens
The Montgomery Guard or Guards
The Palmetto Guard
The Phoenix Rifles or Riflemen
The Richardson Guard
The South Carolina College Cadets
The Sumter Guards, the Gamecocks
The Union Light Infantry

THE 18TH REGIMENT, SOUTH CAROLINA MILITIA

Company E, the Dorchester Company
The Goose Creek Company

THE 26TH REGIMENT, SOUTH CAROLINA MILITIA

The Calhoun Guards
The Chester Rifles

THE 33ᴿᴰ REGIMENT, SOUTH CAROLINA MILITIA

The All Saints Riflemen, All Saints Rifles
Blantons Cross Roads Volunteers
Bull Creek Rangers
The Carolina Greys
Conwayboro Palmetto Guards
Cool Springs Home Guard
Dog Bluff Home Guards
Floyd Guerillas
Waccamaw Guerillas
The Waccamaw Light Artillery
Wachitaw Rifles
The Watchesaw Riflemen

THE 36ᵀᴴ REGIMENT, SOUTH CAROLINA MILITIA

The Johnson Volunteers
Lawson's Fork Volunteers
The Morgan Rifles
Pacolet Volunteers
The Spartanburg Light Infantry

THE 1ˢᵀ BATTALION/1ˢᵀ REGIMENT, SOUTH CAROLINA CAVALRY

Company A, the Abbeville Troop
Company B, the Ferguson Rangers, the Spartanburg and Laurens Rangers, the Enoree Rangers
Company C, the Edgefield and Barnwell Rangers, the Edgefield Rangers
Company D, the Chester Troop
Company E, the Fort Motte Rangers
Company F, the Allen Hussars
Company G, L.J. Johnson's Cavalry
Company H, Robin Jones's Cavalry
Company I, the Round O Troop

THE 2ND REGIMENT, SOUTH CAROLINA CAVALRY

Company A, the Boykin Rangers, the Hampton Scouts, Boykin's Independent Company, South Carolina Cavalry, the Mounted Rangers, the Independent Mounted Rangers
Company B, the Beaufort District Troop, Beaufort Dragoons
Company C, the Congaree Rangers
Company D, the Wassamassaw Cavalry, Wassa Massaw Rangers
Company E, Dean's Company
Company G, the Bonham Light Dragoons, Lipscomb's Troop
Company H, the Congaree Troop, the Congaree Mounted Riflemen or Rifles, the Congaree Mounted Infantry, the Richland Light Dragoons
Company I, the Edgefield Hussars, the Edgefield Dragoons
Company K, the Brooks Troop, the Brooks Guards, the Brooks Dragoons

THE 2ND BATTALION CAVALRY, SOUTH CAROLINA RESERVES

Company B, the Marion Men of Combahee
Company F, the Savannah River Guard or Guards
The Ashley Dragoons or Ashley Rangers
The Barnwell Dragoons
The Beaufort District Troop
The Calhoun Minute Men, Calhoun Mounted Men
The Colleton Rangers
The Spartan Rangers

THE 3RD REGIMENT, SOUTH CAROLINA CAVALRY

Company A, the Marion Men of Combahee
Company B, the Colleton Rangers
Company C, the Beaufort District Troop
Company C, Captain John H. Howard's Company
Company D, the Barnwell Dragoons
Company E, the Calhoun Minute, Calhoun Mounted Men
Company F, the St. Peter's Guards
Company G, the German Hussars
Company H, the Ashley Dragoons, Ashley Rangers

Company I, the Rebel Troop
Company K, the Savannah River Guards or Guard
Johnson's Section of Horse Artillery, Johnson's Mounted Artillery, Colcock's
  Light Artillery, Colcock's Section Light Artillery

THE 3ᴿᴰ BATTALION, SOUTH CAROLINA CAVALRY

Company B, the Congaree Rangers
Company D, the Wassamassaw Cavalry, Wassa Massaw Rangers

THE 4ᵀᴴ REGIMENT, SOUTH CAROLINA CAVALRY

Company A, the Chesterfield Light Dragoons
Company B, the Palmetto Rangers
Company C, the Calhoun Troop
Company D, St. James Mounted Riflemen, Company A
Company E, previously Company C of the 12ᵗʰ Battalion,
  South Carolina Cavalry
Company F, the E.M. Dragoons
Company G, the Evans Light Dragoons
Company H, the Catawba Rangers
Company I, the Williamsburg Light Dragoons
Company K, the Charleston Light Dragoons

THE 5ᵀᴴ REGIMENT, SOUTH CAROLINA CAVALRY

Company A, the St. Matthews Troop
Company B, the Dixie Rangers
Company C, the Beech Hill Rangers
Company D, the South Carolina Rangers, Carolina Rangers
Company E, the St. James Mounted Riflemen, Company B
Company F, the Lexington Light Dragoons
Company G, the Willington Rangers
Company H, the Santee Guerillas, Santee Rangers
Company K, the Mountain Rangers

THE 6TH REGIMENT, SOUTH CAROLINA CAVALRY

Company A, the Carolina Guerrillas
Company B, the Edgefield Rangers, the Edgefield Partisan Rangers
Company E, the Laurens Partizans
Company F, the Cadet Company, the Cadet Troop, the Cadet Rangers, The
 Citadel Troop
Company H, the Yeadon Rangers

THE 7TH REGIMENT, SOUTH CAROLINA CAVALRY

Company A, the Marion Men of Winyah, Company A
Company B, the Rutledge Mounted Riflemen
Company C, the McKissick Rangers, McKissick's Rangers
Company D, the Congaree Mounted Guard, the Congaree Mounted
 Riflemen, the Congaree Cavaliers
Company E, the Newberry Rangers, the Palmetto Light Dragoons
Company F, the Marion Men of Winyah, Company B
Company G, the Rutledge Mounted Riflemen
Company H, the Kirkwood Rangers, the Kirkwood Cavalry, the Kirkwood
 South Carolina Cavalry, the Kirkwoods, the Camden Rangers
Company I, the Claremont Cavalry
Company K, the Wateree Mounted Rifles, Boykin's Company Mounted
 Rifles, the Boykin Rangers

THE 10TH BATTALION, SOUTH CAROLINA CAVALRY

Company A, the Palmetto Rangers
Company B, the Calhoun Troop
Company C, the Evans Light Dragoons
Company D, the Catawba Rangers, the Lancaster Troop, the Lancaster
 Cavalry, the Catawba Guards

THE 12TH BATTALION, SOUTH CAROLINA CAVALRY

Company A, the Chesterfield Light Dragoons
Company B, the Williamsburg Light Dragoons
Company D, the E.M. Dragoons
The Waccamaw Light Artillery

THE 14TH BATTALION, SOUTH CAROLINA CAVALRY

Company A, the Santee Guerillas, Santee Rangers
Company B, the St. Matthews Troop
Company C, the Light Dragoons

THE 16TH BATTALION, SOUTH CAROLINA CAVALRY

Company A, the Carolina Guerrillas
Company B, the Edgefield Rangers, the Edgefield Partisan Rangers
Company E, the Laurens Partizans
Company F, the Cadet Company, the Cadet Troop, the Cadet Rangers

THE 17TH BATTALION, SOUTH CAROLINA CAVALRY

Company A, the South Carolina Rangers, Carolina Rangers
Company B, the Willington Rangers
Company C, the Dixie Rangers
Company D, the Beech Hill Rangers

THE 19TH BATTALION, SOUTH CAROLINA CAVALRY

Company A, Kirk's Company, South Carolina Partisan Rangers, the May
  River Troop
Company B, Captain E.S. Keitt's Company Mounted Riflemen, South
  Carolina Volunteers
Company C, Kirk's Squadron of Partisan Rangers, Company B
Company D, Captain J.J. Steele's Company
Company E, the Ripley Rangers

INDEPENDENT CAVALRY ORGANIZATIONS

Captain Manning J. Kirk's Company, South Carolina Partisan Rangers,
  Kirk's Partisan Rangers, the May River Troop
The Etiwan Rangers
The German Hussars
Keitt's Mounted Riflemen

The North Santee Mounted Rifles
The Pickens Rangers, the Aiken Mounted Infantry
The Ripley Rangers
The Stono Scouts, Stono Rangers

THE 1ST BATTALION/1ST REGIMENT, SOUTH CAROLINA ARTILLERY REGULARS

Company A, the Sumter Battery, the Calhoun Battery, the Calhoun Artillery, the Calhoun Flying Artillery, the Light Battery
Company B, the Brooks Flying Artillery

THE 2ND BATTALION/2ND REGIMENT, SOUTH CAROLINA ARTILLERY

Company C, the Edisto Artillery
Company D, the Inglis Light Artillery
Company E, the Allen Guards
Company F, the Carolina Artillery
Company G, the Silverton Artillery
Company I, the Orangeburg Artillery

THE 3RD BATTALION, SOUTH CAROLINA LIGHT ARTILLERY

Company A, the Furman Artillery, Earle's Battery Light Artillery
Company B, the Columbia Flying Artillery, the Columbia Artillery, the Blake Artillery
Company C, the Wilson Light Artillery, Culpeper's Light Battery
Company D, the Wagner Light Artillery, Kanapaux's Light Artillery
Company E, the Yeadon Light Artillery
Company F, the Chesnut Light Artillery
Company G, the DeSaussure Light Artillery, the DePass Light Battery
Company I, Bowden's Battery Light Artillery
Company K, Richardson's Company

THE 18TH BATTALION, SOUTH CAROLINA ARTILLERY

The Beauregard Louisiana Artillery
The German Artillery, Company B
The Gist Guard, Gilchrist's Independent Company, South Carolina Heavy Artillery

The Horry Light Artillery, the Alston Light Artillery
Mathewes's Artillery
The McQueen Light Artillery, Gregg's Battery
The Palmetto Guard Artillery, the Palmetto Guards, the Buist Light Artillery
The Pee Dee Artillery, McIntosh's Battery

INDEPENDENT ARTILLERY BATTERIES

The Beaufort Volunteer Artillery
Beauregard's Battery–South Carolina Artillery, T.B. Ferguson's Company,
    Light Artillery
Brooks Guard Battery Artillery, Captain Fickling's Company, South Carolina
    Artillery, Fickling's Battery–Brooks Light Artillery, South Carolina;
    Rhett's Company, Rhett–Fickling's Battery
The Calhoun Artillery
The Chesterfield Light Artillery
The German Artillery Battalion, SCV
The German Light Artillery, the German Flying Artillery, the Charleston
    German Artillery, Captain Bachman's Company, South Carolina Artillery–
    German Light Artillery, Captain William K. Bachman's Battery
The Gist Guard Light Artillery, Captain Gilchrist's Company–the Gist
    Guard–South Carolina Heavy Artillery, Robert C. Gilchrist's Company,
    South Carolina Heavy Artillery
The Lafayette Artillery, Kanapaux's Battery—Lafayette Light Artillery—
    South Carolina, the Lafayette Light Artillery
The Macbeth Light Artillery, Captain Jeter's Company, South Carolina
    Light Artillery, Robert Boyce's Company, South Carolina Light Artillery
The Marion Artillery, the Marion Light Artillery, SCV
The Mathewes Artillery, Captain Mathewes's Company, South Carolina
    Heavy Artillery, Mathewes's Battery, Mathewes's Independent
    Company, F.N. Bonneau's Company Artillery, SCV, Confederate States
    Provisional Army
The McQueen Light Artillery
The Palmetto Light Artillery, Captain Garden's Company—the Palmetto
    Light Battery—South Carolina Light Artillery, the Palmetto Light
    Battery; Garden's Battery, SCV, Confederate States Provisional Army
The Pee Dee Light Artillery, Captain Zimmerman's Company, the Pee Dee
    Artillery, South Carolina Artillery, Captain McIntosh's Battery, Captain
    McIntosh's Company Light Artillery, Captain Brunson's Company, South
    Carolina Light Artillery

The Santee Light Artillery, Captain Christopher Gaillard's Company, Light Artillery, SCV, Gaillard's Light Artillery

Stephen D. Lee's Battery–South Carolina Artillery

The Waccamaw Light Artillery, Captain Mayham Ward's Battery, Captain Joshua Ward's Company, South Carolina Light Artillery

The Washington Artillery, Captain George H. Walter's Company, South Carolina Light Artillery, Walter's Battery–the Washington Artillery, Walter's Company–the Washington Artillery, Walter's Light Battery

The Washington Artillery, Captain Hart's Company of Horse Artillery, Hart's Battery, the Washington Light Artillery, Lee's Battery of Hampton's Horse Artillery, Halsey's Battery

INFANTRY COMPANIES WITH UNKNOWN REGIMENTAL OR BATTALION AFFILIATIONS

The Anderson Home Guard

The Anderson's Mills Home Guard

The Battleground Home Guard

The Bethel Guards

The Boy Cavalry

The Broad River Light Infantry

The Brooks Boys

The Bull Swamp Guards

The Burke Sharpshooters

The Carolina Greys

The Carolina Home Guards

The Charleston Guard

The Chesterfield Eagles

The Chichester Guards

The Citizen Guards

The City Guard of Charleston

The Claremont Vigilance and Military Volunteer Committee

The Confederate Guards

The Confederate Stars

The Davis Guards

The Dean Guards

The Edgefield Reserves

The Gasper Guards

The Georgetown Home Guard

The Georgetown Reserves

The Golden's Creek Company

The Greenville Home Guard
The Greenville Home Guards–State Troops
The Greenville Riflemen
Gregg Light Infantry
The Hanging Rock Home Guards
The Home Guard
The Home Guard of Charleston
The Home Guards of Edgefield District
The Home Guards of Yorkville
The Hope Guard
The Hudson Street Guard
The Independent Blair Guards
The Independent Men of Waxhaws
The Keitt Guard
The Lanham Guards
The Lynches Creek Home Guards
The Magrath Guard
The Manigault Guards
The Marion Men
The Mile Creek Home Guard
The Miles Grenadiers
The Mountain Creek Home Guards
The Mountain Guards
The Mountain Rangers
Old Men's Home Guards
The Palmetto Reserve Guards #6
The Pendleton Home Guard
The Pleasant Hill Guard
The Pleasant Lane Home Guards
The Port Royal Guards
The Pumpkin Town Home Guard, the Mountain Rangers
The Rebel Guard
The Rich Hill Guards
The Snow Creek Vigilant Committee
The Snow Hill Guards
The Southern Boys
The Southern Guards
The St. George's Volunteers
The St. Paul's Home Guards
The Sumter Cadets
The University Riflemen

The Village Creek Home Guard
The Walhalla Riflemen
The Walhalla State Guards
The Wild Cat Vigilant Company
The Yeadon Blues

CAVALRY ORGANIZATIONS WITH UNKNOWN REGIMENTAL OR BATTALION AFFILIATIONS

The Abbeville Squadron
The Anderson Troop
The Ashepoo Guerillas
The Black River Troop
The Claremont Troop, the Sumter Cavalry
The Columbia Mounted Rifles
The Combahee Rangers
Farmer's Rangers
Home Guard of Cavalry in St. Paul's Parish
The Horry Hussars
The Jefferson Nullifiers
The Little River Rangers
The Lone Star Dragoons
The Mountain Cavalry
The Mounted Minute Men
The Newberry Chargers
Patterson's Rangers
The Richland Rangers
The Salem Mounted Men
The Saluda Rangers, the Saluda Sentinels
The Southern Rights Dragoons
The Spartan Rangers, the Seneca Rangers
The Spartan Troop

ARTILLERY ORGANIZATIONS WITH UNKNOWN REGIMENTAL OR BATTALION AFFILIATIONS

The Camden Artillery
The Fairfield Artillery
The Georgetown Artillery
The McDuffie Artillery

NOTES

Introduction

1. William J. Rivers, "Annual Report of the State Historian of Confederate Records For The Year 1899." Microcopy 13, Roll 29, South Carolina Department of Archives and History.

Overview

1. Charles E. Cauthen, *South Carolina Goes to War, 1860–1865*, 113. (Hereafter cited as Cauthen, *South Carolina Goes to War*.); Alexander S. Salley, comp., *South Carolina Troops in Confederate Service*, 1: 429. (Hereafter cited as Salley, *SC Troops*.)
2. *Acts of the General Assembly of the State of South Carolina, passed in November and December 1860 and January 1861*, 848. (Hereafter cited as *Acts*.)
3. *Acts*, 849.
4. Cauthen, *South Carolina Goes to War*, 114.
5. Confederate Historian, "Annual Report For The Year 1899, " 9, South Carolina Department of Archives and History. (Hereafter cited as Confederate Historian, "Annual Report.")
6. The county system of subdivision was not adopted until 1868.
7. Lockwood Tower, ed., *A Carolinian Goes To War, The Civil Narrative of Arthur Middleton Manigault, Brigadier General, C.S.A., R.*, 5. (Hereafter cited as Tower, *A Carolinian Goes To War*.)
8. Johnson Hagood, *Memoirs of the War of Secession, From the Original Manuscripts of Johnson Hagood*, 27. (Hereafter cited as Hagood, *Memoirs*.)
9. Charles E. Cauthen, ed., *Journals of the South Carolina Executive Councils 1861 and 1862*, 4. (Hereafter cited as Cauthen, ed., *Journals*.)
10. Cauthen, *South Carolina Goes to War*, 114.
11. Ibid.; Douglas Southall Freeman, *Lee's Lieutenants*, 1, 518. (Hereafter cited as Freeman, *Lee's Lieutenants*.)
12. Cauthen, ed., *Journals*, 17, 18; Salley, *SC Troops*, 1:1; United States War Department, *The War of the Rebellion: A Compilation of the Official Records of the Union and Confederate Armies*, series 4, volume 1, page 913. (Hereafter cited as *OR*. It should be noted that some volumes in this series are broken into parts, while some are not. Entries for volumes with parts are listed with a series, a volume, a part and a page number or numbers; entries for volumes without parts are listed only with a series, a volume and a page number or numbers.)
13. *Acts*, 854; *OR*, 4, 1, 914.
14. Confederate Historian, "Annual Report," 11.
15. *OR*, 4, 1, 914.
16. Ibid.
17. *Charleston Mercury*, 12-30-1861. (Hereafter cited as *CM*.)
18. *OR*, 1, 1, 265
19. Southern Historical Society Papers, 14, 51. (Hereafter cited as SHSP.)
20. Salley, *SC Troops*, 3:284; Cauthen, ed., *Journals*, 67, 68; Cauthen, *South Carolina Goes to War*, 135.
21. Confederate Historian, "Annual Report," 24.
22. Cauthen, ed., *Journals*, 77–79.

23. United Daughters of the Confederacy, South Carolina Division, *Recollections and Reminiscences, 1861–1865 through World War 1*. 9, 242. (Hereafter cited as *RR*.)
24. Confederate Historian, "Annual Report," 26.
25. Cauthen, *South Carolina Goes to War*, 116; *OR*, 4, 1, 412.
26. Confederate Historian, "Annual Report," 30.
27. *Lancaster Ledger*, 9-4-61. (Hereafter cited as *LL*.)
28. Cauthen, *South Carolina Goes to War*, 136.
29. *Camden Confederate*, 11-15-1861. (Hereafter cited as *TCC*.)
30. Cauthen, *South Carolina Goes to War*, 137.
31. *OR*, 4, 1, 779; *TCC*, 12-20-61.
32. Cauthen, *South Carolina Goes to War*, 138.
33. Confederate Historian, "Annual Report," 44.
34. *CM*, 12-18-61.
35. Confederate Historian, "Annual Report," 46.
36. Ibid.
37. *CM*, 2-19-62.
38. Ibid.
39. Cauthen, ed., *Journals*, 102
40. *CM*, 5-1-62; *Edgefield Advertiser*, 5-7-62. (Hereafter cited as *EA*.)
41. *OR*, 4, 1, 973; Cauthen, *South Carolina Goes to War*, 144; *CM*, 5-1-62.
42. *OR*, 4, 1, 963.
43. Cauthen, *South Carolina Goes to War*, 144.
44. *EA*, 3-19-62.
45. *CM*, 5-1-62; Cauthen, ed., *Journals*, 305.
46. *OR*, 4, 1, 975.
47. *CM*, 3-13-62; Cauthen, ed., *Journals*, 107.
48. *CM*, 3-13-62.
49. Cauthen, ed., *Journals*, 103; *OR*, 4, 1, 973–975; *EA*, 3-19-62.
50. *CM*, 5-1-62.
51. Cauthen, ed., *Journals*, 127.
52. *CM*, 4-21-62; Cauthen, ed., *Journals*, 154.
53. Ibid.
54. *OR*, 4, 1, 1062.
55. Confederate Historian, "Annual Report," 47, 57, 58; *CM*, 5-1-62.
56. *Yorkville Enquirer*, 9-17-62. (Hereafter cited as *YE*); *EA*, 9-1-62.
57. D. Augustus Dickert, *History of Kershaw's Brigade*, 105. (Hereafter cited as Dickert, *Kershaw's Brigade*.)
58. *CM*, 4-21-62; *LL*, 10-8-62.
59. Dickert, *Kershaw's Brigade*, 332.
60. *Charleston Daily Courier*, 2-9-64. (Hereafter cited as *CDC*.)
61. *OR*, 1, 35, 1, 518, 577.
62. J.F.J Caldwell, *The History of a Brigade of South Carolinians*, 170.
63. *Daily Southern Carolinian*, 2-22-64. (Hereafter cited as *DSC*.)
64. *CM*, 7-12-62.
65. Confederate Historian, "Annual Report," 58
66. Ibid., 25.
67. Ibid., 57–58.
68. Cauthen, *South Carolina Goes to War*, 110.
69. Confederate Historian, "Annual Report," 25, 53.
70. *LL*, 10-8-62.
71. Cauthen, ed., *Journals*, 154.
72. Ibid.
73. *LL*, 7-30-62.
74. *CM*, 5-16-62; Cauthen, ed., *Journals*, 154–156; *TCC*, 5-2-62.
75. *YE*, 8-13-62.
76. Cauthen, ed., *Journals*, 154.

77. *CM*, 5-16-62; Cauthen, ed., *Journals*, 154; *YE*, 6-24-63.
78. Cauthen, ed., *Journals*, 228.
79. Ibid., 172.
80. Ibid., 173.
81. *CM*, 11-6-62.
82. Cauthen, ed., *Journals*, 154; *TCC*, 8-22-62.
83. *CDC*, 10-3-62.
84. *OR*, 4, 2, 155–56.
85. Ibid., 4, 2, 176.
86. *YE*, 11-12-62.
87. Cauthen, ed., *Journals*, 293; *TCC*, 11-14-62.
88. Cauthen, *South Carolina Goes to War*, 161.
89. *OR*, 1, 53, 281; Judith N. McArthur and Orville Vernon Burton, *A Gentleman and An Officer—A Military and Social History of James B. Griffin's Civil War*, 262. (Hereafter cited as McArthur, *Griffin*.)
90. McArthur, *Griffin*, 266.
91. *YE*, 2-11-63.
92. *OR*, 1, 14, 784–785.
93. Ibid., 1, 14, 816.
94. Cauthen, ed., *Journals*, 228.
95. *TCC*, 7-25-62.
96. Cauthen, *South Carolina Goes to War*, 146.
97. *TCC*, 11-14-62.
98. Cauthen, ed., *Journals*, 292.
99. *OR*, 4, 2, 580–582; *TCC*, 7-31-63; *Triweekly Watchman*, 7-18-63.
100. *OR*, 1, 28, 2, 145.
101. Ibid., 4, 2, 580.
102. Ibid., 1, 28, 2, 145.
103. *Greenville Southern Enterprise*, 7-30-63; Cauthen, *South Carolina Goes to War*, 192; *LL*, 6-24-63; *OR*, 1, 28, 2, 144.
104. *OR*, 1, 28, 2, 145; *YE*, 6-24-63.
105. *OR*, 1, 28, 2, 145.
106. *LL*, 7-15-63; *OR*, 4, 3, 38–39.
107. *OR*, 3, 38–39; 4, 2, 665; *YE*, 6-24-63; 7-29-63; *Carolina Spartan*, 8-27-63. (Hereafter cited as *CS*.)
108. *CM*, 8-14-63.
109. *OR*, 1, 28, 2, 339; 4, 2, 1058.
110. Ibid., 1, 28, 2, 339.
111. Ibid., 1, 35, 1, 562; 4, 2, 1058; *CM*, 2-15-64.
112. Lloyd Halliburton, *Saddle Soldiers, The Civil War Correspondence of General William Stokes 4th South Carolina Cavalry*, 125 (Hereafter cited as Halliburton, *Saddle Soldiers*.); *Sumter Watchman*, 1-18-63.
113. *OR*, 1, 35, 2, 456.
114. *DSC*, 3-15-64.
115. *LL*, 3-2-64; *EA*, 2-24-64.
116. *YE*, 3-2-64.
117. Cauthen, *South Carolina Goes to War*, 194.
118. *EA*, 2-24-64.
119. *YE*, 3-23-64.
120. *DSC*, 4-8-64.
121. *YE*, 6-15-64.
122. Ibid., 6-22-64.
123. Ibid., 7-13-64
124. Ibid., 7-20-64.
125. *EA*, 8-17-64; *LL*, 12-18-64.
126. *EA*, 1-4-65; *Compiled Service Records of Confederate Soldiers Who Served in Organizations from the State of South Carolina*, National Archives and Records Administration, M267, 391. (Hereafter cited as *CSR*.)

127. *RR*, 7, 27.
128. *CM*, 9-6-64.
129. *YE*, 3-29-65.
130. *EA*, 4-19-65
131. Ibid.
132. Ibid., 4-5-65.
133. Confederate Historian, "Annual Report," 84.
134. Ibid., 80.
135. Randolph W. Kirkland Jr, *Broken Fortunes—South Carolina Soldiers, Sailors & Citizens Who Died in the Service of Their Country and State in the War for Southern Independence, 1861–1865*, xiv. (Hereafter cited as Kirkland, *Broken Fortunes*.)
136. Confederate Historian, "Annual Report," 84.
137. *CM*, 4-21-62.
138. *Confederate Veteran*, 34, 221. (Hereafter cited as *CV*.)
139. *Due West Telescope*, 5-2-62. (Hereafter cited as *DWT*.)

Chapter 1

1. *CD*, 3-10-62.
2. *CDC*, 3-5-62.
3. *CM*, 2-24-62.
4. Ibid., 3-18-62.
5. *CDC*, 4-21-62; *CM*, 4-22-62.
6. *CDC*, 5-5-62; *CM*, 5-6-62.
7. *OR*, 1, 28, 1, 441; *CM*, 8-24-63.
8. Robert K. Krick, *Lee's Colonels, A Biographical Register of the Field Officers of the Army of Northern Virginia*, 149. (Hereafter cited as Krick, *Lee's Colonels*.)
9. *OR*, 1, 28, 1, 395, 441.
10. *CM*, 4-22-62; *CDC* 4-21-62; 5-5-62.
11. Confederate Historian, "Annual Report," 57.
12. *CM*, 5-6-62; *CDC*, 5-5-62.
13. *OR*, 1, 28, 1, 544.
14. *CDC*, 8-5-63; *CM*, 7-20-63; 8-5-63; 8-6-63; 8-11-63.
15. *CM*, 8-14-63.
16. Ibid., 10-1-61; 6-17-62.
17. Ibid., 8-8-61.
18. Krick, *Lee's Colonels*, 56.
19. *CDC*, 3-25-62.
20. *CM*, 6-17-62.
21. Ibid., 8-14-63.
22. Confederate Historian, "Annual Report," 69.
23. *CM*, 2-24-62.
24. *CDC*, 3-25-62.
25. W. Chris Phelps, *Charlestonians in War: the Charleston Battalion*, 134. (Hereafter cited as Phelps, *Charleston Battalion*.)
26. *OR*, 1, 28, 2, 396; *CDC*, 8-20-63.
27. *CDC*, 8-20-63.
28. *CM*, 3-19-61.
29. Confederate Historian, "Annual Report," 68.
30. *CM*, 7-20-63; 7-23-63; *OR*, 1, 28, 1, 544.
31. RR5, 324.
32. *CM*, 7-23-63; 8-14-63.
33. Confederate Historian, "Annual Report," 70.
34. *CM*, 5-11-61.
35. *CDC*, 6-18-62.
36. *CM*, 5-21-61; 6-19-62.

37. *CDC,* 3-25-62.
38. Ibid., 6-18-62; *CM,* 6-17-62; 6-19-62; *YE,* 6-26-62.
39. *CM,* 6-18-62.
40. Confederate Historian, "Annual Report," 70.
41. *CDC,* 3-25-62; *CM,* 3-25-62.
42. Phelps, *Charleston Battalion,* 60.
43. Ibid., 88.
44. *OR,* 1, 28, 2, 161.
45. Ibid., 1, 28, 1, 471; *CM,* 6-17-62; 8-19-63.
46. Confederate Historian, "Annual Report," 70.
47. Ibid., 69.
48. *CDC,* 3-25-62.
49. *Memory Roll: Rolls of South Carolina Volunteers in the Confederate States Provisional Army,* South Carolina Department of Archives and History, Microcopy No. 16. (Hereafter *Memory Roll.*)
50. *CM,* 6-17-62.
51. Phelps, *Charleston Battalion,* 150.
52. Confederate Historian, "Annual Report," 70.
53. *OR,* 1, 28, 2, 396.
54. *CDC,* 8-20-63; *CM,* 8-17-63.
55. *OR,* 1, 28, 2, 388.
56. *CM,* 4-15-62.
57. Ibid., 6-4-62.
58. *OR,* 1, 14, 582.
59. *CDC,* 7-21-62; *OR,* 1, 28, 2, 162.
60. Ibid., 1, 14, 265.
61. Ibid., 1, 14, 873.
62. Ibid., 1, 14, 970.
63. Ibid., 1, 28, 1, 372, 543.
64. *CM,* 7-20-63.
65. *OR,* 1, 28, 1, 390; 1, 28, 2, 211; 1, 2, 2, 246.
66. Ibid., 1, 28, 1, 381, 385.
67. Ibid., 1, 28, 2, 249, 518.
68. *CM,* 8-24-63; 8-27-63; *CDC,* 8-27-63.
69. *OR,* 1, 28, 1, 395, 498.
70. Ibid., 1, 28, 1, 400; 1, 28, 2, 327; .
71. Confederate Historian, "Annual Report," 69.
72. Record and Roll of the German Fusiliers, Confederate Historian, South Carolina Department of Archives and History, S108118.
73. *OR,* 1, 28, 1, 131; 1, 28, 2, 367.

Chapter 2

1. *CM,* 6-3-64
2. *OR,* 1, 47, 2, 1070.
3. Ibid., 1, 28, 2, 326, 368.

Chapter 3

1. Warren Ripley, *The Battle of Chapman's Fort, May 26, 1864,* vii. (Hereafter cited as Ripley, *Chapman's Fort.*)
2. Confederate Historian, "Annual Report," 46.
3. Ripley, *Chapman's Fort,* vi.
4. Ibid., vii.
5. *CV,* 24, 342.
6. *CM,* 9-3-63.
7. *Memory Roll.*
8. E. Frank Melton, *War Between the States,* 279. (Hereafter cited as Melton, *War.*)

9. UDC, *RR*, 6, 290.
10. Ibid.
11. *CDC*, 12-5-61.
12. *CM*, 8-5-64.
13. *CDC*, 12-5-61.
14. Ibid., 12-5-61; *CM*, 12-2-61.

Chapter 4

1. *OR*, 1, 53, 257.
2. Ibid., 1, 14, 575.
3. Ibid.
4. UDC, *RR*, 6, 290.

Chapter 5

1. *CM*, 11-27-61.
2. Stewart Sifakis, *Compendium of the Confederate Armies—South Carolina and Georgia*, 78. (Hereafter, Sifakis, *Compendium*.)
3. *OR*, 1, 47, 3, 773.
4. *CM*, 4-24-61.
5. Dickert, *Kershaw's Brigade*, 103.
6. Ibid., 104.
7. *CM*, 4-24-61; 10-14-64.
8. *CDC*, 3-28-61.
9. Dickert, *Kershaw's Brigade*, 149.
10. *CDC*, 9-24-64; Freeman, *Lee's Lieutenants*, 3, 581.
11. *CDC*, 11-1-64.
12. *CM*, 10-14-64.
13. *Register of Confederate Soldiers, Sailors, and Citizens Who Died in Federal Prisons and Military Hospitals in the North, 1861–1865*, National Archives and Records Administration; *CSR*, M267, 231; SHSP, 27, 105; DeWitt Boyd Stone Jr., *Wandering to Glory*, 230. (Hereafter cited as Stone, *Wandering*.)
14. Dickert, *Kershaw's Brigade*, 423.
15. *CM*, 4-24-61; *CV*, 35, 389.
16. *CDC*, 3-28-61.
17. Dickert, *Kershaw's Brigade*, 274.
18. Ibid., 278.
19. SHSP, 13, 392.
20. Dickert, *Kershaw's Brigade*, 251; Krick, *Lee's Colonels*, 255.
21. *CM*, 7-21-63; 8-18-63; 9-4-63; Krick, *Lee's Colonels*, 255.
22. *CDC*, 8-18-63; 9-4-63.
23. Dickert, *Kershaw's Brigade*, 251.
24. SHSP, 4, 183.
25. *CSR*, M267, 233.
26. Dickert, *Kershaw's Brigade*, 285-6.
27. *CM*, 4-24-61.
28. Dickert, *Kershaw's Brigade*, 284.
29. *CM*, 7-18-62; South Carolina Department of Archives and History, *Roll of the Dead, South Carolina Troops Confederate States Service*. (Hereafter, SCDAH, *Roll of the Dead*.)
30. *CSR*, M267, 232.
31. *CDC*, 11-1-64.
32. *CM*, 4-24-61.
33. Ibid., 7-21-63.
34. *CDC*, 11-1-64.
35. *CM*, 4-24-61; 10-17-63.
36. Ibid., 10-17-63.
37. *Daily Southern Guardian*, 9-7-63 (Hereafter cited as *DSG*); *CM*, 7-20-63; 7-21-63; 8-28-63.

38. *CDC,* 10-22-63.
39. Ibid.
40. *CM,* 10-2-63; *Confederate Military History Extended Edition, Volume 6, South Carolina,* 735. (Hereafter cited as *CMH.*); *CV,* 24, 271.
41. *CSR,* M267, 232.
42. *CM,* 4-24-61.
43. Ibid.
44. *CSR,* M267, 232.
45. *CM,* 7-21-63.
46. Ibid., 7-18-62.
47. Ibid., 4-24-61.
48. UDC, *RR,* 6, 359.
49. *CM,* 4-24-61; UDC, *RR,* 10, 6.
50. *CM,* 2-11-62.
51. *CSR,* M267, 231.
52. *CM,* 4-24-61.
53. UDC, *RR,* 6, 359.
54. *CSR,* M267, 230.
55. Kirkland, *Broken Fortunes,* 250.
56. *CM,* 7-18-62; 7-20-63; 7-21-63; Eleanor D. McSwain, ed., *Crumbling Defenses or Memoirs and Reminiscences of John Logan Black,* 51. (Hereafter cited as McSwain, *Crumbling Defenses.*)
57. McSwain, *Crumbling Defenses,* 52.
58. Ibid, 53.
59. *CM,* 12-8-63.
60. *CSR,* M267, 229.
61. Melton, *War,* 26.
62. *CM,* 4-18-61; 4-24-61.
63. *CSR,* M267, 233.
64. *CMH,* 726.
65. UDC, *RR,* 1, 400.
66. UDC, *RR,* 1, 412.
67. *CM,* 4-24-61.
68. Dickert, *Kershaw's Brigade,* 149.
69. *CM,* 7-18-62; 7-21-63.
70. *CSR,* M267, 230.
71. Dickert, *Kershaw's Brigade,* 484.
72. *CSR,* M267, 233.
73. UDC, *RR,* 5, 244.
74. *CDC,* 4-20-61.
75. Dickert, *Kershaw's Brigade,* 484.
76. *CM,* 7-18-62.
77. Melton, *War,* 56.
78. *CMH,* 511.
79. *CM,* 7-20-63.
80. Ibid., 11-30-63.
81. *CDC,* 11-30-63.
82. *CM,* 6-3-61.
83. Ibid., 7-22-61.
84. *CV,* 4, 6.
85. UDC, *RR,* 1, 411.
86. Ibid., 6, 359.
87. *CDC,* 4-18-61; 4-29-61; *CM,* 4-19-61; 5-2-61;
88. *CM,* 5-24-61.
89. UDC, *RR,* 6, 359.
90. *CM,* 6-15-61.

91. Ibid.
92. Guy R. Everson and Edward H. Simpson Jr. eds., *Far, Far from Home—The Wartime Letters of Dick and Tally Simpson, 3rd South Carolina Volunteers*, 33. (Hereafter cited as Everson, *Far from Home*.)
93. *CM*, 2-27-62.
94. *CMH*, 464.
95. Everson, *Far from Home*, 106.
96. Ibid., 109.
97. Ibid., 113.
98. Ibid.
99. Ibid., 125; *CM*, 6-13-62.
100. *CM*, 6-3-62.
101. Ibid., 6-27-62; Everson, *Far from Home*, 132.
102. *CM*, 7-23-62; 7-24-62.
103. Ibid., 9-10-62; *CDC*, 9-10-62.
104. *CM*, 10-2-62; 1-1-63; *EA*, 10-8-62.
105. *CM*, 10-2-62.
106. *CDC*, 12-22-62.
107. Mac Wycoff, *A History of the 2nd South Carolina Infantry, 1861–1865*, 58. (Hereafter cited as Wycoff, *2nd South Carolina Infantry*.)
108. *CM*, 12-29-62.
109. Wycoff, *2nd South Carolina Infantry*, 61.
110. Ibid., 84.
111. SHSP, 4, 183.
112. Ibid., 13, 210.
113. *CM*, 7-20-63.
114. *LL*, 11-4-63; SHSP, 16, 377.
115. Freeman, *Lee's Lieutenants*, 3,229; Mac Wyckoff, *A History of the 3rd South Carolina Infantry 1861–1865*, 135.
116. *CDC*, 10-24-63; Everson, *Far from Home*, 283; *CM*, 9-26-63.
117. *CM*, 10-2-63.
118. SHSP, 16, 387.
119. *CM*, 12-22-63.
120. *CDC*, 12-29-63.
121. SHSP, 16, 390.
122. Ibid., 7, 129.
123. *CM*, 5-31-64.
124. Freeman, *Lee's Lieutenants*, 3,506; *CM*, 6-13-64; 6-20-64.
125. *CDC*, 7-19-64.
126. Freeman, *Lee's Lieutenants*, 3,506.
127. *CDC*, 7-19-64.
128. *CM*, 8-3-64; 8-8-64; *CDC*, 8-9-64.
129. *CDC*, 9-24-64.
130. *CM*, 10-24-64.
131. *OR*, 1, 47, 2, 1074.
132. Ibid., 1, 47, 2, 262, 1282.
133. Ibid., 1, 47, 1, 1111.

Chapter 6

1. Cauthen, ed., *Journals*, 172.
2. *OR*, 1, 53, 257.
3. *CM*, 11-28-62.
4. UDC, *RR*, 8, 393.
5. *Horry Dispatch*, 2-6-62.
6. Ibid., 10-3-61.
7. *CM*, 5-24-62.

8. Ibid.
9. Ibid.
10. Ibid., 1-20-63.
11. Ibid., 5-24-62.
12. *Horry Dispatch*, 2-6-62; *CM*, 5-24-62.
13. *Horry Dispatch*, 10-3-61.
14. *CM*, 5-24-62.
15. *Horry Dispatch*, 2-6-62.
16. *CM*, 5-24-61.
17. Ibid., 5-24-62.
18. Ibid.
19. Ibid.
20. Ibid., 6-17-62.
21. Ibid., 5-24-62.
22. *Horry Dispatch*, 2-6-62; 10-3-61.
23. *CM*, 5-24-62.
24. *CSR*, M267, 239.
25. *OR*, 1, 6, 426.

Chapter 7

1. *CDC*, 6-8-61.
2. *OR*, 4, 1, 414.
3. J.R. Tolar, "A History of Company B, 10th Regiment, SCV," 2. (Hereafter cited as Tolar, Company B.)
4. *CM*, 2-24-63; 10-5-63.
5. Ibid., 10-5-63; 12-8-63; C.I. Walker, *Rolls and Historical Sketch of the Tenth Regiment, So. Ca. Volunteers in the Army of the Confederate States*, 96. (Hereafter cited as Walker, *Rolls*.)
6. *CM*, 2-18-64; Walker, *Rolls*, 107; *CDC*, 2-18-64.
7. *CDC*, 6-8-61.
8. Ibid., 7-29-62.
9. *LL*, 3-4-63.
10. Tower, *A Carolinian Goes To War*, 181.
11. Ibid., xii.
12. Ibid., xiii.
13. *CDC*, 9-6-61.
14. Ibid., 6-8-61.
15. Tower, *A Carolinian Goes To War*, 60.
16. *CM*, 2-24-63; 12-8-63.
17. Ibid., 2-24-63.
18. Ibid., 7-29-64; *CDC*, 7-30-64.
19. Manigault, 227.
20. *CM*, 10-17-64.
21. Thigpen, *Potter's Raid*, 293.
22. *CM*, 6-8-61; *CDC*, 6-8-61.
23. *CM*, 1-5-61; 5-23-61; 6-7-61.
24. *For Love of a Rebel*, Arthur Manigault Chapter of the U.D.C., 17. (Hereafter cited as *For Love of a Rebel*.)
25. *CM*, 9-5-61.
26. Walker, *Rolls*, 72; S. Emanuel, "A historical Sketch of the Georgetown Rifle Guards," speech, Microfiche, SC 973.7457, Fiche 113. (Hereafter cited as Emanuel, "Sketch.")
27. Walker, *Rolls*, 80.
28. *CM*, 3-10-64.
29. Tower, *A Carolinian Goes To War*, 144; UDC, *RR*, 12, 356.
30. Tower, *A Carolinian Goes To War*, 60.
31. *CM*, 2-24-63.

32. Ibid., 12-2-63.
33. *CDC,* 3-11-64.
34. Tower, *A Carolinian Goes To War,* 144
35. Walker, *Rolls,* 107.
36. *CM,* 7-25-64.
37. *CV,* 3, 326; 19, 459; Walker, *Rolls,* intro.
38. *CDC,* 8-15-64.
39. *CV,* 6, 335.
40. UDC, *RR,* 5, 598; *CV,* 18, 233.
41. *CV,* 35, 103.
42. *CM,* 1-5-61; SHSP, 13, 495.
43. *Horry Dispatch,* 5-23-61; UDC, *RR,* 5, 598.
44. UDC, *RR,* 5, 598; Walker, *Rolls,* 70–72.
45. *CDC,* 9-16-61.
46. *CM,* 1-16-61; Cauthen, *South Carolina Goes to War,* 80.
47. *CM,* 4-18-61.
48. Ibid., 4-27-61.
49. *Horry Dispatch,* 5-23-61.
50. UDC, *RR,* 5, 598; *CM,* 5-23-61.
51. *CM,* 7-23-61.
52. *CDC,* 7-24-61.
53. UDC, *RR,* 7, 196.
54. UDC, *RR,* 5, 502; UDC, *RR,* 6, 290.
55. *CM,* 1-10-61.
56. UDC, *RR,* 5, 598.
57. *Horry Dispatch,* 5-23-61.
58. Ibid.
59. *Acts,* 934.
60. Walker, *Rolls;* Emanuel, "Sketch."
61. *CM,* 1-27-60.
62. *CDC,* 4-4-62.
63. Ibid.
64. *CM,* 1-5-61; 5-23-61; C6-7-61; *Horry Dispatch,* 5-23-61.
65. *CM,* 6-1-61; 6-7-61.
66. *CM,* 1-5-61; 2-8-64; C. Vann Woodward and Elisabeth Muhlenfeld, *The Private Mary Chesnut, The Unpublished Civil War Diaries,* 331. (Hereafter cited as Woodward, *Mary Chesnut.*)
67. *CDC,* 4-4-62.
68. Walker, *Rolls,* 80; *CDC,* 7-29-62.
69. *CDC,* 6-16-62.
70. *CDC,* 10-23-62.
71. *LL,* 12-24-62; Emanuel, "Sketch."
72. SCDAH, *Roll of the Dead; CM,* 2-2-64; *CDC,* 1-30-64.
73. *CDC,* 1-30-64; Tower, *A Carolinian Goes To War,* 29.
74. *CDC,* 10-5-63.
75. *CM,* 10-5-63.
76. *CV,* 15, 263; *CDC,* 8-15-64.
77. Tower, *A Carolinian Goes To War,* 55.
78. Emanuel, "Sketch."
79. *CV,* 34, 46.
80. Ibid., 21, 225.
81. Tolar, *Company B.*
82. *Horry Dispatch,* 5-23-61.
83. Tolar, *Company B.*
84. *CV,* 2, 225.
85. *CDC,* 10-5-63; *CM,* 10-5-63.

86. *CDC,* 7-30-64.
87. *CV,* 21, 225.
88. Ibid.
89. *Horry Dispatch,* 5-23-61.
90. *CDC,* 7-29-62.
91. Ibid., 10-5-63.
92. Walker, *Rolls,* 22; *CM,* 10-5-63; 6-17-64.
93. Confederate Historian, "Annual Report," 28.
94. *CM,* 11-30-61.
95. *CDC,* 7-29-62.
96. Ibid., 10-5-63.
97. *CM,* 10-5-63.
98. *CDC,* 8-15-64.
99. Ibid., 7-11-62.
100. *CM,* 11-5-60.
101. *CV,* 18, 233; *CM,* 6-21-64.
102. *Horry Dispatch,* 5-23-61.
103. SCDAH, *Roll of the Dead.*
104. *CDC,* 10-5-63.
105. *Horry Dispatch,* 5-23-61.
106. *CDC,* 7-29-62.
107. Ibid., 10-5-63.
108. UDC, *RR,* 12, 356.
109. *CM,* 10-5-63.
110. *Horry Dispatch,* 8-29-61.
111. Ibid.
112. Ibid.; *CDC,* 7-29-62.
113. *CM,* 1-14-63.
114. *CDC,* 10-5-63.
115. *CM,* 10-5-63.
116. *Horry Dispatch,* 5-23-61; Tolar, *Company B*; Walker, *Rolls,* 71.
117. *Horry Dispatch,* 5-23-61.
118. Kirkland, *Broken Fortunes,* 259.
119. Tower, *A Carolinian Goes To War,* 58, 60.
120. Gary R. Baker, *Cadets in Gray,* 67. (Hereafter cited as Baker, *Cadets.*)
121. *CDC,* 10-5-63.
122. *Abbeville Press,* 6-5-63. (Hereafter cited as *AP,*)
123. Tolar, Company B; Walker, *Rolls,* 72.
124. *CDC,* 7-29-62.
125. *CM,* 1-14-63.
126. *CDC,* 10-5-63.
127. *CM,* 6-30-61.
128. Ibid., 9-7-61.
129. Ibid., 6-6-61.
130. *CDC,* 10-5-63.
131. Baker, *Cadets in Gray,* 67;
132. *CM,* 1-14-63; 10-24-64; *CDC,* 8-15-64.
133. UDC, *RR,* 12, 356.
134. *Cyclopedia of Eminent and Representative Men of the Carolinas of the Nineteenth Century,* 325. (Hereafter cited as *Cyclopedia.*)
135. UDC, *RR,* 12, 356.
136. *CDC,* 10-5-63.
137. *CM,* 10-5-63.
138. *Horry Dispatch,* 2-6-62.
139. Tolar, *Company B.*

140. *CDC,* 7-29-62; UDC, *RR,* 12, 356.
141. *CDC,* 10-5-63; *CM,* 10-5-63.
142. *CMH,* 655; *Cyclopedia,* 235.
143. Sifakis, *Compendium,* 82.
144. Tower, *A Carolinian Goes To War,* xiii; SHSP, 12, 152; *CDC,* 10-17-63.
145. Sifakis, *Compendium,* 82.
146. *OR,* 1, 47, 3, 734.
147. Ibid., 1, 47, 1, 1064.
148. *CDC,* 2-23-61.
149. *CM,* 4-18-61.
150. UDC, *RR,* 5, 599.
151. *CM,* 7-23-61.
152. *CDC,* 9-6-61.
153. UDC, *RR,* 8, 372, 6, 615.
154. Ibid., 5, 599.
155. *OR,* 1, 6, 352.
156. Ibid., 1, 6, 418.
157. UDC, *RR,* 8, 452.
158. *OR,* 1, 6, 426.
159. *CM,* 4-13-62; UDC, *RR,* 8, 453; Tower, *A Carolinian Goes To War,* 7.
160. *Horry Dispatch,* 5-8-62.
161. *DWT,* 7-4-62; *CM,* 5-20-62; UDC, *RR,* 8, 453.
162. *CDC,* 7-29-62.
163. Tower, *A Carolinian Goes To War,* 55, 61.
164. *CM,* 3-30-63.
165. *CDC,* 3-7-63; *CM,* 3-21-63, *CDC,* 2-18-63.
166. *CV,* 15, 263; 28, 128.
167. *CDC,* 3-7-63; UDC, *RR,* 9, 168.
168. *CM,* 1-14-63; *CDC,* 2-18-63.
169. *CM,* 2-24-63.
170. *AP,* 2-20-63.
171. Ibid., 5-15-63, 6-5-63, 6-19-63, 6-26-63, 7-3-63.
172. Ibid., 7-10-63, 7-17-63.
173. Walker, *Rolls,* 98.
174. *CDC,* 10-17-63.
175. *CM,* 10-1-63.
176. Ibid., 5-30-64.
177. Ibid.
178. UDC, *RR,* 5, 358; Tower, *A Carolinian Goes To War,* 265.
179. Tower, *A Carolinian Goes To War,* 219.
180. Ibid., 251.
181. Walker, *Rolls,* 132.
182. Emanuel, "Sketch."

Chapter 8

1. *CM,* 2-27-61; 5-13-61.
2. Ibid., 6-29-61; *OR,* 4, 1, 414.
3. *CM,* 11-15-61.
4. *LL,* 8-7-61.
5. *CM,* 5-5-62.
6. *CDC,* 11-8-61.
7. Ibid., 5-12-62.
8. Hagood, *Memoirs,* 204.
9. *CM,* 5-11-61; 5-25-61.
10. Ibid., 9-3-63.

11. Ibid.
12. Ibid.
13. *EA*, 9-16-63.
14. *CM*, 5-21-61; 5-25-61.
15. Ibid., 5-25-61.
16. Krick, *Lee's Colonels*, 82.
17. *CM*, 5-5-62; *CDC*, 5-12-62.
18. Halliburton, *Saddle Soldiers*, 61; Hagood, *Memoirs*, 205.
19. *CSR*, M267, 248.
20. Krick, *Lee's Colonels*, 130.
21. *CM*, 5-5-62; *CDC*, 5-12-62.
22. Hagood, *Memoirs*, 205.
23. *CM*, 5-5-62; *CDC*, 5-12-62.
24. *CM*, 10-24-62; 11-7-62.
25. *CDC*, 11-14-62.
26. *CSR*, M267, 249.
27. *CMH*, 668.
28. *OR*, 1, 28, 1, 136.
29. Hagood, *Memoirs*, 205.
30. *Memory Roll*.
31. Ibid.
32. *CM*, 7-1-61.
33. Ibid., 2-7-61.
34. *CMH*, 679.
35. *CM*, 6-24-61.
36. Ibid., 5-14-61.
37. Ibid., 9-25-61.
38. Ibid., 7-25-61.
39. *CDC*, 5-12-62.
40. *CM*, 11-14-64.
41. *DSC*, 6-14-64; Hagood, *Memoirs*, 261.
42. *CM*, 7-9-62; 12-23-64.
43. Ibid., 10-15-64.
44. Neil Baxley, *No Prouder Fate: The Story of the 11th South Carolina Volunteer Infantry*, 214. (Hereafter cited as Baxley, *No Prouder Fate*.)
45. *CM*, 5-24-64; 6-14-64; 12-24-64; Baxley, *No Prouder Fate*, 125.
46. *DSC*, 5-28-64.
47. *CM*, 6-14-64; 12-24-64.
48. *OR*, 1, 28, 2, 444.
49. *CM*, 8-19-61; SHSP, Index; *CV*, 27, 64.
50. *CM*, 11-7-62.
51. Ibid., 1-30-65; *CDC*, 2-2-65.
52. *CM*, 6-24-61.
53. Ibid., 1-6-64.
54. Ibid., 8-22-62, 11-25-62.
55. Ibid., 3-16-63, 3-23-63.
56. Ripley, *Chapman's Fort*, 303.
57. Baxley, *No Prouder Fate*, 188.
58. Salley, *SC Troops*, 1:430.
59. *CDC*, 7-26-61.
60. *CM*, 6-3-62.
61. *CDC*, 5-12-62; *CM*, 6-3-62.
62. *CDC*, 8-23-61; *CMH*, 427, 768.
63. *CM*, 7-27-61.
64. Ibid.

65. Ibid., 9-29-64.
66. *CDC,* 6-25-61.
67. *OR,* 1, 6, 24.
68. *CM,* 1-6-62.
69. Ibid., 5-24-64; 12-2-64.
70. Ibid., 6-15-64.
71. *CDC,* 10-6-64; *CV,* 7, 317; *CM,* 12-2-64.
72. *CM,* 12-2-64.
73. *OR,* 1, 14, 283; 1, 28, 2, 444.
74. *CM,* 6-7-61; 2-15-62; *CDC,* 9-4-61.
75. *CM,* 6-7-61.
76. Ibid., 6-7-61.
77. Sifakis, *Compendium,* 83.
78. *OR,* 1, 28, 2, 368.
79. *CM,* 7-8-61; 7-9-61.
80. *CM,* 8-1-61; *OR,* 4, 1, 414.
81. *OR,* 1, 6, 14.
82. *CM,* 11-12-61.
83. Ibid., 12-9-61.
84. *OR,* 1, 14, 25; *CM,* 6-3-62.
85. *OR,* 1, 14, 31.
86. Ibid., 1, 14, 112.
87. *CM,* 7-10-62.
88. *YE,* 8-27-62; *CM,* 8-22-62.
89. Baxley, *No Prouder Fate,* 66.
90. *CM,* 10-24-62; 10-29-62; 1-8-64; *CDC,* 10-28-62.
91. *CM,* 10-28-62.
92. Baxley, *No Prouder Fate,* 71.
93. *CM,* 2-6-63.
94. Ibid., 4-25-63.
95. *OR,* 1, 14, 282.
96. Ibid., 1, 28, 1, 149.
97. Ibid., 1, 14, 288.
98. *CM,* 6-6-63; *OR,* 1, 14, 309.
99. *OR,* 1, 28, 1, 592.
100. Ibid., 1, 28, 1, 74.
101. Ibid., 1, 28, 2, 245.
102. Ibid., 1, 28, 2, 245, 346.
103. Ibid., 1, 28, 2, 729.
104. Ibid., 1, 28, 2, 367.
105. Ibid., 1, 28, 1, 131.
106. Ibid., 1, 28, 1, 136.
107. Ibid., 1, 28, 1, 139, 145, 627, 629.
108. Ibid., 1, 28, 2, 467-8; *CM,* 10-13-63.
109. *OR,* 1, 28, 2, 601.
110. Ibid., 1, 35, 1, 557-8.
111. Ibid., 1, 35, 1, 622.
112. Hagood, *Memoirs,* 172; Halliburton, *Saddle Soldiers,* 129; *CM,* 3-7-64; 3-11-64.
113. *OR,* 1, 35, 1, 372; 1, 35, 2, 436; *CM,* 4-30-64.
114. *OR,* 1, 35, 2, 454.
115. Ibid., 1, 35, 2, 518.
116. Ibid., 1, 35, 2, 454.
117. Ibid., 1, 35, 2, 518.
118. Ibid.
119. SHSP, 16, 179.

120. *CV,* 25, 458.
121. *CM,* 5-13-64; *CV,* 23, 458.
122. *CM,* 5-24-64; 6-2-64.
123. Ibid., 5-16-64; 6-2-64.
124. *CDC,* 5-23-64.
125. *CM,* 5-23-63; SHSP, 16, 190.
126. *CM,* 5-23-64; 5-24-64; 5-26-64; 6-2-64.
127. Ibid., 6-2-64; 6-13-64.
128. *CDC,* 8-13-64.
129. *DSG,* 7-14-64.
130. *CM,* 7-29-64; *CDC,* 7-29-64; 8-13-64; Confederate Historian, "Annual Report," 72.
131. *CM,* 8-26-64.
132. Hagood, *Memoirs,* 473.
133. *CM,* 10-18-64.
134. Ibid.
135. Ibid., 11-8-64.
136. *CDC,* 1-25-65; *CM,* 1-23-65.
137. *CM,* 1-30-65.

Chapter 9

1.   SHSP, 14, 51.
2.   Ibid., 16, 133.
3.   *CM,* 12-21-61.
4.   *CDC,* 2-20-62.
5.   Ibid., 3-31-62.
6.   Ibid.
7.   Cauthen, ed., *Journals,* 164.
8.   *CDC,* 5-2-62; *CM,* 5-2-62; SHSP, 16, 134.
9.   SHSP, 18, 134.
10. Ibid., 16, 134; *EA,* 6-25-62; *CDC,* 6-17-62; 6-19-62.
11. SHSP, 14, 35; 16, 151.
12. *CDC,* 5-9-62; *EA,* 6-25-62.
13. *OR,* 1, 14, 103.
14. *CM,* 5-2-62.
15. Cauthen, ed., *Journals,* 164.
16. *CM,* 5-2-62; Cauthen, ed., *Journals,* 164.
17. *CM,* 6-24-61.
18. Ibid., 6-20-61.
19. Ibid., 2-24-62.
20. *CDC,* 5-9-62.
21. *CM,* 10-2-61; 2-24-62.
22. *CDC,* 5-9-62.
23. *CV,* 35, 103.
24. SHSP, 10, 134.
25. Ibid., 10, 134; *CM,* 2-20-64.
26. *CM,* 5-2-62; 6-2-64.
27. Ibid., 7-31-61.
28. *CDC,* 2-24-62; *CM,* 2-26-62; 4-21-62.
29. *CM,* 7-31-61.
30. William Valmore Izlar, *A Sketch of the War Record of the Edisto Rifles, 1861–1865,* 33. (Hereafter cited as Izlar, *Sketch.*)
31. SHSP, 16, 134; Confederate Historian, "Annual Report," 57; Izlar, *Sketch,* 33; *CV,* 21, 350; 32, 420.
32. UDC, *RR,* 5, 131.
33. SHSP, 18, 134.

34. *CM*, 6-13-64.
35. *CDC*, 2-25-64.
36. *CM*, 6-13-64.
37. Confederate Historian, "Annual Report," 57.
38. *CM*, 4-10-62.
39. Ibid., 4-30-62.
40. Ibid., 5-20-62.
41. SHSP, 16, 128.
42. *CDC*, 5-1-62; 5-9-62.
43. *OR*, 1, 14, 103; *DSG*, 6-18-62.
44. SHSP, 16, 151.
45. Ibid.

Chapter 10

1.   *CM*, 12-18-61.
2.   Ibid., 11-27-61; 3-21-62.
3.   Ibid., 12-4-61; 3-21-62.
4.   Ibid., 3-21-62.
5.   Hagood, *Memoirs*, 205.
6.   *CM*, 3-21-62.
7.   Ibid., 3-14-62.
8.   Ibid., 11-30-61; 3-21-62.
9.   Ibid., 5-16-64; 5-23-64.
10. Ibid., 10-14-64.
11. Ibid., 3-14-62; *DSG*, 5-31-64.
12. *DSG*, 5-31-64; *CM*, 5-16-64; 9-12-64; Henry Kershaw DuBose, *The History of Company B, 21st Regiment (Infantry) SCV C.S.P.A.*, 55. (Hereafter cited as DuBose, *Company B*.)
13. *CDC*, 5-16-64.
14. DuBose, *Company B*, 55.
15. Hagood, *Memoirs*, 205; *CDC*, 11-3-64.
16. *CM*, 3-14-62.
17. Ibid., 6-24-64.
18. Hagood, *Memoirs*, 205.
19. *CDC*, 5-28-64.
20. Ibid., 3-9-64.
21. Ibid., 2-4-65.
22. *CM*, 7-13-63.
23. Ibid., 7-11-63.
24. Melton, *War*, 72.
25. DuBose, *Company B*, 119.
26. Hagood, *Memoirs*, 384.
27. UDC, *RR*, 12, 373; Allan D. Thigpen, *Recollections of Potter's Raid*, 59. (Hereafter cited as Thigpen, *Potter's Raid*.)
28. Thigpen, *Potter's Raid*, 59-61.
29. UDC, *RR*, 12, 373.
30. SHSP, 16, 151.
31. *CDC*, 2-26-63; 5-9-62.
32. *CM*, 7-13-63; 5-16-64.
33. Ibid., 7-13-63; 5-16-64; 6-6-64; SCDAH, *Roll of the Dead*; UDC, *RR*, 3, 494; Kirkland, *Broken Fortunes*, 87.
34. *CM*, 2-21-62.
35. Sketch of Co. F. 21st. Regiment, SCV, Miscellaneous Historical Sketches, 1868–1898. South Carolina Department of Archives and History, S108121.
36. UDC, *RR*, 12, 438.
37. SHSP, 16, 173.

38. *CM,* 7-11-63.
39. Ibid., 5-16-64.
40. Ibid., 5-23-64.
41. SHSP, 16, 173.
42. *CM,* 8-5-63.
43. Ibid., 7-11-63.
44. *DSC,* 5-26-64.
45. Melton, *War,* 88
46. *CDC,* 2-3-63; *CM,* 2-4-63.
47. *CDC,* 2-10-63.
48. *CM,* 5-16-64.
49. Ibid., 7-11-63; 7-13-63.
50. *CDC,* 11-30-63.
51. *CM,* 11-30-63; 5-9-64; *CDC,* 5-6-64.
52. *DSC,* 5-26-64.
53. Ripley, *Chapman's Fort,* 304.
54. *CDC,* 5-24-64.
55. Ibid., 5-23-64; Kirkland, *Broken Fortunes,* 266.
56. *CM,* 6-24-64.
57. *CDC,* 2-4-65.
58. *CM,* 5-16-64; 5-23-64.
59. SCDAH, *Roll of the Dead; CV,* 36, 286.
60. SCDAH, *Roll of the Dead; CM,* 5-16-64; Hagood, *Memoirs,* 388.
61. *CDC,* 2-4-65.
62. Sifakis, *Compendium,* 97.
63. *OR,* 1, 28, 2, 368.
64. *CM,* 3-22-62; Tower, *A Carolinian Goes To War,* 11.
65. *OR,* 1, 6, 418, 426.
66. *CDC,* 4-17-62.
67. *CM,* 10-31-62; *OR,* 1, 14, 823.
68. *CM,* 7-11-63.
69. Ibid., 7-11-63; 7-17-63.
70. *OR,* 1, 28, 1, 72, 413.
71. Ibid., 1, 28, 1, 414.
72. Ibid., 1, 28, 2, 212, 231, 245.
73. Ibid., 1, 28, 1, 383.
74. Ibid., 1, 28, 1, 496.
75. Ibid., 1, 28, 1, 388, 393.
76. Ibid., 1, 28, 2, 325.
77. Ibid., 1, 28, 2, 367.
78. Ibid., 1, 28, 2, 468, 603; 1, 35, 1, 559; 1, 35, 2, 469.
79. *CM,* 3-7-64.
80. *OR,* 1, 35, 1, 603.
81. Ibid., 1, 35, 1, 190, 206.
82. Ibid., 1, 35, 1, 196, 200.
83. Ibid., 1, 35, 2, 454.

Chapter 11

1. *CM,* 7-11-62.
2. Ibid., 12-18-61.
3. *LL,* 11-27-61; *CM,* 9-26-61; *CDC,* 7-19-62.
4. *CM,* 9-20-64.
5. Ibid., 1-1-62; 9-2-64.
6. Ibid., 3-2-64; *CDC,* 3-7-64.
7. *CDC,* 5-8-62.

8. *CM*, 6-21-62.
9. Ibid., 5-26-62; *CDC*, 5-8-62.
10. Krick, *Lee's Colonels*, 187.
11. Historical Sketch of the 5th. South Carolina Cavalry, Miscellaneous Historical Sketches, 1866–1898, South Carolina Department of Archives and History, S108121; *CMH*, 626.
12. Ibid.
13. *CM*, 1-26-64.
14. Krick, *Lee's Colonels*, 167.
15. *Triweekly Watchman*, 7-5-61; 5-22-63.
16. *CM*, 5-26-62.
17. Ibid., 9-9-62; UDC, *RR*, 8, 415.
18. *OR*, 1, 28, 2, 589.
19. UDC, *RR*, 3, 4.
20. *Triweekly Watchman*, 7-5-61.
21. Stone, *Wandering*, 180.
22. *CM*, 5-28-62; 7-11-62.
23. Ibid., 9-9-62.
24. Kirkland, *Broken Fortunes*, 299.
25. *CM*, 5-26-62.
26. *CDC*, 9-10-62; UDC, *RR*, 9, 14.
27. *CM*, 9-9-62; 9-13-62; UDC, *RR*, 8, 416.
28. R.A. Brock and Philip Van Doren Stern, *The Appomattox Roster*, 403. (Hereafter cited as Brock, *The Appomattox Roster*); SHSP, 15, 403.
29. *CM*, 6-24-64; 9-2-64; *CDC*, 6-24-64.
30. *DSG*, 8-31-64; *CM*, 7-16-64; 9-2-64; *CDC*, 9-3-64.
31. *CDC*, 9-3-64.
32. Brock, *The Appomattox Roster*, 403.
33. *CM*, 9-9-62; 10-9-62.
34. *CDC*, 9-13-62; Kirkland, *Broken Fortunes*, 239.
35. *CM*, 10-9-62; Krick, *Lee's Colonels*, 286.
36. *CDC*, 10-27-62; 11-3-62.
37. Ibid., 10-27-62.
38. Krick, *Lee's Colonels*, 286.
39. Ibid., 286.
40. Stone, *Wandering*, 35.
41. *CM*, 8-5-61; 1-1-62; 1-3-62.
42. Ibid., 1-3-62.
43. Ibid., 9-18-61; 1-3-62; SHSP, Index.
44. *CDC*, 9-10-62.
45. *CM*, 9-13-62; Gordon C. Rhea, *Carrying the Flag*, 71.
46. *CM*, 7-11-62; 9-27-62.
47. Ibid., 9-9-62.
48. Ibid., 6-24-64.
49. Ibid., 9-27-61; 1-1-62.
50. Ibid., 9-17-61.
51. *CDC*, 9-3-64.
52. *CSR*, M267, 335.
53. *CM*, 1-1-62; 10-13-62.
54. *CDC*, 10-1-61; *CM*, 10-14-62.
55. *CM*, 7-11-62.
56. Ibid., 6-24-64.
57. Ibid., 8-11-64.
58. *CDC*, 10-21-61; 6-9-62.
59. SHSP, Index.
60. *CSR*, M267, 332.

61. Ibid.
62. *CM,* 7-11-62; 6-24-64.
63. *CSR,* M267, 332.
64. *CM,* 7-11-62.
65. Ibid., 9-9-62.
66. *CDC,* 2-25-64.
67. *CM,* 6-24-64.
68. Ibid., 10-20-61.
69. *CDC,* 6-9-62; 11-11-62.
70. *CM,* 10-26-61.
71. Ibid.
72. Ibid., 7-11-62.
73. Ibid., 9-9-62.
74. *CV,* 8, 284; *CM,* 11-30-61.
75. *CM,* 7-11-62.
76. *CDC,* 10-232-62.
77. *CM,* 12-29-62.
78. *CV,* 8, 284.
79. *CSR,* M267, 334.
80. *CMH,* 627.
81. Ibid., 470; UDC, *RR,* 7, 343; *CM,* 7-19-61.
82. UDC, *RR,* 1, 456, 7, 343.
83. *Triweekly Watchman,* 7-5-61.
84. *CM,* 7-19-61.
85. *CM,* 7-11-62.
86. *CMH,* 471.
87. UDC, *RR,* 8, 416.
88. *CDC,* 6-9-62; *Sumter Watchman,* 1-25-65; UDC, *RR,* 3, 505.
89. UDC, *RR,* 3, 505.
90. Ibid.
91. *CM,* 7-11-62.
92. *CM,* 9-9-62.
93. UDC, *RR,* 3, 506; Thigpen, *Potter's Raid,* 68.
94. *CM,* 6-24-64.
95. Sifakis, *Compendium,* 91.
96. UDC, *RR,* 6, 406.
97. Sifakis, *Compendium,* 92.
98. *CM,* 9-26-61.
99. Stone, *Wandering,* 20.
100. *CM,* 9-27-61; *CDC,* 9-27-61.
101. *CM,* 10-4-61; 10-26-61.
102. UDC, *RR,* 3, 505.
103. *CM,* 4-7-62; 5-26-62.
104. UDC, *RR,* 3, 505.
105. *CDC,* 5-8-62.
106. UDC, *RR,* 8, 409.
107. *OR,* 1, 14, 582.
108. Ibid., 1, 14, 587.
109. Ibid.; Sketches of the 23rd. Regiment, SCV, Miscellaneous Sketches, South Carolina Department of Archives and History, S108121. (Hereafter cited as Sketches of the 23rd Regiment, SCDAH, S108121.)
110. *OR,* 1, 14, 587.
111. Samuel N. Thomas Jr. and Jason H. Silverman, eds., *A Rising Star Of Promise: The Civil War Odyssey of David Jackson Logan, 17ᵗʰ South Carolina Volunteers, 1861–1864,* 40. (Hereafter cited as Thomas, *Rising Star.*)

112. UDC, *RR*, 8, 410.
113. Ibid., 11, 12; W.H. Edwards, *A Condensed History of the Seventeenth Regiment, SCV C.S.P.A.*, 15. (Hereafter cited as Edwards, *Seventeenth Regiment*.)
114. Stone, *Wandering*, 28, 36.
115. *CM*, 9-8-62; *CDC*, 8-30-62; 9-27-62.
116. Sketches of the 23rd Regiment, SCDAH, S108121.
117. *LL*, 9-17-62; *CM*, 9-9-62; 9-10-62; 9-20-64; 9-27-64.
118. Robert J. Stevens, *Captain Bill, The Records and Writings of Captain William Henry Edwards (and others) Company A, 17th Regiment South Carolina Volunteers, Confederate States of America*, 27. (Hereafter cited as Stevens, *Captain Bill*.)
119. *CM*, 9-9-62.
120. Ibid., 9-13-62; 9-25-62; Stone, *Wandering*, 56.
121. *YE*, 1-28-63; UDC, *RR*, 11, 14.
122. Everson, *Far from Home*, 159; Thomas, *Rising Star*, 54.
123. Thomas, *Rising Star*, 56.
124. *Triweekly Watchman*, 1-5-63; *CM*, 12-23-62.
125. *Triweekly Watchman*, 1-5-63.
126. *YE*, 2-18-63.
127. *DSG*, 4-18-63.
128. *YE*, 4-22-63.
129. *CM*, 5-9-63.
130. UDC, *RR*, 8, 421; Sketches of the 23rd Regiment, SCDAH, S108121.
131. *LL*, 7-1-63.
132. *YE*, 8-5-63.
133. Ibid.
134. Ibid., 8-12-63.
135. Ibid., 9-9-63; *OR*, 1, 28, 2, 255.
136. *YE*, 8-26-63; 9-9-63; 9-16-63; *CM*, 8-18-63.
137. *OR*, 1, 28, 2, 309, 325.
138. Ibid., 1, 28, 2, 327, 345, 367; UDC, *RR*, 2, 215.
139. *OR*, 1, 28, 2, 590.
140. UDC, *RR*, 8, 433.
141. *YE*, 10-11-63; 10-28-63.
142. Ibid., 10-25-63.
143. *OR*, 1, 28, 2, 444, 468, 587, 529.
144. Ibid., 1, 28, 2, 444, 467, 587.
145. *YE*, 11-11-63.
146. *OR*, 1, 28, 2, 587-9.
147. Ibid., 1, 28, 2, 590.
148. *YE*, 11-11-63; *OR*, 1, 28, 2, 468, 587.
149. *OR*, 1, 28, 1, 160, 637.
150. Ibid., 1, 35, 1, 557-9.
151. Ibid., 1, 28, 2, 467, 587, 601; 1, 35, 1, 558.
152. Ibid., 1, 28, 2, 467, 529, 587, 601; OR1, 35, 1, 557.
153. Ibid., 1, 35, 1, 189-191.
154. Ibid., 1, 35, 1, 191.
155. Ibid., 1, 35, 1, 604.
156. Ibid., 1, 35, 1, 191.
157. Ibid., 1, 35, 1, 194-203.
158. Ibid., 1, 35, 1, 204.
159. Ibid., 1, 35, 1, 192.
160. Sketches of the 23rd Regiment, SCDAH, S108121.
161. *OR*, 1, 35, 1, 194, 196.
162. Ibid., 1, 35, 1, 196, 200.
163. Ibid., 1, 35, 1, 204.

164. Ibid., 1, 35, 1, 621.
165. *CM,* 2-24-64.
166. *OR,* 1, 35, 1, 372; 1, 35, 2, 422, 427, 430.
167. Ibid., 1, 35, 2, 435.
168. Ibid., 1, 35, 2, 436.
169. Ibid., 1, 35, 1, 193, 633.
170. Ibid., 1, 35, 2, 426.
171. *CMH,* 740; *CM,* 5-16-64; 5-21-64.
172. UDC, *RR,* 1, 89.
173. *YE,* 5-11-64; *OR,* 1, 35, 2, 425.
174. *YE,* 5-11-64.
175. Ibid., 5-19-64; 6-8-64.
176. Ibid., 6-1-64; 6-8-64; *DSG,* 5-31-64; *CDC,* 6-4-64; *CM,* 5-28-64.
177. *CM,* 6-24-64.
178. *EA,* 6-29-64; *CDC,* 7-20-64.
179. Joshua Hilary Hudson, *Sketches and Reminiscences,* 41. (Hereafter cited as Hudson, *Sketches.*)
180. *YE,* 8-17-64.
181. *LL,* 8-9-64.
182. *EA,* 8-10-64.
183. *CM,* 11-9-64.
184. Stevens, *Captain Bill,* 1, 62.

Chapter 12

1. *EA,* 6-25-62.
2. *OR,* 1, 14, 103.
3. Confederate Historian, "Annual Report," 59.
4. *CM,* 1-8-63.
5. SHSP, 14, 51.
6. Ibid., 14, 42.
7. *CDC,* 6-3-64.
8. SHSP, 14, 43.
9. Ibid., 14, 35–62.
10. *CV,* 23, 458; *CM,* 5-23-64.
11. *CM,* 5-23-64; *CDC,* 5-25-64.
12. *CDC,* 7-15-64.
13. Hagood, *Memoirs,* 226.
14. Thigpen, *Potter's Raid,* 227.
15. Hagood, *Memoirs,* 206.
16. Izlar, *Sketch,* 48.
17. SHSP, 16, 194; *DSG,* 6-6-64.
18. *CM,* 6-15-64; 6-24-64; Hagood, *Memoirs,* 263.
19. Izlar, *Sketch,* 60.
20. Hagood, *Memoirs,* 263.
21. *CM,* 7-7-64.
22. Kirkland, *Broken Fortunes,* 132; Hagood, *Memoirs,* 388.
23. Hagood, *Memoirs,* 206.
24. Ibid., 263.
25. Izlar, *Sketch,* 60.
26. SHSP, 14, 43.
27. *CM,* 2-21-60.
28. Ibid., 6-24-61.
29. Ibid., 6-20-61.
30. Ibid., 2-24-62.
31. Ibid., 5-5-62.
32. Ibid., 7-17-63; *CV,* 11, 419.

33. *CSR*, M267, 344.
34. *DSC*, 5-26-64.
35. Hagood, *Memoirs*, 230; *CV*, 11, 419.
36. SHSP, 16, 191; *CM*, 5-26-64.
37. *CDC*, 5-26-64.
38. Ibid., 1-25-65.
39. *CV*, 11, 419.
40. Izlar, *Sketch*, 106.
41. *CM*, 10-2-61.
42. Ibid., 2-24-62.
43. *Cyclopedia*, 486.
44. *CM*, 2-20-64.
45. *CV*, 35, 103.
46. *CM*, 5-2-62; 6-2-64.
47. *CSR*, M267, 344.
48. *CM*, 2-20-64; *CDC*, 2-20-64.
49. *CM*, 5-26-64.
50. Ibid., 6-2-64; *CV*, 35, 103.
51. *CDC*, 2-2-65.
52. *CM*, 9-7-63.
53. Ibid., 8-29-64.
54. Ibid., 9-27-64; 9-29-64; 10-22-64; *CDC*, 10-22-64.
55. *CM*, 9-10-63; 8-29-64.
56. Ibid., 7-31-61.
57. Ibid., 2-26-62.
58. Ibid., 4-21-62.
59. Ibid., 7-31-61.
60. *CSR*, M267, 349.
61. *CM*, 12-15-63.
62. Mac Wycoff, Website on South Carolina in the Civil War, http://www.members.ripod.com/
     mwycoff/. (Hereafter cited as Wycoff, Website.)
63. *CM*, 7-17-63.
64. *CM*, 5-16-64; *DSC*, 5-28-64.
65. *CM*, 7-29-64.
66. Ibid., 8-29-64.
67. Hagood, *Memoirs*, 300.
68. SHSP, 16, 134; Confederate Historian, "Annual Report," 57; Izlar, *Sketch*, 33; *CV*, 21, 350; 32,
     420.
69. Izlar, *Sketch*, 33.
70. UDC, *RR*, 5, 131.
71. *CM*, 9-7-63; *CMH*, 668.
72. *CDC*, 2-2-65.
73. *CV*, 21, 350; *Cyclopedia*, 350.
74. Confederate Historian, "Annual Report," 57.
75. *CM*, 4-10-62.
76. Ibid., 4-30-62.
77. Ibid., 5-20-62; *OR*, 1, 28, 1, 568; *CDC*, 10-15-62.
78. *CSR*, M267, 345.
79. *CM*, 9-9-63.
80. Ibid., 5-23-64; Hagood, *Memoirs*, 230.
81. *CV*, 23, 458.
82. Izlar, *Sketch*, 51.
83. *CDC*, 5-25-64.
84. UDC, *RR*, 2, 578.
85. SHSP, 14, 35, 16, 151.
86. UDC, *RR*, 12, 373.

87. *CSR*, M267, 343.
88. *CM*, 9-10-63.
89. Ibid., 9-10-63.
90. SHSP, 16, 134.
91. *CDC*, 2-25-64.
92. *CM*, 6-13-64.
93. Ibid.
94. *DSG*, 9-9-63; *CM*, 9-10-63; 1-25-65.
95. *CM*, 1-25-65.
96. Ibid.
97. *OR*, 1, 28, 2, 368.
98. Ibid., 1, 14, 103.
99. SHSP, 14, 37.
100. *CM*, 10-11-62; 11-4-62.
101. SHSP, 16, 152.
102. *OR*, 1, 14, 742.
103. *CM*, 1-29-63; 1-25-65; *CDC*, 1-24-63.
104. *CM*, 4-15-63.
105. *OR*, 1, 14, 289.
106. UDC, *RR*, 5, 516.
107. *CM*, 7-17-63; *CDC*, 7-17-63.
108. *OR*, 1, 28, 1, 81, 593, 595.
109. Ibid., 1, 28, 2, 245, 325.
110. Ibid., 1, 28, 1, 559; *CDC*, 9-9-63; 9-10-63; *CM*, 9-7-63.
111. Izlar, *Sketch*, 40.
112. *OR*, 1, 28, 1, 563; Ripley, *Chapman's Fort*, 38.
113. *OR*, 1, 28, 1, 136, 627.
114. Ibid., 1, 28, 2, 367.
115. *CM*, 11-2-63; John Johnson, *The Defense of Charleston Harbor including Fort Sumter and the Adjacent Islands, 1863–1865*, 172.
116. *OR*, 1, 28, 2, 467-8.
117. Ibid., 1, 28, 1, 154, 634.
118. Ibid., 1, 28, 1, 174, 180.
119. *CM*, 12-15-63.
120. *OR*, 1, 28, 1, 188; 1, 28, 2, 603.
121. *CM*, 1-29-64; *OR*, 1, 35, 1, 78.
122. *OR*, 1, 35, 1, 78.
123. Ibid., 1, 35, 1, 181, 187.
124. Ibid., 1, 35, 1, 189, 192.
125. Ibid., 1, 35, 1, 192, 195.
126. Ibid., 1, 35, 1, 196.
127. Ibid., 1, 35, 1, 200.
128. Ibid., 1, 35, 1, 206.
129. *CM*, 4-15-64.
130. *OR*, 1, 35, 2, 454; *CM*, 7-7-64; Ripley, *Chapman's Fort*, 144.
131. SHSP, 16, 179.

Chapter 13

1. *OR*, 1, 53, 257; *CM*, 11-4-62; 11-28-62.
2. *CM*, 2-9-64.
3. *OR*, 1, 53, 257; *CM*, 11-28-62.
4. *OR*, 1, 28, 2, 590.
5. *CSR*, M267, 354.
6. Hudson, *Sketches*, 60.
7. Edwards, *Seventeenth Regiment*, 47.
8. Stone, *Wandering*, 239.

9. Krick, *Lee's Colonels*, 349.
10. *CM*, 11-28-62.
11. UDC, *RR*, 9, 12.
12. Stone, *Wandering*, 180.
13. *OR*, 1, 53, 257; *CM*, 11-28-62.
14. *CSR*, M267, 350.
15. Krick, *Lee's Colonels*, 78; UDC, *RR*, 7, 66.
16. *CMH*, 701.
17. *CSR*, M267, 353.
18. *CMH*, 700.
19. Brock, *The Appomattox Roster*, 403.
20. *CM*, 11-28-62.
21. *CSR*, M267, 354.
22. Hudson, *Sketches*, 41.
23. *CM*, 11-28-62.
24. Ibid., 2-13-64.
25. Ibid., 9-29-64; *CDC*, 2-16-65.
26. *CSR*, M267, 351.
27. *CM*, 11-28-62.
28. Ibid., 5-28-64; UDC, *RR*, 9, 595.
29. Brock, *The Appomattox Roster*, 403.
30. *CM*, 1-20-63.
31. Ibid., 5-24-62.
32. Ibid., 11-28-62.
33. Ibid., 5-28-64.
34. *DSG*, 5-31-64.
35. Brock, *The Appomattox Roster*, 403.
36. *CM*, 11-28-63.
37. *CSR*, M267, 350.
38. *CM*, 8-4-63; 2-26-64.
39. *CSR*, M267, 350.
40. *CM*, 5-28-64; 8-2-64.
41. Ibid., 11-28-62.
42. Ibid., 2-16-64.
43. Ibid., 6-17-62.
44. Ibid., 11-28-62.
45. Kirkland, *Broken Fortunes*, 59.
46. *CM*, 11-28-62.
47. Ibid.
48. *CMH*, 700.
49. *CM*, 11-28-62; *CV*, 12, 544.
50. *CV*, 12, 544.
51. *CMH*, 699.
52. Sifakis, *Compendium*, 92.
53. *CM*, 11-4-62.
54. Ibid.
55. *OR*, 1, 14, 744.
56. Ibid., 1, 14, 823.
57. *CM*, 5-9-63.

Chapter 14

1. *CM*, 8-24-63.
2. *CDC*, 10-6-63.
3. UDC, *RR*, 3, 68.
4. *CM*, 8-26-64.

5. Krick, *Lee's Colonels*, 149.
6. Hagood, *Memoirs*, 207.
7. Phelps, *Charleston Battalion*, 10.
8. *CM*, 8-14-63.
9. Ibid., 5-16-64; 5-23-64; 6-2-64.
10. *CDC*, 8-26-64.
11. Ibid., 9-18-64.
12. *CM*, 8-26-64; 11-15-64.
13. *CDC*, 11-14-64.
14. Krick, *Lee's Colonels*, 56.
15. Hagood, *Memoirs*, 208.
16. Ibid.
17. Ibid.
18. *CM*, 5-24-64.
19. UDC, *RR*, 11, 286.
20. *CSR*, M267, 356.
21. Hagood, *Memoirs*, 208.
22. *CM*, 3-25-62.
23. Ibid., 10-7-63; Phelps, *Charleston Battalion*, 60.
24. *CM*, 6-17-62; 8-19-63.
25. Ibid., 5-16-64; 6-24-64.
26. Confederate Historian, "Annual Report," 72; SCDAH, *Roll of the Dead*; *CM*, 6-29-64; 7-13-64.
27. Hagood, *Memoirs*, 270.
28. *CM*, 7-13-64.
29. *CDC*, 7-15-64.
30. Hagood, *Memoirs*, 279.
31. *CM*, 7-13-64; 7-19-64.
32. Ibid., 3-25-62.
33. Ibid., 10-7-63.
34. *Memory Roll*; *CM*, 7-19-64.
35. *CM*, 6-17-62.
36. Ibid., 10-7-63.
37. Ibid., 5-23-64; 7-19-64; Phelps, *Charleston Battalion*, 94.
38. *CM*, 7-19-64; SCDAH, *Roll of the Dead*.
39. *CDC*, 7-25-64.
40. *CM*, 7-4-64; *CDC*, 7-2-64.
41. Kirkland, *Broken Fortunes*, 41.
42. *CM*, 5-11-61.
43. Ibid., 3-25-62.
44. Ibid., 10-7-63.
45. Ibid., 6-18-64; 7-14-64.
46. Hagood, *Memoirs*, 270.
47. *CM*, 1-23-65; *CMH*, 506.
48. *CM*, 10-7-63.
49. Ibid., 7-4-64.
50. Robert Chisolm, Papers, Greenville County Public Library Microfiche, SC973.7457, fiche 123.
51. *CM*, 10-7-63.
52. *CV*, 12, 124; *CM*, 5-24-64.
53. *CV*, 12, 124.
54. Ripley, *Chapman's Fort*, 308.
55. *CM*, 10-7-63.
56. *OR*, 1, 35, 2, 518.
57. *DSC*, 7-21-64; *CM*, 7-4-64; *CDC*, 7-29-64.
58. *CV*, 7, 317; *CM*, 9-29-64.
59. *CM*, 10-4-64; SHSP, 17, 46.
60. *CM*, 12-2-64.

61. Ibid., 7-23-63; 8-14-63.
62. Ibid., 10-7-63.
63. Hagood, *Memoirs,* 279; *CM,* 7-4-64; *CDC,* 7-15-64; 7-29-64.
64. *CV,* 7, 317.
65. *CM,* 9-29-64; *CDC,* 10-6-64.
66. *CM,* 12-2-64; *CV,* 7, 317.
67. J. Ogden Murray, *The Immortal 600,* 150.
68. *CM,* 9-26-64.
69. Ibid., 8-14-63.
70. Ibid., 10-7-63.
71. Ibid., 8-17-63.
72. Ibid., 10-7-63.
73. *OR,* 1, 28, 2, 368.
74. UDC, *RR,* 7, 17.
75. *OR,* 1, 28, 2, 444.
76. Ibid., 1, 28, 2, 603; 1, 35, 1, 557–9.
77. Ibid., 1, 28, 1, 174, 640.
78. Ibid., 1, 28, 1, 180, 188.
79. Ibid., 1, 35, 1, 178, 181.
80. Ibid., 1, 35, 1, 557–9; 1, 35, 2, 418.
81. Ibid., 1, 35, 1, 187, 191.
82. Ibid., 1, 35, 1, 192.
83. Ibid., 1, 35, 1, 195–6.
84. Ibid., 1, 35, 1, 196.
85. Ibid., 1, 35, 1, 200, 206.
86. Ibid., 1, 35, 2, 454; *CM,* 7-7-64.
87. Ibid., 1, 35, 2, 518.

Chapter 15

1. *CDC,* 3-20-62.
2. *CM,* 1-11-61.
3. Ibid., 4-7-63; *Memory Roll.*
4. *CM,* 5-31-61; 4-7-63.
5. Ibid., 5-1-61; 5-9-61.
6. *CMH,* 595.
7. Wycoff, *2nd South Carolina Infantry,* 18; *CM,* 2-12-62.
8. *CM,* 1-11-61.
9. Ibid., 6-18-61.
10. Ibid., 7-23-61.
11. *CDC,* 7-30-61.
12. *OR,* 1, 35, 2, 474.
13. Ripley, *Chapman's Fort,* 195; SHSP, 2, 202; *OR,* 1, 35, 1, 158.
14. *CM,* 8-10-61.
15. *CM,* 10-17-61.
16. *CV,* 12, 219; *CMH,* 868.
17. *CM,* 8-23-61.
18. *CV,* 12, 219.
19. *CM,* 8-10-61; 8-23-61.
20. Ibid., 8-23-61; *CMH,* 762, 361.
21. *CMH,* 868.
22. *CM,* 7-15-63.
23. Ibid., 7-17-63.
24. Ibid., 2-21-62; *CDC,* 2-21-62.
25. *CM,* 2-21-62; Compiled Service Records of Confederate Soldiers Who Served in Organizations from the State of South Carolina, National Archives and Records Administration. M267, 361. (Hereafter cited as CSR.)

26. *Acts*, 873.
27. *OR*, 1, 35, 2, 549.
28. *CM*, 9-5-61.
29. *CDC*, 1-13-62.
30. *CM*, 12-7-60; 9-7-61.
31. Ibid., 11-6-60.
32. Ibid., 1-10-61.
33. Ibid., 1-21-61.
34. Ibid., 2-23-61; *CM*, 4-17-61.
35. Ibid., 4-18-61.
36. Ibid., 4-23-61.
37. Ibid., 9-18-61.
38. Ibid., 4-24-61; 10-2-61; 1-1-62.
39. Bruce S. Allardice, *More Generals in Gray*, 248.
40. Hudson, *Sketches*, 32; *LL*, 11-27-61; *Horry Dispatch*, 9-26-61.
41. *LL*, 11-27-61.
42. *Horry Dispatch*, 9-26-61.
43. *CM*, 10-31-61.
44. Ibid., 11-27-61.
45. Ibid.
46. Ibid., 11-30-61.
47. Ibid., 10-24-61; *CDC*, 11-23-61.
48. *CDC*, 2-26-63.
49. *CM*, 5-8-62.
50. *CDC*, 11-23-61; *CM*, 12-4-61; *OR*, 1, 6, 360.
51. *OR*, 1, 6, 360.
52. *CM*, 3-21-62.
53. Ibid.

Chapter 16

1. *CM*, 5-19-62.
2. Ibid.
3. Ibid., 9-3-62.
4. Ibid., 5-19-62.
5. *CDC*, 2-24-62.
6. *CM*, 5-19-62.
7. Ibid.
8. Ibid., 4-11-62.
9. Ibid., 1-12-61.
10. Ibid., 1-30-62.
11. *CDC*, 2-24-62; *CM*, 2-26-62; 3-13-62.
12. *CDC*, 2-24-62.
13. *CM*, 4-3-62; *OR*, 1, 14, 487.
14. *CM*, 5-19-62.
15. Ibid., 6-24-62.
16. Ibid., 3-31-62.
17. Sifakis, *Compendium*, 46.
18. *OR*, 1, 14, 25.

Chapter 17

1. *CM*, 9-3-62.
2. Ulysses Robert Brooks, ed., *Stories of the Confederacy*, 221.
3. Ibid., 224.
4. *CM*, 5-19-62.
5. *CV*, 27, 211; Brooks, *Stories*, 221.

6. Thigpen, *Potter's Raid*, 207.
7. Ripley, *Chapman's Fort*, 301.
8. McSwain, *Crumbling Defenses*, 97.
9. *CM*, 5-19-62.
10. *OR*, 1, 35, 1, 269.
11. Ripley, *Chapman's Fort*, 300.
12. *OR*, 1, 35, 1, 149.
13. *CM*, 9-3-62.
14. Ibid., 3-31-62.
15. Ibid.
16. *CSR*, M267, 16.
17. *CM*, 6-24-62.
18. *CSR*, M267, 18.
19. Brooks, *Stories*, 221.
20. Kirkland, *Broken Fortunes*, 45.
21. *CM*, 4-3-62.
22. *CM*, 12-10-60; 5-19-62.
23. *OR*, 1, 14, 487.
24. *CM*, 9-3-62.
25. Ibid., 9-19-64.
26. Ibid., 2-20-61; 12-22-63.
27. Ibid., 9-3-62.
28. *OR*, 1, 35, 1, 441.
29. Ibid., 1, 14, 487.
30. *CM*, 5-1-61.
31. Ibid., 5-16-89.
32. Ibid., 4-24-61.
33. Ibid., 5-1-61; 1-30-62.
34. Ibid., 2-27-62.
35. *CDC*, 3-13-62.
36. *CM*, 4-8-62; *CDC*, 4-10-62.
37. *CM*, 4-8-62.
38. *OR*, 1, 14, 487.
39. *CM*, 3-13-62.
40. Ibid., 2-25-62; 9-5-64.
41. *CDC*, 2-24-62; *CM*, 2-26-62; 3-13-62.
42. *OR*, 1, 14, 487.
43. *CMH*, 678.
44. *OR*, 1, 14, 487.
45. Brooks, *Stories*, 224.
46. *CM*, 1-30-62.
47. *OR*, 1, 14, 487.
48. *CM*, 9-3-62.
49. Ibid., 1-12-61.
50. *OR*, 1, 28, 2, 602.
51. Brooks, *Stories*, 223; *OR*, 1, 35, 2, 464.
52. *OR*, 1, 35, 2, 464.
53. Brooks, *Stories*, 223.
54. *OR*, 1, 44, 875.
55. Ibid., 1, 44, 997.
56. Sifakis, *Compendium*, 20.
57. *OR*, 1, 44, 875.
58. Ibid., 1, 47, 3, 712.
59. Ibid., 1, 47, 1, 1065.
60. Brooks, *Stories*, 223.

61. *CM*, 5-16-1889.
62. Brooks, *Stories*, 224.
63. Thomas, *Rising Star*, 33.
64. *CDC*, 8-19-62.
65. *CM*, 10-27-62; 1-8-64; *OR*, 1, 14, 180; *CDC*, 10-27-62.
66. *OR*, 1, 14, 660.
67. Johnson, *Charleston Harbor*, 36; *OR*, 1, 14, 822.
68. *OR*, 1, 14, 309.
69. Ibid., 1, 28, 1, 149; 1, 28, 2, 169.
70. Ibid., 1, 28, 2, 246, 326, 467.
71. Ibid., 1, 28, 1, 751
72. Ibid., 1, 28, 2, 602.
73. Ibid., 1, 31, 1, 558.
74. *CM*, 2-11-64; 2-15-64; *OR*, 1, 35, 1, 558.
75. *OR*, 1, 35, 2, 457.
76. Brooks, *Stories*, 227.
77. *OR*, 1, 35, 2, 599.
78. Ibid., 1, 35, 1, 441.
79. *CDC*, 8-27-64; *OR*, 1, 35, 1, 441.
80. *OR*, 1, 35, 1, 124; SHSP, 2, 194.
81. *CMH*, 679.
82. Ripley, *Chapman's Fort*, 200.
83. *OR*, 1, 35, 2, 644.
84. *CM*, 12-10-64.
85. Brooks, *Stories*, 223.
86. *CM*, 12-16-64.
87. *OR*, 1, 44, 961; UDC, *RR*, 11, 352.
88. *The Civil War in Western South Carolina December 1864–January 1865*, 9. (Hereafter cited as *The Civil War in Western SC*.)
89. Brooks, *Stories*, 228.
90. *OR*, 1, 44, 970.
91. Ibid., 1, 44, 993; *The Civil War in Western SC*, 24.
92. Brooks, *Stories*, 225.
93. *OR*, 1, 47, 2, 1033.
94. Ibid., 1, 47, 2, 1053, 1081.
95. CM, 2-2-65.
96. *OR*, 1, 47, 2, 1182.
97. Ibid., 1, 47, 2, 1197.
98. Brooks, *Stories*, 225.
99. *OR*, 1, 47, 2, 1421.
100. Ibid., 1, 47, 3, 753.
101. Brooks, *Stories*, 226, 230.
102. *OR*, 1, 47, 1, 1065.

Chapter 18

1. *CDC*, 12-28-62.
2. *CM*, 12-23-62; 12-27-62.
3. Ibid., 12-23-62.
4. Ibid., 12-27-62.
5. Halliburton, *Saddle Soldiers*, 153.
6. Ulysses Robert Brooks, ed., *Butler and His Cavalry in the War of Secession 1861–1865*, 332.
7. *CV*, 7, 317; *CM*, 12-27-62.
8. *OR*, 1, 14, 307.
9. *CM*, 2-10-64.
10. *CDC*, 10-6-64; *CM*, 6-25-64.

11. *CM,* 12-2-64; *CDC,* 12-16-64; Krick, *Lee's Colonels,* 130.
12. UDC, *RR,* 9, 496.
13. *CMH,* 727.
14. Ibid.; Halliburton, *Saddle Soldiers,* 183.
15. UDC, *RR,* 9, 496.
16. *CM,* 6-6-64.
17. UDC, *RR,* 7132; UDC, *RR,* 9, 497; Halliburton, *Saddle Soldiers,* 183.
18. UDC, *RR,* 9, 497.
19. Halliburton, *Saddle Soldiers,* 183.
20. *CDC,* 1-24-62.
21. Ibid.; *CM,* 1-6-64.
22. *CM,* 5-6-62; 12-27-62.
23. *CSR,* M267, 24.
24. *CM,* 1-6-64.
25. Ibid., 12-27-62; 6-6-64.
26. Calhoun, "Liberty," 149.
27. Ibid., 183.
28. Brooks, *Butler,* 198, 300.
29. *CV,* 24, 342; *CM,* 12-27-62; 6-6-64.
30. *CDC,* 9-21-64; *CV,* 24, 78.
31. *CV,* 7, 317.
32. *CM,* 8-4-64.
33. *CDC,* 10-6-64.
34. *CM,* 12-2-64; *CV,* 24, 79; *CDC,* 12-16-64.
35. *CV,* 24, 373.
36. Ibid., 24, 78, 373.
37. Ibid., 24, 79, 373.
38. *CM,* 12-27-62.
39. *CSR,* M267, 26.
40. *CM,* 6-6-64.
41. Ibid., 12-27-62.
42. *CSR,* M267, 27.
43. *CM,* 6-6-64.
44. UDC, *RR,* 3, 49, 3, 395.
45. *CM,* 1-6-64; *Memory Roll.*
46. *CM,* 12-27-62; 6-6-64; William Stokes, "Sketch of Co. G, 4th South Carolina Cavalry," South Carolina Department of Archives and History, S108121. (Hereafter cited as "Sketch of Co. G, SCDAH, S108121.)
47. *LL,* 2-5-62; 5-10-64.
48. *CM,* 1-6-64.
49. Ibid., 12-27-62; 6-6-64.
50. Ibid., 12-27-62; 6-6-64.
51. Ibid., 4-24-61.
52. Halliburton, *Saddle Soldiers,* 52.
53. UDC, UDC, *RR,* 9, 241; Halliburton, *Saddle Soldiers,* 142.
54. *CM,* 2-15-62.
55. Ibid., 5-15-62.
56. *YE,* 6-5-62.
57. *CM,* 1-6-64.
58. *CV,* 24, 538.
59. *CM,* 6-6-64.
60. Sifakis, *Compendium,* 43.
61. *OR,* 1, 47, 1, 1065.
62. Ibid., 1, 14, 822, 921.
63. *CM,* 12-23-62; Halliburton, *Saddle Soldiers,* 63.

64. *OR*, 1, 14, 824.
65. Ibid., 1, 14, 282.
66. Halliburton, *Saddle Soldiers*, 83.
67. *OR*, 1, 14, 287.
68. Ibid.; UDC, *RR*, 8, 405.
69. Halliburton, *Saddle Soldiers*, 85.
70. *CM*, 4-24-63; Halliburton, *Saddle Soldiers*, 84.
71. *OR*, 1, 14, 294.
72. Ibid., 1, 14, 308.
73. Ibid., 1, 28, 2, 326, 602; 1, 35, 1, 558.
74. Ibid., 1, 28, 1, 149; 1, 28, 2, 326, 467, 602; 1, 35, 1, 558.
75. Ibid., 1, 28, 729.
76. Halliburton, *Saddle Soldiers*, 111; *LL*, 12-2-63; *OR*, 1, 28, 729, 746.
77. Halliburton, *Saddle Soldiers*, 131; *OR*, 1, 35, 2, 362.
78. *OR*, 1, 35, 2, 402.
79. *LL*, 5-10-64.
80. Halliburton, *Saddle Soldiers*, 138.
81. "Sketch of Co. G," SCDAH, S108121.
82. Halliburton. *Saddle Soldiers*, 180; Stokes, "Sketch of Co. G," SCDAH, S108121; Edward L. Wells, *A Sketch of the Charleston Light Dragoons, from the earliest formation of the corps*, 34–37. (Hereafter cited as Wells, *Sketch of CLD*.)
83. *CM*, 5-20-64; 6-6-64; *CDC*, 9-21-64.
84. Wells, *Sketch of CLD*, 41.
85. *CM*, 6-6-64; 8-25-64; *CDC*, 9-21-64; Wells, *Sketch of CLD*, 51–53.
86. Halliburton, *Saddle Soldiers*, 149; Brooks, *Butler*, 192.
87. Stokes, "Sketch of Co. *G*," SCDAH, S108121.
88. Ibid.
89. *CV*, 2, 178.
90. Halliburton, *Saddle Soldiers*, 164.
91. Freeman, *Lee's Lieutenants*, 3, 589; Halliburton, *Saddle Soldiers*, 166.
92. Brooks, *Butler*, 303ff; Stokes, "Sketch of Co. *G*," SCDAH, S108121.
93. *CM*, 10-12-64.
94. *CM*, 11-2-64; Halliburton, *Saddle Soldiers*, 179; *CDC*, 11-3-64.
95. *CDC*, 12-8-64; Baker, *Cadets in Gray*, 129.
96. Halliburton, *Saddle Soldiers*, 186.
97. Ibid., 191.
98. Ibid., xiii; Stokes, "Sketch of Co. G," SCDAH, S108121;
99. Halliburton, *Saddle Soldiers*, 199.
100. UDC, *RR*, 8, 450; Thigpen, *Potter's Raid*, 3.

Chapter 19

1. *CM*, 1-27-63.
2. Brooks, *Stories*, 234.
3. *CM*, 1-27-63; *CDC*, 1-29-63.
4. *CM*, 1-27-63.
5. A,B. Mulligan, *My Dear Mother and Sisters, The Civil War Letters of Captain A.B.* Mulligan *Company B, 5th South Carolina Cavalry, Butler's Division, Hampton's Corps, 1861–1865*, 82. (Hereafter Mulligan, *My Dear Mother*.")
6. *CV*, 16, 183.
7. *CM*, 9-1-64.
8. *CV*, 16, 183.
9. Halliburton, *Saddle Soldiers*, 173; C.M. Calhoun, "Liberty Dethroned," 143. (Hereafter cited as Calhoun, "Liberty.")
10. Calhoun, "Liberty," 143.
11. *CV*, 16, 183.
12. Halliburton, *Saddle Soldiers*, 174.

13. Calhoun, "Liberty," 151.
14. Brooks, *Butler*, 474.
15. *CDC*, 6-3-64; *DSC*, 6-14-64.
16. Mulligan, *My Dear Mother*, 141.
17. *CM*, 9-1-64.
18. Ibid., 10-31-64; Halliburton, *Saddle Soldiers*, 178.
19. Brooks, *Butler*, 372.
20. *CDC*, 11-4-64.
21. *CM*, 10-31-64; 11-4-64.
22. Calhoun, "Liberty," 148; *CDC*, 11-4-64.
23. Mulligan, *My Dear Mother*, 141.
24. *CDC*, 9-6-64; Halliburton, *Saddle Soldiers*, 167.
25. Confederate Historian, "Annual Report," 78.
26. Halliburton, *Saddle Soldiers*, 167.
27. Brooks, *Butler*, 66.
28. *CV*, 18, 483.
29. Mulligan, *My Dear Mother*, 166.
30. Ibid., 167.
31. *CMH*, 539.
32. Brooks, *Butler*, 541; *CV*, 18, 483.
33. *Memory Roll.*
34. *CM*, 7-23-60.
35. Ibid., 2-7-61; UDC, *RR*, 7, 358.
36. UDC, *RR*, 7, 207.
37. *CDC*, 11-3-64.
38. Mulligan, *My Dear Mother*, 171. In 1969, Mulligan's daughter taught seventh grade science to the author at Columbia's Keenan Junior High School.
39. *CM*, 1-28-62.
40. *CDC*, 4-5-62.
41. SCDAH, *Roll of the Dead.*
42. *CM*, 3-10-64; 5-27-64.
43. Ibid., 3-10-64; *CDC*, 3-10-64.
44. *CM*, 5-27-64; *CDC*, 5-27-64.
45. Kirkland, *Broken Fortunes*, 371.
46. Melton, *War*, 279.
47. *CDC*, 12-9-61; *YE*, 1-31-61.
48. Ibid., 12-9-61.
49. Ibid., 2-14-62.
50. *CM*, 11-3-62; 5-27-64; 7-22-64.
51. Ibid., 3-19-64; 5-27-64.
52. UDC, *RR*, 7, 358.
53. *CM*, 5-27-64.
54. Bill Brasington, Website, "South Carolina State Troops Seed Corn Units, 1864–1865," wwww:// geocities.com/sc_seedcorn.
55. *CSR*, M267, 32.
56. Sifakis, *Compendium*, 43.
57. Ibid., 44.
58. *OR*, 1, 47, 1, 1065.
59. Mulligan, *My Dear Mother*, 70.
60. Ibid., 80.
61. Ibid., 96.
62. Ibid., 115.
63. *OR*, 1, 14, 283.
64. Johnson, *Charleston Harbor*, 36; *OR*, 1, 14, 283.
65. *OR*, 1, 14, 822.

66. Ibid., 1, 28, 159; 1, 28, 2, 162.
67. Ibid., 1, 28, 591.
68. Sifakis, *Compendium*, 45.
69. *OR*, 1, 28, 386, 439.
70. Ibid., 1, 28, 2, 245.
71. Ibid., 1, 28, 2, 245, 325, 367, 467, 601.
72. *CM*, 1-29-64; *OR*, 1, 35, 1, 558.
73. *YE*, 3-9-64.
74. *OR*, 1, 35, 2, 362.
75. Ripley, *Chapman's Fort*, 136.
76. *CDC*, 8-25-64.
77. *CM*, 5-26-64; 5-27-64; *CMH*, 720; *CDC*, 8-24-64.
78. *CM*, 7-22-64; *CDC*, 6-3-64; 9-21-64.
79. *DSG*, 6-6-64; *CDC*, 9-21-64.
80. Brooks, *Butler*, 190.
81. Halliburton, *Saddle Soldiers*, 149; Brooks, *Butler*, 192.
82. *CV*, 2, 178.
83. Mulligan, *My Dear Mother*, 143.
84. *CDC*, 9-6-64.
85. Freeman, *Lee's Lieutenants*, 3,589; Halliburton, *Saddle Soldiers*, 166.
86. Mulligan, *My Dear Mother*, 144.
87. Brooks, *Butler*, 303ff.
88. *CDC*, 10-12-64.
89. *CM*, 10-12-64.
90. Ibid., 11-2-64; *CDC*, 11-3-64.
91. *CDC*, 12-8-64; Baker, *Cadets in Gray*, 129.
92. Halliburton, *Saddle Soldiers*, 184, 186.
93. *CDC*, 12-28-64; 1-6-65.
94. Confederate Historian, "Annual Report," 77.
95. *OR*, 1, 47, 2, 1183.
96. *EA*, 5-17-65.
97. *CV*, 28, 170.
98. Brooks, *Butler*, 541; *CV*, 18, 483.

Chapter 20

1. UDC, *RR*, 10, 3.
2. Confederate Historian, "Annual Report," 66.
3. *OR*, 1, 14, 115.
4. Ibid., 1, 6, 426.
5. Ibid.
6. Ibid.; Roster of Officers, Confederate Historian, South Carolina Department of Archives and History, S108079.
7. *CM*, 12-27-62.
8. UDC, *RR*, 9, 496; *CMH*, 727.
9. *OR*, 1, 6, 426.
10. *CM*, 8-27-64.
11. Ibid., 12-27-62.
12. UDC, *RR*, 3, 491.
13. Sifakis, *Compendium*, 47.
14. *OR*, 1, 6, 426.
15. *CM*, 11-12-62; UDC, *RR*, 8, 405, 10, 3.
16. UDC, *RR*, 8, 405, 10, 3.
17. *OR*, 1, 14, 114.
18. Ibid., 1, 14, 921.
19. UDC, *RR*, 8, 406.

Chapter 21

1. *CM*, 3-25-62.
2. *CDC*, 4-14-62.
3. *CM*, 3-25-62.
4. *OR*, 1, 14, 38, 112, 602
5. *CDC*, 4-11-62; *CM*, 4-14-62.
6. *CDC*, 4-14-62.
7. Ibid., 6-18-61.
8. *CM*, 6-11-61; 9-4-61; *CDC*, 6-11-61.
9. *CMH*, 677; *CM*, 3-10-64; *CDC*, 3-10-64.
10. *CDC*, 4-14-62; 3-10-64; 4-21-64; *CM*, 3-10-64.
11. *CM*, 3-10-64.
12. Ibid., 2-15-62; *CDC*, 2-14-62.
13. *CM*, 2-18-62.
14. Ibid., 3-31-62.
15. Ibid.
16. *CDC*, 4-11-62.
17. Cauthen, ed., *Journals*, 155.
18. Mulligan, *My Dear Mother*, 33.
19. *CM*, 11-3-62.
20. Mulligan, *My Dear Mother*, 15-16; *CDC*, 2-17-62.
21. *CM*, 2-15-62; *CDC*, 4-11-62.
22. Mulligan, *My Dear Mother*, 15.
23. *CDC*, 2-17-62; Mulligan, *My Dear Mother*, 15.
24. Mulligan, *My Dear Mother*, 34.
25. *CM*, 5-24-62.
26. *CDC*, 4-5-62.
27. Ibid., 4-11-62.
28. *CM*, 1-28-62.
29. Ibid., 9-18-61; 5-23-62.
30. *CDC*, 4-28-62.
31. Mulligan, *My Dear Mother*, 16, 24.
32. *CM*, 5-30-62; Halliburton, *Saddle Soldiers*, 32.
33. *CM*, 6-14-62; *OR*, 1, 14, 38.
34. Mulligan, *My Dear Mother*, 28.
35. *CM*, 8-27-62.
36. Ibid., 1-6-64; Mulligan, *My Dear Mother*, 51.
37. Mulligan, *My Dear Mother*, 58.
38. *OR*, 1, 14, 700.

Chapter 22

1. Tower, *A Carolinian Goes To War*, 11.
2. *CM*, 1-14-63.
3. Ibid., 6-2-62.
4. *OR*, 1, 28, 2, 325, 367, 467, 601; 1, 35, 1, 558; 1, 35, 2, 598, 644.
5. Ibid., 1, 44, 875.
6. *CM*, 10-23-60.
7. Tower, *A Carolinian Goes To War*, 11.
8. *OR*, 1, 6, 352.
9. Ibid., 1, 6, 426.
10. *CM*, 5-31-62.
11. *CDC*, 7-28-62; *CM*, 4-21-62; 8-1-62.
12. *OR*, 1, 28, 1, 159; 1, 28, 2, 246, 327, 467, 602; 1, 35, 1, 558.
13. Ibid., 1, 35, 2, 362.

14. *CM*, 51-61; 5-16-89.
15. Ibid., 4-24-61.
16. Ibid., 5-1-61; 1-30-62.
17. Ibid., 2-27-62.
18. Ibid., 4-8-62.
19. *CDC*, 2-24-64; *CM*, 2-22-64.
20. *OR*, 4, 2, 82-83.
21. *CM*, 10-27-62; 1-6-64; *CDC*, 10-28-62.
22. *OR*, 1, 28, 1, 592.
23. Ibid., 1, 28, 2, 246, 326, 602; 1, 35, 1, 558.
24. Ibid., 1, 35, 2, 457.
25. Ibid., 1, 35, 1, 169.
26. Ibid., 1, 35, 2, 598, 644; 1, 44, 875.
27. Ibid., 1, 44, 890.
28. Ibid., 1, 44, 909.
29. Ibid., 1, 44, 970.
30. Ibid., 1, 44, 992, 999; 1, 47, 2, 989.
31. Ibid., 1, 47, 2, 1206.
32. *CM*, 4-24-61.
33. Halliburton, *Saddle Soldiers*, 52.
34. *OR*, 1, 1, 36; UDC, *RR*, 9, 241.
35. *OR*, 1, 53, 173.
36. *CDC*, 2-14-62; *CM*, 2-15-62.
37. *CDC*, 3-27-62.
38. *CM*, 5-15-62; *CDC*, 5-15-62.
39. *YE*, 6-5-62.
40. *OR*, 1, 14, 624.
41. *CM*, 1-6-64; *CDC*, 1-25-62.
42. *CV*, 24, 538.
43. *CM*, 9-18-61.
44. Ibid., 9-17-61.
45. Cauthen, ed., *Journals*, 128.
46. *CM*, 11-10-60; UDC, *RR*, 8, 371.
47. UDC, *RR*, 8, 371.
48. *Acts*, 868.
49. *CM*, 4-26-61.
50. *OR*, 1, 53, 158.
51. *CDC*, 9-9-61; *CM*, 9-10-61.
52. Louise Haskell Daly, *Alexander Cheves Haskell, The Portrait of a Man*, 239. (Hereafter cited as Daly, *Portrait*.)
53. *CM*, 10-2-61.
54. Ibid., 9-29-61.
55. Ibid., 10-22-61.
56. *CDC*, 1-15-62; *CM*, 1-15-62.
57. *CDC*, 1-15-62; *CM*, 1-15-62.
58. *CM*, 2-17-62.
59. Ibid., 5-30-62; *OR*, 1, 14, 31.
60. *CM*, 8-2-62.
61. Ibid., 10-27-62; 1-6-64; *OR*, 1, 14, 624; *CDC*, 10-25-62.
62. *CM*, 12-16-62.
63. Ibid., 5-29-63.
64. Ibid.
65. *OR*, 1, 14, 298.
66. Ibid., 1, 28, 1, 149; 1, 28, 2, 246, 326, 467, 602; 1, 35, 1, 558; 1, 35, 2, 346.
67. Ibid., 1, 28, 1, 174.

68. Ibid., 1, 35, 2, 357.
69. Ibid., 1, 35, 2, 362.
70. Ibid., 1, 35, 2, 402.
71. *CDC*, 5-5-64.
72. Laylon Wayne Jordan and Elizabeth H. Stringfellow. *A Place Called St. John's: The Story of John's, Edisto, Wadmalaw, Kiawah, and Seabrook Islands of South Carolina*, 142.
73. *CSR*, M267, 56.
74. *OR*, 1, 14, 202.
75. Ibid., 1, 28, 1, 149; 1, 28, 2, 169, 246, 326, 467, 544.
76. Ibid., 1, 28, 2, 603; 1, 35, 1, 559; 1, 35, 2, 458, 599.
77. *CM*, 2-15-64.
78. *OR*, 1, 35, 2, 447.
79. *CM*, 8-22-64; Ripley, *Chapman's Fort*, 229; *OR*, 1, 35, 1, 269.
80. *OR*, 1, 44, 875; 1, 47, 2, 1071.
81. Ibid., 1, 47, 1, 1061.
82. *CMH*, 597.

Chapter 23

1. *CM*, 7-21-62.
2. Ibid., 11-4-62.
3. *OR*, 1, 28, 2, 325.
4. Ripley, *Chapman's Fort*, viii.
5. *CM*, 7-21-62.
6. *CSR*, M2367, 84.
7. *CV*, 24, 342.
8. *CM*, 9-3-63.
9. *OR*, 1, 47, 2, 1142.
10. Ripley, *Chapman's Fort*, 247.
11. Ibid., xiii.
12. *CM*, 7-21-62.
13. Ibid., 8-14-63.
14. A.P Ford and M.J. Ford, *Life in the Confederate Army*, 52. (Hereafter cited as Ford, *Life*.)
15. *OR*, 1, 14, 201.
16. *CM*, 7-21-62.
17. *CM*, 8-8-64.
18. Ripley, *Chapman's Fort*, 155.
19. *CM*, 7-21-62.
20. Ibid., 8-8-64.
21. *CM*, 5-1-61; 5-9-61.
22. Ford, *Life*, 7.
23. *CM*, 2-10-62; *CDC*, 2-10-62.
24. *CDC*, 6-17-62.
25. *CM*, 5-10-61.
26. *CMH*, 489; *CDC*, 1-23-63.
27. *CM*, 1-21-63; 1-23-63; 9-7-64.
28. Ripley, *Chapman's Fort*, 181.
29. *CMH*, 725.
30. Ripley, *Chapman's Fort*, 318.
31. Woodward, *Mary Chesnut*, 210.
32. *OR*, 1, 44, 875.
33. *OR*, 1, 44, 997.
34. Ibid., 1, 47, 2, 1070.
35. Ibid., 1, 47, 1, 1063.
36. Ford, *Life*, 13.
37. *CM*, 10-23-62; 11-4-62.

38. Ibid., 2-2-63; *OR*, 1, 14, 201.
39. *CDC*, 2-11-63.
40. *OR*, 1, 14, 822.
41. Ibid., 1, 28, 2, 245, 325.
42. Ripley, *Chapman's Fort*, 1.
43. *CDC*, 7-17-63.
44. *OR*, 1, 28, 1, 454, 467, 518; 1, 28, 2, 213.
45. Ibid., 1, 28, 1, 439, 494.
46. Ibid., 1, 28, 1, 383, 400.
47. *CM*, 8-14-63; *OR*, 1, 28, 2, 325.
48. *OR*, 1, 28, 1, 557.
49. Ibid., 1, 28, 2, 367.
50. Ibid., 1, 28, 2, 468-9.
51. Ibid.
52. Ibid., 1, 28, 2, 563; 1, 53, 20.
53. Ibid., 1, 28, 2, 603; 1, 35, 1, 559.
54. Ripley, *Chapman's Fort*, 120.
55. *OR*, 1, 35, 1, 642.
56. Ibid., 1, 35, 2, 457.
57. Ibid., 1, 35, 2, 598.
58. Ripley, *Chapman's Fort*, 155.
59. *OR*, 1, 35, 1, 400.
60. Ibid., 1, 35, 2, 599, 645.
61. *CM*, 9-7-64.
62. *OR*, 1, 35, 2, 598, 645.
63. *CM*, 2-11-65.
64. Ford, *Life*, 45.
65. *OR*, 1, 47, 3, 781.

Chapter 24

1. SHSP, 26, 233.
2. *Memory Roll.*
3. *CM*, 2-11-64.
4. Ibid., 12-11-63; 12-15-63.
5. UDC, *RR*, 11, 10.
6. *CM*, 5-15-63.
7. Ibid., 12-9-61.
8. Ibid., 5-30-62; 6-9-62.
9. *OR*, 1, 14, 112.
10. Ibid., 1, 14, 118; Johnson, *Charleston Harbor*, Appendix A, iv; *CDC*, 8-22-62.
11. *YE*, 8-27-62; CC 8-29-62.
12. *CM*, 10-24-62; *CDC*, 10-25-62.
13. *OR*, 1, 14, 282; *CM*, 4-11-63.
14. Ibid., 1, 28, 1, 149; 1, 28, 2, 246, 326, 467, 602; 1, 35, 1, 558; 1, 35, 2, 457, 599, 544.
15. Ibid., 1, 28, 1, 592.
16. Ibid., 1, 44, 875.
17. *CM*, 12-5-64; *The Civil War in Western SC*, 8.
18. *OR*, 1, 44, 993, 1000.
19. Ibid., 1, 44, 997.
20. Ibid., 1, 47, 2, 1071.
21. Ibid., 1, 47, 1, 1064; 1, 47, 3, 732.
22. Ibid., 1, 47, 1, 1085; 1, 47, 3, 780; *EA*, 4-5-65.
23. Krick, *Lee's Colonels*, 95.
24. *OR*, 1, 47, 1, 1066.
25. *CM*, 9-19-61.

26. *Triweekly Watchman*, 2-9-62.
27. *CDC*, 2-10-63; Sifakis, *Compendium*, 16.
28. *OR*, 1, 47, 2, 1069.
29. Sifakis, *Compendium*, 16.
30. *CM*, 1-11-61.
31. Ibid., 4-7-63; *Memory Roll*.
32. *CM*, 5-1-61; 5-9-61.
33. Ibid., 5-13-61.
34. *CMH*, 595.
35. Wyckoff, *2nd South Carolina Infantry*, 18; *CM*, 2-12-62; 6-6-62; *CV*, 3, 281.
36. *CM*, 7-21-62.
37. *CMH*, 595.
38. *CM*, 2-20-64.
39. Ibid., 7-2-62.
40. Ibid., 2-11-63.
41. *CDC*, 2-12-63.
42. Ibid.
43. *CV*, 1, 3, 38.
44. *CM*, 7-18-63.
45. Ibid., 3-24-62.
46. Ibid., 6-2-62.
47. *CMH*, 596.
48. *CM*, 7-4-62; *CDC*, 7-4-62.
49. *CM*, 9-29-62.
50. Ibid., 6-19-63.
51. Ibid., 7-1-61; Brooks, *Stories*, 293.
52. *CM*, 2 7-61.
53. Ibid., 5-15-61; 7-1-61.
54. *CMH*, 679.
55. *CM*, 6-24-61.
56. *CDC*, 6-24-61; Brooks, *Stories*, 293.
57. *OR*, 1, 32, 3, 693.
58. *CM*, 11-1-64.
59. *OR*, 1, 30, 1, 230.
60. Baker, *Cadets in Gray*, 19.
61. *CM*, 7-15-63; 7-17-63; Baker, *Cadets in Gray*, 19.
62. *CM*, 11-1-64.
63. Sifakis, *Compendium*, 17.
64. *OR*, 1, 24, 3, 1041.
65. Ibid., 1, 30, 2, 14; 1, 30, 4, 516.
66. Ibid., 1, 30, 1, 230; 1, 30, 2, 244 .
67. Ibid., 1, 31, 3, 620.
68. Ibid., 1, 31, 2, 660; 1, 31, 3, 807; 1, 31, 3, 827, 886.
69. Ibid., 1, 32, 2, 820, 589; 1, 32, 3, 687, 871; 1, 39, 2, 826, 857;1, 45, 1, 669; *CM*, 11-1-64.
70. L.M. Bell, ed., *Rebels In Grey, Soldiers from Pickens District 1861–1865*, 81.
71. Walter Brian Cisco, *States Right Gist, A South Carolina General of the Civil War*, 91; *OR*, 1, 14, 822, 925.
72. *CM*, 5-22-63.
73. *OR*, 1, 24, 3, 883, 920.
74. Ibid., 1, 52, 2, 485.
75. Ibid., 4, 2, 816.
76. Ibid., 1, 30, 2, 14.
77. Ibid., 1, 31, 2, 402, 480–487; Eugene W. Jones, Jr., *Enlisted for The War, The Struggles of the Gallant 24th Regiment, South Carolina Volunteers, Infantry 1861–1865*, 138.
78. *YE*, 12-9-63.

79. *OR,* 1, 32, 3, 693-5, 731.
80. *CM,* 11-1-64.
81. *OR,* 1, 39, 1, 826.
82. Ibid.
83. Ibid., 1, 45, 1, 479.
84. *CM,* 10-9-61; Confederate Historian, "Annual Report," 61
85. *CM,* 8-18-60; 7-24-61.
86. Ibid., 7-24-61.
87. Ibid., 11-11-61.
88. *CSR,* M267, 106.
89. *OR,* 1, 1, 36.
90. *CM,* 10-9-61.
91. Ibid., 8-18-60; 2-20-61; 6-17-62.
92. *CDC,* 4-28-62.
93. *CM,* 6-17-62.
94. *CDC,* 6-17-62; *CMH,* 747; *CM,* 6-17-62.
95. *OR,* 1, 44, 997.
96. Ibid., 1, 47, 2, 1071.
97. Ibid., 1, 28, 2, 161.
98. Ibid., 1, 44, 875; 1, 47, 2, 1073.
99. Ibid., 1, 44, 997.
100. Ibid., 1, 14, 581; *CDC,* 10-6-62.
101. *OR,* 1, 14, 822.
102. Ibid., 1, 28, 1, 159; OR1, 28, 2, 246.
103. Ibid., 1, 28, 2, 325, 367, 467, 601; 1, 35, 1, 559; 1, 35, 2, 457, 598.
104. Ibid., 1, 35, 1, 170; SHSP, 2, 202.
105. *OR,* 1, 35, 2, 644.
106. Ibid., 1, 44, 875.
107. Ibid., 1, 44, 974, 1000.
108. Ibid., 1, 47, 3, 782.
109. *CDC,* 4-28-62.
110. *OR,* 1, 14, 822.
111. *CMH,* 569; *OR,* 1, 28, 1, 159; 1, 28, 2, 246, 327, 468, 602; 1, 35, 1, 558; 1, 35, 2, 457, 644.
112. *CM,* 10-10-63.
113. Brooks, *Stories,* 278.
114. *CM,* 8-23-61.
115. Ibid., 9-18-61.
116. Ibid., 1-1-62; UDC, *RR,* 12, 151.
117. *CSR,* M267, 362.
118. *CM,* 9-9-61.
119. Brooks, *Stories,* 279.
120. *CSR,* M267, 362.
121. *CM,* 2-20-64.
122. *OR,* 1, 44, 997.
123. Ibid., 1, 44, 875.
124. Ibid., 1, 44, 997.
125. Ibid., 1, 47, 2, 1071.
126. *CDC,* 7-18-62.
127. *CM,* 7-15-62.
128. *CDC,* 12-28-62.
129. *CMH,* 673.
130. *CM,* 10-10-63.
131. *OR,* 1, 35, 2, 357.
132. Ibid., 1, 28, 2, 602; 1, 35, 1, 558; 1, 35, 2, 457, 559; 35, 2, 644.
133. Ibid., 1, 44, 446.

134. Brooks, *Stories*, 281.
135. *OR*, 1, 47, 3, 781.
136. *CV*, 10, 274; *CMH*, 673; Brooks, *Stories*, 281.
137. *The Civil War in Western SC*, 36.
138. *CM*, 2-20-62.
139. *CDC*, 3-3-62.
140. Ibid., 4-8-62.
141. Ibid., 9-16-64.
142. *OR*, 1, 28, 1, 511.
143. *CDC*, 8-31-63.
144. *OR*, 1, 28, 1, 511–518.
145. Ibid., 1, 28, 1, 580.
146. Ibid., 1, 28, 1, 465.
147. Ibid., 1, 28, 1, 478; *CDC*, 8-31-63.
148. *CDC*, 8-31-63.
149. Ibid., 9-16-64.
150. Ibid., 8-31-63.
151. *CM*, 2-19-62.
152. *OR*, 1, 28, 2, 161.
153. Sifakis, *Compendium*, 19.
154. *OR*, 1, 44, 875.
155. Ibid., 1, 44, 997.
156. Ibid., 1, 47, 2, 1070.
157. *CDC*, 6-2-62.
158. *Triweekly Watchman*, 6-4-62; Hagood, *Memoirs*, 88.
159. *OR*, 1, 28, 2, 162.
160. *CM*, 4-13-63.
161. *OR*, 1, 28, 1, 372.
162. Ibid., 1, 28, 2, 211, 231.
163. Ibid., 1, 28, 2, 245.
164. Ibid., 1, 28, 1, 385.
165. Ibid., 1, 28, 1, 551.
166. *CM*, 8-13-63; *OR*, 1, 28, 1, 499, 500; 1, 28, 2, 325.
167. *OR*, 1, 28, 2, 368.
168. Ibid., 1, 28, 2, 468, 603; 1, 35, 1, 558; 1, 35, 2, 458, 469.
169. Ibid., 1, 35, 1, 220.
170. Ibid., 1, 35, 2, 644.
171. *CM*, 7-21-62.
172. Ibid., 8-8-64.
173. Ibid., 7-21-62.
174. Ibid., 8-8-64.
175. *Cyclopedia*, 436.
176. *CM*, 8-8-64; *CDC*, 8-9-64.
177. Welbum J. Andrews, *Sketch of Company K, 23rd SCV in the Civil War from 1862 to 1865*, repr. 3, 505.
178. *CDC*, 11-21-64.
179. MS11-16-64; *CDC*, 11-21-64.
180. Ibid.
181. Sifakis, *Compendium*, 12.
182. *OR*, 1, 28, 1, 479.
183. SHSP, 26, 236.
184. *CM*, 2-8-62.
185. *CDC*, 2-27-62; *CM*, 2-27-62.
186. *CDC*, 12-5-64.
187. Ibid., 2-24-64.
188. Ibid., 3-14-62; *CM*, 3-14-62

189. *CDC*, 2-24-64.
190. *CM*, 2-24-64; *CDC*, 2-24-64.
191. *OR*, 1, 44, 875.
192. Ibid., 1, 44, 997.
193. Ibid., 1, 47, 1, 1065.
194. *CDC*, 10-27-62; 10-28-62; *CM*, 10-27-62; 11-4-62.
195. *OR*, 1, 28, 1, 149; 1, 28, 2, 246, 325, 467, 602; 1, 35, 1, 558; 1, 35, 2, 457, 599, 644.
196. Ibid., 1, 44, 993; *The Civil War in Western SC*, 24.
197. *OR*, 1, 44, 1000.
198. Ibid., 1, 47, 2, 1007.
199. *CMH*, 463.
200. *OR*, 1, 47, 3, 781.
201. *CM*, 3-26-60; 5-23-61.
202. Ibid., 3-14-61.
203. Ibid., 7-18-61.
204. Ibid.
205. Ibid., 3-4-64.
206. *OR*, 1, 44, 997.
207. Ibid., 1, 44, 875.
208. Ibid., 1, 44, 997.
209. Ibid., 1, 47, 2, 1070.
210. Ibid., 1, 47, 1, 1064.
211. Ibid., 1, 14, 19.
212. Ibid., 1, 14, 576, 822; 1, 28, 1, 149.
213. Ibid., 1, 28, 1, 198.
214. Ibid., 1, 28, 74.
215. *CDC*, 7-17-63.
216. *OR*, 1, 28, 2, 245.
217. Ibid., 1, 28, 1, 499; 1, 28, 2, 325.
218. Ibid., 1, 28, 2, 367, 469.
219. Warren Ripley, *Siege Train, The Journal of a Confederate Artilleryman in the Defense of Charleston*, 100; *OR*, 1, 28, 2, 563; 1, 53, 20.
220. *OR*, 1, 28, 2, 603.
221. Ibid., 1, 35, 1, 559.
222. Ibid., 1, 35, 1, 610.
223. *CM*, 2-15-64; Johnson, *Charleston Harbor*, 221; *OR*, 1, 35, 1, 145.
224. *CM*, 3-4-64.
225. *OR*, 1, 35, 2, 458, 599, 645.
226. Ibid., 1, 35, 1, 264-266; *CM*, 7-11-64.
227. *OR*, 1, 47, 2, 1169.
228. Ibid., 1, 47, 3, 781.
229. Ibid., 1, 14, 276.
230. Woodward, *Mary Chesnut*, 210.
231. *CSR*, M267, 102.
232. *OR*, 1, 28, 2, 161.
233. Ibid., 1, 44, 875.
234. Ibid., 1, 44, 997.
235. Ibid., 1, 47, 2, 1071.
236. *CM*, 11-28-61.
237. *CMH*, 682.
238. Hagood, *Memoirs*, 87.
239. *OR*, 1, 28, 2, 62.
240. *CM*, 4-13-63; *OR*, 1, 14, 276.
241. *OR*, 1, 28, 2, 223.
242. Ibid., 1, 28, 1, 385; 1, 28, 2, 245.

243. Ibid., 1, 28, 1, 383, 409, 500.
244. Ibid., 1, 28, 1, 398.
245. Ibid., 1, 28, 2, 325.
246. Ibid., 1, 28, 2, 367, 468, 603.
247. Ibid., 1, 35, 1, 558; 1, 35, 2, 457.
248. Ibid., 1, 35, 1, 400.
249. Ibid., 1, 35, 2, 645.
250. *CMH*, 619.
251. UDC, *RR*, 9, 169.
252. UDC, *RR*, 5, 502, 6, 290.
253. Ibid., 6, 290.
254. *CM*, 3-21-63.
255. Ibid.
256. Baker, *Cadets in Gray*, 67.
257. *CV*, 15, 263; *CV*, 28, 128.
258. UDC, *RR*, 9, 168.
259. *OR*, 1, 44, 875.
260. Ibid., 1, 44, 997.
261. *CV*, 30, 227.
262. UDC, *RR*, 6, 290.
263. Ibid.
264. Ibid..
265. *OR*, 1, 14, 822.
266. *CM*, 4-9-63; UDC, *RR*, 5, 505.
267. *OR*, 1, 28, 2, 162.
268. Ibid., 1, 28, 2, 246, 327, 467.
269. Ibid., 1, 28, 2, 601; 1, 35, 1, 558.
270. Ibid., 1, 35, 1, 377.
271. Ibid., 1, 35, 2, 457, 644.
272. Ibid., 1, 44, 890.
273. Ibid., 1, 47, 3, 782.
274. UDC, *RR*, 6, 290.
275. *CM*, 2-22-61.
276. UDC, *RR*, 5, 194.
277. *CV*, 9, 501; *CM*, 6-13-61; 7-10-61; *CMH*, 620.
278. *CM*, 6-28-61; 12-11-61.
279. *OR*, 1, 6, 336.
280. *CM*, 6-28-61; Record and Roll of the Washington Light Artillery, Confederate Historian, South Carolina Department of Archives and History, S108079. (Hereafter cited as Roll of Washington Light Artillery, SCDAH, S108117.)
281. *CDC*, 3-11-62.
282. *CM*, 3-12-64; *CDC*, 3-10-64.
283. *CM*, 3-6-64.
284. *OR*, 1, 44, 997.
285. Ibid., 1, 44, 875.
286. Ibid., 1, 44, 997.
287. Ibid., 1, 47, 2, 1071.
288. Ibid., 1, 47, 1, 1063.
289. *CMH*, 765.
290. Roll of Washington Light Artillery, SCDAH, S108117.
291. Ibid.; *CV*, 9, 501.
292. UDC, *RR*, 5, 194.
293. Baker, *Cadets in Gray*, 44.
294. *OR*, 1, 14, 823.
295. Ibid., 1, 6, 113-123; *CM*, 4-1-62.

296. Roll of Washington Light Artillery, SCDAH, S108117.
297. Hagood, *Memoirs*, 104.
298. Roll of Washington Light Artillery, SCDAH, S108117.
299. *OR*, 1, 28, 2, 169.
300. Ibid.
301. *CM*, 7-13-63; 7-15-63; *Triweekly Watchman*, 7-17-63.
302. Brooks, *Butler*, 120; *OR*, 1, 28, 1, 19, 199.
303. *OR*, 1, 28, 2, 246, 326, 467, 601; 1, 35, 1, 558; O1, 35, 2, 456, 599, 645.
304. Ibid., 1, 28, 1, 737.
305. *CM*, 3-12-64; *CDC*, 3-10-64.
306. *CM*, 7-11-64; *OR*, 1, 35, 1, 267.
307. *CDC*, 2-18-65; Roll of Washington Light Artillery, SCDAH, S108117.
308. *OR*, 1, 47, 3, 78.
309. *CMH*, 765.
310. Ibid., 620.
311. *CM*, 2-22-61.
312. *CV*, 9, 501.
313. *CM*, 6-13-61; 7-10-61; *CMH*, 620; *CV*, 9, 501; UDC, *RR*, 5, 194.
314. *CM*, 6-28-61.
315. Ibid., 5-20-61.
316. *CDC*, 5-31-61.
317. *CM*, 6-13-61.
318. Ibid., 6-10-61.
319. Brooks, *Stories*, 247.
320. *CV*, 5, 333.
321. *Cyclopedia*, 224-225.
322. *CDC*, 3-12-62.
323. *CV*, 9, 501.
324. *CM*, 2-2-64.
325. *CDC*, 11-5-64; Calhoun, "Liberty," 149.
326. *CV*, 13, 240; *CMH*, 620.
327. Brooks, *Stories*, 271.
328. *OR*, 1, 47, 1, 1065.
329. CM 6-13-61.
330. Ibid., 6-27-61.
331. McArthur, *Griffin*, 169; *CV*, 29, 414.
332. *McArthur, Griffin*, 193.
333. Brooks, *Stories*, 272.
334. *CMH*, 622.
335. Freeman, *Lee's Lieutenants*, 3, 10.
336. McSwain, *Crumbling Defenses*, 19.
337. Brooks, *Butler*, 177.
338. Brooks, *Stories*, 265.
339. Ibid., 265.
340. Brooks, *Butler*, 321.
341. *CDC*, 11-5-64.
342. *OR*, 1, 47, 2, 1300.
343. *CMH*, 725.
344. *CM*, 1-4-61; 3-2-61; 4-23-61.
345. *CMH*, 725.
346. *CM*, 5-10-61.
347. Ibid., 5-2-61; 5-14-61.
348. Ibid., 6-29-61.
349. Ibid., 5-29-62.
350. *CV*, 25, 224.

351. *CMH,* 725; *CV,* 25, 177; 25, 224.
352. SHSP, 50, 439, 442.
353. *CV,* 25, 225.
354. Joseph Woods Brunson, *Pee Dee Light Artillery of Maxcy Gregg's (Later Samuel McGowan's) Brigade First South Carolina Volunteer (Infantry) CSA. A Historical Sketch and Roster,* 7. (Hereafter cited as Brunson, *Pee Dee Artillery.*)
355. *CV,* 20, 204; 25, 177, 224.
356. Brunson, *Pee Dee Artillery,* 28.
357. *DSC,* 3-16-64.
358. Sifakis, *Compendium,* 33.
359. *OR,* 1, 47, 1, 1063.
360. Freeman, *Lee's Lieutenants,* 1,512.
361. *CDC,* 9-24-62.
362. Daly, *Portrait,* 80.
363. *CV,* 19, 429.
364. Brunson, *Pee Dee Artillery,* 6.
365. *CM,* 12-24-62.
366. Brunson, *Pee Dee Artillery,* 8.
367. *OR,* 1, 35, 2, 598.
368. *CMH,* 729; Brunson, *Pee Dee Artillery,* 30; *OR,* 1, 47, 3, 781.
369. *CDC,* 4-29-62; *OR,* 1, 1, 310.
370. *CM,* 1-9-62; *DSG,* 1-10-62.
371. *CDC,* 4-29-62.
372. *OR,* 1, 6, 418, 426.
373. *Horry Dispatch,* 4-11-61.
374. Thigpen, *Potter's Raid,* 26.
375. *OR,* 1, 44, 875; 1, 47, 2, 1073.
376. Ibid., 1, 1, 310.
377. *Horry Dispatch,* 4-11-61.
378. Ibid.
379. *CM,* 8-1-62.
380. *OR,* 1, 14, 114; *CDC,* 8-18-62.
381. *OR,* 1, 14, 822.
382. *CM,* 11-12-62.
383. *OR,* 1, 14, 762.
384. Ibid., 1, 28, 2, 159, 246, 327, 468, 602; 1, 35, 1, 558; 1, 35, 2, 457, 598, 644.

Appendix 1

1. *CS,* 2-28-61; *CM,* 2-25-60.
2. *CM,* 1-11-61.
3. Ibid., 2-22-61.
4. Ibid., 3-1-61.
5. Ibid., 3-14-61.
6. Ibid., 3-27-61; *YE,* 4-4-61.
7. *CM,* 6-5-61.
8. *YE,* 1-24-61.
9. *CM,* 6-13-61.
10. Ibid., 7-13-61.
11. Ibid., 7-2-61.
12. Ibid., 8-16-61; *CDC,* 4-13-63.
13. *CM,* 8-19-61.
14. Ibid., 9-19-61.
15. Ibid., 9-23-61.
16. Ibid., 10-4-61.
17. Ibid., 12-25-61.

18. Ibid., 1-29-62.
19. Ibid., 4-14-62.
20. Ibid., 5-12-63.
21. Ibid., 6-3-64.
22. Ibid., 1-19-65.
23. SHSP, Index.
24. UDC, *RR*, 7, 23.
25. Ibid., 10, 337.
26. *DSG*, 9-4-63.
27. *YE*, 1-10-61.
28. Ibid., 1-17-61.
29. Thomas, *Rising Star*, 177.
30. *YE*, 1-24-61; *Keowee Courier (Walhalla)*, 1-12-61; 6-29-61.
31. *YE*, 1-24-61.
32. Ibid.
33. Ibid., 1-31-61.
34. Ibid., 2-21-61.
35. Ibid., 2-28-61.
36. Ibid., 4-25-61; *CM*, 5-6-61.
37. *YE*, 5-30-61.
38. *Keowee Courier (Walhalla)*, 2-2-61.
39. *EA*, 5-22-61.
40. Ibid., 6-12-61; 7-3-61.
41. Ibid., 6-19-61.
42. Ibid., 6-26-61.
43. Ibid., 7-3-61.
44. Ibid., 7-10-61.
45. Ibid., 8-7-61.
46. Ibid., 7-8-63.
47. Ibid., 7-21-64; *CDC*, 9-15-64.
48. *EA*, 3-22-65.
49. *Keowee Courier (Walhalla)*, 6-29-61.
50. Ibid., 6-29-61.
51. Ibid., 7-6-61.
52. Ibid., 7-13-61.
53. Ibid.
54. Ibid., 7-20-61.
55. Ibid.
56. Ibid.
57. *LL*, 5-1-61.
58. Ibid., 5-22-62.
59. Ibid.
60. Ibid., 5-29-61.
61. Ibid., 5-12-61.
62. Ibid.
63. Ibid., 9-18-61.
64. PM1-3-61.
65. *Greenville Southern Enterprise*, 7-2-63.
66. Ibid.
67. *LL*, 4-30-62.
68. *Anderson Intelligencer*, 2-7-61.
69. Ibid., 2-21-61.
70. *AP*, 9-20-61.
71. *OR*, 1, 47, 2, 1073.
72. *CDC*, 5-2-61.

73. Ibid., 5-31-61.
74. Ibid., 8-26-61.
75. Ibid., 8-30-62.
76. *For Love of a Rebel*, 50.
77. Ibid, 103.
78. Wycoff, Website.
79. Brooks, *Stories*, 293.
80. Wycoff, Website
81. Ibid.
82. Ibid.

Appendix 2

1. Halliburton, *Saddle Soldiers*, 130.
2. *CM*, 1-12-61.
3. *Anderson Intelligencer*, 1-3-61, 1-10-61.
4. *Keowee Courier (Walhalla)*, 1-19-61.
5. *CM*, 1-31-61.
6. Ibid., 2-22-61.
7. Ibid., 4-19-61.
8. Ibid., 6-1-61.
9. Ibid., 10-9-61.
10. UDC, *RR*, 7, 343.
11. *Triweekly Watchman*, 7-27-63.
12. *CM*, 11-14-63.
13. *CMH*, 687.
14. Ibid.
15. *Acts*, 878.
16. Cauthen, ed., *Journals*, 190.
17. *YE*, 1-10-61; *DSG*, 1-8-61; 5-4-61.
18. *Anderson Intelligencer*, 1-10-61; *Keowee Courier (Walhalla)*, 1-19-61.
19. *Keowee Courier (Walhalla)*, 1-12-61.
20. *EA*, 1-30-61.
21. Ibid., 2-27-61.
22. Ibid., 9-4-61.
23. *Keowee Courier (Walhalla)*, 6-15-61.
24. *Triweekly Watchman*, 8-14-63; 9-18-63.
25. *CDC*, 1-17-65.
26. *AP*, 1-4-61.

Appendix 3

1. Baker, *Cadets in Gray*, 155.
2. *CMH*, 437.
3. *CM*, 10-29-62.
4. Ibid., 1-6-64.
5. Ibid., 6-27-61.
6. Ibid., 9-19-61.
7. James J. Baldwin, *The Struck Eagle—A Biography of Brigadier General Micah Jenkins, and A History of the Fifth South Carolina Volunteers and the Palmetto Sharpshooters*, 75.
8. *Acts*, 934.
9. *For Love of a Rebel*, 17.
10. Tower, *A Carolinian Goes To War*, 12.

BIBLIOGRAPHY

Abbeville Banner

Abbeville Press

Acts of the General Assembly of the State of South Carolina, passed in November and December 1860 and January 1861. Columbia, South Carolina: Charles P. Pelham, 1861.

Allardice, Bruce S. *More Generals in Gray*. Baton Rouge: Louisiana State University Press, 1995.

Anderson Intelligencer

Andrews, Robert W. *The Life and Adventures of Captain Robert W. Andrews of Sumter, South Carolina*. Boston, Massachusetts: E.P. Whitcomb, 1887.

Andrews, Welburn J. *Sketch of Company K, 23rd SCV in the Civil War from 1862–1865*. Richmond, Virginia: Whittet and Shepperson, n.d. Repr. South Carolina Division, United Daughters of the Confederacy. *Recollections and Reminiscences 1861–1865 through World War I*.

Armstrong, James. *The Carolina Light Infantry's Record in the Great War*. Charleston, South Carolina: Walker, Evans, and Cogswell, 1912.

Austin, J. Luke. *General John Bratton: Sumter to Appomattox In Letters to His Wife*. Sewanee, Tennessee: Proctor's Hall Press, 2003.

Baker, Gary R. *Cadets in Gray*. Columbia, South Carolina: Palmetto Bookworks, 1989.

Baldwin James J. *The Struck Eagle—A Biography of Brigadier General Micah Jenkins, and A History of the Fifth South Carolina Volunteers and the Palmetto Sharpshooters*. Shippensburg, Pennsylvania: Burd Street Press, 1996.

Barnwell Sentinel

Batson, Steve. Website on the 16th Regiment, SCV. http://www.geocities.com/BourbonStreet/Square/3873/franklina.html.

Baxley, Neil. *No Prouder Fate: The Story of the 11th South Carolina Volunteer Infantry*. Bloomington, Indiana: AuthorHouse, 2005.

Bell, L.M., ed. *Rebels In Grey, Soldiers from Pickens District 1861–1865*. Clemson, South Carolina: Joyce's Print Shop, 1984.

Benson, Susan Williams, ed. *Berry Benson's Civil War Book, Memoirs of a Confederate Scout and Sharpshooter*. Athens: The University of Georgia Press, 1992.

Boykin, Edward Mortimer. *The Falling Flag*. New York: E.J. Hale and Son, 1874.

Boykin, Richard Manning. *Captain Alexander Hamilton Boykin, One of South Carolina's Distinguished Citizens*. Repr. Camden, South Carolina: J.J. Fox, 1991.

Boyles, J.R., Lt. *Reminiscences of the Civil War, Company C, 12th Regiment, SCV*. Columbia, South Carolina: R. L. Bryan Co., 1890.

BIBLIOGRAPHY

Boylston, Raymond P. *Butler's Brigade, That Fighting Civil War Cavalry Brigade from South Carolina*. Raleigh, North Carolina: Jarrett Press and Publications, 2000.

Bradshaw, Timothy E., Jr. *Battery Wagner, The Siege, The Men Who Fought and The Casualties*. Columbia, South Carolina: Palmetto Historical Works, 1993.

Brasington, Bill. Website "South Carolina State Troops Seed Corn Units, 1864–1865." Website deals with reserves and state troops. www://geocities.com/sc_seedcorn.

Brennan, Patrick. *Secessionville, Assault on Charleston*. Campbell, California: Savas Publishing Company, 1996.

Brock, R.A., and Philip Van Doren Stern. *The Appomattox Roster*. New York: Antiquarian Press, Ltd. 1962.

Brooks, Ulysses Robert, ed. *Butler and His Cavalry in the War of Secession 1861–1865, 1909*. Repr. Camden, South Carolina: J.J. Fox, 1991.

———. *Stories of the Confederacy*. Columbia, South Carolina: The State Company, 1912.

Brown, Joseph N., Col. "Account of the Battle of Gettysburg." Speech given in Anderson, South Carolina. March 23, 1901. (Available from the Greenville County Public Library. Microfiche SC 973.7457, Fiche 109.)

———. An Address Delivered on the Battle of the "Bloody Angle" at the November 1900 Meeting of the Robert E. Lee Chapter of the Daughters of Confederacy May 12, 1864. Anderson, South Carolina: The Association Publishing Company, 1900.

Brown, Varina D. *A Colonel at Gettysburg and Spotsylvania*. Columbia, South Carolina: The State Company, 1931.

Brunson, Joseph Woods, Sgt. *Pee Dee Light Artillery of Maxcy Gregg's (Later Samuel McGowan's) Brigade First South Carolina Volunteers (Infantry) C.S.A. A Historical Sketch and Roster*. University of Alabama: Confederate Publishing Company, 1983.

Buzhardt, Beaufort Simpson. "Diary of Beaufort Simpson Buzhardt." (Available from the Greenville County Public Library. Microfiche 973.7457, fiche 89.)

Caldwell, J.F.J. *The History of a Brigade of South Carolinians*. Philadelphia: King and Baird Printers, 1866. Repr. Dayton, Ohio: Morningside Press, 1984.

Calhoun, C.M. *Liberty Dethroned*. N.p., n.d. (Available from author.)

Camden Confederate

Carolina Spartan

Cauthen, Charles E. *South Carolina Goes to War, 1860–1865*. Chapel Hill: University of North Carolina Press, 1950.

———, ed. *Journals of the South Carolina Executive Councils 1861 and 1862*. Columbia: South Carolina Archives Department, 1956.

Charleston Daily Courier

Charleston Mercury

Chisolm, Robert. Papers. N.p., n.d. (Available from the Greenville County Public Library. Microfiche SC 973.7457, fiche 123.)

Cisco, Walter Brian. *States Rights Gist, A South Carolina General of the Civil War*. Shippensburg, Pennsylvania: White Mane Publishing Company, 1991.

The Civil War in Southwestern South Carolina December 1864–January 1865. Montmorenci, South Carolina: Western Carolina Historical Research, 1997.

Clary, James B. *A History of the 15th South Carolina Infantry 1861–1865*. Cary, NC: James B. Clary in cooperation with the South Carolina Department of Archives and History, 2007.

Coker, James Lide. *History of Company G, Ninth S.C. Regiment, Infantry, South Carolina Army and of Company E, Sixth S.C. Regiment, Infantry, South Carolina Army*. Greenwood, South Carolina: The Attic Press, Repr. 1979.

Confederate Military History Extended Edition, Volume 6, South Carolina. Wilmington, North Carolina. Broadfoot Publishing, 1987.

Confederate Veteran, Nashville, Tennessee. 40 vols.

Conrad, James L. The Sad History of 'Shanks' Evans." *The Civil War Times Illustrated*, Vol. 22 (Sept. 1983): 32–38.

Coward, Asbury, N.J. Bond, and O.L. Coward, eds. *The South Carolinians*. New York: Vantage Press, 1968.

Crute, Joseph H., Jr. *Units of the Confederate Army*. Midlothian, Virginia: Derwent Books, 1987.

Cyclopedia of Eminent and Representative Men of the Carolinas of the Nineteenth Century. Vol. 1. Madison, Wisconsin: Brant and Fuller, 1892.

Daily South Carolinian

Daily Southern Guardian

Daly, Louise Haskell. *Alexander Cheves Haskell, The Portrait of a Man*. Wilmington, North Carolina: Broadfoot Publishing Company, 1989.

Darlington Southerner

Davis, Nora M., comp. *Military and Naval Operations in South Carolina 1860–1865: A Chronological List, With References to Sources of Further Information*: South Carolina Archives, 1959.

Davis, Sam. Conversation with author.

Dedmondt, Glenn. *Southern Bronze, Captain Garden's (S.C.) Artillery Company During the War Between the States*. Columbia, South Carolina: Palmetto Bookworks, 1993.

Dickert, D. Augustus. *History of Kershaw's Brigade*. Dayton, Ohio: Morningside House, 1988.

Douglas, David G. *A Boot Full of Memories: Captain Leonard Williams, 2nd South Carolina Cavalry*. Camden, South Carolina: Gray Fox Publishing, 2003.

DuBose, Henry Kershaw. *The History of Company B, 21st Regiment (Infantry) SCV C.S.P.A.* Columbia, South Carolina: The R.L. Bryan Company, 1909.

Due West Telescope

Dunlop, W.S. *Lee's Sharpshooters or, The Forefront of Battle*. W.S. Dayton, Ohio: Morning House Inc, 1988.

Edgefield Advertiser

Edwards, W.H., Capt. *A Condensed History of the Seventeenth Regiment, SCV, C.S.A.* Columbia, South Carolina: The R.L. Bryan Company, 1908.

Elliott, Charles P., Maj. "Elliott's Brigade and how it held the Crater at the Battle of Petersburg. Speech given 5 December 1895. The Fitz William McMaster Collection. (Available from the Greenville County Public Library. Microfiche SC 973.7457, Fiche 113.)

Emanuel, S. "A Historical Sketch of the Georgetown Rifle Guards." Speech delivered on 17 November, 1909. (Available from the Greenville County Public Library. Microfiche 973.7457, fiche 100.)

Estilow, L.E., ed. "Doing My Duty—The Wartime Experiences of John S. Hard 1861–1863." Unpublished. (Available from author.)

Evans, Clement, ed. *Confederate Military History Extended Edition*, Vol. 6, *South Carolina*. Atlanta: Confederate Publishing Company, 1899. Repr. Wilmington, North Carolina: Broadfoot Publishing Company, 1987.

Everson, Guy R., and Edward H. Simpson Jr., eds. *Far, Far from Home—The Wartime Letters of Dick and Tally Simpson, 3rd South Carolina Volunteers*. New York: Oxford University Press, 1994.

Ewell, S.P.H. *Recollections of War Times*. Bamberg, South Carolina: The Bamberg Herald Printers, 1895.

For Love of a Rebel. Georgetown, South Carolina: The Arthur Manigault Chapter of the U.D.C., 1964.

Ford, A.P., and M.J. Ford. *Life in the Confederate Army*. New York: The Neale Publishing Company, 1905.

BIBLIOGRAPHY

Freeman, Douglas Southall. *Lee's Lieutenants*. 3 vols. New York: Charles Scribner's Sons, 1944.

Garlington, J.C. *Men of the Time, Sketches of Living Notables, A Biographical Encyclopedia of Contemporaneous South Carolina Leaders*. Spartanburg, South Carolina: Garlington Press, 1902.

Gibson, John Mendinghall. *Those 163 Days; A Southern Account of Sherman's March from Atlanta to Raleigh*. New York: Bramhall House, 1961.

Greenville Mountaineer

Greenville Patriot and Mountaineer

Greenville Southern Enterprise

Hagood, James R. "Memoirs of the First South Carolina Regiment of Volunteer Infantry in the Confederate War for Independence from April 12, 1861 to April 10, 1865." Unpublished MS. Columbia: South Caroliniana Library.

Hagood, Johnson. *Memoirs of the War of Secession, From the Original Manuscripts of Johnson Hagood*. Columbia, South Carolina: The State Company, 1910.

Halliburton, Lloyd. *Saddle Soldiers, The Civil War Correspondence of General William Stokes 4th South Carolina Cavalry*. Orangeburg, South Carolina: Sandlapper Publishing Company, 1993.

Heller, J. Roderick, and Carolynn Ayres Heller, eds. *The Confederacy Is on Her Way Up the Spout, Letters to South Carolina 1861–1864*. Columbia: University of South Carolina Press, 1998.

Henderson, E. Prioleau. *Autobiography of Arab, E. Prioleau Henderson*. Oxford: The Guild Bindery Press, 1901. Repr. Camden, South Carolina: J.J. Fox, 1991.

Horry Dispatch

Howard, Robert M. *Reminiscences*. Columbus, Georgia: Gilbert Printing Company, 1912.

Hoyt, James A. *The Palmetto Riflemen, Company B, 4th Regiment SCV and Company C, Palmetto Sharpshooters*. Greenville, South Carolina: Hoyt and Keys Printers, 1886.

Hudson, Joshua Hilary. *Sketches and Reminiscences*. Columbia, South Carolina: The State Company, 1903.

Inglesby, Charles. *Historical Sketch of the First Regiment of South Carolina Artillery (Regulars)*. Charleston, South Carolina. Walker, Evans, and Cogswell, n.d.

Izlar, William Valmore. *A Sketch of the War Record of the Edisto Rifles, 1861–1865*. Columbia, South Carolina: The State Company, 1914.

Johnson, John. *The Defense of Charleston Harbor including Fort Sumter and the Adjacent Islands, 1863–1865*. Charleston, South Carolina: Walker, Evans, and Cogswell, 1890.

Jones, Eugene W. Jr. *Enlisted For The War, The Struggles of the Gallant 24th Regiment, South Carolina Volunteers, Infantry, 1861–1865*. Highstown, New Jersey: Longstreet House, 1997.

Jordan, Laylon Wayne, and Elizabeth H. Stringfellow. *A Place Called St. John's: The Story of John's Edisto, Wadmalaw, Kiawah, and Seabrook Islands of South Carolina*. Spartanburg, South Carolina: The Reprint Company, 2003.

Keowee Courier (Walhalla)

Kirkland, Randolph W., Jr. *Broken Fortunes—South Carolina Soldiers, Sailors and Citizens Who Died in the Service of Their Country and State in the War for Southern Independence, 1861–1865*. Charleston: The South Carolina Historical Society, 1995.

Krick, Robert K. *Lee's Colonels, A Biographical Register of the Field Officers of the Army of Northern Virginia*. 3d ed. rev. Dayton, Ohio: Morningside House, 1991.

Lancaster Ledger

Laurensville Herald

Lewis, Richard, Lieutenant. *Camp Life of a Confederate Boy*. Charleston, South Carolina: News and Courier Press, 1883.

Lexington Dispatch

Longacre, Edward G. *Gentleman and Soldier*. Nashville, Tennessee: Rutledge Hill Press, 2003.

BIBLIOGRAPHY

Lynch. Harriet P. *Reminiscences and Sketches of Confederate Times*. Columbia, South Carolina: The R.L. Bryan Company, 1909.

Marion Star

McArthur, Judith N., and Orville Vernon Burton. *A Gentleman and An Officer-A Military and Social History of James B. Griffin's Civil War*. New York: Oxford University Press, 1996.

McDaniel, J.J. "Diary of the Battles, Marches, and Incidents of the 7th South Carolina Regiment." N.p., n.d. (Available from the Greenville County Public Library. Microfiche 973.7457, fiche 99.)

McSwain, Eleanor D., ed. *Crumbling Defenses or Memoirs and Reminiscences of John Logan Black, Colonel, C.S.A.* Macon, Georgia: J.W. Burke Company, 1960.

Melton, E. Frank. *War Between The States*. Hartsville: Old Darlington District, South Carolina Genealogical Society, 2002.

Mixson, Frank M. *Reminiscences Of A Private*. Columbia, South Carolina: The State Company, 1910.

Mulligan, A.B. *My Dear Mother and Sisters, The Civil War Letters of Captain A.B. Mulligan, Company B, 5th South Carolina Cavalry, Butler's Division, Hampton's Corps, 1861–1865*. Spartanburg, South Carolina: The Reprint Company, 1992.

Murray, J. Ogden. *The Immortal 600*. New York: The Neale Publishing Company, 1905.

National Archives and Records Administration. *Compiled Service Records of Confederate Soldiers Who Served in Organizations from the State of South Carolina* (CSR). Microcopy 267.

———. Register of Confederate Soldiers, Sailors, and Citizens Who Died in Federal Prisons and Military Hospitals in the North, 1861–1865. Microfilm publication. M918 (973.742).

Nichols, Wesley. *The Autobiography of Wesley Nichols*. N.p., n.d. (Available from the Greenville County Public Library. Microfiche SC 973.7457, Fiche 111.)

Phelps, W. Chris. *Charlestonians in War: the Charleston Battalion*. Gretna, Louisiana: Pelican Publishing Company, 2004.

Reid, Jesse W. *History of the Fourth Regiment, S.C. Volunteers, from the Commencement of the War until Lee's Surrender*. Greenville, South Carolina: Shannon and Company, 1891. Repr. Dayton, Ohio: Morningside Bookshop, 1975.

Rhea, Gordon C. *Carrying the Flag*. New York: Basic Books, 2004.

Ripley, Warren. *The Battle of Chapman's Fort, May 26, 1864*. Green Pond: Ashepoo Plantation, 1978.

———. *Siege Train, The Journal of a Confederate Artilleryman in the Defense of Charleston*. Columbia: University of South Carolina Press, 1986.

Rivers, William J. *Rivers's Account of the Raising of Troops in South Carolina for State and Confederate Service 1861–1865*. Columbia, South Carolina: The Bryan Printing Company, State Printers, 1899.

Salley, Alexander S., comp. *South Carolina Troops in Confederate Service*. 3 vols. Columbia, South Carolina: The R.L. Bryan Company, 1913, 1914, 1930.

Sellers, William W. *A History of Marion County, South Carolina, from its earliest times to present— 1901*. Columbia, SC: R.L. Bryan Company, 1902.

Sifakis, Stewart. *Compendium of the Confederate Armies—South Carolina and Georgia*. New York: Facts on File, 1995

Smith, C.F. *Jeremiah Smith and the Confederate War*. Spartanburg, South Carolina: The Reprint Company, 1993.

South Carolina Department of Archives and History.

———. Adjutant and Inspector General. "History of Charleston Zouave Cadets." 1904. 1 vol. N.d.

Roster of 14th South Carolina Infantry. 2 vols. N.d.

BIBLIOGRAPHY

———. Comptroller General. Confederate Pension Applications Division, 1910–1926. Nos. 1941–2202 (Charleston-Cherokee). Microfilm Roll CW1231 (AD1149), No. 1995.

———. Confederate Historian.

"Annual Report For The Year 1899." *South Carolina Reports and Resolutions 1868–1900, regular session 1900.* Microcopy 13, Roll 29.

Memory Roll: Rolls of South Carolina Volunteers in the Confederate States Provisional Army. 5 vols. Microcopy 16, 1993.

Record and Roll of the German Fusiliers. 1 vol. 1904.

Record and Roll of the Washington Light Artillery, 1905. 1 vol.

Roster of Officers. N.d. 1 vol.

———. Miscellaneous Historical Sketches, 1866–1898. S108121.

Albergotti, W. Greer. "Sketch of Company F, 2nd Battalion, South Carolina State Troops." N.d.

Alston, Butler P. "Sketch of the 6th South Carolina Infantry." 1878.

Hammond, W.A. "Sketch of Company B, 37th Virginia Cavalry." 1898.

"Historical Sketch of the 5th South Carolina Cavalry." 1866. S108121.

James, A.A. "Brief History of the 18th. South Carolina Volunteers." N.d.

Lucas, J.J. "Sketch of Lucas's Battalion of Heavy Artillery." 1882.

Roll of Company G, 22nd South Carolina Infantry. 1884.

Roster of the 17th South Carolina Infantry (Partial). N.d.

Rion, J.H. "History of the 6th Regiment, South Carolina Infantry," n.d.

"Sketch of Company F, 21st South Carolina Infantry." N.d.

"Sketch of the 2nd South Carolina Artillery Regiment." N.d.

"Sketches of the 23rd South Carolina Infantry." 1891.

Stokes, William. "Sketch of Company G, 4th South Carolina Cavalry." N.d.

———. *Roll of the Dead, South Carolina Troops Confederate States Service.* 1994.

South Carolina Historical Magazine

Southern Historical Society. Southern Historical Society Papers. 52 vols. Richmond, Virginia, 1876–1959.

Starr, Linda Sparks. *W.R. Rankin, Manassas to Appomattox.* Norman, Oklahoma: Linda Sparks Starr, 1990.

The State

Stevens, Robert J. *Captain Bill, The Records and Writings of Captain William Henry Edwards (and others) Company A, 17th Regiment, South Carolina Volunteers, Confederate States of America.* 3 vols. Richburg, South Carolina: The Chester District Genealogical Society, 1985–1990.

Stone, DeWitt Boyd, Jr. *Wandering to Glory.* Columbia: University of South Carolina Press, 2002.

Sumter Watchman

Taylor, John S. *Sixteenth South Carolina Regiment CSA from Greenville County, South Carolina.* Private printing, 1964.

Thigpen, Allan D. *Recollections of Potter's Raid.* Sumter, South Carolina: Gamecock City Printing, 1999.

Thomas, John P. *Career and Character of General Micah Jenkins, C.S.A.* Columbia, South Carolina: The State Company, 1903.

Thomas, Samuel N., Jr., and Jason H. Silverman, eds. *A Rising Star of Promise: The Civil War Odyssey of David Jackson Logan, 17th South Carolina Volunteers, 1861–1864.* Campbell, California: Savas Publishing Company, 1998.

Tolar, J.R. "A History of Company B, 10th Regiment, SCV" (Available from the Greenville County Public Library. Microfiche 973.7457, fiche 101.)

Tompkins, D.A. *Company K, 14th SCV* Charlotte, North Carolina: Charlotte Observer Printing Publishing House, 1897. (Available from the Greenville County Public Library. Microfiche SC 973.7457, Fiche 110.)

BIBLIOGRAPHY

Toole, Gasper Loren. *Ninety Years in Aiken County*. Private printing, 1961.

Tower, Lockwood, ed. *A Carolinian Goes To War, The Civil Narrative of Arthur Middleton Manigault, Brigadier General, C.S.A., R.* Columbia: University of South Carolina Press, 1983.

Triweekly Watchman

United Daughters of the Confederacy. South Carolina Division, *Recollections and Reminiscences 1861–1865 through World War I.* 9 vols.

United States War Department. *The War of the Rebellion: A Compilation of the Official Records of the Union and Confederate Armies.* 128 vols. Washington, DC.: Government Printing Office, 1891–1895. (It should be noted that some volumes in this series are broken into parts, while some are not. Entries for volumes with parts are listed in the endnotes with a series, a volume, a part, and a page number or numbers; entries for volumes without parts are listed only with a series, a volume, and a page number or numbers.)

Walker, C.I. *Rolls and Historical Sketch of the Tenth Regiment, So. Ca. Volunteers in the Army of the Confederate States by C.I. Walker, Late Lieut. Col. of the Regt. To which is added An Historical Sketch of the Georgetown Rifle Guards Company A, 10ᵗʰ South Carolina by Sol. Emanuel.* South Carolina: Walker, Evans, and Cogswell, 1881. Repr. Alexandria, Virginia: Stonewall House, 1985.

Warner, Ezra J. *Generals in Blue, Lives of the Union Commanders*. Baton Rouge: Louisiana State University Press, 1986.

———. *Generals in Gray, Lives of the Confederate Commanders*. Baton Rouge: Louisiana State University Press, 1986.

Welch, Spencer G. *A Confederate Surgeon's Letters to his Wife.* New York: Neale Publishing Company, 1911.

Wellman, Manly Wade. *Giant in Gray, A Biography of Wade Hampton of South Carolina*. New York: Charles Scribner's and Sons, 1949.

Wells, Edward L. *Hampton and His Cavalry in '64*. Richmond, Virginia: B.F. Johnson, 1899.

———. *A Sketch of the Charleston Light Dragoons, From the Earliest Formation of the Corps.* Charleston, South Carolina: Lucas, Richardson, and Company, 1888.

Wise, Stephen R. *Gate of Hell, Campaign for Charleston Harbor, 1863*. Columbia: University of South Carolina Press, 1994.

Woodward, C. Vann and Elisabeth Muhlenfeld. *The Private Mary Chesnut, The Unpublished Civil War Diaries*. New York: Oxford University Press, 1984.

Woodward, T.W. "History of the 6ᵗʰ Regiment, S.C. Volunteers." Speech. Columbia, South Carolina: Presbyterian Publishing House, 1883.

Wyckoff, Mac. *A History of the 2ⁿᵈ South Carolina Infantry 1861–1865*. Fredericksburg, Virginia: Sergeant Kirkland's Museum and Historical Society, 1994.

———. *A History of the 3ʳᵈ South Carolina Infantry 1861–1865*. Fredericksburg, Virginia: Sergeant Kirkland's Museum and Historical Society, 1995.

———. Website on South Carolina in the Civil War. http://www.members.tripod.com/mwycoff/.

Yorkville Enquirer

INDEX